# The Sword & The Serpent

## About the Authors

Osborne Phillips is the pen name of Leon Barcynski. Leon is an internationally recognized authority on the mainstream Western mysteries and at one time was Grand Master of the International Order Aurum Solis. In addition to his lifelong practical involvement in the Western magickal arts, he has a consuming passion for the spiritual disciplines of Hinduism and Buddhism. He is particularly interested in the phenomenon of psychism, to which he has devoted many years of research, and in the psychology of religious mystical experience. Among his other interests are caving, archaeology, astronomy, and science fiction. He currently lives in the United Kingdom where he shares his life and aspirations with his partner, Sandra.

Melita Denning was the pen name of the late Vivian Godfrey Barcynski. Vivian, who passed into the Greater Life in 1997, was for many years Grand Master of the Order Aurum Solis. Under her direction and with her encouragement, the Order's program of making public aspects of its rites and teachings was inaugurated; and she was the inspiring genius of *The Magical Philosophy*, to which she contributed much high wisdom and poetic beauty. In addition to her magickal research and writings, Vivian was a brilliant historian. Her research into medieval and Renaissance aspects of the Ogdoadic Tradition was extensive and profound; and for her study of the history and ritual of the Knights Templar she was invested Dame d'Honneur by the Sovereign Military Order of the Temple of Jerusalem in 1967.

## To Write to the Author

If you wish to contact the author or would like more information about this book, please write to the author in care of Llewellyn Worldwide and we will forward your request. Both the author and publisher appreciate hearing from you and learning of your enjoyment of this book and how it has helped you. Llewellyn Worldwide cannot guarantee that every letter written to the author can be answered, but all will be forwarded. Please write to:

Osborne Phillips
℅ Llewellyn Worldwide
2143 Wooddale Drive, Dept. 0-7387-0810-0
Woodbury, MN 55125-2989, U.S.A.
Please enclose a self-addressed stamped envelope for reply,
or $1.00 to cover costs. If outside U.S.A., enclose
international postal reply coupon.

Many of Llewellyn's authors have websites with additional information and resources. For more information, please visit our website at http://www.llewellyn.com.

# The Sword & The Serpent

## The Two-Fold Qabalistic Universe

# DENNING & PHILLIPS

Llewellyn Publications
Woodbury, Minnesota

SECOND EDITION REVISED, 2005
first printing, 2005

FIRST EDITION, 1975. SECOND EDITION, 1988.


Cover design by Ellen L. Dahl
Flames © PhotoDisc
Lightning © Digital Stock
Sword and Serpent  illustration © 2005 Jon Hunt

Llewellyn is a registered trademark of Llewellyn Worldwide, Ltd.

Library of Congress Cataloging-in-Publication Data
Denning, Melita.
    The sword & the serpent: the two-fold Qabalistic universe / Melita Denning & Osborne Philips.—2nd ed.
        p. cm.
    ISBN 0-7387-0810-0 (alk. paper)
        1. Cabala.  I. Phillips, Osborne. II. Title.

BF1611.D43  2005
135'.47–dc22                                                          2005050434

Llewellyn Publications
A Division of Llewellyn Worldwide, Ltd.
2143 Wooddale Drive, Dept. 0-7387-0810-0
Woodbury, MN 55125-2989
www.llewellyn.com


Printed in the United States of America

# Other Books by the Authors

*Voudon Fire: The Living Reality of Mystical Religion,* 1979
*The Inner World of Fitness* (by Melita Denning), 1986

The Practical Guide Series
   *Practical Guide to Astral Projection,* 1979
   *Practical Guide to Creative Visualization,* 1980
   *Practical Guide to the Development of Psychic Powers,* 1981
   *Practical Guide to the Magick of Sex,* 1982
   *Practical Guide to the Magick of Tarot,* 1983
   *Practical Guide to Creative Moneymaking,* 1992

   *Magical States of Consciousness,* 1985
   *The Magical Philosophy: The Foundations of High Magick* (Volume 1), 1991
   *Mysteria Magica* (Volume 3), 1986 and 2004
   *Planetary Magick, 1989*
   *Entrance to the Magical Qabalah* (Thoth Publications, UK), 1997

The Magical Philosophy
   (reprinted as combined volumes [see above])
   Book I. *Robe and Ring,* 1974
   Book II. *The Apparel of High Magic,* 1975
   Book III. *The Sword and the Serpent,* 1975
   Book IV. *The Triumph of Light,* 1978
   Book V. *Mysteria Magica,* 1982

# Contents

*Chapter III—The Emanations*

*Chapter VI — Some Discursive Reflections on the Paths*

*Chapter VII — Channels of Force*

*Chapter VIII—The Magical Art*

# Book IV  The Triumph of Light
## (Part One)

Chapter II — The Astral and Mental Bodies

*Chapter III — The Higher Self*

*Chapter IV—The Trine of Spirit*

*Chapter V—Epilogue to Part I*

(Part Two)

*Chapter 1—The Subrational Foundation*

### III — The Finnish Knife

### IV — Fee Fi Fo Fum

# AUTHORS' NOTE TO THE SECOND EDITION

A new freedom of approach is becoming manifest in the occult world: a freedom we hail, not only because it characterizes our Aquarian times, but also because it is in itself *magical*, an advance in the self-aware decision-making of the individual. The first edition of *The Magical Philosophy* was prepared in the light of this realization, and this second edition proceeds further in the same vital spirit.

*The Magical Philosophy* is, certainly, a presentation of the teachings and practices of the Aurum Solis: equally, it is designed for the student of magick who lacks the opportunity, or the desire, to participate in formal lodge-type workings. It provides an introduction to, and a means of progression in, the mainstream Western Mystery Tradition, which is both compatible with group working and viable for the individual aspirant.

Here we must particularly express our indebtedness to our publisher, Carl Llewellyn Weschcke. As we make final adjustments to this volume of the new edition, we reflect that we have known and worked with Carl for sixteen years. His warm friendship, his unbiased promotion of occult teachings, and his personal concern that magick should be truly "available to all," have been, and continue to be, a major inspiration to us.

His wishes, and ours, accompany this book for your happy success in magical attainment.

Denning and Phillips
Twin Cities
March, 1987

# INTRODUCTION
## *Step into Magick!*

The world of magick awaits you. It can be thought about, written about, represented in pictures or diagrams, but the reality of magick exists in life and action. Magick is within you, a part of your essential being, and you need but to bring it forth and to surround yourself with it, so as to live magickally.

As far back in time as we find evidence of human activities, and earlier than that without any doubt, people performed magickal rites. Often they used no instruments, or they had only a stick as a sign of authority or a stone to carve a shape or symbol. No temple was available, so they used a cavern or a grove of trees or a bare mountain top, and here they practiced magick and, evidently, potent magick.

At first, the gestures and utterances that gave expression to ancient people's inner power must have been guided by natural impulse, as are the magickal actions done spontaneously by children; but early magicians learned quickly from experience that rhythmic gesture and utterance, which developed into dancing and chanting, would strengthen the current of power even more. The examples of the natural world were the ancient person's teacher: the creativity of the recurring seasons and of the actions of sexuality, the exhilarating rhythm of the seashore, the vitality of awakening and the repose of sleep, even the presence of life itself as indicated by the rhythms of breathing and of the beating heart. We know that magicians learned how the ritual wearing of masks could block the everyday tribal self from confusing the magickal will of the individual, and how channels of power could be formed by incising patterns, probably like those of their dances, upon the hidden walls of caverns. As the ancient people lived so close to the earth, directly within the influences of the earth and the heavens, we can be certain that their psychic perceptions were no less acute than those of the animals: noncorporeal influences, of elemental and human and, in some instances, of higher origin, would not have been strange to them. To such influences they would have learned to make reverence through acts of propitiation or petition or to offer a pact, as might seem fitting. But, apart from these acts involving other beings, they learned above all to strengthen and develop their own inner selves, to express and to fulfill their will by means of magick.

Among a number of prehistoric representations in caverns, which can be interpreted as showing one or the other of these types of working, there are some that almost certainly indicate acts of the developed will of the individual or of the group, effective without recourse to an external discarnate power; and there are other markings that seem distinctly to imply an appeal to an external power. Each of these types of workings is indicated among the various examples of prehistoric art that are presented by Norbert Casteret in his book *Ten Years Under the Earth.**

As examples of figures that show the gathering or the manifestation of personal power, we may instance Casteret's mention of various masked and dancing figures, and supremely the famous masked sorcerer of the cavern of Trois Freres. Another aspect of personal magick is cited by him in his account of representations in the caverns of Montespan. The prehistoric people here were much concerned with the multiplication of horses, and in one of several depictions of pregnant mares, a right hand is incised upon the shoulder of the animal: "a true symbol," writes Casteret, "of man's domination over the animal." From the magickal viewpoint, we would add, the symbol indicates more than the mere fact of domination: the hand represents the will of the magician, the desire and intention to possess such creatures.

* *Ten Years Under the Earth*, J. M. Dent & Sons, London 1939, is an English compilation from two books by Norbert Casteret: *Dix ans sous terre* and *Au fond des gouffres*.

By contrast, the record of the prints of mutilated hands in a cavern near Luchon and Saint Bernard-de-Comminges, described by Casteret in another chapter of his book, suggests altogether another form of magickal, or magico-religious, activity.

In a primitive culture where the life of the individual and the welfare of the community were largely dependent upon manual strength and skill, surely nobody would attempt to increase inner power by maiming the physical instrument of those abilities. Even as a token of mourning—an interpretation suggested by Casteret—the act seems, in context, inappropriate, though it may have been considered necessary as a means of appeasement to the shade of the departed. But, just as probably, these amputations of joints of one or several digits upon the hand may have been made with some hope of benefit in return for the sacrifice—benefit either to the sacrificer or to others—perhaps to the whole community. And in that case, to what discarnate being or beings, or to what force were the offerings addressed? The answer remains unknown, but the question is a valid one. At all events, it is certain that the people of the caverns, and certainly those of other primitive ways of life less able to leave an enduring record—those of the deep forests, the open steppes, and the prairies—explored and understood the fundamentals of different types of magick and put them to practical use with a success that encouraged them to explore and practice further. And they survived. Through untold ages, without many things that we consider necessities of life, with no material help but such medicinal herbs and crude surgery as they might discover, among beasts stronger than they and more effectively equipped with natural weaponry, and through extreme changes of climate and of environment, the human race survived: growing in dexterity and knowledge, coming in process of time to build great civilizations and to create numerous works of beauty and utility. But always, in whatever time or place, the arts of magick accompanied it, and are found, in one form or another, everywhere upon earth today.

With the growth of civilization, and the interchange of knowledge among peoples, the arts of magick have also become greater in scope, more articulate, and more interrelated in teaching. These advances are typified by the Qabalah, the mighty system of the western world that has been formulated in a diversity of nations and centuries by people of high mystical and magickal development. In this system, wherein the present book has its subject matter, the ancient wisdom abides within us, with the life-giving realities that are embodied in the natural world. The Tree of Life, the basic glyph of the Qabalah, links the Qabalah directly with those realities:. Alternatively, the Tree can be considered a plan of the entire universe, the cosmos spiritual and material, and the individual human psyche and personality.

In traditional magickal writing, that integral human unit is termed the *microcosm*. You are a microcosm: that is, the universe in miniature.

Truly, your life is of one fabric with that of the universe, at its nonmaterial and spiritual levels as well as at the material level. It is from this primal unity of person and universe that our great aspirations spring: the longing to know and to experience the reality of the mystery that encompasses us, but also of the mystery of selfhood that is within us—for each of these mysteries reflects the other.

The very fact of the reflected likeness, the unity of pattern, gives us a key to both mysteries—to both psychological and mystical understanding. And it is this same unity, giving us our inner key to the outer universe, that makes magick possible. It is this that makes the magick of the Qabalah, in particular, a coherent system—a sane system despite the tremendous scope of its perceptions—in which the magician does not move blindly but with a comprehension ever increasing, yet without ever losing the uplifting sense of wonder and of adventure that are rightfully a part of life itself.

In Qabalah teachings the levels of being, both inner and outer, are counted as four. These levels admittedly flow into one another, rather as the colors of the spectrum, which are counted as seven, flow into each other so that we have blue-green and yellow-green, orange-red and purple-red, and an infinity of delicate variations besides.

The four great levels of being that are distinguished in the Qabalah are known as the Four Worlds. In this sense, the term is always given an initial capital, to distinguish it from the worlds that are the planets, or from such expressions as "the world of music" or "the world of commerce." The Worlds are here given their Hebrew names and brief descriptions of their functions in descending order, for they are often pictured as distinct layers that increase in density from the highest to the lowest.

## Aulom ha-Atziluth

The World of Atziluth. This is the world of the divine, and can, as a whole, be simply defined as the Supreme Being: God. But when the Qabalist says, "God is One," it is to be understood that this One is not a sterile and isolated unit but is an entire world, that is to say, an entire universe—perhaps many universes—of intense spiritual existence-action, beyond the power of any human mind to comprehend. The entire world of Atziluth is of the divine nature, God. It is likewise the world of the divine mind, and also the domain of the numberless archetypal concepts, known or unknown to us, which subsist within that mind. These concepts, with all else in Atziluth, being wholly of the divine nature, are altogether without any kind of imagery.

## Aulom ha-Briah

The World of Briah. Below the world of the divine, and less purely spiritual in nature, is the world of mind: here "mind" in the broad sense of the word, is distinct from the divine mind. In the highest experiences of it, however, this is not simply the world of the plodding processes of logic, of induction and deduction, but rather of mind in its fullness, luminous, swifter even than light. Apart from these functions, apart also from the multitude of "archetypal images" that are to be found in it, Briah is the natural abode of the most powerful and majestic living beings, divine in origin but variously imaged by human understanding. Such are those whom we term collectively the archangels: although each of them exists by a separate and distinct sending-forth of the divine mind. Briah is also the world of the gods, beings that have originated as high perceptions envisioned by human minds, and that by reason of their near-identity with certain concepts in the divine mind have gained a glorious and living potency, illimitably beyond any reality that human creativity alone could bestow.

## Aulom ha-Yetzirah

The World of Yetzirah. Below the world of Briah, and much denser and more complex in structure, is Yetzirah, the astral world. The scope of this world extends from high emotion-forms that, in their beauty and sincerity, are scarcely to be distinguished from pure thoughtforms, down to the so-called "etheric" and lower astral levels that exist below the normal range of human consciousness and that are, in some aspects, inimical to it. It is "the world behind this world," where images of past and present merge with images of the future-that-is-to-be and the future-that-perhaps-may-be. It is also the natural region of numerous living beings. Just as the great archangels have their abode in the world of Briah, so Yetzirah is the abode of the angels, those bright and ethereal beings who sometimes singly, sometimes in the shining clusters that we call "choras," perform their varied works. At the different levels of this world abide, moreover, the many kinds of elementals, nature-spirits—the elevated and noble beside the simple and earthly. Beside these again, Yetzirah is frequented by human presences, whether shades of the departed or astral forms of dreamers and others whose consciousness, by art or by spontaneous impulse, are for a time liberated from their corporeal bonds.

We may comment, too, that this, the "astral light", as it is often named, is the world of most powerful creative imagination and also of most false illusion, a perilous but indispensable field of magickal action. In its essential nature it is the region of the great undifferentiated matrix of astral life-force, from which ephemeral beings continually arise and to which they continually return, and from the scintillating current of which embodied beings can draw refreshment and new vitality.

## Aulom ha-Assiah

The World of Assiah. The fourth and lowest of these worlds, and also the most dense and complex in structure, is the material world. By this term is meant the entire universe in its material aspect: our planet. Earth with all that is upon it, around or within it; our sun and solar system; the boundless seething marvel of other suns and systems, galaxies, nebulae and the rest that lies beyond; likewise, the atomic and subatomic structures of matter itself. We have said that the worlds merge, one into another. This is very easily discerned when we consider the misty borderland between the astral and the material levels of existence, between the worlds of Yetzirah and of Assiah. Of the subatomic structures, physical science can measure the properties: but what of the energy-stuff that composes them? Can that basic substance, in itself immeasurable, be called material? And, on a more subtle and more intimate level, to which world—astral or material—are we to ascribe the forces with which the healer or dowser works?

But our preliminary survey of the universe cannot be considered even reasonably complete until we define the place in it of the living human being—the magician, actual or potential.

Human nature is truly as complex as that of the external universe itself, not only in its main plan but in its extension. The universe's Four Worlds exist in us, and we in them; and we can, and should, be fully alive and aware in each of the four levels. Each level—one material and three nonmaterial—correspond to the external four worlds, and are to be looked for in the composition of the individual person.

## The Guph

Plainly the physical body belongs to, and is part of, the material world. We are born of earthly parentage; we must nourish our bodies with the produce of Earth, we must breathe Earth's atmosphere; and at the last, when the body is no longer animated, it returns naturally to the components of this globe. This book has but little concerning the Guph, the physical body in itself, but some aspects of the relationship of body and psyche are essential in magickal development and working. In the individual person, as also in the external universe, the material level and the lower astral are as one in their action. For in the hidden life of cell, gland, and nerve, the action of the body and that of the psyche are inseparably mingled.

## The Nephesh

The whole of the emotional-instinctual functioning of the psyche, from its simplest reaction with sensory perceptions to its highest and most sublimated emotions, is encompassed by the Hebrew term *Nephesh*. The Nephesh is composed of astral substance, and is native to the astral world, the world of Yetzirah. It can participate in all the rich and luminous experience of that world; it can likewise be captivated by its enticements of fantasy and illusion. The Nephesh delights in symbolism and disguise, as it demonstrates often in our dream-life that is its special domain. It is in many respects childlike—truly the eternal child—and in all aspects of life, magickal as well as mundane, it needs the control of the higher functions of the psyche to keep its play from straying into folly or danger. For the Nephesh, of itself, has in its innocence neither rational nor moral direction. Assuredly of all the functions of the psyche, it is, if gently guided with love and wisdom, the most accessible source of creativity and inspiration: it is the source of the creative impulses of the arts—including art magick—and of the "working hypotheses" of science. But in the fulfillment of this imaginative creativity, the action of the brain and of the directing rational mind must play their parts.

## The Ruach

Above the Nephesh is the rational mind, which is comprised within the meaning of the Hebrew term *Ruach*. Rationality is not the entire life and function of the Ruach, but is the most evident aspect of the Ruach in the developing personality. Essentially, the Ruach represents the conscious function of the psyche in forming judgment and decision; but since it is to guide and direct the Nephesh, how well can it do so if its decisions are to be based entirely on sensory experience and other information gathered, and probably to some degree biased, by the Nephesh itself?

The answer is that the Ruach, although the central and governing function of the psyche, is not the highest. The Ruach is native to the world of Briah, the mental world, and should be nourished with the substance of that world. Through the pressures of our civilization, however, and the need to follow a specialized career, the great potential of the mind is often unperceived, so that its higher reaches remain unexplored. Briah is the world in which divine and human creativity need to meet and mingle; and in the action of the Ruach, the divine influence must participate.

## The Neshamah

The psyche as a whole has, by right, its part in the divine life as well as in the life of the lower worlds. The higher self, as it is often called, although abiding in the world of Atziluth, is linked to the personality most strongly in a spiritual bond of love and light. Gradually from that source, as the inner life of the psyche develops and matures, the aspiring Ruach are given understanding, wisdom, and power for the wholeness and true fulfillment of the personality in all the worlds. The inner structure, so to call it, of the higher self is, thus, an exalted and glorious matter; but in its wholeness, in its active and most evident aspect, it is often named in Qabalistic terms as the Triune Neshamah, or simply as the Neshamah.

We, dwelling corporeally in the world of Assiah, are surrounded with the powers and influences of all the worlds and we should, of our inherent nature, be charged with them, to use them for happy achievement in our lives and the realization of our true will. Mystics of every faith declare that the power and glory of God are to be found everywhere; the philosophers tell us that the mind can direct its attention, and thus its presence, where it will. Psychology and parapsychology alike are still exploring, even clinically, the demonstrable powers of the psyche without having found any limit to them; and likewise, without boundaries, is the physiological study of interventions of the psyche. Ideally, all these spheres of activity and power are open to you.

The levels of the external universe, as we have said, flow into one another without rigid lines of demarcation, even as do the colors of the spectrum. Even so, united in purpose and vitality should be the varied aspects of your bodily and psychic life. So also, true to its own nature at each level, should be the interaction of your bodily and psychic life with the life of the greater universe, the cosmos that is all about you and pervades you.

# Book III
# The Sword and The Serpent

This revised Book III
is lovingly dedicated to the
memory of the Princess Maria
Therese Jalowiecka, artist,
and initiate of Aurum Solis in
her chosen name Bhanora.

# CONTENTS

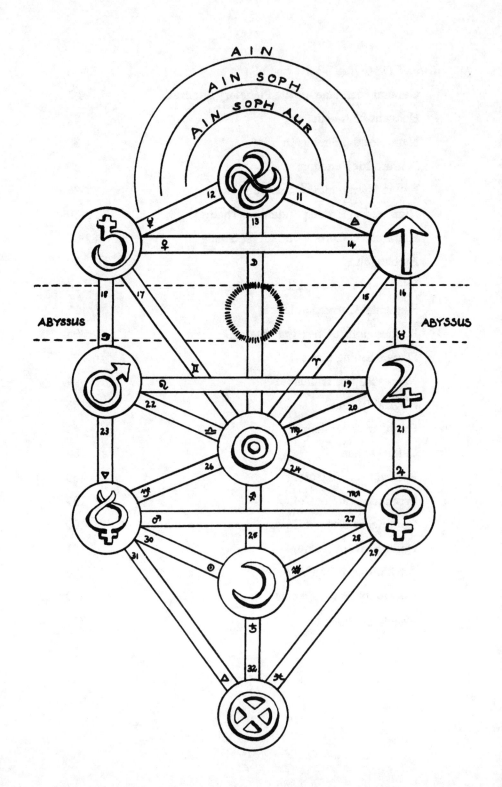

CHAPTER I

The three Veils of Negative Existence: the underlying origin and dynamism of the complex web of positive existence.

The World of Atziluth, the world of Deity: the Divine Mind and the formless Archetypes subsisting therein.

The World of Briah, the plane of archetypal images. Vital importance of connection with true archetypal images in the development of certain religions. The possibility of works of High Magick which are dependent on the Briatic link.

The World of Yetzirah, the Astral Plane or Astral Light. Yetzirah as the world immediately "underlying" or "behind" the material universe. Interaction of the astral and material levels. The true inhabitants of the World of Yetzirah.

The World of Assiah equates to the entire material universe. The confusion which is frequent in older writings, between terms denoting this planet upon which we dwell and terms denoting our solar system with all the stars beyond.

The Tree of Life, a glyph intended for interpretation by the rational beings of this planet. Importance to the student of the symbols and the patterns of relationship shown forth in the World of Assiah. Qabalah and Gnosis.

1

Emanation of the Ten Sephiroth. The Way of Return.

The Qliphoth as unbalanced and distorted sephirothic forces. Parallel between their development and that of "splinter personalities" in human beings.

## CHAPTER I
## THE EMANATIONS

אי'ן

אי'ן סוף

אי'ן סוף אור

The complex web of life which is charted by the Qabalah, conceals an underlying origin and dynamism which is supremely elevated and most austerely simple. The popular concept of a God as ultimate origin of all things is replaced by a state of "negative existence." The most remote aspect of that state, beyond which the human mind cannot conceive of anything further from life as we know it, is termed Ain, "the negative." The next phase, still at a stupendous remove, is named Ain Soph, "without limit" or "the Infinite"; and this is just so far formulated, so to put it, that although completely impersonal it may be described as the Qabalist's ultimate attribution of God. The third phase of negative existence is called Ain Soph Aur, "Infinite Light," and this is almost upon the brink of those states of existence of which the human mind can in some manner conceive. Not quite upon that brink, since every word for "infinite" or "limitless" contains in its structure the idea of a limit or boundary to be effaced. That which in its primal nature has no limit, is thus not truly thinkable. It cannot, indeed, be defined, for to *define* anything is to state its limits. Without quantitative statements, however, something of these notions can be conveyed in terms of relationships, as in that sentence of Marsilio Ficino, "Light is the shadow of God."

These three "negative" modes of Being are generally named by Qabalists, the Veils of Negative Existence. Any concepts or images, therefore, which the foregoing comments may have created in the mind, are to be regarded likewise as "veils," indicating the presence of a concealed truth, but hardly more than that.

Ain, Ain Soph, Ain Soph Aur, from these inscrutable, comes forth the Kether of Atziluth, the "Bountiful Giver," whence the Emanations of the positive universe progressively unfold.

עולם האאצילות

The World of Atziluth is the ultimate of most religious thought: it is the World of those true Archetypes which subsist in the Divine Mind, far beyond the archetypal images which man has formulated for them. Considering this from the viewpoint of the human mind looking towards it from the material world, we can say that the World of the Divine is the world of pure abstraction, of complete dissociation from all shape or form. This is the meaning of the word Atziluth, from the Hebrew verb אצל AtzL, meaning "to remove" or "to abstract." As examples, those archetypal forces which we commonly name from the Seven Planets, thus linking them to the names and characters associated with them in Greco-Roman mythology, have their high essences in Atziluth: and these essences can better be named, not from the mythological images but by titles indicating their archetypal significance:

| | |
|---|---|
| ♄ | Changeless Stability |
| ♃ | Majestic Beneficence |
| ♂ | Valiant Strength |
| ☉ | Lifegiving Splendour |
| ♀ | Celestial Love |

&#9791;    Spirit of Wisdom

&#9790;    Change and Becoming

Besides these, there are the two highest Archetypes, and that of Malkuth. Of these, something will presently be indicated.

The Archetypes in general are to some extent discernable to man in his highest states of awareness, in terms of their significances, which imply also certain relationships: when the seer comes down somewhat from that height he images them, therefore, as Father, Mother, Child, Lover, Priest, or by some other term describing such relationships. The ten divine Archetypes of the World of Atziluth are of the greatest importance in our study, not only as modes of Divine Being, but also because they are the highest and most perfect types of the Ten Sephiroth. Man has seen the reflection of these essences on level after level down to the material world, and proliferating throughout the material world, and has framed thereon systems of symbolism to chart his own way of return to the heights.

It is noteworthy here, although the fact will become much clearer as we proceed, that the emanations of a Sephirah may be received in a different "plane" or "world," but nevertheless they always represent the same Sephirah. The reflections down through the worlds of the Divine Archetype of the Sephirah Hod, for instance, may be manifested by god-forms, by various spiritual beings, by "astral" or material phenomena, by human beings or other living creatures; but all these manifestations, insofar as they are truly "Mercurial" or "Hermetic" in nature, are attributable to the Sephirah Hod, and help to constitute the manifestation of Hod at their level. In this sense, we may say that it is the Sephiroth which link the Worlds.

## עולם הבריאה

Next below Atziluth is the World of Briah, the realm wherein dwell the Archangels and all great Gods "to whom men prayed or pray." The name of this World is derived from the Hebrew verb בָּרָא BRA, meaning "to create." As this name indicates, it is the World of Forms. It is the plane of the great archetypal images, as distinct from the Archetypes themselves which are beyond form.

Briah is the "World of Creation" when considered in its relationship to the plane of Atziluth, but its relationship to the plane immediately below it is expressed by another name. Since Yetzirah is the World of Emotion, Briah is the Intellectual World. This distinction is important, since Yetzirah, the Astral Light, also has its images, which are extremely numerous in view of the fact that to Yetzirah belong most of the forms whose origin is on the material level. Most of the images in Yetzirah are activated by emotions arising from the material world, and frequently these are of so confused a character that, although we may ascribe them in a general way to one or another Sephirah, they cannot be completely drawn into the sphere of that Sephirah and so cannot rise higher. The images in Briah, however, are truly oriented and have become linked to the Archetypes which give them a new impulse. Thereafter, they are known and contemplated by the higher human faculties.

This transition is very marked in the development of certain religions. A religion may begin as a not very enlightened, not very inspiring cult, fostered by a group of devotees who want hope or healing, rain for their crops or victory in battle, or something equally mundane and obvious. It happens that their chosen god or goddess approximates to one of the archetypal images which the subconscious or unconscious mind can recognise. Because of this unconscious and therefore subrational identification, the cult spreads and prospers, and the astral image of the deity becomes tremendously strengthened; but all that informs it at this stage will probably be the emotional impulses and motivations of the worshippers.

Then a change occurs. It may be due to the spiritual genius of one man, or to the adventure of an entire people; but in some way the worshippers are brought into contact with a vision of the higher planes. The astral image of their deity, hitherto activated only by the aspirations of the worshippers, now becomes a channel for, and a vehicle of, the true divine power of the corresponding Archetype in Atziluth. It is this which brings maturity to a religious system. The simple relation between deity and worshippers, which existed in earlier times, gives place to a more elaborate theology now that an increasing number of spiritual values are discerned. The form of the deity becomes established in Briah, the Intellectual World; as long as the cult continues, and probably for long afterwards, this form remains as a means by which contact can be established with the Archetype. Eventually, if that particular channel remains long unused, the archetypal force will be withdrawn and the Briatic link will dissolve. Thereafter anyone desiring to invoke the deity will have to work arduously from basic principles to establish what will in fact be a new cult. This may not succeed, owing to fundamental changes in methods of approach or modes of thought; nevertheless, it is occasionally a matter for awe, to see what living echoes from ancient time can be reawakened by one who has the authentic keys and who has worked patiently to re-establish the link.

| | |
|---|---|
| Atziluth | The World of the Divine |
| Briah | The Mental Plane or Intellectual World |
| Yetzirah | The Astral Light |
| Assiah | The Physical Universe |

## עולם היצירה

The World below Briah is the World of Yetzirah, and is what is generally known as the Astral Plane or Astral Light. Be it noted that the Astral Plane is altogether distinct from the material universe which is the World of Assiah. The

Astral Plane is the "substance" of the World of Assiah: that is
to say, the World of Yetzirah immediately underlies the
material universe and is in a certain sense causal to the
material universe. Changes take place in the World of
Yetzirah before becoming manifest in the world of matter; in
this fact lies the secret of much magick and of much
clairvoyance. To have a true and lasting significance,
however, the chain of causality should not be merely
Assiah-Yetzirah-Assiah, but should descend or should be
caused to descend in due stages from the World of Atziluth.
As has already been stated, Yetzirah is thronged with images
arising from Assiah; most of these are formed spontaneously
by emotion, some are formed by thought and may be created
deliberately. The images in Yetzirah tend to shift continually,
and emotion can move and change them as the wind moves
and changes cloud-forms; but thought can fix them.

Besides these shifting images, Yetzirah has its true
inhabitants: Potencies and Forces of various natures; Spirits
of the Solar, Lunar and the several planetary Spheres; and
Elementals, associated with one or other of the four
Elements in the Sphere of Malkuth in the World of Yetzirah.

## עולם העשיّה

The World of Assiah, the Material World, is the last of the
Four Worlds in the order of causality, the most dense in
fabric, and the lowest in mode of existence.

Many Qabalists through the centuries have tried to limit
the significances of the whole material universe to the Sephirah
Malkuth in Assiah. This is partly the result of a clinging, no
longer justifiable, to the old mode of thought, which made no
distinction between world and universe. One word could
signify either this planet, or everything as far as the Sphere of
Fixed Stars. *Kosmos* meant either world or universe to Plato,
*mundus* meant either to Cicero, and some people have failed to
revise their thinking since. In Qabalistic philosophy a further

cause of confusion has been the arrangement of the Tree of
Life into "Three Triangles." We shall return to that point
later. To bring our view of the World of Assiah up to date, we
must see it as coextensive with the material universe as now
conceived. The Sephirah Tiphareth, in Assiah, for example, is
represented in the Solar System by the Sun; likewise every
nebula is a sublime symbol of the First Sephirah. At the same
time it is true that every vortex of ocean or of desert is a
lesser symbol of Kether, just as in considering the human
body as Microcosm we would say Tiphareth is represented by
the heart. In the modern Qabalistic philosophy of the Aurum
Solis, Assiah *is* Matter: it is the material manifestation of
those forces whose pattern is established on the Inner Causal
Planes. (Atziluth, Briah and Yetzirah).

Here certain questions are fruitless. One such question is
this: "To us, this Earth to which we are native represents the
Sephirah Malkuth, while the planet Venus (for example)
represents the Sephirah Netzach; but what would be the
situation for a native of Venus?"

The only answer which can be given to this, is to point
out that the Tree of Life is a glyph developed by inhabitants
of this Earth for their own use, and that the symbols
associated with it are derived entirely from the universe as
seen and experienced by inhabitants of this Earth. We do not
doubt that among the teeming myriads of worlds which are
clustered throughout the universe, other forms of life exist,
with modes of consciousness developed in terms of their own
environment. We, however, the inhabitants of Earth, are so
conditioned by our own particular nook of the universe as to
be unable to conceive of other modes. It is useless to regret
such limitations, nor indeed should we do so; for this very
conditioning has given to us the means by which we chiefly
learn. Some vibrations impinge upon our senses as colour,
others as sound; we perceive forms, we can reflect upon
purposes and contingencies. Thus, clue by clue, we learn

somewhat to read "in nature's infinite book of secrecy."

The other question which is sometimes uselessly asked comes from the student who has been attracted by the neat diagrams and tabulations of forces and attributes representing the Sephiroth in the other worlds, but who perceives, inevitably, that the World of Assiah is quite otherwise: attributions and manifestations are scattered through the material universe without perfection, without sequence. "Why is Assiah so different?" this student asks.

Again, the question itself is at fault. The questioner has mistaken the order of things. The multiple symbolisms of the World of Assiah give it the very quality which indicates the validity of the Tree as a pattern of relationships; as has previously been shown, man has worked from symbols pre-eminently, expanding his ideas and knowledge from that basis. An abstraction is, literally, something which has been abstracted or drawn forth from its material associations; until this process has become familiar, therefore, it is virtually impossible for man to reason in pure abstractions, and, in fact, any textbook of philosophy is filled with examples and analogies drawn from the material world to help the mind follow the line of reasoning. In such books, when a concept is needed which has no direct counterpart in the material world, a favourite example is a blue swan. It is not very difficult to imagine a blue swan; but the reason is that we are picturing the well-known form of a swan, and adding to it the even more familiar quality of blueness. Thus the human mind always works, in close stages from the known to the unknown.

Thus the sequences and patterns of relationship which we perceive in the material world, indicate to our minds certain ideas and concepts which have their own true reality, but at which we have first arrived by knowing their material counterparts. Our concept of Beauty, for instance, is drawn forth from our experience of beautiful beings and things; but

the essential reality of Beauty exists as an Archetypal Power
in the Divine Mind, and the existence of this Power is the
true reason why our minds are able to perceive beauty where
they might otherwise have discerned only mathematical
balance, for example, or biological aptness, or a certain
refraction of light. Our concept of Motherhood, too, is drawn
from our experience of that relationship, and Freud rightly
points out that this concept will have a dark as well as a
bright aspect: maternal severity, the mother who administers
discipline and withholds indulgences, is as "real" as the
maternal bounty of her who guides and encourages her
children with gifts which foster in them a more adult understanding. Often in the material world, both aspects are seen
in the same mother; and the Archetype of Motherhood in
the Divine Mind has these two aspects also. Thus an understanding of the Tree of Life gives us a means of contemplating the forces which it represents: the material world
illustrates for us the Archetypal Powers in action, and then
the pattern of the Archetypal Powers gives us a further clue
by which we can penetrate more deeply into the lessons of
the material world without losing our way. Similarly we
may learn to read maps by comparing a map with a living
landscape; but, this achieved, we can take a larger map and
use it in our exploration of territory which before was quite
unknown to us.

In the case of the Tree, that is by no means the end of
the matter; because here we have four "territories" or levels
charted, not merely one; and although the diagram of the
Tree is a true guide to each level, the experiences of the levels
are different and distinct. They are much more different, for
example, than a tract of northern forest in summer and in
winter: the map representing that land does not change,
although in one season it represents a green, shaded country
divided by streams of flowing water, and in winter it
represents a land of white snow and bare boughs, where one

can travel directly onwards over the ice. The geographical features, also, do not change. So likewise with the Tree of Life: the Ten Sephiroth do not change, although in Assiah they are manifested by a diversity of material symbols, in Yetzirah by the shifting visions of the Astral Light, in Briah by the potent and awesome presence of the Archetypal Images, in Atziluth by the entire reality of the primal Archetypes in the Divine Mind.

Although from the viewpoint of man in the material world, it can be stated that the World of Atziluth, the Divine Mind, is the ultimate abstraction, far more important is that order of reality in which Atziluth is true and vital Being, from which the three other Worlds successively derive existence. The work of Jung and his school on the archetypal images present in the deeper levels of the human mind, far beyond the reach of the conscious inventive processes, points to the presence in these images, or in the process of their formulation, of great common factors, spiritual realities pre-existing, to be modified in their manifestation by the conditions of the individual psyche. The data of the psychologists is limited to the results of their investigations; therein lies the integrity and the value of their work. But the writings and pictorial representations produced by men in ancient times are as valid a subject of investigation as the products of today, and Jung, who became a keen collector of the scripts and artefacts of the Gnosis, was fully aware of the unity of evidence from age to age as to the nature of the spiritual substructure.

The Qabalah and the Gnosis are, in essence, one: the Gnosis having been developed from the main body of Qabalistic tradition by minds predominantly Greek in training and outlook, more free in speculation than the Jewish, and naturally more apt to multiply mythologies. Yet the unbiased student of the documents will find that interaction between Greek and Hebrew thought has been great and fertile. Here, the exact tracing of origins and

identification of traditions is not our concern: out of the
body of resultant teaching which has been preserved to the
present time, it is our task to state that which has come to us
as a living reality; and of which we are convinced, not merely
by its intellectual validity and richness, but by what is for us
the acid test: as the basis of a magical system, it works.

The Divine Mind, then, has brought the universe into
being according to its own intrinsic pattern. Force is balanced
by Form, Mercy by Severity; kinetic force is balanced by
static through the whole series of archetypes in the Divine
Mind itself. We cannot intellectually know those archetypes
as they are, for our intellects are not equipped to know Being
which is purely Act, and such is the nature of an Archetype;
but we can attain to the state of glimpsing the reality of their
existence, for certain penetrating thinkers and seers have
after intensive preparation done so. These divine and stupendous forces are conceived of as having successively come into
existence and into balance; for man has from ancient times
traced in the fundamental nature of spiritual forces that
principle which Augustine in his mode, and Hegel later in his
different mode, adopted and enunciated: the fact that any
spiritual force will first bring into being its true opposite, and
then, balance having been achieved, will conjoin with that
opposite to bring into being a product of the two. This causes
a new imbalance, so that new pairs of opposites, new unions
and new resultants follow. Thus far Hegel's theory of thesis,
antithesis and synthesis. It makes for an indefinite development, unless and until presumably the initial impulse is either
exhausted or balanced out.

In the development of the universe, it has been
perceived that different factors supervene. In the World of
Atziluth we contemplate a force, indeed a schema of forces,
completely spiritual and totally *living*. This schema of forces
having attained a pattern of perfectly balanced relationships,
becomes closed at that point: the World of Atziluth is

complete. The initial Source of Power is, however, inexhaustible. There follows an outpouring of force to the formation of the World of Briah, which consequently becomes filled, not directly with the Divine Mind but, rather, with the powers of the Divine Mind; the process of opposition and union of forces, however, is repeated at this level until the World of Briah is completed. So the remaining two Worlds in turn come into being. At last, however, the World of Assiah having been brought about, a reflux current may be discerned. The material universe, and in a particular manner the mind of man, projects its astral creations back into Yetzirah. Man discerns the possibility of the Way of Return. A very small proportion of the human race has found that possibility immediately attractive, although as a distant prospect it wins the assent of a larger number.

Thus Spirit is conceived of as descending into Matter by a process of involution, and returning thence to Source by a process of evolution. Here, for some students, a difficulty arises. If the process of evolution will in due time inevitably take its course, what avails the Great Work whose avowed goal is precisely similar: to carry us forward upon the Way of Return?

There is really no adequate answer to that question, because it is all a matter of individual temperament and character. Some spirits will strive, some will avoid effort. We believe that the greater the effort, the shorter the road, but also we believe that those who seek the Work now, and the Wonder, shall find greater work and greater wonder. Even if this should not be so, still we see that the ultimate symbol before us is not the Circle, but the Spiral. From this we infer, that though we return to our origin, it is not our business to arrive there even as we were in the beginning; we cannot truly fulfill our destiny unless we have wrought somewhat in ourselves and in the worlds. Yet even if there were no destiny to fulfill, the Wonder would still lead us.

In the plan of the universe that we have been considering, there are two other questions which predominantly arise. One is, What becomes of the totality of energy from the inexhaustible Source?

Quite simply, we do not know and it not our business to know. We know Power, Force, Energy, is always there and can always be "brought down" by one who has the necessary understanding. However, in a universe where, on the material level, the number of stars probably exceeds 1,000,000,000,-000,000,000,000, it is evident that the outlets of such energy are more vast and more numerous than we could suspect.

Another question associated with this one concerns the unbalanced aspects of force brought into being at the various stages of development of the Sephiroth in the Worlds below Atziluth. This applies to the development of all the Sephiroth: but let us take a specific example at the stage when Chesed (whose Divine Archetype we have named as Majestic Beneficence) has emerged, but has not yet produced its opposite, Geburah (whose Divine Archetype we have named as Valiant Strength); at this stage, such an imbalance exists. There is a surplus of Chesed-force, and this is, so to say, thrown off by the Sephirah which maintains its own true character and dignity without distortion; but that which is thrown off becomes a caricature of the Sephirah, a separate entity whose imbalance and exaggeration are made permanent by its dissociation from the developing schema of the Tree.

A clear distinction is important here, between the creation of this outlawed product of unbalanced force, termed a Qliphah, and the emergence of the normal antithesis or synthesis. In the first place, each of the Ten Sephiroth differs completely in significance from the others, whereas the Qliphah thrown off by a sephirothic force is of the same general import as that force, differing only by exaggeration and imbalance. Thus the Sephirah of Chesed, as we have seen,

produces its antithesis, the Sephirah of Geburah: Order
produces Energy. But the Qliphah, or rather, the Qliphoth
(for these splinter-forces tend always to further breakdown
and disunion) of Chesed are characterised as Weakness and
Decay of Strength, the Qliphoth of Geburah as Cruelty and
Barbarity.

It may further be asked, whether we should not expect
the qliphothic forces to balance one another as the sephirothic forces do? In fact, we can see clearly from their effects
in mundane life that this is not so. Not all the harshness
in the world can temper one jot of the hesitancy and
sentimentality; not all the weakness, or abdication of
authority, can mitigate savagery and malice.

The process of formation of the Qliphoth has a parallel
in the processes of the human psyche. Jung has shown that in
the psyche, at a depth which cannot be called "personal,"
there exist the great archetypal images to which we have
already referred. These images are demonstrably related to
the true Archetypes; and although, in dreams for instance,
they may sometimes move in the personal levels of the
psyche and participate in actions which reflect personal
conditions, still their more profound character is manifest.

We are not at the moment concerned with the majority
of these archetypal images in the psyche, but with those
which are termed Animus and Anima. If the subject be a
male, the conscious personality takes the place of Animus,
but a figure representing Anima may be seen as an objective
character. If the subject be a female, the conscious
personality takes the place of Anima, and a corresponding
sequel follows. This pair of opposites play an important part
in the normal development of the personality, and
correspond in their major aspects to the Supernal Sephiroth
Chokmah and Binah:* it is noteworthy that Anima-Binah,

*For further development of this study see Book IV.

whether she appear in her bright or dark aspect, is still felt to be one and the same Mother, whereas Animus-Chokmah is multiplex as the host of the stars, his material symbol. Besides these true archetypal functions, however, there is frequently to be found another character regarded as distinct from the main personality; this is termed the Shadow. In an imperfectly developed personality, this often takes an equal or even a greater part in the inner drama. It is not opposite in sex from the subject; in reality it is a part of the conscious personality, but having been thrown off and disowned it has developed a pseudo-character of its own, with some repressed attributes of the conscious personality in an exaggerated form. It may be seen either as an arch-enemy or as a powerful friend (much as the medievals considered their "Devil"), but the therapist's task in either case is to lead the subject by degrees to recognize that these attributes are really his own, and that the Shadow, unlike the true archetypal image, has no licit existence.

If we compare this to the position of the Qliphoth in the schema of the universe, we see that their relation to the Sephiroth is in each case very much that of a splinter-personality to the main consciousness. The Qliphoth have not, in fact, their own qliphothic Archetypes, but are dissociated developments from the true Archetypes in the Divine Mind.

In the light of this parallelism in the consequences of imbalance, the wholeness of the pattern of the sephirothic powers in each of the Four Worlds can be seen as a necessity, that the equilibrium among those powers may be maintained. For a universe as for an individual person the greatest good lies in balance, not in the excess of any impulse.

Zohar I, 8b notably illustrates the point in mythocosmic terms. Here the qliphothic power appears, certainly not as an exponent of "evil" as this is conceived of in modern theologies, but as a divinely originating force which has lost its harmony and balance with other such forces. In the mythic narrative of the passage in question (which is a reflection upon the second

Book of Samuel, chapter 11), the qliphothic leader Dumah, named as commanding myriads of destroying angels, presents himself before the Holy One to demand the destruction of King David. Dumah is here represented as an uncompromising upholder of strict justice and literalism: the divine Arbiter defeats his logical arguments, not by meeting them on their own ground, but by holding to a comprehensive archetypal overview. Divine omniscience, and David's allotted destiny, combine to take the matter out of the hands of unmitigated, single-sighted rigor, and sephirothic balance is maintained.

We can turn from this far-off imagery, however, to trace the action and interaction of the true sephirothic powers in the very making of our material world.

## CHAPTER II

The traditional symbols in Assiah of the sephirothic Powers.

A more direct demonstration of the sephirothic functions in Assiah, which can be perceived with the aid of a more up-to-date knowledge of the material universe.

*(N.B. All sephirothic processes can be traced at any level of existence. To give useful limits to the vast scope envisaged by the rest of this chapter, the functions of the Sephiroth of the First Triad are here considered in terms of the coming into existence of the material universe, the functions of the Sephiroth of the Third Triad, together with the Sun-sphere, in terms of processes upon this planet Tellus which is our home, as far as the emergence of life. For the general significance of the sephirothic Triads, see pages 37-38.)*

Space as representative of Negative Existence: the first showing forth in space of the function of Kether as an increasing field of energy manifesting as white heat of incomparable intensity. Emergence of the Chokmah phase: the Big Bang. Development from energy particles through to the cooling of tenuous gases: the Binah phase. Development of conditions representative of the Sephiroth below the Abyss. The coming into being of our Sun and of the planets associated with it.

19

Forces which act directly upon this planet.

Lines of force set up in quasi-organic radial or segmented
forms: before life is present, the patterns in which life is
maintained become established.

The single-celled organism.

The sciences and living reality: magical development through
knowledge and experience. The magician as artist.

Awareness at all levels. Objectivity and inner response. The
powers which have shaped us, indicators of the means to
our willed attainment.

# CHAPTER II
## THE EMANATIONS

*Genesis I: 1-20, Revised*

In chapter VIII of *The Apparel of High Magick*, brief reference is made to the symbols in Assiah of the sephirothic Powers.

|    | Sephirah | Cosmic Symbol in Assiah | Hebrew Name of Symbol |
|----|----------|-------------------------|------------------------|
| 1  | Kether   | Spiral Nebula           | Rashith Ha-Gilgalim   |
| 2  | Chokmah  | Sphere of Fixed Stars   | Masloth               |
| 3  | Binah    | Planet Saturn           | Shabbathai            |
| 4  | Chesed   | Planet Jupiter          | Tzedeq                |
| 5  | Geburah  | Planet Mars             | Madim                 |
| 6  | Tiphareth| The Sun                 | Shemesh               |
| 7  | Netzach  | Planet Venus            | Nogah                 |
| 8  | Hod      | Planet Mercury          | Kokab                 |
| 9  | Yesod    | The Moon                | Levanah               |
| 10 | Malkuth  | Tellus (Planet Earth)   | Cholem Yesodoth       |

These traditional symbols, if considered with the type of understanding in which they were conceived, have a unique power and do in fact reveal a great deal of the sephirothic processes. Kether, Primal Unity, the "First Swirlings," is typified by the Spiral Nebula: the image is of an intense white brilliance, whirling with that swift inner motion which is usually seen to precede either formulation or fission. In the event, it is fission. From Kether is produced Chokmah, the Second Glory: this however manifesting not as

21

one Light but as many, an outpouring torrent of chaotic
dynamism in the Sphere of the Zodiac. Binah, the Third
Sephirah, is typified by the slow-moving, huge and cold
planet of Saturn. The Saturn of mythology is an elder deity;
with his deposition by Jupiter, the "Golden Age" is closed
and the reign of the actively manifest begins. In the sequence
of the Sephiroth in Assiah from Chesed to Yesod, the
mythologies of Chaldaea, Greece and Rome are interwoven
with astronomical and astrological lore.

When we proceed to the Malkuth of Assiah, as
represented by this planet upon which we dwell, we find that
the influences of all the other Sephiroth, and indeed of all
the Worlds, do truly, from our viewpoint, converge upon us.
They manifest around us, and in us, in the most intricate
complexity. The symbolic indicators in Assiah of the
sephirothic Powers are still the heavenly bodies associated
with them from ancient times; they remain unchanged and of
prime importance in our schema. However, among the
attendant throng of ideas, we can discern other developments
of the sephirothic forces in Assiah. For instance:

### Prima Materia and Big Bang

Space, initially, in this connotation, symbolizes the Ain
Soph: negative existence. A number of physicists in past
generations have made the mistake of trying to identify
Space with a hypothetical aspect of positive existence, as for
example, an ether; but the negative attribution is needed to
fulfill all the conditions. Out of that Negation appears the
First Sephirah, Kether: הגלגלים ראשית . Movement
indicates the presence of energy, and energy is the potential
of matter. Whence comes this first impulse? Not *ex nihilo:*
certainly it is not the offspring of the unchanging void.
"Nothing will come of nothing: speak again." Here is the
mysterious but essential nexus between the Worlds: energy
pouring through from the Astral Light at a point which is at

first truly without dimension. This energy is not the out-flung imbalance of a single Sephirah: it holds concentrated in its single brilliance the influences of all the Sephiroth as these have been developed and balanced in the three Worlds down to Yetzirah. It is thus a true Kether-force, אור פשוט,* coming into material manifestation as an increasing field of energy manifesting as white heat of incomparable intensity.

The force-fields increase as tremendous areas of electrical tension. The critical point is reached: that which the Qabalists have termed the emergence of Chokmah, and the physicists have dignified as the Big Bang! A vast field of primal force disintegrates in the unheard cataclysms of massive electrical explosion. Myriad upon myriad electrons suddenly released recoil upon themselves, spin, revolve about one another; some exchange charges, becoming protons, neutrons or other energy particles. The first varied associations are formed, becoming stabilised as atomic structures: some of a few such infinitesimal particles, others of greater numbers. These first atoms hurled in great clouds through space make up what can only be conceived of as the most tenuous of gases, but a gas is atomic matter. The tremendous development of our universe has begun.

The primal gas cannot be supposed a pure element; the atoms contained therein are representative of all the elements in chaotic mixture. We have previously pointed out that Saturn is the visible symbol of the force of Binah because Saturn is pre-eminently huge, cold, and emblematic of formative constriction: but now our contemplation witnesses the action of a higher, invisible representative of the Binah-function in our universe. The primal gas is hurled outward from the centre of explosion into the void, and now the

* AVR PShVT, Pure Light, a traditional title of Kether.

Binah phase supervenes. Still at white heat, it has neverthe-less lost temperature considerably, and contraction and an increase in density ensue. Long have the Qabalists spoken of a "sterile Mother" without being deterred by the paradox, and in this they are right, for this aspect of Binah is typified by the contracting of the radiant torrent of Chokmah in the cold womb of Space into which it has been poured. Yet Binah is also to us a bright and fruitful Mother, for it is her tempering and formative power which makes possible the development of all that sustains our life.

It is said of the Supernals that they are separated from the rest of the Tree by an immeasurable abyss. This is true in Assiah of the inceptive Supernal manifestations we have been discussing, as it is true in another sense upon the higher planes.

The Supernal forces in the World of Assiah manifest on an awesome scale. To gather something of the vastness of the outpoured forces we must consider distance in terms of light, which travels at a speed of approximately one hundred and eighty-six thousand miles a second. If we were to travel from our star (the Sun) to the next nearest star, Proxima Centauri, it would take us four light years; that is, it would take us four years travelling at the speed of light. But our star and Proxima Centauri are only two among the estimated one hundred thousand million and more stars in our galaxy. This huge concourse of stars is itself separated in space from other galaxies by tremendous distances. For instance, the spiral galaxy Andromeda, which is a "near" neighbour, is about two million light-years from us: two million years at one hundred and eighty-six thousand miles a second. It is estimated that there are thousands of millions of galaxies.

Returning now to our consideration of the involutionary forces, the emergence of matter to a recognizable condition brings us from the realm of the

Supernals into that of active manifestation. At each level, the Abyss marks a clear distinction between one mode of being and another. This shift of attention on our part does not mean that the action of the Supernals can be presumed to have ceased. It never ceases, at any level. Kether is still the Source, Chokmah the Supernal Father; the action of Binah continues in restricting and in giving form. Under her influence, therefore, Matter continues to contract.

On the level of action in the far-flung Prima Materia in Space, other forces come into play: gravitational attraction, represented by Chesed, and centrifugal repulsion, represented by Geburah. Every particle, great or small, in the universe, has a gravitational attraction to every other particle; every moving particle has a tendency to escape from the gravitational pull. The attraction is of Chesed, orderer and law-giver; the escape tendency is of Geburah, disruptive, catalytic, not only balancing Chesed but also strongly modifying the power of Binah. The great gaseous masses, still travelling outward from the site of the explosion, are moving continually further from each other and are becoming each more dispersed and attenuated. Taking one of these vast clouds of gas as an example, we see that it begins to revolve upon its centre (we are here considering only the formation of a spiral galaxy). The area of the cloud as a whole continues to increase, but the atoms of which it is composed are at the same time drawn towards one another in groups and agglomerations by the forces of attraction and gravitational pull. Inevitably, therefore, a considerable part of the cloud is torn into fragments, each fragment of glowing vapour developing its own gravitational centre, and contraction about this centre produces a new increase in internal temperature. Thus, in the particular series of sephirothic manifestations we are considering, begins the Tiphareth phase: from the incandescent, fragmenting, coalescing deluge of star-stuff, the stars are born. One of these stars is our Sun.*

The exact cause which brought our Solar System† into being is a subject of scientific doubt, but this doubt is of no importance in the main line of development which we are following. The cause is in any case within the order of the attractions and repulsions already existing. A probable hypothesis is that in the separation of the portion of vapour-cloud which formed the Sun, fluctuations and vortices were set up which produced ancillary focal centres, the origin of fragments which, being so much smaller, cooled to a far greater extent. Whether we accept this hypothesis or some other, certain it is that fragments of such material began orbiting about our Sun.

We are here examining natural processes which in their actual development flow gradually, each into the next, during countless ages, but sephirothic phases can nevertheless be distinguished therein. Initially these nascent planets are white hot and gaseous, but in due course they cool towards solidification. Here we identify two further sephirothic functions which have entered successively into the pattern, to participate in determining the planets' character and structure: Netzach and Hod. The powers we have previously named continue their action upon the orbiting material; but now within it, Netzach, Force, combines and elaborates; Hod, Form, separates and distinguishes. In the amorphous fluid spheroid, moulded by external and internal forces, chemical reactions gradually lead to an agglomeration of solid compounds, a dissolving of chemical salts, a separation of

* This chapter is not a scientific treatise, and is concerned only with illustrating the principal action of the Sephiroth in cosmic terms. To our regret we cannot here enter into such manifestations as neutral hydrogen, galactic nebulae, interstellar matter, supernovae, irregular galaxies and other phenomena. We are simply presenting a neat universe in which every dancer gets a partner.

† At this point we must begin to limit our comments to particular examples in which we see the action of the Sephiroth in the sequence of causality leading to the phenomenon of an inhabited planet: specifically, the Planet Tellus.

solid masses from liquid, a throwing off of gases. Then, as when solidity is approached in any cooling material, we see the mingled molecules separating out to form crystals and masses of their particular substances, manifesting their distinctive natures.

These processes likewise continue, but in their entirety we contemplate a composite structure, a geological whole. These vast crystalline aggregates are mountain ranges; these accumulated mineral solutions are seas. The Yesod phase, synthesis of the work of Netzach and Hod, is before us: a violent drama in which the actors are the whirling, raging, frenzied forces of nature.

It is a well-known axiom in Qabalistic philosophy that "every Sephirah contains a Tree"; so that all the sephirothic processes can be traced within the function of Hod, for instance, or within the function of Chesed, or of any other Sephirah. It must, however, be borne in mind that although we can easily identify secondary sephirothic functions within a particular phase of involution or evolution, this is an artificial simplification. The repeating patterns of sephirothic functions continue side by side and ad infinitum throughout the manifest Worlds; on the physical plane, the various processes can be traced through to sub-microscopic level.

Thus far we have traced the course of involution, but in Malkuth the tide turns: with Malkuth the involutionary processes are completed, and the processes of evolution begin.

We see a world, a mineral ball suspended in space, reflecting from its surface the light of the Sun. All movement, all manifestation in this world is of chemical or of physical origin. This world is all the geological structure which is to be clothed with the green and the rich colours of fertile earth when its Malkuth phase supervenes; it is all the mineral potential which would provide the basis for that manifestation. But whence comes life?

Now we see our world as the fulfilment of all the sephirothic forces converging upon it. Cosmic rays are bombarding it, the Sun is beating down on it, causing the solid and liquid minerals of the surface to vaporise continually, forming and re-forming clouds in the atmosphere. Here there is an echo of the supernal pattern: clouds increase, electrical tension builds up, and lightning begins to play among them.

The descent of the Lightning Flash is one of the great Qabalistic symbols of the advent of life. When these physical lightnings of which we are writing strike, there is neither man nor any other corporeal being to witness them or to perceive their importance. Yet harbingers of life indeed they are. As the lightnings flash again and again, gases are produced in the atmosphere, to be washed down by rain with their resulting compounds into the seas, the rivers, the lakes. Many chemical substances, furthermore, are transmuted by radioactivity, which at this early period subsists in a considerable number of metals and other minerals later found only in an inert, exhausted form. Thus in the early history of the world, the great waters become stored with compounds of carbon, oxygen, hydrogen, nitrogen, phosphorus, including nitric acids, hydrocarbons and amino acids, and giving rise to innumerable others.

For how many ages this stage of development continues we cannot say; but amino acids and other nitrogen compounds are the foundation of protein, and protein molecules are the foundation of life, to which the other chemicals are also necessary. The Sun, the Tiphareth force, rays down its warm and vital light upon the seas. There the amino acids and the other minerals react and conjugate, bound up with the hydrocarbon colloids. The tensions in colloidal droplets, the inherent molecular rhythms of crystalline substances, provide recurring lines of force in radial and segmented quasi-organic forms; long before life is present, the patterns in which life is maintained are established. And then at last, almost imperceptibly, the new factor is produced: life has come into being. From the colloidal droplet, the single-celled organism evolves in the protozoic slime. Here is a notable effect of the Netzach influence: life from the waters! This is the true primal manifestation in Malkuth, of Venus Anadyomene.

We need not trace the emergence of the evolving life-force any further; indeed, to cover its every aspect would be beyond us. A good textbook on biological prehistory should provide the student with plenty of material for an exercise in identifying the sephirothic influences in the natural agencies which impinge on this earth. Astronomy and astrology, too, afford matter for reflective study which no aspirant to magical understanding and power should neglect.

These last-named subjects cannot for their full effectiveness be acquired from text-book and ephemeris only; even though the illustrations in modern astronomic studies, and the exactitudes of the ephemeris, are in their own ways indispensable. Magick is an art rather than a science: and although the painter or sculptor of, say, the human form will be helped considerably by knowledge of anatomy to interpret what he sees, a true mastery of the art will come only from contemplating the living figure. So also the magician, aspiring to work with and through the forces of the universe, will attain the grand vision and dominion of that art only through contemplation of the living kosmos.

It may be necessary to remove oneself from the city's glare to achieve this contemplation in physical reality, but this is in all respects effort well spent. Astrological concepts which may have seemed very theoretical will spring into the vital reality of personal experience. Perhaps for instance the student sees two planets approaching conjunction: the more distant luminary—more distant, in scientific fact, by many millions of miles—looking as it were over the shoulder of the nearer one, and approaching more closely in perspective until their light comes to the observer in what is virtually a single blended beam.

Or astronomic happenings which are of little consequence in relation to the boundless immensities of the night sky can be seen, and inwardly felt, by the watcher as disturbing the physical and astral ambience with all their primitive force. Such an occurrence might be a lunar eclipse, or the return of a comet. To explain these things in the domain of reason is not rightly to explain them away in the emotional-instinctual domain, any more than scientific understanding should destroy our delight in seeing a rainbow or our awe at the elemental magnificence of a great storm.

For the magician needs by practice and habitude to be aware, and in control, at all levels of consciousness. On the one hand, sending the gaze of eye and of mind into vast starry distances, he should be able without losing wonder to review the discoveries of science, to ponder the nature of nebula and "black hole", and be able to dare—more logically than many scientists—to seek the truth of the unanswered questions by following evidence and reason without compromise, wherever they lead. On the other hand he should be consciously aware that with all this he is a child of this small solar system which exists almost marginally to its galaxy: he is a sentient being upon whom the powers of this Sun, this Moon and these planets most immediately act: and that in all his life, as in the magical art, it is through these limitations, these types of a grander scheme, that he finds his own greatness.

# CHAPTER III

*This chapter elucidates some considerations arising from Chapters I and II.*

Traditional Hebrew names of the Ten Sephiroth, together with their meanings and inalienable numbers.

Involutionary order of the Emanations: the Sword.

General significations of the Ten Sephiroth.

The Three Columns: the Column of Mercy, the Column of Severity, and the Column of Equilibrium. The Sephiroth thereon.

The Three Triads. The Composite Tree. The Way of Return: the Serpent.

The great Gate-Sephiroth of the Column of Equilibrium. In gaining a higher level of consciousness by these Gates, the practitioner does not lose the faculties associated with the lower level.

Rising on the Planes: a brief description of the experience of this exercise.

31

Tiphareth, the pre-eminent Gate-Sephirah through which power descends, and through which the initiate passes to Adepthood.

Daath, the hidden Gate.

Hymn to All the Gods:  Proclus, its author, seeks through knowledge of the holy writings to find help upon the Way of Return.

The Fourfold Tree:  a description of a diagram sometimes seen which makes for confusion in some respects but creates a great sense of the continuity of the Worlds. "Each Sephirah unfolds from the preceding phase as a new modality but without spatial separation."

Further concerning unbalanced forces:  dependence of the Qliphoth upon the true Archetypes. A plea for the Environment.

## CHAPTER III
## THE EMANATIONS

The Ten Sephiroth, or Emanations of Deity, have Hebrew names which give a key, but no more than a key, to their significances. In fact, any name or title given to a Sephirah must be a simple abstraction, since its content should hold good of that Sephirah in any of the Four Worlds.

The traditional names of the Sephiroth are translated as follows:

|  | Transliteration | Translation |
|---|---|---|
| 1 | Kether | Crown |
| 2 | Chokmah | Wisdom |
| 3 | Binah | Understanding |
| 4 | Chesed, Gedulah | Mercy, Magnificence |
| 5 | Geburah | Strength |
| 6 | Tiphareth | Beauty |
| 7 | Netzach | Victory |
| 8 | Hod | Splendour |
| 9 | Yesod | Foundation |
| 10 | Malkuth | Kingdom |

The Sephiroth, when they are referred to by number, are always numbered as here shown in their descending, or *involutionary*, order, because this is their own order of emanation. Later in this chapter the "Way of Return", the *evolutionary* order, is introduced: and even there, although for

33

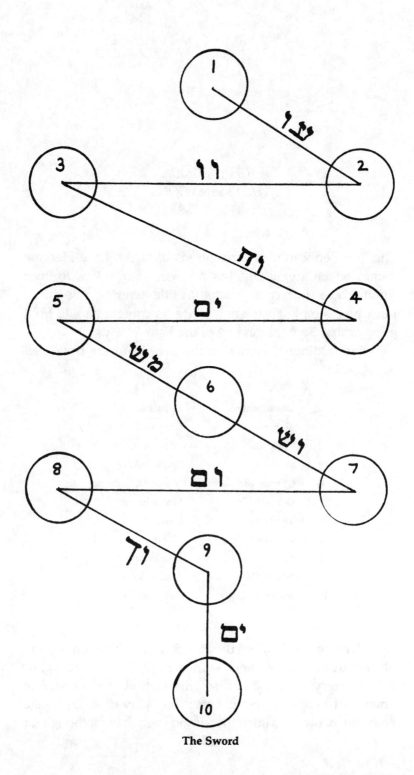

The Sword

example its starting point is in Malkuth, that Sephirah is still, in that context as in every other, the Tenth.

The involutionary order of the Emanations is symbolized by the diagram of the Sword* on page 34. We see that the descending force passes from Kether to Chokmah, and thence across to Binah; over to Chesed as lightning leaps across a vast valley, and back to Geburah; thence diagonally through Tiphareth, that great centre of transformation, and continuing in the same line to Netzach, the natural complement to Geburah; across once more to Hod, the balancer of the Tiphareth-charged energies of Netzach, and thence to Yesod upon the midline, Hod and Netzach being equilibrated; vertically down now to Malkuth, the realisation and fulfillment of the forces gathered in Yesod.

In order to understand more deeply the meanings of the Sephiroth in their various relationships, we may thus identify the types of force represented by them:

1   Unity
2   Expansion
3   Constriction
4   Order
5   Energy
6   Equilibrium
7   Combination
8   Separation
9   Conception
10  Resolution

From a contemplation of the diagram of the Tree and the various patterns to be perceived therein, certain key concepts emerge. For instance, it can be seen that the Sephiroth are shown as situated upon three verticals, the Three Columns.

*For the signification of the Hebrew letters on the diagram of the Sword, see Appendix E.

Severity          Equilibrium          Mercy

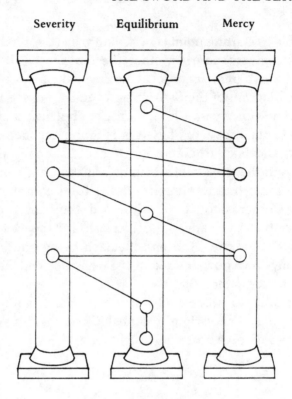

Here the Column of Mercy is represented by Expansion, Order, and Combination; the Column of Severity by Constriction, Energy and Separation; the Column of Equilibrium by Unity, Equilibrium, Conception and Resolution: Conception in this series being the equivalent of the alchemical Projection. The central column shows Kether, Tiphareth, Yesod and Malkuth; to one side of it is the column of Chokmah, Chesed and Netzach, to the other side is that of Binah, Geburah and Hod. From what has previously been said, it will be evident that the columns are formulated in such a manner as to play the parts of Thesis, Antithesis, Synthesis. The Columns of Mercy and of Severity, as we have shown, represent far more than is usually implied in the words by which they are named: the first stands for all that gives and maintains life at whatever level, the second for all that restrains, guides or conditions the life-force. The Column of Equilibrium is the expression of balance and harmony between these reciprocal influences; nevertheless it too is a vital part of the pattern, for the balance and harmony are not a mere cancelling-out of influences, but always, at whatever level, produce a creative force.

Another manner of considering the pattern of the Tree is concerned with the individual distinctions of the Sephiroth. This is the system of the Three Triads.

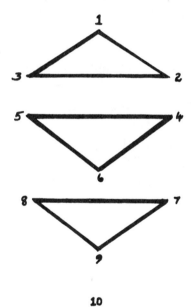

The first Triad: Kether, Chokmah, Binah, the Three Supernals. Kether is the source of all things; Chokmah is outpoured Force, the Archetypal Male; Binah, the constrictive or formative influence, the Archetypal Female. Chokmah and Binah are a perfectly balanced pair of opposites.

The second Triad: Chesed, Geburah, Tiphareth. The Sephirah Chesed is universal order; it represents masculine authority and is a manifestation within the Column of Mercy;

it is the Male as Lawgiver. The balancing force in this case is
another male image, dynamic Energy, although situated in
the feminine Column of Severity; for here we have the Male
as Warrior, and although admittedly this image is more
violent, so equally the implications of discipline and of
obligation are more narrow. The great difference which
distinguishes this pair of opposites from the Supernal pair, is
that both Chesed and Geburah stand in a direct relationship
to action and experience, in which the influence of the
Supernals is indirectly causal. As in other sephirothic
distinctions, this should hold good no matter which of the
Four Worlds we are considering, since it is implicit in the
function and nature of the Sephiroth themselves. The third
point of this Triad is Tiphareth, the "solar" sphere, and here
again we enter into a new involvement with the motivation
and action of human life, albeit we are considering, for
instance, man's relationship to the World of the Divine.
Tiphareth, the synthesis in one sense of Mercy and Strength,
but in another sense of Wisdom and Understanding, can but
show forth aspects of self-sacrifice. Tiphareth, the reflection
of Kether, is truly the child also of Chokmah and Binah: it is
the Logos, the power of the spiritual force raying its
splendour down into the lower Sephiroth.

The third Triad is made up of Netzach, Hod and Yesod.
Netzach and Hod are here the balanced opposites: Netzach is
force, Hod is form. Netzach gives the all-encompassing
emotional drive, the unbounded maternal life-current; Hod
gives intellectual precision of purpose, apt judgment of
opportunity, analytical deployment of means. Neither
Netzach alone, nor Hod alone, could arrive at the perfect
conception of a project. The synthesis of Netzach and Hod,
however, is Yesod, the reality of that conception; for Yesod,
in every one of the Four Worlds, is the sphere of generation.

At this stage it seems appropriate to deal with the
theory, which has inspired both truth and error, of the

Composite Tree. Stated briefly, this theory refers the Supernal Sephiroth to the World of Atziluth, the Second Triad to Briah, the Third Triangle to Yetzirah, and the Sephirah Malkuth to Assiah.

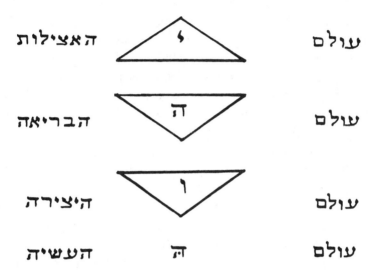

| | | |
|---|---|---|
| הָאֲצִילוּת | י | עוֹלָם |
| הַבְּרִיאָה | ה | עוֹלָם |
| הַיְצִירָה | ו | עוֹלָם |
| הָעֲשִׂיָּה | הָ | עוֹלָם |

This is by no means a modern view of the Tree; it is implicit in a number of the Zoharic texts for example, and appears in scattered references in the writings of Giovanni Pico della Mirandola (1463-1494) who, besides being the devoted student of the texts themselves, received also the oral instruction of several Rabbinic teachers of European repute. From these and other sources, more modern writers have copied the concept without regard to its true meaning and purpose.

In considering the Sephiroth objectively, the "Composite" interpretation has no place. All the ten modes of being which are the Sephiroth, exist in each of the Four Worlds. This does not multiply the number of those modes of being. If we say, for example, "Beauty exists in the World of the Divine, in the Intellectual World, in the Astral Light and in earthly manifestation," that does not mean that there are four different and distinct qualities called Beauty. Without doubt a different type of beauty exists in each of the worlds, but to divorce these four completely from any common factor, any underlying unity of the word Beauty, would make the attribution quite meaningless. The same applies to Strength or Splendour or any other sephirothic attribution. Despite evident differences of application in the Four Worlds, there is a recognisable thread of identity running through the different levels as we contemplate the meaning of Strength in the Divine World, in the Intellectual World and so on. It becomes evident thereby that the Ten Sephiroth do in fact exist in the Four Worlds, each world in its own kind being fulfilled by them; nor, in fact, do Qabalists ever explicitly contradict this view, which is manifestly their true teaching.

It is likewise possible, without at all contradicting this true teaching, to trace a degree of correspondence between the Worlds and the sephirothic Trines.

It is when we consider man's Way of Return that the "Composite" view of the Tree rightfully comes into its own. The changes of level on the journey of Evolution are by no means haphazard, but are the consequence of certain highly potent magical properties of the Sephiroth of the Column of Equilibrium. The natural progress of the Soul upon the Way of Return must here be distinguished from the conscious, magical, accelerated progress of the initiate; in a word, the natural progress of evolution is characterised by the gradual, often unrecognised unfoldment within the psyche of cosmic awareness.* The Way of Return, or of Evolution, is conceived of as beginning from the Malkuth of Assiah, the material world in which we physically dwell, to retrace, broadly speaking, the course of Involution, so that ultimately the

---

* There is, of course, on the natural way of progress always the "natural initiate," the person who without guidance or deliberation does in fact come into direct contact with sephirothic forces; but apart from this exceptional case, the way of natural development is not by that direct contact.

highest spiritual level is reached. In the diagram of the Serpent on page 42 this concept is indicated by the twining of the enigmatic coils about each Path in due turn.* Here there are several necessary conventions, since it would be impossible to state diagrammatically the variations in each case; therefore, each Path is shown as being visited once only.

In real life, however, there are many returns and visitations; any part of the progress may take many lifetimes, and in no lifetime does man dwell continually at the highest level that he attains; always "the bow must be sometimes unstrung," to quote a traditional phrase. The essential point which we wish to clarify here is that the Way of Return envisages a rising through the Worlds at the same time as an ascent by the Paths, and always it is through the influence of the Sephiroth upon the column of Equilibrium that such a change of level is caused. Naturally, in terms of evolution, the treading of the Thirty-Second Path from the Malkuth of Assiah does not necessarily signify that one has left physical life for the Astral, but that through development of the faculties, through the first "venture into the realm of the subconscious," the psyche is opened to the subtle influences of the Astral World; and thus with the continuing progress. Similarly, it is not anticipated that the Adept who gains the Briatic consciousness through the mysteries of Tiphareth will lose thereby the more ordinary levels.

An interesting example of the change of level indicated by the Three Triangles is afforded by the technique known as Rising on the Planes, in which the consciousness is exalted by means of a series of key symbols. Fundamentally, the great difference between the exercise of Rising on the Planes and the evolutionary Way of Return is that in the exercise, which

---

*Although shown as issuing from Malkuth, the starting point of the evolutionary journey, the Serpent is not depicted as entering any Sephirah on its upward course. The sole purpose of the diagram is to indicate the ideal sequence in which the Paths of the Tree are to be taken: a progression which, in its fullness, necessarily brings the psyche to experience the magical virtues of all the Sephiroth in due and potent succession.

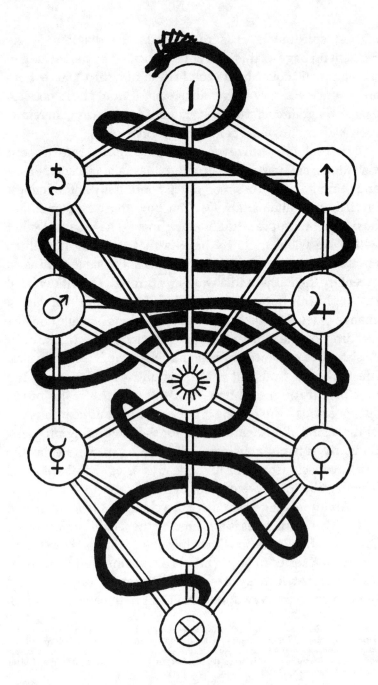

**The Serpent**

is a mystical rather than a magical experience, only the Column of Equilibrium is followed, and then no higher than Tiphareth. The great point of resemblance between the exercise and the evolutionary process, however, is that it is precisely these Gate-Sephiroth upon the Column of Equilibrium through which the consciousness rises to higher worlds. In Rising on the Planes, one's consciousness "ascends" from Malkuth by the 32nd Path, to the Yesod of Yetzirah, then by the 25th Path directly from Yesod. It is in the mystical experience of Tiphareth in Briah that the journey culminates. One feels oneself rising vertically, swiftly but as through immeasurable space. There is an intuition of vast altitudes, of speeding upwards, lost to all sense of time, until suddenly one breaks through into the Sephirah.

After Rising on the Planes, as with all magical operations in which a change in the level of consciousness is effected, one must not omit the willed return to normality. This can be difficult, for there is that within the psyche of the practitioner which does not wish to return to earthly life, being content to bask elsewhere.

Tiphareth is the Sephirah which above all others is the Gate of the Worlds. This Sephirah is the great Gate by which power descends, not only from the Kether of each World to its lower Sephiroth, but also from the higher Worlds to the lower. Thus it comes about that a Divine Being incarnating in the Malkuth of Assiah, appears as a solar hero. This same Sephirah gives the Adept access to Briah; but the key of the Gate on the upward route—the Sacrament of Tiphareth so to speak, which the Adept consummates—is death: understood as a sacrificial death. Ritually enacted it may be, but the validity of the ritual form is contingent upon, and linked to, the spiritual reality underlying it. Be it noted here that physical death does not automatically result in awareness of the Briatic level; this depends on the state of evolution of the individual. From the initiation of Tiphareth the Adept "rises" into the World of Briah. From that point, the further Sephiroth thereof, Geburah and Chesed, await him upon great steeps of ascent.

Higher than Briah it is not in any case for us to pursue the matter, since Atziluth is the plane of Divinity itself. There are, in fact, no further Gates upon the Tree of Life (excepting the great ultimate, Kether) since Daath is never shown regularly as a Sephirah. It is to be observed, however, that Daath does also lie upon the Column of Equilibrium and is stated to be in a different dimension (that is, to represent a state of being of a different order) from the other Sephiroth. Daath is "the hidden Gate" which takes the Adept across the Abyss and beyond the limit of normal human modes of knowledge; but this Gate is well-guarded, and he who before his time dares the "Adventure of the Abyss," as the Master Therion calls it, will find the Secret Door sealed with a seal of power that all his art cannot break. From the confusion of the Abyss shall such a one be cast back upon his true level. What further consequences may result from his presumption are impossible to determine. To prevent grave misconception, therefore, is Daath not shown upon our diagram of the Serpent.

### HYMN TO ALL THE GODS

*O Gods, ye who guide the course of holy Wisdom, hear me!*

*Ye who kindle in human souls the flame of return, who lead them back to the Immortals: ye who bestow in your festal songs which are secret initiations, the power to win free from the dark cavern of ignorance:*

*Hear me, great Lords of Freedom!*

*Grant me by knowledge of the holy writings, by dispersal of the night which encircles me, a high and true perception: that I may truly know the incorruptible God, and the man that I am.*

*Let me never as a supreme misfortune, in forgetfulness turn my face from you: never may a dread retribution bind me to earthly life, or my soul to its icy deeps:*

*For my desire is not to linger therein.*

*Hear me then O Gods, Sovereigns of the Radiant Wisdom: and reveal to*
*one who hastens on the ascending Path of Return, the ecstasies and the*
*initiations which are enshrined in the divine words.*

                                        Proclus (trans. by O.P. and M.D.)

There are other aspects of the Sephiroth upon the Tree which must be mentioned. One important aspect of the Sephiroth is their microcosmic application in terms of the human psyche. This microcosmic manifestation of the sephirothic forces will be dealt with at length in Book IV, *The Triumph of Light,* a study of psychology and magick.

Another aspect of the Tree, whose consideration belongs to this chapter, is in fact impossible to explain fully. What follows here must be taken as a basis for meditation, therefore, rather than as a plainly literal exposition.

One sometimes sees a diagram in which the Sephiroth are shown set out as upon the Tree, four times over, one series below the other, so that the Malkuth of each World in turn becomes the Kether of the next. The descending power is traced, as in our illustration of the Sword, down through the Sephiroth in Atziluth; then as a continuous line down through the Sephiroth of Briah, and so on. When it reaches the Malkuth of Assiah, there is usually some indication that the force is transmitted from thence to the Qliphoth. This diagram brings out some aspects of the matter very clearly, albeit at the expense of others. It shows beautifully the blossoming of World after World, each coming into being at its own level after the completion of the previous World. The primary causal Emanations unfold in the World of Atziluth. From each Emanation proceeds the next, until the Malkuth of Atziluth which completes that World. Then begins the unfoldment of the World of Briah, according to the archetypal pattern established in Atziluth. Initially, the whole potential of Briah is comprehended within the Kether of Briah, the phase of being which immediately follows the completion of Atziluth. The diagram makes difficulties,

however, because at first glance it suggests the existence of
four series of Sephiroth, and in any case it indicates no
particular connection between, say, Hod in Assiah and Hod
in Yetzirah. In attempting to represent the Four Worlds in a
two-dimensional diagram, a difficulty seems inevitable which
is similar to, though more acute than, the difficulty which
besets cartographers in presenting a two-dimensional map of
the material world: in conveying one truth, another is always
found to have been completely falsified.

The fact is that the principal value of all such diagrams
is to be found in their use as aids or mnemonics for those
who have already grasped something of the qualities
represented. We may take the several presentations of the
Tree and reflect upon them so as to gain a composite mental
picture of the truths indicated by each, but the more
important thing for us now is to consider the realities of the
Worlds and of the Sephiroth, so that these vital symbols may
gain new meaning for us. A characteristic scene, a
characteristic human figure or enactment, an emotional or
intellectual quality, should spring to the imagination, and will
do so with practice; but even these impressions are in danger
of becoming dead stereotyped "counters" unless revitalised
by magical and meditative use. *Each Sephirah unfolds from
the preceding phase as a new modality but without spatial
separation.* When the Sephiroth are known by experience as
realities, the diagrams present no problems.

The Sephirah Hod has as its chief symbol in Assiah a
superb planet which, for brilliance as well as from its position
in the heavens, is frequently mistaken for Venus. The planet
Mercury, however, is not taken to represent the forces of
Nature triumphant, as Venus is, but the formative mind
receiving and adapting spiritual illumination: that is, a
masculine potency with certain feminine characteristics. (It is
noticeable here how spontaneously one Sephirah is
interpreted in terms of relationship to another.) Among the
other material symbols of Hod we have herbs of medicinal

virtue, a translucent gem with fire in its heart, and a cold liquid which is in reality a molten metal; in each case it is potency hidden in latency, again indicative of intellectual force. On the astral level, therefore, Hod is typified by the bi-formed, the androgynous, the mysterious: Centaur and Sphynx and the winged Pegasus all have distinct connotations in the realm of intellect, representing Learning, Enigma and Inspiration respectively. (In Greek myth the Centaurs were regarded as particularly skilled in medicine, in mathematics, and in the music of the lyre; which last was classically regarded as akin to mathematics, and as an invention of Hermes.) In the World of Briah, the God-forms of Hod include Thoth and Hermes. There is thus no difficulty in identifying the manifestations of Hod in the different worlds as being interrelated, and the same is true of each Sephirah. One could add to the traditional diagrams of the Tree another, representing each Sephirah as a vast cylindrical column standing with its base in Assiah, its shaft rising through the mists of Yetzirah and the star-like forms of Briah, to its capital in Atziluth. This image also, however, while showing some aspects of the matter clearly, would assuredly obscure others.

Upon the subject of the Qliphoth, this consideration of each Sephirah as a mode of being, rather than as a circle on a diagram, throws further light upon the affinity existing between the Qliphoth of a particular Sephirah, and the Sephirah itself. This is a matter which is frequently mis-understood. It is often assumed, for instance, that if the sephirothic forces of Chesed induce generosity (as they do), then the qliphothic forces of Chesed will induce miserliness. This is altogether an error: the qliphothic quality correspond-ing to the generosity of Chesed is prodigal extravagance. The ideal, the Archetype, is exactly the same in the case of the virtue and of the vice. Thus, to illustrate further, with Hod whose characteristics are intellect and analysis: the cor-responding qliphothic aspect would not be stupidity, but instead, a heartless and hypercritical curiosity. Qliphothic aspects exist in Briah, Yetzirah and Assiah, their manifestation varying with the level. There are not, however, any Qliphoth of the World of Atziluth: Atziluth is entirely the World of the Divine Mind, which is infinite, and there are not and cannot be two Infinite Minds; neither in the one Divine Mind is there place for qliphothic Archetypes.

There is a particular aspect of imbalance on the material level which especially commands our attention at the present time. It has become amply clear that every serious mind, and still more, every aspirant to occult wisdom, must take thought for this our planet. Hitherto, through the ages, our predecessors have been able to draw strength and inspiration, spiritual as well as physical nutriment, from this Earth in whose sphere we work. The tragic crisis of our times is that unless the doom can be averted, all the natural beauty and bounty of a world which we have supposed our birthright, but which has been left too long a prey to ignorant and greedy exploitation, will be lost to us forever. To all dwellers upon Earth such a state of things is calamitous; to those who work with the natural forces, and who as an essential condition of the work must love those forces, the threat combines on a major scale something of the crumbling of the foundations of one's home, with the fatal sickness of a sister. It behoves us to devote our most urgent attention to this question.*

* With the publication of this new edition, this paragraph is urgently emphasized, and support of organizations concerned with the welfare of the natural world is strongly recommended by the authors.

# CHAPTER IV

Any Being which we may require to contact in our magical work, can be considered as relating to one or other of the Sephiroth, in one or other of the Worlds.

The Supernal Sephiroth, transcending magical operation yet continually influencing it. The dual significance of Binah-Saturn and the high importance of the forces of limitation in creative work.

The Sephiroth of the Manifest Powers:—
    The nature of Chesed.
    The nature of Geburah.
    The nature of Tiphareth, with a brief inquiry into the nature of beauty.
    The nature of the Sephirah of Netzach; the inapplicability of moral values to the Sephiroth below Tiphareth.
    The nature of Hod, which when associated with the vitality of Netzach becomes the most magical of all the Sephiroth.
    The nature of Yesod, and its essential relationship to the World of Yetzirah.
    The nature of Malkuth, the Bride, the Lower Mother.

The Elementals, and the magician's responsibility towards them.

49

Deific forces and the Tree of Life: male forces discussed in relation to the Sephiroth Chokmah, Geburah, Chesed, Tiphareth and Hod; female forces discussed in relation to Binah, Netzach, Yesod and Malkuth. The Mystery of the Sophia.

## CHAPTER IV
## THE EMANATIONS

From what precedes, it is evident that any possible Power, or any possible Being, of no matter what kind, that we may wish to contact in our magical work, can be considered within the scope of one or other of the Ten Sephiroth in one or other of the Four Worlds. A further survey of the Sephiroth from this viewpoint should emphasise the value of these categories.

The Three Supernal Sephiroth are beyond the range of magical operations in the strict sense of the words; nevertheless, their presence should never be forgotten or disregarded. Kether is ever the true source of Power, and in certain procedures it is necessary to bring energy through the "microcosmic Kether," that is, through the Kether-center above the head of the individual. Of Chokmah and Binah, the primal Paternal and Maternal Forces, more will be said presently; it remains true that the Supernals do not directly come into practical work, but their mystical significance, and thus their indirect influence in the practical realm, is immense. Binah indeed, besides this high maternal aspect, also comes into our reckoning as the Sphere of Saturn, with the beings and influences thereof: the austerity and limiting tendencies of Binah are strongly reflected in the Saturnian characteristics, but this sphere is thereby denoted as vitally important for those who accept the limitations of matter and work with them as a medium for their aspiration

51

to the heights: that is, primarily for artists and for ceremonial magicians. As for everyone else, it can be indicated that the centuries in which the Saturnian limitation could be dismissed as "malefic" are at an end; in the present age, the possibilities of achievement have broadened so far that nobody can truly do everything well. While one-sidedness is to be avoided, some degree of selection is needed as never before. Success in any endeavour is gained by a wise choice of voluntary limitations. To be "qualified" is, as the word itself signifies, to be "limited" suitably. The Saturnian powers, therefore, are to be regarded certainly with the reverence due to the powers of a Supernal Sephirah, but should by no means be ignored or shunned in craven fear.

When we come to the Sephiroth of the Manifest Powers, the situation is clearer: the nature of each Sephirah associates it with a particular type of magical working. Chesed, the Sphere of Jupiter, is particularly the Sephirah of the merciful and peaceful King, Priest and Lawgiver. By rites of this Sephirah we celebrate the deific powers of fatherhood and of the heavens: Zeus or, equally, his brother Poseidon, or the Etruscan Tinia. Operations concerned with mercy or prosperity, the interests of the defendant in legal matters, the responsibilities of civic leadership, all show forth various aspects of this sphere. Everything used in the rites should reflect the majestic and mystical qualities of Chesed, of such kingly names as Melchisedek and Solomon, of the particular authority and sublimity which De Quincey found in the words *Consul Romanus.*

Geburah, the Sphere of Mars, is the Sephirah of the Warrior-King, of divine justice and strength, Ares, Ate, Mars, Oghma, Elohim Gebor, in their particular cosmogonies. We may prepare a path for the mighty Kamael, we may call upon those burning Seraphim who touched the lips of Isaiah with glowing coals. For this is the sphere of those who go forth against that which is ill done: the surgeon no less than the knight-errant, the prosecutor or plaintiff in legal matters, those responsible for the initiative in any civil or military campaign against injustice. We may recall the lurid elaborations of the Temple of Mars in Chaucer's "Knight's Tale"; these are too fanciful to be in keeping with the true spirit of Geburah, but the setting of stark steel and scarlet is correct, with all that makes for Spartan austerity, simplicity, and disciplined power.

Tiphareth is the Sphere of the Sun. Magically it is the sphere of transmutation and metamorphosis, that great good which is seen from the exterior as the privation of sacrifice. The three great God-concepts of Tiphareth are the child, the crowned king and the sacrificed god, and all these are different phases of one reality: for the king is a divine king, who is in due course sacrificed, to be reborn as the child. These three phases make up the solar cycle, and in turn show forth the inception of Adepthood. To this Sephirah, therefore, are attributed the triumphant and the mournful, the child and the adult gods of incarnation and of rebirth, Dionysus, Osiris, Adonis, Mithras, Jesus, the Child Horus; Harpocrates if we look to later Egypt, and, if we look to the East, Krishna. The Hebrew God of this Sephirah is Yahveh Eloah V'Daath, a phrase variously interpreted, but evidently signifying "The God of the Four Elements in Manifestation and Knowledge." The applicability of this title is shown by the position of Tiphareth, not only on the straight way between Kether and Malkuth, but also located centrally upon the Tree. Tiphareth is the heart of the Tree, the great meeting-place of the forces which work *through* matter, with those which work *upon* it.

The name of the Sephirah itself, Tiphareth, means Beauty: and this when understood gives an insight into its nature. Characteristically, it was in reality to the God of Tiphareth that St. Augustine addressed himself when he wrote, "Too late I loved thee, O thou Beauty ancient yet ever

new! . . . and behold, thou wert within, and I abroad. . ." The
whole of that great twenty-seventh section of the tenth book
of the *Confessions* is an inspired perception of the nature of
Tiphareth.

What, then, is Beauty, that it should hold this central
place in the plan of our philosophy? It has been said, that in
all true beauty there is some strangeness of proportion—a
statement which must imply that the greater component of
beauty is not this strangeness, but is a familiar predictability
of proportion; both qualities are necessary. Augustine's
words express something of this: "ancient, yet ever new."
Catullus, to whom beauty was the beauty of woman, in his
own way contributes to our verdict, in that poem which
denies to the perfectly proportioned Quintia the description
"beautiful": "I grant she is blonde, tall and straight . . . but
she has no charm, not one grain of salt in all her stature." It
is precisely a combination of perfect proportion with the
"grain of salt" which Gerard Manley Hopkins points out, in
his unfinished essay on the nature of beauty, as constituting
the beauty of a horse-chestnut leaf. This leaf has five or seven
radiating leaflets, all except the central one being ovate in
shape, and progressively increasing in size from the outside to
the central leaflet, which not only is the largest but is
adorned with a bold terminal point. The regular increase in
size of the similar leaflets, combined with the originality of
the central one, give a fine example of beauty of form which
would be marred, as Hopkins points out, if either the
harmony or the contrast were lacking. Although he never
finished the essay, if one studies his poems it is not difficult
to complete the line of thought. "Pied Beauty," and "The
Sea and the Skylark," most clearly state it outright; but,
submerged, it runs like a purple thread through the tapestry
of this devoted student of Duns Scotus. He would say that
the recognised, the known-from-of-old, combines with the
fresh uniqueness and surprise of the present moment to show

forth Beauty which is, furthermore, Divine Beauty. We can add that this Divine Beauty is Tiphareth, for in this Sephirah the eternal and the temporal flash and fuse into unity.

Tiphareth is then the especial Sephirah of consecration, whether of persons or of things. It is both the Sephirah through which life strikes down into matter, and that which draws it forth again.

In moving from Tiphareth to Netzach, we move into that group of Sephiroth which represent what may be called "purely natural forces." There is often some confusion as to the exact difference between the sephirothic forces above and below Tiphareth, particularly as the difference has to be stated in terms equally applicable to all the Worlds. This it is, then, which holds good in Assiah, in Yetzirah, in Briah and in Atziluth: that with regard to Tiphareth and to the forces above Tiphareth, one type or another of moral value can be contemplated; but below Tiphareth, such considerations would be incongruous. This, doubtless, is the reason why MacGregor Mathers calls the trine of Chesed, Geburah and Tiphareth the "Moral World," and Dion Fortune calls it the "Ethical Triangle"; but it seems less needful to stress that aspect of the matter, than to point out that below Tiphareth the concepts of moral obligation do not apply.

Netzach is the Sphere of Venus; the Hebrew God-name in this Sephirah is Yahveh Tzabaoth, God of Hosts, and the name of the Sephirah itself signifies Victory. To this sphere are ascribed joyous and gentle god-forms: Aphrodite and Hathor, Bast and La Sirène, as well as the beautiful and terrible ones, Maeve and Astarte, and tower-crowned Cybele. These are deities of the great sustaining powers of nature and, life-giving and beneficient though they are, their "terrible" aspects proceed from the fact that they are at all levels without moral or human bias. This truth hardly needs enlarging upon: magical work is potent in this sphere, but wishful thinking emphatically is not. Less evolved forms of life are frequently better equipped for survival, and the powers, even the deific powers, of the Sephiroth below Tiphareth do not spontaneously change the course of nature for our benefit; whereas those who work in harmony with these powers find success in their endeavours, even though the morality of their actions may not be above question. The early part of the Old Testament affords a number of examples of this kind. An understanding of the forces of Netzach also gives us the key to such Biblical utterances as "The sins of the fathers shall be visited upon the children." The amorality of this statement scandalises many people quite needlessly: we have here a highly perceptive utterance concerning the forces affecting human life and happiness, and if one wished to criticise it, it would not be appropriate to say, as some folk try to, "A just God would not permit such a thing!" One has to look at the conditions of disease, pollution, poverty and neurosis into which children often are in fact born as a result of the misdeeds of past generations, and to perceive that where the Divine Mind is set at nought in the lower Sephiroth, it cannot be invoked in the higher. This is a paramount principle in magical work. For many of the malcontents, however, the test is too great: having failed to comprehend or to master Netzach, they take refuge in the scepticism of Hod.

It must not be concluded from this that the Sephirah Hod is without magick: it is in some ways the most truly magical of all the Sephiroth, but it is so only in conjunction with the vitality and force of Netzach. If we follow the course of the Sword, we trace the flow of power from Netzach in the Column of Mercy to Hod in the Column of Severity; we may say that this power transmitted by Netzach is intellectually formulated to the purposes of Hod. The masculine intellect is thus receptive, here, to the feminine life-transmitting principle, and this situation is the key to a number of androgynous representations of Mercury, to be found especially in alchemical documents. Conformably with this idea, the Divine Name Yahveh Tzabaoth associated with Netzach, is balanced in Hod by Elohim Tzabaoth: if the former is the God-of-the-elements of Hosts, the latter is Goddess-God of Hosts. The God-forms of Hod are those associated with the scientific aspect of mind; the principal examples are Mercury, Hermes and Thoth. Hod signifies Splendour: and the especial splendour of Hod consists in the mental perception of that fulness of life and of life-forces which come from Tiphareth through Netzach, now as it were crystallized into intelligibility, flooding the consciousness not with an undefined ecstasy but with thronging ideas, winged inspirations. Netzach works with the forces of nature, Hod with the forces of mind.

We must see the operations of Hod not only in this relationship with Netzach, but also in relation to the next Sephirah in descent: Yesod, the Sephirah in which the forces of Netzach and of Hod resolve before the projection of Malkuth. If Intellect is to dominate this fusion of Mind and Instinct, it must be Intellect backed wholeheartedly by Emotion. The magician must not only know, but feel, the essential rightness of his work: rightness in the sense that a passage of music must be "right," the placing of forms in a painting must be "right." The underlying structure in both these examples is mathematical, yet mathematical correctness is insufficient unless a person sensitive in these matters can "feel" it to be so. The result otherwise would be what popular language in one of its flashes of insight calls *barren* intellectual exercise: and it is not the business of magick to be barren. To justify its existence, magick must ever be fruitful of result.

If result is to be manifest in Malkuth, then, it must be fulfilled in Yesod. Yesod—Foundation—is the great Gate-Sephirah of Yetzirah, the Astral World. The identification is so close, that Qabalistic authors frequently

write of Yesod as Yetzirah, and vice versa. The Hebrew
God-names in this Sephirah are El Shaddai and El Chai: God
the Omnipotent, the Living God—most potent names to
express the Divine Archetype of this magically potent sphere.
The God-forms are likewise most powerful: the Three-formed
Goddess (Diana the Bow-Maiden, Selene of the Silver Disc,
Hecate of the Waning Moon); also the Fertility God,
frequently horned, whether Minos of the Bull, for example,
or Cern-Owain (Cernunnos) of the Stag-antlers. The Moon is
of prime importance in magical working, because of the
highway of ascent from the Malkuth of Assiah through the
Yesod of Yetzirah. The Malkuth of Yetzirah is primarily the
underlying substance of this world as it is, but it is by nature
static. The powers of Malkuth resolve and establish the
influences they receive, and to effect change which is to
manifest in Malkuth we must work through the power of
Yesod, which is dynamic; it is no good hammering with one's
will on the doors of the things that are. Though we work
within Malkuth and the action of our rite takes place on the
physical plane, yet must our rite have its astral counterpart;
this is not to imply that every operation will be of a lunar
nature, but quite simply that our magick must be lifted into
the Astral World through the great Gate-Sephirah. From
Yesod, the "Treasure-house of Images," the concourse of
forces awakened and called forth by our rite is projected
back into the Malkuth of Yetzirah, and thence, if our magick
be such, into the Malkuth of Assiah. This is precisely the
reason why all students of magick are warned not to perform
any operation "in the dark of the Moon." In those few days
of each lunar cycle between the disappearance of the waning
Moon and the reappearance of the new Moon, the impetus
which is needed to lift the work into the Sphere of Yesod is
lacking: the purposes and components of the rite, falling
back upon themselves therefore, may well end in chaos.*

* CAVE CANEM!

Yesod is then a most powerful factor in magical work, but there are two reasons why some people tend to be afraid of it. One reason is that associated with the Yesod of Yetzirah there is a great deal of illusion, which is, naturally, encountered by the student as soon as he begins to progress in any serious work. The only sure methods of countering this are, first, to provide a channel as soon as possible for the higher forces of Yesod; secondly, to work with patience and with that real humility which does not consist in under-estimating oneself, but which does consist in getting on with one's work and so allowing no spare attention for fantasy and self-congratulation. The second difficulty with Yesod is the predominantly sexual nature of many of its connotations. This, again, is a factor which is likely to strike many at their first venture out of the sphere of everyday consciousness; and anyone who has encountered the wide realms of wild imaginings which surround the whole subject of sex, will readily sympathise with those who are alarmed thereby. However, the student is not bidden to cast himself adrift on that turbulent sea; none should in any case embark thereon without a clear sense of purpose and direction. Safeguards against the various kinds of unbalanced force which may be encountered are set up at the necessary stages of the work. Unbalanced force within oneself is, however, the chief peril; and those who are fascinated by some particular element, or by some particular subject, or who are drawn more than is usual by the new or the full Moon, must beware how they place themselves within the power of that which would dominate them.

To those who ordinarily have their feet planted firmly upon the Earth, however, the Moon is the marvellous opener of the Gate of Enchantment, the friend who whispers, "Come forth with me to the Carnival of Masks, which precedes the ascent to the stars! Life is more than you have guessed. It dances and whirls in the height, to be caught in the mirroring bosom of time: caught, to be reborn in a myriad sparkles, a myriad flashes of crystalline light: yet the least of these flashes, even to the most evanescent, is Life again. Come forth with me!"

Malkuth is the Sephirah of Completion: the Tenth Sephirah, making up the perfect number. Malkuth is the Kingdom, the Bride, the Lower Mother. The Hebrew God associated therewith is Adonai Melek or Adonai Ha-Aretz, simply the Lord King or the Lord of the Earth. The Archangel of Malkuth, Sandalphon, is the only one of the Archangelic Powers to be represented in female form. The chief God-forms of Malkuth are Ceres and Demeter, and those similar Earth-Mothers who are found in every cosmogony:* gracious and generous goddesses, and withal of high dignity, for they participate in that mystery which is expressed in Qabalistic tradition by the words, "Malkuth sitteth upon the Throne of Binah." Thus the Bride becomes the Supernal Mother: Demeter, Mother of Barley, becomes Mother of the Mysteries.

In the World of Yetzirah, Malkuth is especially the home of the Elemental Spirits. True it is that in ascending, the magician does not ordinarily touch upon their abodes; the path of his aspirations, as we have indicated, is from the Malkuth of Assiah to the Yesod of Yetzirah. He may, however, wish to make particular excursions into the world of the Elementals, by means of scrying for example or of other techniques, either simply for the sake of the great beauty and interest to be found in that world and its inhabitants, or with a further view also to summoning their assistance on occasion. It is normal magical practice, whenever a force is "brought down," to call upon the Elementals to be present and to take part in the rite. The purpose of this is that they may help to complete the process of "earthing" and stabilising the force in the Malkuth of Yetzirah; and they on their side are very willing to assist, since contact with an affinitive force is a great joy to them.

* See also ch. VII for further discussion of the nature of Malkuth forces in magical working.

The Elementals of Fire have a natural affinity to the forces of Geburah and Netzach; the Elementals of Water, to the forces of Chesed and Hod; the Elementals of Air, to the forces of Tiphareth and Yesod; and the Elementals of Earth, to Malkuth and to the Saturnian forces of Binah.* Let them therefore rejoice and exult in their especial ways as they welcome the invoked potency; and, the rite concluded, let them be released with thanks and benediction to continue in their own mode of existence.

Man has a considerable and frequently unconscious talent for developing the individuality, in human terms of reference, of any creature to which he gives his attention. People who have made a pet of an animal, especially an animal of a kind not usually chosen, are often surprised at the extent of this development. The same thing is found with regard to human beings, when a child or an adult who has been disregarded in a large group is for some reason singled out: the personality often blossoms into self-awareness in a startling manner which is not reversible, so that there is a definite sense of cruelty in returning the subject to an environment in which he or she was previously quite contented. The same principle applies to those Elementals who assist the magician. Sometimes it will happen that certain ones become known to him as individual beings; when this occurs, it can generally be assumed that the conversion to human terms of reference has already begun, but it will depend very much upon the magician how far the process is to be continued. No definite rules can be laid down here, but, besides the question of responsibility for the Elemental, it also behoves the magician to examine carefully whether the

---

* It is here recognised that the Supernals are the "Roots of the Elements": Kether, Root of Air; Chokmah, Root of Fire; Binah, Root of Water. For practical work, however, the recognition of the affinity of the Element Earth with Saturn is a *sine qua non*. In many aspects of the Tree, it becomes evident that a distinction must be made between Binah as a Supernal Sephirah and Binah as a Planetary Sephirah: the attributions of Hera, the Celestial Queen, are quite distinct from those of Chronos.

element represented is out of balance in his own character. Either a preponderance or a deficiency can be a danger signal. Nevertheless, all these matters receiving their due consideration, it remains true that the innocence, happiness and strange knowledge shown by Elemental beings often afford delight and refreshment to the magician who has come to know them.

Having so far surveyed the magical aspects of the Sephiroth, we can observe that the deific forces associated with five of the Sephiroth are represented principally by male forms, and four by female.

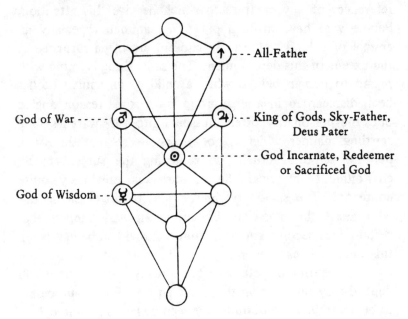

Kether, besides being unmanifest, is the source of all and is therefore regarded as universal in nature. The All-Father, representing the Divine Archetype of Chokmah, is likewise unmanifest. The idea which most people have of that Archetype is represented by the Sephirah next below Chokmah on the Pillar of Mercy: Chesed, known in the cosmogonies as the Sky-Father and King of the Gods. Zeus (whose name is cognate with Theos and Deus) and Jupiter (whose name signifies Deus-Pater) are characteristic manifestations of the Sky-Father, patriarchal, all-seeing and benign. The God of War, representing the Archetype of Geburah, provides the balancing qualities of courage and resolved purpose. It is natural that the fierce qualities of Geburah, combined with the benignity and paternal responsibility of Chesed, should combine to produce the self-sacrificing valour of Tiphareth. This would complete the male attributions of the Sephiroth, but that there is one more function to fulfill: that of teacher and messenger. This function is fulfilled by Hod, the reflection of Chesed through Tiphareth, for the work of Hod is by nature merciful, though necessarily brought into form and discipline under the influence of Binah and Geburah.

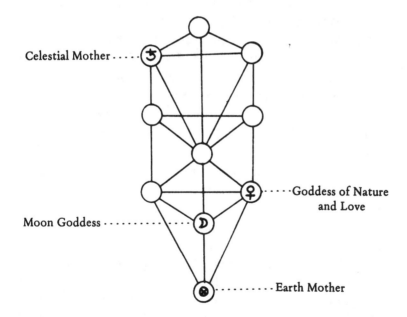

Consideration of the Goddesses gives us quite another pattern. The Great Goddess, the Celestial Mother, when reflected through "the prism of Tiphareth," gives as it were three partial likenesses: the Goddess of Nature in Netzach, the Moon-Goddess in Yesod, and the Earth-Mother in Malkuth. Just as Hod contains a reflection through Tiphareth of Chesed, so those dominant and even fierce aspects which we have observed in Netzach are reflections through Tiphareth of Geburah. As we have indicated, however, it can be said of all manifestations of the Goddess that they are fundamentally one, and thus the student of mythology will sometimes find it extremely difficult to decide whether certain aspects belong to one or another of these Sephiroth. Most important, however, is the reflection of the Saturnian Goddess right down to Malkuth. There is a great mystery here, and one whose misinterpretation has caused centuries of contention and anguish of heart to the Western world. The descent of the Divine Force of the Third Sephirah to the Tenth was presented in the Greco-Judaic cosmogonies of the Eastern Mediterranean as the descent of the Sophia, Holy Wisdom, into the material world. This was in fact to declare her the formative principle of the material world, so that this involution should have been regarded as an essential part of the cosmic process. Unfortunately, however, by a not uncommon confusion of ideas, the early Christian Gnostics regarded the material world as a pre-existing and corrupt condition into which the Sophia descended, and more unfortunately still they therefore declared her descent to be a sin.

This interpretation was not only false, it was pernicious. Followed to its logical conclusions, it would have closed the Way of Return to all incarnate beings. The rest of the Greek world rejected the interpretation, but the storm lacked a focal point and did not burst as yet. Although the initial philosphic groundwork became blurred, the popular certainty held that the Divine Mind's perfect concept, by which all matter was framed, had never fallen into sin. (Similarly, as a plain fact, the *Prima Materia* itself can never, in any sense of the word, be corrupted, since it is the pure energy underlying all phenomena.)

This is not the place to trace the bitter controversies and contentions which raged for centuries over the myth which developed as The Immaculate Conception of the Blessed Virgin Mary, when this doctrine was brought in Crusading times from the East to Europe; but it is at least illuminating in understanding the emotions involved, if we know the confusion of ideas which it set out to combat in the first place. It also gives us a key to the reason underlying the development of the corresponding myth, that of the Assumption. For as we know, the Bride has to be taken up again to the World of the Supernals, and to be set upon the Throne of Binah.

The foregoing is a general survey of the sephirothic powers and of some of their applications in magical working. It contains many points for the serious attention of the reader, but in its very abundance it presents what may well seem a formidable medley of names from different cosmogonies, with facts concerning different levels of existence. These names and facts should be borne in mind, but now we must extend the framework upon which our philosophy rests.

# CHAPTER V

Sephirothic and Goetic Powers of the Hebrew hierarchical cosmogony: their indications and names.

The Hebrew Divine Names transliterated, with their significances. Magical use of these names as sephirothic formulae.

Exceptional character of the Hebrew system in the clear distinction made between Atziluthic and Briatic representatives of a divine force. Names of the sephirothic Archangels.

The Choras, that is to say the assemblages of angelic beings of Yetzirah. The first chapter of Ezekiel and its references to the Choras of Kether and Chokmah. The Choras of Binah and of the remaining Sephiroth.

Biblical Adam and Adam Kadmon: the transition from involution to evolution as a moment in the existence of Cosmic Man.

Bringing down power: different procedures are indicated for different purposes. Intelligences and Spirits of the Planetary Spheres. Angels of the Decans and Quinances. Permutations of the Tetragrammaton. Ruling Planetary Forces and Elemental names.

The Qliphoth. Relationship of qliphothic forces to the corresponding Sephiroth. The qliphothic hierarchy as mirror-image of the sephirothic: limitations of the parallel.

The Abyss in context of the goetic powers: the Kingdom of Chaos and the disintegration of personality.

The Prince of Chaos, the infernal rulers below the Abyss, and the demonic aspects of zodiacal forces. The Cohorts of the Qliphoth.

The Magical Images, the "indigenous God-forms of the Qabalistic sub-structure," the Images of the Divine Archetypes. Methods of introducing them in magical working.

Correspondences to be employed not only correctly but validly. Pantheons not to be mixed. Whatever Atziluthic names are chosen as Formulae, from whatever religious or magical system, complete harmony required between these and all materials, instruments and methods of working.

Divine names composed of vowels in certain ancient cults: their treatment.

Greek Names of Power and Formulae.

The Olympic Planetary Spirits.

# CHAPTER V
## THE EMANATIONS

*Lucis et caliginis potestates*


### Key to Table

1 Sephiroth and Paths
2 God-Names
3 Archangels (Sephiroth)
4 Archangels (Elements)
5 Archangels (Signs)
6 Choras
7 Angels (Ruling Sephiroth
    and 7 Paths contingent)
8 Angels (Ruling Elements)
9 Angels (Ruling Signs)
10 Lesser Angels (Sephiroth and Paths)
11 Lesser Angels (Elements)
12 Lesser Angels (Signs)
13 Heavenly Arch Ascendant
    Decans and Quinances
14 Heavenly Arch Succedent
    Decans and Quinances
15 Heavenly Arch Cadent
    Decans and Quinances
16 Planetary Intelligences
    (Sephiroth and 7 Paths)
17 Planetary Spirits
    (Sephiroth and Paths)

69

18  Palaces
19  Zodiacal Goetia (Cadent)
20  Zodiacal Goetia (Succedent)
21  Zodiacal Goetia (Ascendant)
22  Infernal Habitations
23  Cohorts of the Qliphoth
24  Qliphothic Princes

## Key to Alphabet

| Letter | Name | Transliteration |
|--------|------|-----------------|
| א | Aleph | A |
| ב | Beth | B |
| ג | Gimel | G |
| ד | Daleth | D |
| ה | Heh | H |
| ו | Vau | V |
| ז | Zain | Z |
| ח | Cheth | Ch |
| ט | Teth | T |
| י | Yod | Y |
| ךכ | Kaph | K |
| ל | Lamed | L |
| םמ | Mem | M |
| ןנ | Nun | N |
| ס | Samekh | S |
| ע | Ayin | O |
| ףפ | Peh | P |
| ץצ | Tzaddi | Tz |
| ק | Qoph | Q |
| ר | Resh | R |
| ש | Shin | Sh |
| ת | Tau | Th |

# THEURGIA

בריאה     אצילות

| 1 | | 2 | | 3 | |
|---|---|---|---|---|---|
| 1 | כתר | 1 | אהיה | 1 | מטטרון |
| 2 | חכמה | 2 | יה | 2 | רציאל |
| 3 | בינה | 3 | יהוה אלהים | 3 | צפקיאל |
| 4 | חסד | 4 | אל | 4 | צדקיאל |
| 5 | גבורה | 5 | אלהים גבור | 5 | כמאל |
| 6 | תפארת | 6 | יהוה אלוה ודעת | 6 | רפאל |
| 7 | נצח | 7 | יהוה צבאות | 7 | האניאל |
| 8 | הוד | 8 | אלהים צבאות | 8 | מיכאל |
| 9 | יסוד | 9 | שדי אל חי | 9 | גבריאל |
| 10 | מלכות | 10 | אדני מלך: יי הארץ | 10 | סנדלפון |
| 11 | אלף | 11 | יהוה | | |
| 12 | בית | 12 | אלהים צבאות | | |
| 13 | גמל | 13 | אל חי | | |
| 14 | דלת | 14 | יהוה צבאות | | |
| 15 | הא: הה | 15 | אלהים גבור | | |
| 16 | וו | 16 | יהוה צבאות | | |
| 17 | זין | 17 | אלהים צבאות | | |
| 18 | חית | 18 | שדי | | |
| 19 | טית | 19 | אלוה | | |
| 20 | יוד | 20 | אלהים צבאות | | |
| 21 | כף | 21 | אל: אב | | |
| 22 | למד | 22 | יהוה צבאות | | |
| 23 | מים | 23 | אל | | |
| 24 | נון | 24 | אלהים גבור | | |
| 25 | סמך | 25 | אל | | |
| 26 | עין | 26 | יהוה אלהים | | |
| 27 | פא: פה | 27 | אלהים גבור | | |
| 28 | צדי | 28 | יהו | | |
| 29 | קוף | 29 | אל | | |
| 30 | ריש | 30 | אלוה ודעת | | |
| 31 | שין | 31 | אלהים | | |
| 32 | תו | 32 | יהוה אלהים: אימא | | |
| 32 bis | תו | 32 bis | אדני | | |
| 31 bis | שין | 31 bis | יהשוה: אגלא: אהיה | | |
| DAATH | דעת | DAATH | אליון | | |

| | בריאה | | בריאה | | יצירה |
|---|---|---|---|---|---|
| **4** | | **5** | | **6** | |
| 1 | | 1 | | 1 | חיות הקדש |
| 2 | | 2 | | 2 | אופנים |
| 3 | | 3 | | 3 | אראלים |
| 4 | | 4 | | 4 | חשמלים |
| 5 | | 5 | | 5 | שרפים |
| 6 | | 6 | | 6 | מלכים |
| 7 | | 7 | | 7 | אלהים |
| 8 | | 8 | | 8 | תרשישים |
| 9 | | 9 | | 9 | כרובים |
| 10 | | 10 | | 10 | אשים |
| 11 | רוחיאל | | | | |
| 12 | | | | | |
| 13 | | | | | |
| 14 | | | | | |
| 15 | | 15 | מלכידאל | | |
| 16 | | 16 | אסמודאל | | |
| 17 | | 17 | אמבריאל | | |
| 18 | | 18 | מוריאל | | |
| 19 | | 19 | ורכיאל | | |
| 20 | | 20 | המליאל | | |
| 21 | | | | | |
| 22 | | 22 | זוריאל | | |
| 23 | מיאל | | | | |
| 24 | | 24 | ברכיאל | | |
| 25 | | 25 | אדוכיאל | | |
| 26 | | 26 | הנאל | | |
| 27 | | | | | |
| 28 | | 28 | כאמבריאל | | |
| 29 | | 29 | אמניציאל | | |
| 30 | | | | | |
| 31 | אשיאל | | | | |
| 32 | | | | | |
| 32 bis | אופיריאל | | | | |
| 31 bis | | | | | |
| DAATH | | | | | |

| יצירה | יצירה | יצירה | | | |
|---|---|---|---|---|---|
| **7** | | **8** | | **9** | |
| 1 | | | | | |
| 2 | | | | | |
| 3 | כשיאל | | | | |
| 4 | סחיאל | | | | |
| 5 | זמאל | | | | |
| 6 | מיכאל | | | | |
| 7 | אנאל | | | | |
| 8 | רפאל | | | | |
| 9 | גבריאל | | | | |
| 10 | | | | | |
| 11 | | 11 | אריאל | | |
| 12 | | | | | |
| 13 | | | | | |
| 14 | | | | | |
| 15 | | | | 15 | איאל |
| 16 | | | | 16 | טואל |
| 17 | | | | 17 | גיאל |
| 18 | | | | 18 | כעאל |
| 19 | | | | 19 | עואל |
| 20 | | | | 20 | ויאל |
| 21 | | | | | |
| 22 | | | | 22 | יהאל |
| 23 | | 23 | תרשים | | |
| 24 | | | | 24 | סוסול |
| 25 | | | | 25 | סויעסאל |
| 26 | | | | 26 | כשניעיה |
| 27 | | | | | |
| 28 | | | | 28 | אנסואל |
| 29 | | | | 29 | פשיאל |
| 30 | | | | | |
| 31 | | 31 | שרף | | |
| 32 | | | | | |
| 32 bis | | 32 bis | כרוב | | |
| 31 bis | | | | | |
| DAATH | | | | | |

| יצירה 10 | יצירה 11 | יצירה 12 |
|---|---|---|
| 1 | | |
| 2 | | |
| 3 עתאל | | |
| 4 לכאל | | |
| 5 מפאל | | |
| 6 תראל | | |
| 7 עראל | | |
| 8 רבאל | | |
| 9 זגאל | | |
| 10 | | |
| 11 | 11 חסן | |
| 12 | | |
| 13 | | |
| 14 | | |
| 15 | | 15 שרהיאל |
| 16 | | 16 ארזיאל |
| 17 | | 17 סראיאל |
| 18 | | 18 פכיאל |
| 19 | | 19 שרטיאל |
| 20 | | 20 שלתיאל |
| 21 | | |
| 22 | | 22 חדקיאל |
| 23 | 23 טליהד | |
| 24 | | 24 סאיציאל |
| 25 | | 25 סמקיאל |
| 26 | | 26 סריטיאל |
| 27 | | |
| 28 | | 28 צכמקיאל |
| 29 | | 29 וכביאל |
| 30 | | |
| 31 | 31 אראל | |
| 32 | | |
| 32 bis | 32 bis פורלאך | |
| 31 bis | | |
| DAATH | | |

יצירה

| 13 | | | | | |
|---|---|---|---|---|---|
| 1°—10° | | 1°—5° | | 6°—10° | |
| 1 | | | | | |
| 2 | | | | | |
| 3 | | | | | |
| 4 | | | | | |
| 5 | | | | | |
| 6 | | | | | |
| 7 | | | | | |
| 8 | | | | | |
| 9 | | | | | |
| 10 | | | | | |
| 11 | | | | | |
| 12 | | | | | |
| 13 | | | | | |
| 14 | | | | | |
| 15 | זזר | 15 | והואל | 15 | דניאל |
| 16 | כרמדי | 16 | מבהיה | 16 | פויאל |
| 17 | סגרש | 17 | ומבאל | 17 | יההאל |
| 18 | מתראוש | 18 | איעאל | 18 | חבויה |
| 19 | לוסנהר | 19 | והויה | 19 | יליאל |
| 20 | אננאורה | 20 | אכאיה | 20 | כהתאל |
| 21 | | 21 | | 21 | |
| 22 | טרסני | 22 | יזלאל | 22 | מבהאל |
| 23 | | 23 | | 23 | |
| 24 | כמוץ | 24 | לוויה | 24 | פהליה |
| 25 | מזרח | 25 | נתהיה | 25 | האאיה |
| 26 | מסנין | 26 | לכבאל | 26 | ושריה |
| 27 | | 27 | | 27 | |
| 28 | כסף | 28 | אניאל | 28 | חעמיה |
| 29 | בהלמי | 29 | וליה | 29 | ילהיה |
| 30 | | | | | |
| 31 | | | | | |
| 32 | | | | | |
| 32 bis | | | | | |
| 31 bis | | | | | |
| DAATH | | | | | |

יצירה

| 14 | | | | | |
|---|---|---|---|---|---|
| 11°—20° | | 11°—15° | | 16°—20° | |
| 1 | | | | | |
| 2 | | | | | |
| 3 | | | | | |
| 4 | | | | | |
| 5 | | | | | |
| 6 | | | | | |
| 7 | | | | | |
| 8 | | | | | |
| 9 | | | | | |
| 10 | | | | | |
| 11 | | | | | |
| 12 | | | | | |
| 13 | | | | | |
| 14 | | | | | |
| 15 | בכורמיה | 15 | החשיה | 15 | עממיה |
| 16 | מנחראי | 16 | נממיה | 16 | יילאל |
| 17 | שהרני | 17 | ענואל | 17 | מחיאל |
| 18 | רהרץ | 18 | ראהאל | 18 | יבמיה |
| 19 | זחעי | 19 | סיטאל | 19 | עלמיה |
| 20 | ראיהיה | 20 | הזיאל | 20 | אלריה |
| 21 | | 21 | | 21 | |
| 22 | סהרנץ | 22 | הריאל | 22 | הקמיה |
| 23 | | 23 | | 23 | |
| 24 | נינרוהר | 24 | נלכאל | 24 | יייאל |
| 25 | והרין | 25 | ירתאל | 25 | שאהיה |
| 26 | יסיסיה | 26 | יחויה | 26 | להחיה |
| 27 | | 27 | | 27 | |
| 28 | אברדרון | 28 | רהעאל | 28 | ייזאל |
| 29 | איתן | 29 | סאליה | 29 | עריאל |
| 30 | | | | | |
| 31 | | | | | |
| 32 | | | | | |
| 32 bis | | | | | |
| 31 bis | | | | | |
| DAATH | | | | | |

יצירה

| 15 | | | | | |
|---|---|---|---|---|---|
| 21°—30° | | 21°—25° | | 26°—30° | |
| 1 | | | | | |
| 2 | | | | | |
| 3 | | | | | |
| 4 | | | | | |
| 5 | | | | | |
| 6 | | | | | |
| 7 | | | | | |
| 8 | | | | | |
| 9 | | | | | |
| 10 | | | | | |
| 11 | | | | | |
| 12 | | | | | |
| 13 | | | | | |
| 14 | | | | | |
| 15 | סטנדר | 15 | ננאל | 15 | ניתאל |
| 16 | יסגנוץ | 16 | הרחאל | 16 | מצראל |
| 17 | ביתון | 17 | דמביה | 17 | מנקאל |
| 18 | אלינכור | 18 | הייאל | 18 | מומיה |
| 19 | סהיבה | 19 | מהשיה | 19 | ללהאל |
| 20 | מספר | 20 | לאויה | 20 | חהעיה |
| 21 | | 21 | | 21 | |
| 22 | שהדר | 22 | לאואל | 22 | כליאל |
| 23 | | 23 | | 23 | |
| 24 | נתרודיאל | 24 | מלהאל | 24 | חהויה |
| 25 | אבוהא | 25 | רייאל | 25 | אומאל |
| 26 | יסגריברודיאל | 26 | כוקיה | 26 | מנדאל |
| 27 | | 27 | | 27 | |
| 28 | גרודיאל | 28 | הההאל | 28 | מיכאל |
| 29 | סטריף | 29 | עשליה | 29 | מיהאל |
| 30 | | | | | |
| 31 | | | | | |
| 32 | | | | | |
| 32 bis | | | | | |
| 31 bis | | | | | |
| DAATH | | | | | |

| | יצירה | | יצירה |
|---|---|---|---|
| **16** | | **17** | |
| 1 | | | |
| 2 | | | |
| 3 | אגיאל | 3 | זזאל |
| 4 | יופיל | 4 | חסמאל |
| 5 | גראפיאל | 5 | ברצבאל |
| 6 | נכיאל | 6 | סורת |
| 7 | הגיאל | 7 | קדמאל |
| 8 | טיריאל | 8 | תפתרתרת |
| 9 | מלכה בתרשישים | 9 | חשמודאי |
| 10 | | | |
| 11 | | | |
| 12 | 260 | 12 | 2080 |
| 13 | 1917 | 13 | 369 |
| 14 | 49 | 14 | 175 |
| 15 | | | |
| 16 | | | |
| 17 | | | |
| 18 | | | |
| 19 | | | |
| 20 | | | |
| 21 | 136 | 21 | 136 |
| 22 | | | |
| 23 | | | |
| 24 | | | |
| 25 | | | |
| 26 | | | |
| 27 | 325 | 27 | 325 |
| 28 | | | |
| 29 | | | |
| 30 | 111 | 30 | 666 |
| 31 | | | |
| 32 | 45 | 32 | 45 |
| 32 bis | | | |
| 31 bis | | | |
| DAATH | | | |

עשיה—יצירה

| 18 | |
|---|---|
| 1 | ראשית הגלגלים |
| 2 | מסלות |
| 3 | שבתאי |
| 4 | צדק |
| 5 | מאדים |
| 6 | שמש |
| 7 | נוגה |
| 8 | כוכב |
| 9 | לבנה |
| 10 | חלם יסודות* |
| 11 | רוח |
| 12 | כוכב |
| 13 | לבנה |
| 14 | נוגה |
| 15 | טלה |
| 16 | שור |
| 17 | תאומים |
| 18 | סרטן |
| 19 | אריה |
| 20 | בתולה |
| 21 | צדק |
| 22 | מאזנים |
| 23 | מים |
| 24 | עקרב |
| 25 | קשת |
| 26 | גדי |
| 27 | מאדים |
| 28 | דלי |
| 29 | דגים |
| 30 | שמש |
| 31 | אש |
| 32 | שבתאי |
| 32 bis | ארץ |
| 31 bis | את |
| DAATH | סף |

*The title *Cholem Yesodoth* is authentic: see second footnote, page 93.

# GOETIA

| 19 | | | |
|---|---|---|---|
| | 26°—30° | | 21°—25° |
| 1 | | | |
| 2 | | | |
| 3 | | | |
| 4 | | | |
| 5 | | | |
| 6 | | | |
| 7 | | | |
| 8 | | | |
| 9 | | | |
| 10 | | | |
| 11 | | | |
| 12 | | | |
| 13 | | | |
| 14 | | | |
| 15 | רונוו | 15 | אנדראש |
| 16 | פרנאש | 16 | כימער |
| 17 | געף | 17 | דכארביא |
| 18 | צולם | 18 | אנדרומאל |
| 19 | מאלף | 19 | ושאגו |
| 20 | ופר | 20 | ולפר |
| 21 | | 21 | |
| 22 | וינא | 22 | פימון |
| 23 | | 23 | |
| 24 | העגנת | 24 | שעיר |
| 25 | בלעם | 25 | אליגוש |
| 26 | מערם | 26 | באתין |
| 27 | | 27 | |
| 28 | ושו | 28 | מוראץ |
| 29 | נפל | 29 | נבר |
| 30 | | | |
| 31 | | | |
| 32 | | | |
| 32 bis | | | |
| 31 bis | | | |
| DAATH | | | |

יצירה

| 20 | | | |
|---|---|---|---|
| | 16°—20° | | 11°—15° |
| 1 | | | |
| 2 | | | |
| 3 | | | |
| 4 | | | |
| 5 | | | |
| 6 | | | |
| 7 | | | |
| 8 | | | |
| 9 | | | |
| 10 | | | |
| 11 | | | |
| 12 | | | |
| 13 | | | |
| 14 | | | |
| 15 | בים | 15 | ולו |
| 16 | עשתרת | 16 | אנדראלף |
| 17 | אשמודאי | 17 | בליעל |
| 18 | מרחוש | 18 | דנטאליון |
| 19 | האלף | 19 | אגאר |
| 20 | פוכלור | 20 | מארב |
| 21 | | 21 | |
| 22 | שץ | 22 | ברבמטוש |
| 23 | | 23 | |
| 24 | וול | 24 | גוסיון |
| 25 | פורך | 25 | לריך |
| 26 | כאין | 26 | בוטיש |
| 27 | | 27 | |
| 28 | גמור | 28 | פרשון |
| 29 | וריאץ | 29 | אימה |
| 30 | | | |
| 31 | | | |
| 32 | | | |
| 32 bis | | | |
| 31 bis | | | |
| DAATH | | | |

יצירה

| 21 | | |
|---|---|---|
| | 6°—10° | 1°—5° |
| 1 | | |
| 2 | | |
| 3 | | |
| 4 | | |
| 5 | | |
| 6 | | |
| 7 | | |
| 8 | | |
| 9 | | |
| 10 | | |
| 11 | | |
| 12 | | |
| 13 | | |
| 14 | | |
| 15 | גלאסלבול | 15 זגן |
| 16 | ברית | 16 פלער |
| 17 | פראש | 17 אמדור |
| 18 | פורפור | 18 שאר |
| 19 | פנץ | 19 בעל |
| 20 | רעם | 20 כמיגין |
| 21 | | 21 |
| 22 | שבנוך | 22 אמון |
| 23 | | 23 |
| 24 | ביפרן | 24 בואר |
| 25 | כרוכל | 25 בלאת |
| 26 | אלוך | 26 זפר |
| 27 | | 27 |
| 28 | ערבם | 28 שלוש |
| 29 | און | 29 יפוש |
| 30 | | |
| 31 | | |
| 32 | | |
| 32 bis | | |
| 31 bis | | |
| DAATH | | |

| עשיה—יצירה | | יצירה | | בריאה | |
|---|---|---|---|---|---|
| **22** | | **23** | | **24** | |
| 1 | | 1 | | 1 | |
| 2 | אבדון | 2 | סתרות | 2 | רומה* |
| 3 | | 3 | | 3 | |
| 4 | צלמות | 4 | רפאים | 4 | השטן |
| 5 | שעירמות | 5 | קטבים | 5 | המלך |
| 6 | טיטהיון | 6 | תגערים | 6 | אשמדי |
| 7 | גי הנם | 7 | שעירים | 7 | הילל |
| 8 | בארשחת | 8 | תרפים | 8 | סמאל |
| 9 | | 9 | עירים | 9 | לילית |
| 10 | שאול | 10 | נעימות | 10 | בליעל |
| 11 | | | | | |
| 12 | | | | | |
| 13 | | | | | |
| 14 | | | | | |
| **15** | | | | | |
| 16 | | | | | |
| 17 | | | | | |
| 18 | | | | | |
| 19 | | | | | |
| 20 | | | | | |
| 21 | | | | | |
| 22 | | | | | |
| 23 | | | | | |
| 24 | | | | | |
| 25 | | | | | |
| 26 | | | | | |
| 27 | | | | | |
| 28 | | | | | |
| 29 | | | | | |
| 30 | | | | | |
| 31 | | | | | |
| 32 | | | | | |
| 32 bis | | | | | |
| 31 bis | | | | | |
| DAATH | | | | | |

* See Zohar I, 8b. The specified domain of operation is plainly a poetic term for the "underworld" generally: compare Zohar I, 59a.

In order to work a magical system, it essentially must be possible to call the forces connected therewith, powerfully and appropriately, to the focal point of the magical purpose. From a consideration of the Four Worlds in their sephirothic manifestations, it is seen that if a force is to be brought down from the Divine World to the material level (to express this aspect of magick in a very general way), then, at the least, four Words of Power are indicated: a God-name for the Atziluthic level, an Archangelic name for the Briatic level, the name of an angelic Chora in Yetzirah, and the name of the particular "Palace of Assiah" that is the principal symbol in Assiah to which this Power is attributed. Obviously there will be variations in this plan, conformably to particular purposes, but for the present we are concerned with the main framework of the general procedure. Likewise we are first and foremost considering the Sephiroth, since these are the great cosmic forces of the universe.

Let us begin, therefore, with the Divine Names, Words of Power referred to the Sephiroth in Atziluth. The Hebrew names shown in the Table may be rendered as follows:

1. *EHEIEH.* This Name is interpreted as "I am"; otherwise occurring as *Eheieh Asher Eheieh,* "I am that I am". It is an expression of pure Being, of Positive Existence unqualified by past or future tense, by any moral or conceptual limitation: Godhead in full Reality.

2. *YAH.* This Name, attributed to the Sephirah of Supernal Fatherhood, is one of the simplest and most ancient forms of those mysterious vowel-names which occur among Chaldaean and cognate peoples: we may compare the Babylonian EA. More will be put forward presently concerning this type of Deity-name; for the present it suffices that the Name with which we are here concerned, if uttered reverently and magically, is of great potency.

3. *YHVH ELOHIM.** Of the two components of this

---

*Some authorities give the name for Binah simply as ALHIM, ascribing YHVH ALHIM to Daath.

Name, the former, YHVH, is another of the vowel-names
alluded to above. For magical purposes it is pronounced as
YAHVEH, as YOD HEH VAU HEH, or is expressed by the
Greek word TETRAGRAMMATON, signifying simply a
Word of Four Syllables. In the present case for instance it
would be entirely a matter for personal decision, whether to
pronounce YAHVEH ELOHIM, YOD HEH VAU HEH
ELOHIM, or TETRAGRAMMATON ELOHIM. The word
TETRAGRAMMATON was much honoured in medieval
magick, and affords an interesting example of the way in
which a word, intended in the first place as a substitute for a
Name of Power, becomes a Name of Power itself. The second
component of the Divine Name in Binah, ELOHIM, is a
masculine plural form of a feminine noun, ELOAH, Divine
Majesty. It will be observed that this word ELOHIM occurs in
all the God-names of the Column of Severity, which is the
"feminine" Column of the Tree.

  4. *EL* simply signifies God. It has the force of a proper
name, as we see clearly by the use given to the corresponding
Arabic form ALLAH; and the use of the Name EL to govern
Chesed, the Sphere of Jupiter, makes it interesting to recall
that Zeus and Jupiter are likewise not personal names in
origin, meaning simply God and Father-God. This accurately reflects the character of Chesed: children do not
usually address their father by name, nor subjects their
king, and exceptions indicate cession from the archetypal
pattern.

  5. *ELOHIM GEBOR.* The second component of this
Name is clearly related to the name of the Sephirah
GEBURAH, which signifies Strength; thus this Name may be
rendered "Elohim the Warrior."

  6. *YHVH ELOAH V'DAATH.* This Name is variously
interpreted. We may say "God of Majesty and Knowledge,"
but the most obviously significant fact concerning this Name
is that it brings together in the centre of the Tree
characteristic words related to all three Columns: the Divine

Names YHVH and ELOAH, and the name of the "Invisible Sephirah" upon the central Column, DAATH. In Kether we have Divine Force unconditioned; in Tiphareth we have that same Divine Force which has assumed the character of each of the higher Sephiroth, now gathered together again into unity for its transmission in manifestation to the lower Sephiroth.

7. *YHVH TZABAOTH,* God of Hosts. This Divine Name is attributed to Netzach, the Sephirah whose name means Victory. Its significance has been discussed in the preceding chapter.

8. *ELOHIM TZABAOTH:* Divine power of command in latency; the forces of Order in the manifest spheres.

9. *SHADDAI, EL CHAI:* the Omnipotent, Living God. The Name SHADDAI is of great antiquity; it is one of the oldest Hebrew epithets of Divinity, so that although usually translated "Almighty" or "Omnipotent," its exact meaning has become lost in the mists of time. Nevertheless, on account of its venerable associations this is a most potent Name of Power. It is linked here with another great title of God, EL CHAI, the Living God, which implies not only the living presence of this Divine Force, but also the character of this Sephirah in transmitting and imparting life.

10. *ADONAI MELEK* or *ADONAI HA-ARETZ.* The first word of these Divine Names, ADONAI, is another example of the development of such a Name. This word means originally Lord, and could be used even as a secular title. In these two Divine Names associated with Malkuth, the significance is simply that of a title, Lord King in the first example, Lord of the Earth in the second. However, as is well known, ADONAI has acquired the force of a Divine Name in its own right: modern Jewish custom avoids, except in actual prayer, the use of this word which was earlier employed as a substitute for the unspoken name YHVH; in the mythology of the Eastern Mediterranean the title appears as a Divine

proper name in the Greek form Adonis; and in medieval Judeo-Christian magick, associations of great potency accrued to the form ADONAY.

We are not bound to the exactitudes of Jewish theology in using these Names. Certainly the archetypal forces which they represent should be understood as deeply as possible, but it is more than doubtful whether the modern Western mind is helped to the type of understanding needed for magical purposes, by the tortuosities of rabbinical metaphor and veiled utterance found in the older mystical texts. To utter one of these sephirothic Divine Names, then, is from our viewpoint *a Formula, an expression of something of that essential concept of the Sephirah, which is held in being in the Divine Mind.* No image is attached to it, and only the starkest utterance; knowing inwardly what we mean thereby, *we should not* mentally whisper an interpretation even in the inmost awareness at the time of invocation. The Name should be all. We are carried up to its utterance by the form and the purpose of the ritual, by the symbolism of incense and colour and all that has been brought together to point the way.

This invocation of the Atziluthic reality of the force leads to the next step, the Briatic level, which here takes a form distinctive to the Hebrew cosmogony. Really, the theological distinction here is only a matter of emphasis. Any Briatic entity, although originating, as regards form, in the human mind's representation of a true Archetype descried within the Divine Mind, yet is far more than a Yetziratic creation, inasmuch as the Briatic entity so corresponds in character to the Archetype as to become a channel or vehicle for that Divine Force. In Jewish, Pagan and Christian theologies alike, the human element in this form-making generally passes unremarked. In the Jewish system, in contrast to Pagan systems, a clear distinction has been made between the Atziluthic and the Briatic levels. The Atziluthic level, in itself incomprehensible to the human mind, is represented by the Divine Names to betoken the Archetypes; the Briatic level thereby becomes the "Messenger" of the Atziluthic force. In the Pagan systems, no distinction is made between the Briatic form and the archetypal force which informs it. Nevertheless, in Jewish esotericism, and in the monastic traditions of the Near East and of Byzantium, an understanding has been handed down that the Old Testament references to archangelic beings are a veiled allusion to actual Divine presence. (Notable examples are the Fourth Companion in the Fiery Furnace; the three Angels entertained by Abraham.) The names of the great Archangels are the following:

| 1 | Kether | Metatron |
|---|---|---|
| 2 | Chokmah | Ratziel |
| 3 | Binah | Tzaphqiel |
| 4 | Chesed | Tzadqiel |
| 5 | Geburah | Kamael |
| 6 | Tiphareth | Raphael |
| 7 | Netzach | Haniel |
| 8 | Hod | Mikael |
| 9 | Yesod | Gebriel |
| 10 | Malkuth | Sandalphon |

The sigils of the Archangels of the planetary Sephiroth (that is, numbers 3 through 9) as drawn from the XIX century *Liber Siderum Pragae* and employed by the Aurum Solis, are as follows:

3. TZAPHQIEL

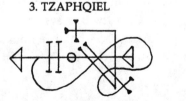

4. TZADQIEL

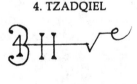

### 5. KAMAEL

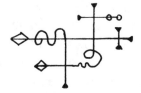

### 6. RAPHAEL

### 7. HANIEL

### 8. MIKAEL

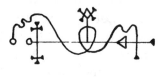

### 9. GEBRIEL

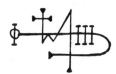

When we proceed to the sephirothic forces in Yetzirah, we find that the Hebrew cosmogony here presents us with a different picture. In Yetzirah, the Astral World, we have primarily Choras of congregated beings, rather than uniquely individual entities: there are the Chaioth ha-Qadesh, the Holy Living Ones of Kether, and the Auphanim, that is to say the Wheels, of Chokmah, their form suggesting that great Wheel of the Zodiac which, enclosing the concentric orbits of our Solar System, is the principal Assiatic symbol of their Sephirah. In the first chapter of Ezekiel, we see that the setting for his vision carries him up to the Supernal Sephiroth of Yetzirah, that is to say the highest levels of the Astral World. He beholds the Chaioth ha-Qadesh accompanied by the Aralim, and above their heads the appearance of a "firmament" like ice, as it were a separation between Yetzirah and the World of Briah: into which World his vision presently passes. For then we have "the likeness of a throne" of lapis-lazuli (translated "sapphire" in most versions) and upon the throne "the likeness of the appearance of a man." This, indeed, is one of the rare occasions in Jewish religious writing where a Briatic manifestation is interpreted as a figure representing Divinity and not a messenger thereof. We see the extreme and accurate care taken by Ezekiel to emphasize that this Briatic figure is but "the likeness of the appearance of a man," and then "the appearance of the likeness of the glory of the Lord"; but the voice which comes to the Prophet from this figure gives, he doubts not for an instant, a Divine command.

The beings of the Chora of Binah in Yetzirah are named Aralim, "Thrones," since in the nature of their Sephirah they are primarily passive recipients of the force transmitted from higher levels; while the Chora of Chesed are the Chasmalim, the "Brilliant Ones." They also show forth the character of their Sephirah, the splendour of the Priest-King. The Chora of Geburah are the "Burning Ones," the Seraphim; the beings of the Chora of Tiphareth are Malekim, "Kings." Kings indeed they are, for "all that is beneath the Sun," and the harmony thereof, constitutes their domain. (The aggregation of so many shrines of healing or of divination in classical times to Apollo is a reflection of this dominion.) The Chora of Netzach is that of the Elohim, the "Gods"; nor is it strange that they should bear this title, for they are active in the life-forces and in the triumph thereof. Hod has for Chora the Tarshishim. By some authorities this Chora is given as the Beni-Elohim, "Sons of the Gods." This is a correct attribution; for the so-called "Laws of Nature," and likewise the forms in which these may be embodied (all of which are the work of Hod), are contingent upon the natural forces themselves. We, however, prefer to use for these beings their equally venerable name, Tarshishim, "the Seas"; for the great waters with their tides and currents splendidly represent the rhythms which divide and measure the natural force.*

The Chora of Yesod, the Kerubim, are the "Strong Ones," and in the context of Yesod, "strength" implies virility; not only because of the actual relevance of this Sephirah to matters of sex but also because it is the function of Yesod to bring the Sephirah Malkuth into existence by "projection" (in the alchemical sense) of the combined sephirothic influences: and also continually to fecundate and renew Malkuth by transmission of these influences.† In Biblical descriptions there is a perhaps deliberate avoidance of detail as to the Kerubic form, which is that of a winged human-headed bull not unlike the huge shapes represented in Assyrian sculpture. The guardians set to debar Adam's re-entrance into Eden would have been thus conceived of, and it is significant that between them there is mentioned "a flaming sword which turned every way, to keep the way of the Tree of Life." "Adam," then, is man projected into the material world, at the conclusion of the Path of the Sword; he must fully complete the involutionary process before he is permitted to reascend, just as mystics frequently have to tell the immature would-be disciple that flight from the world is not for him until life's lessons have been learned. For the Adam formed of the dust of the earth in the Biblical story is but an episode in the existence of Cosmic Man, whose name in the Hebrew Qabalah is Adam Kadmon (קדמון), and whose being comprises the totality of manifestation in

*Opinions differ regarding the ascription of Tarshishim: Rabbi Ishmael gives Tiphareth, the Master Therion gives Geburah, and S.R.M.D. gives Netzach. Our ascription to Hod is on the authority of the Targum.

†It is in context of this generative vitality of Yesod that *Cholem Yesodoth*, an important traditional title of Malkuth, is to be interpreted. This title is "Might of the Foundations"; the root ChLM signifying "to make strong" and having connotations of essential life and power. ChLM is also "to dream", the state of dreaming seen anciently as that which strengthens, confirms, activates: that which shows forth an inner potency. Malkuth is the witness, the manifestation, and the returned reflection, of Yesod.

3.   KASSIEL

4.   SACHIEL

5.   ZAMAEL

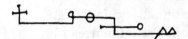

6.   MIKAEL*

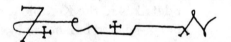

7.   ANAEL

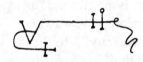

8.   RAPHAEL*

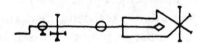

9.   GEBRIEL*

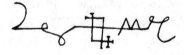

* These Angels are not to be confused with Archangels similarly named.

involution and return.

The Chora of Malkuth is composed of the Ashim, or "Flames." There has been a confused tradition concerning this name. Eliphaz Levi gives it as *Ischim*, and this indicates a confusion between AISh, a man, and ASh, and makes them human spirits; Dion Fortune gives *Ashim*, but translates it as "Souls of Fire"; MacGregor Mathers in *Kabbalah Unveiled* gives both *Ishim* and *Ashim*. AShIM is, however, the true name. Beauty and brilliance, swiftness and energy character-ise the strong and joyous beings of this Chora, who of all the angelic hosts are nearest to that creative fire in which astral force passes over to the material level.

The sephirothic names of the Fourth World complete the main series of Words of Power. These are the "Assiatic Palaces," that is, the names of the heavenly bodies: those chief symbols which act as focal points for the sephirothic forces.

For general sephirothic workings, to bring the power down as far as the Chora may often be all that is needed. There are, however, other beings in Yetzirah which are invoked in particular operations. In the case of the planetary Sephiroth, the Planetary or Ruling Angel is of chief importance. In bringing down a magical force through Yetzirah, the most effective method is not generally found to be the obvious one of addressing the Planetary Angel first and then the Chora. To do this tends to rediffuse the force after it has been concentrated. It is advisable to invoke first the Chora to receive the force from Briah, that it may be balanced, and then to bring it into focus (so to put it) by invocation of the Planetary Angel. With each of these Angels is associated a traditional sigil, indicated on page 94.

For other workings, more complex series of names in Yetzirah are needed: names of Intelligences, and sometimes

of those beings who are described simply as Spirits. In the
case of the Sephiroth which we have been considering, these
are the Planetary Intelligences and Spirits. The Intelligences
are of less power than the Ruling Angels but yet are among
the higher beings of Yetzirah; the Spirits are, of those we
have mentioned, nearest to the material world.

|   | Intelligence | Spirit |
|---|---|---|
| 3 | Agiel | Zazel |
| 4 | Yophiel | Hismael |
| 5 | Graphiel | Bartzabel |
| 6 | Nakiel | Sorath |
| 7 | Hagiel | Qedemel |
| 8 | Tiriel | Tapthartharath |
| 9 | Malkah b'Tarshishim | Chasmodai |

The Intelligences and Spirits represent in different
modes the essential characters of their spheres. Thus Agiel is
lofty, silent and remote, and Zazel is keenly perceptive in
matters of material prosperity; Yophiel and Hismael perceive
directly the needs of a moral situation, but Yophiel with
royal mien emphasises the philosophic or religious interpretation, while Hismael genially assists the social aspect.
Of the Intelligence and the Spirit of Mars, Graphiel is stern
and just, Bartzabel fiery and enthusiastic. Similarly Nakiel
radiates the effulgent light and spiritual generosity of the
Sun-sphere; Sorath, its joy and warmth. Hagiel is the high and
inspiring Lady of Beauty; Qedemel, the translator of beauty
to its more earthly connotations. Tiriel is the Intelligence
of prophecy and of the interpretation of oracles; Tapthar-
tharath, the Spirit of all communication. Finally, Malkah
b'Tarshishim, the Queen upon the Waters, shining with
the serene radiance of the Moon above the sea, is the con-
trolling Intelligence of the Sphere of Change, of birth, of

renewal; Chasmodai dwells within that Sphere of change, and is the veritable Spirit of that fluctuation.

The Elements Air, Water, Fire and Earth are ascribed to the Paths 11, 23, 31 and 32 bis respectively. In the various columns opposite those numbers on our Table, we have the God-name, the Archangel, the Angel Ruling and the Lesser Angel of the Element:

| Key | God-Name | Archangel | Angel | Lesser Angel |
|---|---|---|---|---|
| 11 | Yhvh | Ruachiel | Ariel | Chassan |
| 23 | El | Miel | Tharshis | Taliahad |
| 31 | Elohim | Ashiel | Seraph | Aral |
| 32 bis | Adonai | Auphiriel | Kerub | Phorlak |

We thus derive from the Table a set of names for use in connection with the elemental forces.

The zodiacal forces are attributed to Paths 15, 16, 17, 18, 19, 20, 22, 24, 25, 26, 28 and 29. The correspondences are God-name, Archangel, Angel Ruling Sign, Lesser Angel, Decanate Angel and Quinary Angel. The Decans, of which there are three to each zodiacal sign, are termed respectively Ascendant, Succedent, and Cadent. The Hierarchical Correspondences employed in a particular working should be those of the Ascendant Decan (or) Succedent Decan (or) Cadent Decan, depending upon the Sun's position in the first, second, or final part of the thirty degrees comprising the zodiacal sign. This should be determined exactly by means of an ephemeris. The same care is needed with regard to the Quinance, which further pinpoints the time of the operation since each Decan is made up of two Quinances. When working with such clearly defined forces, failure to ascertain the correct Decan and Quinance could wreck the operation, particularly in such a work as evocation to visible appearance.

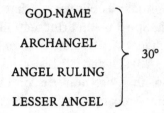

|  | GOD-NAME |  |
|---|---|---|
|  | ARCHANGEL | ⎫ |
|  | ANGEL RULING | ⎬ 30° |
|  | LESSER ANGEL | ⎭ |

| ANGEL OF DECAN<br>(ASCENDANT) | ANGEL OF DECAN<br>(SUCCEDENT) | ANGEL OF DECAN<br>(CADENT) |
|---|---|---|
| 1°-5°        6°-10° | 11°-15°        16°-20° | 21°-25°        26°-30° |

QUINANCES

The zodiac is referred to the Sphere of Chokmah. The Divine Name associated with Chokmah is YH (Yah); thus all the zodiacal forces may be placed under the presidency of this name. Again, the ineffable Tetragrammaton, YHVH, is sometimes ascribed to the Sphere of Chokmah, and the permutation of this name is traditionally held to govern the Zodiac:

| YHVH | ♈ | VHYH | ♎ |
|---|---|---|---|
| YHHV | ♉ | VHHY | ♏ |
| YVHH | ♊ | VYHH | ♐ |
| HVHY | ♋ | HYHV | ♑ |
| HVYH | ♌ | HYVH | ♒ |
| HHVY | ♍ | HHYV | ♓ |

It is felt, however, that the best practice with regard to the presidency of zodiacal signs is to place each House under its ruling planetary force:

| Sign | Ruled by | Sign | Ruled by |
|------|----------|------|----------|
| ♈ | ♂ | ♎ | ♀ |
| ♉ | ♀ | ♏ | ♂ |
| ♊ | ☿ | ♐ | ♃ |
| ♋ | ☽ | ♑ | ♄ |
| ♌ | ☉ | ♒ | ♄ |
| ♍ | ☿ | ♓ | ♃ |

Again, each House may be placed under the presidency of the Elemental Name, associated with the Triplicity to which it belongs:

| | | | | |
|---|---|---|---|---|
| △ | ALHIM (Elohim) | ♈ | ♌ | ♐ |
| ▽ | AL (El) | ♋ | ♏ | ♓ |
| △ | YHVH (Yahveh) | ♊ | ♎ | ♒ |
| ▽ | ADNI (Adonay) | ♉ | ♍ | ♑ |

We pass to that section of the Table which treats of the Qliphoth. Something of their nature has already been explained: the Qliphoth are the unbalanced overplus of their respective sephirothic forces, and therefore represent excessive or extreme degrees of these. We are not here working on the Aristotelian plan, which would associate the deficiency of a quality with that quality, as well as its excess. From the magical viewpoint it would be absurd to regard Irascibility, for example, as a manifestation of the same Archetype as Patience; whereas Weakness must clearly be recognised as a manifestation of that virtue in imbalance, and Irascibility is similarly related to the qualities of Strength and Valour. This point is emphasised because various writers have confused the matter.

Just as the Sephiroth are by no means mere empty philosophic concepts, so it is with the Qliphoth. Almost wherever forces, energies, are found, from the highest levels to the lowest, living beings are found whose existence is a participation in those energies. This, naturally, is true of the imbalanced forces of the Qliphoth just as it is true of the sephirothic forces.

Here ceases the progression to which we have become accustomed, of the Sephiroth through the Worlds. The qliphothic hierarchy takes on the aspect of a kind of mirror-image of the sephirothic hierarchy. On this point, Dante's *Inferno* gives a good picture of the situation, portraying the lower regions as a vast pit in the earth, with the minor transgressors near the surface and the great Princes of Hell in the depths. There are exceptions to the mirror-image. There are no separate Infernal Archetypes, for instance, for the reason already given: the Divine Archetypes set the pattern for all, even for the Infernal Powers. (The student who looks into medieval Grimoires, will find repeatedly that Evil Spirits are commanded by the Divine Names.) It must however be pointed out in this connection, that a progress from the Malkuth towards the Kether of the qliphothic Tree, which is really a descent, does *not* lead the practitioner back to the Divine Archetypes as a progress upward from the Malkuth of the sephirothic Tree would do. It does lead to the Abyss, for the normal or the malignant development of the faculties does not alter their nature, and the limit of those influences which pertain to earthly life is as clearly defined in their qliphothic manifestations as in their sephirothic. They who enter the Abyss in the power of the qliphothic Forces do not pass through Daath to Atziluth, but are assimilated to the Kingdom of Chaos, the realm of Dumah, and their fate is a slow but total disintegration, the utter dissolution of the individual. The horror of this is not fully thinkable by the human mind, so inured is that mind to the idea of its own cohesion; but those who have witnessed the failure of the physical brain, or who have realised the implications of much in the paintings of Goya and of Van Gogh, will guess something of this spiritual decomposition.

Yet at the end there is hope, for though the efforts of millenia may have been wasted, the indestructible Life at the centre of the psyche will create anew the concourse of forces: a new lower self will be evolved which will tread the Path from the beginning.

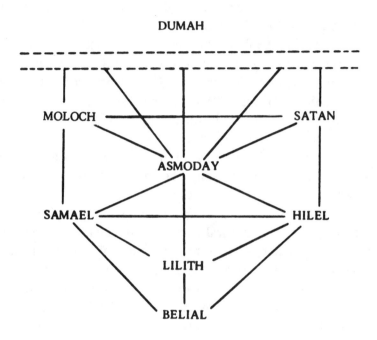

The qliphothic names have been variously given, not so much because of doubts as to their nature as on account of an ancient but regrettable Jewish custom of giving qliphothic ascriptions to the gods of other peoples. Although this custom has struck so much root in the Western tradition as to have been followed **without** question by both Dante and Milton, it goes entirely against the feeling of the enlightened modern magician; nevertheless, as with Moloch whose name is given in our table, there is occasionally no reasonable alternative. The justification here is that, although used as a proper name, Moloch is really a title, and can be used to signify an extreme manifestation of the force implied. Lilith, on the other hand, began her existence among the Sumerians as a "night-monster"; she passed into the Jewish cosmogony from the Babylonian at an early date, and has become a veritable part of the qliphothic tradition. The Aurum Solis scheme of the Princes of the Qliphoth and of their Cohorts is the work of Rabbi Morris Greenberg.

Dumah is the Prince of Chaos: in our scheme there is no attempt to distinguish any parts in the infernal rulership beyond the Abyss. Moloch rules the violent and cruel excess of the Qliphah of Mars: "My sentence is for open war" is the pronouncement which Milton perceptively gives him. Satan is distinctly Jupiter in excess, an aspect which Byron detects, representing Satan as offering his bounties to all who will seem to follow him, regardless of whether they afterwards cheat him. Asmoday, famous in medieval conjuration, is the proud and relentless destructive force symbolized by the tropical sun at noon. Hilel is the Hebrew name of Lucifer, the Venusian "Star of the Morning"; opposite to him is Samael, the Tempter of Eden, Mercurial in his Serpent-symbolism and also in his promise of knowledge. Lilith, the Night-demon, is ascribed to the Moon. Belial is ascribed to the Earth: his signification is of inertia, worthlessness, the most deadening influences of the Earth-sphere.

Corresponding to the Heavenly Arch, the Qliphoth have the demonic aspects of the zodiacal forces. These are the beings (named in our Table) which have been known through the centuries to magicians as the Spirits of the Lemegeton, the Lesser Key of Solomon. Other names there are which are attributed to the qliphothic Zodiac, but they are not given herein, being of no practical relevance to our work.

Besides these again, as there are Choras of sephirothic Spirits, so are there Cohorts of the Qliphoth: they, as we have seen with the other qliphothic powers, represent exaggerated or distorted aspects of the corresponding Sephirah.

The Cohorts of the Qliphoth beyond the Abyss are collectively known as the Sataroth, or Concealers. Neither they nor their habitations have any known form, but the Sataroth have been compared to huge, foul, voracious birds brooding on the slimy and fog-covered steeps of an unscaleable cliff.

The Rephaim, by contrast, are Qliphoth of the depths, of the marine aspect of Chesed: beings which must be described as dead in their corrupt and almost total lack of volition. Like long-drowned corpses they drift in the currents of being; nevertheless, some slight consciousness is theirs, and a dull malevolence.

The Qliphoth of Geburah are the Qetebim, or Destroyers: "the pestilence that walketh in darkness" as composed of a host of evil beings.

The qliphothic Cohort corresponding to Tiphareth is composed of the Taga'arim: these are the Rebukers. To see and to know is the unvarying privilege of the solar force; to use that knowledge in order to proclaim human shortcomings, and to rebuke them, is qliphothic.

The Seirim are the Qliphoth corresponding to Netzach. "And they shall no more offer their sacrifices unto devils . . ." "And he ordained him priests for the high places, and for the devils . . ." In both these biblical passages, Leviticus 17:7 and 2 Chronicles 11:15, the Authorised Version translates the Hebrew word *Seirim* (lit. Satyrs) as "devils."

The Qliphothic forces of Hod are the Teraphim; this word is also used of the idols dedicated to these beings. Experiment with these particular forces led in one instance (known to the present writers) to a series of horrific misfortunes culminating in insanity.

"And it came to pass, when men began to multiply on the face of the earth, and daughters were born unto them, that the Sons of God saw the daughters of men that they were fair; and they took wives of them all which they chose"

(Genesis 6:12). By tradition, the erotic beings here mentioned are the Oirim, the evil Watchers. Among their crew are Shemchozai, A'azel and A'aza.

The qliphothic Cohort of Malkuth, the Na'aimoth, are Spirits of indolence and sloth; their name means "the Pleasant Ones" and their tendency is to accentuate the natural inertia of the Earth-sphere.

This concludes our survey of the main principles of the Hebrew hierarchy in its aspects both theurgic and goetic. This survey is intended for study, for reference and for progressive reflection, as a basis for the student's own explorations. A thoughtful reading of the more mystical passages of the Old Testament—and of the Zohar should these be accessible—will help further to reveal an underlying view of the universe which is ancient, timeless and truly magical: a view which is ethical without dualism, and in which a great wonderment consistently exceeds every other emotion.

The Hebrew hierarchical system is traditional, is potent for those who either have or can induce in themselves the requisite temperament, and raises no particular difficulty beyond the need for exact knowledge of it. All learners should study this Hebrew hierarchy of Atziluthic, Briatic, Yetziratic and Assiatic names, which gives the basic framework of our method and which provides a system of invocation needing no extraneous supplement. However, for various reasons, not every Western magician wishes to work a completely Hebrew system; besides which, such a system inevitably excludes much that is known and that ought to be available for use.

One important series of key concepts which is omitted, although not necessarily so, by the system of invocation above indicated, is the series of Magical Images. These are really what may be called the "indigenous God-forms of the Qabalistic substructure," and their importance can scarcely

be over-emphasised: the Divine Archetypes find direct
expression in them. For Kether we give no such image, since
any would be totally inappropriate to the nature of that
Sephirah: no ritual is performed which could require such an
image, and there is but one semblance in which the Force of
Kether can fittingly be visualised. These, then, are the
Magical Images of the Sephiroth:

| 1 | Kether | White Brilliance |
|---|--------|------------------|
| 2 | Chokmah | Bearded Patriarch |
| 3 | Binah | Celestial Queen |
| 4 | Chesed | Enthroned Priest-King |
| 5 | Geburah | Armed Warrior-King |
| 6 | Tiphareth | Divine Child, Solar King, Sacrificed God |
| 7 | Netzach | Naked Amazon |
| 8 | Hod | Hermaphrodite |
| 9 | Yesod | Ithyphallic Youth |
| 10 | Malkuth | Veiled Maiden |

These Briatic forms open very potent channels of force,
and therefore due care and solemnity should always attend
their use. They can be employed with the Hebrew Divine
Names, the power of EL, for example, being invoked through
the form of the Priest-King.*

The Archetypes in the Divine Mind can, however, be
invoked by other names than the Hebrew God-names. We can
work a sphere without reference to any particular religious
system: we can, for instance, make our Atziluthic invocation
by one of such Formulae as those given in chapter I, building
up the corresponding Magical Image as the channel for the
Divine Force. In working the Sphere of Mars we might invoke:

* The Magical Images may be employed within the framework of the Hebrew
cosmogony, or the Hebrew Divine Names may be employed simply as key words
in connection with the Images; but although the Magical Images may thus be
validly used with the Hebrew cosmogony, they are not essential to it, the forms of
the Archangels being the normal Briatic channels in that system. We are not here
making rules, we are simply reviewing options.

(The Warrior-King stands in his chariot: courage and power are in his gaze. Over his corselet of burnished steel he wears a great red cloak, lined with amber and bright as flame. Upon his head is a helm, surrounded by a crown starred with pentagrams. He holds in his right hand a steel sword with crystal pommel, in his left a great shield. His chariot is of red gold adorned with green. Emeralds flash at his collar and upon his armlets. Like a terrible fire is his aspect, a fire whose scarlet flames flash with points of green.)

*"O Valiant Strength, hear the voice of my justice! In this day and this hour of thy Sphere do I call upon thee. I have covered this altar with scarlet, and in thy Name have I burned opoponax with aloes. Thee do I invoke, with the Sword of steel striking once and thrice and once . . . ."*

Or, for the Sphere of Jupiter, the following:

(The Priest-King is seated upon a throne of lapis-lazuli: he is robed in rich blue, patterned with squares and lozenges of lilac and gold. He wears a crown, over a cap of maintenance of blue. Upon the back of the throne, above his head, stands a great eagle with outstretched wings. Calm and benign is the countenance of the king. In his right hand he holds a sceptre surmounted by a phoenix, in his left an orb of gold surmounted by an equal-armed cross.)

*"Hail to thee, Majestic Beneficence! In this day and this hour of thy Sphere do I place myself within thy protection. For thee this altar is covered with blue of the wide vault of heaven; for thee arises the smoke of cedar and olive. Thee I invoke to be my defence, as I pour this fourfold libation from the bountiful Cup . . . ."*

The full potential of the Qabalah in magical work is not realised by seeing it as a closed system of Hebrew names and Judaic concepts: it is to be understood as a universal substructure denoting the primary forces of Cosmos and Microcosmos. Upon the framework of this substructure we may range in due order names from any pantheon known to us. Thus magick, according to the system of the Qabalah, enables us to invoke or to identify with the power of any deity of any pantheon whatever, so long as we hold to the correct correspondences and so long as we are consistent in our workings. A thorough knowledge of the correspondences does not warrant their use for the mixing of pantheons, nor for the confusion of archetypal images. It would not do to invoke Raphael by the power of Thoth, though both are ascribed to the Sephirah Hod. When the Hebrew hierarchical cosmogony is used, it must be used in its entirety. Thus, to call forth to visible appearance the Spirit of Mars, one would begin with the God-name ALHIM GBVR, call upon the Archangel KMAL, then the Chora ShRPIM and the Angel ZMAL, then the Intelligence of the Sphere, GRAPIAL: these invocations result in a pressure upon the Spirit BRTzBAL to manifest himself. (This is, of course, a very much simplified exposition.) One could not, as a variation, command Bartzabel to visible appearance by a conjuration in the name of Ogoun, the Voudoun Loa corresponding to Geburah. What is forbidden here is not the use of the Voudoun pantheon, but the mingling of cosmogonies. This is common sense, for the Christian bread and wine cannot be transubstantiated by the power of the Celtic Lugh; likewise, Bran is not healed by the mystical spear, but by passing through the Cauldron. Furthermore, that same Cauldron, which was a most potent vessel of healing under the power of Ceriddwyn, certainly became other- wise when Medea lured King Pelias to become mutton served as *agneau à l'hyperborée.*

The question of correct presidency is the most important aspect of successful working that we have at present to consider. It will be obvious of course that archangelic and angelic names can only be included in our invocation if they are under the presidency of a Hebrew God-name.

But if the magician wishes to work with the gods of the various pantheons, how does he draw his work into a central unity, how does he maintain uniformity in his work at the supreme level?

It must be borne in mind that any god who so corresponds to an Archetype as to become a channel for that force, is, though born of the human mind's perception of the Archetype, a veritable function of the Divine Mind. The form of the god is Briatic (and Yetziratic, of course) but the essence of the god, the life of the god, is truly and potently Atziluthic. Taking any god thus, it becomes obvious that the name of that being is a Word of Power that expresses something of the Archetype discerned; and in the context of its own cult, no further Word is needed. There are, indeed, certain operations of magick that necessitate working on this very basis, but it is generally desirable for the magician to maintain uniformity in his working, and it is very possible that the deity in question may not be a part of the cult of the magician's own dedication. It is a fact that, for example, Ogoun, Ares, Mars, Tiw and so on, are each for his own cult a universal manifestation of the Geburah Archetype, but the various names cannot be used indiscriminately. Here, Magical Formulae are necessary to use with the names of the deities so as to draw the working to a central unity, and, in fact, to identify the archetypal essence of the god as a primordial reality.* These Formulae may be the Hebrew Divine Names, or they may be other names of a suitable nature.†

Whatever Atziluthic names are chosen as Formulae, in whatever language, the most exact care must be taken to achieve complete harmony in all materials, instruments and modes of working: water is not offered to Dionysus, nor is a bell sounded for Allah. Some Names of Power there are,

---

* Of course, presidency in this context does not imply superiority, for the essence which is the veritable "life" of a god is precisely the same force which is betokened by the Formula, only it is here "de-personalised," so to speak, and thus universalised.

† The Formulae of the Aurum Solis will be given in a subsequent volume. Our first intention is to present as far as possible the essentials of magical working.

which should be uttered not only with correct pronunciation, but in the correct tones, as the magician may be able to ascertain these: such are some of the Egyptian and other Middle Eastern names, especially such as are composed entirely or almost entirely of vowels: Ea, Iao, Iove, Iah. Or, where the Deity-name itself is not of that nature, there is sometimes a consecrated formula of invocation such as Io, Evoe, or other call having fixed ritual tones. (The basic idea of this is found in all parts of the human race.) In a passage which has become famous in his treatise *Peri Hermeneias*, the Greek writer Demetrios states that the Egyptians of old hymned their gods by means of the seven vowels. This would seem to indicate a distinct tone for each vowel: a theory which accords with known facts of religious and magical practice.

In our tradition, this is the true secret of that supreme Hebrew Name of Power which we render as Yahveh or as Yod Heh Vau Heh, or as Tetragrammaton, the Word of Four Syllables, the proper name of the God of Israel. The mystery concerning this Name was not, as is generally supposed, that it *must not* be pronounced by lay-people in ordinary speech; in fact it *could not* be so pronounced, for the musical tones of its solemn utterance were an integral part of the Name itself. Thus when it is reported in the Mishnah that a certain man was able to write the Divine Name, it is by no means implied that therefore he was also able to utter it. Without the right musical tones, the Name is not truly the Name. True, to speak even the mere sequence of vocables of such a Word of Power, with due solemnity and with serious intent, has much potency; but the full force of utterance is possible only to those who know the Tones.

And though a man know both the Syllables and the Tones, yet without great hardihood, and without full dedication to the Hebrew work, he will not dare once in a lifetime to utter it.

There are names of more general import which can be
used with great power by those who do not wish to bind
themselves to the Hebrew. Again, consistency in one's
method is all important to the strength of one's working.
Mention has already been made of such Formulae as those
to be found in chapter I; names of another kind may be
culled from the *Treatise on the Divine Names* of Dionysius the
Pseudo-Areopagite, who, though he wrote within the
Christian framework, was not as earlier centuries thought a
disciple of St. Paul, but a Neo-Platonist who brought many
of the doctrines of Proclus into the traditions of the medieval
Church. Or the deeper scholar may go to Proclus himself
for the source of these names, which in fact are most august
Greek titles of Divine Attributes: ΠΡΟΩΝ, Primal Being;
ΑΙΩΝΙΟΣ ΖΩΗ, Eternal Life; ΚΡΥΦΙΑ ΓΝΩΣΙΣ, Source of
Wisdom. The transcendent Aleister Crowley developed his
own distinctive system: his magick is a fugue for ten thousand worlds and must be studied as a complete
cosmology. The student interested in the Law of Thelema
must look to Crowley's published works for guidance.
Certain Gnostic names are profoundly potent; nor is this
surprising, since so much informed Greek and Jewish thought
was directed to the formulation of the Gnosis. Examples are
Iao, Abraxas, Agathodaemon, Sophia: glorious Names of
Power, whose use well accords with magical freedom.

If it should be desired to invoke particular beings in
Yetzirah to stabilise the invoked influences, there are the
Elemental Spirits, who, as we have noted are called to
participate in many magical rituals for this purpose. These
are of the Malkuth of Yetzirah. Important also in this respect
is the Elizabethan system of magick of Dee and Kelly, which,
however, goes beyond the purely Yetziratic level (see
Volume 3, Mysteria Magica).

There are other Spirits of the Planetary Spheres of
Yetzirah who can form an effective link in the chain of

invocation. They can be used with any cosmogony, or with none, being without bias in that respect. Little is generally known of them save their names and attributions. In work undertaken with them the authors have found them powerful and beneficent. They are known as the Olympic Planetary Spirits:

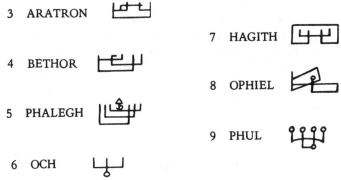

But the universe is thronged with Spirits of every kind; magical writings abound in names given by one or another magician, names of beings which have become known to him and which in some cases have become his especial helpers. The earnest student will in due course find his own.

From these considerations it should be clear that an invocation may be profoundly Qabalistic without in any way obligating the magician to an acceptance of Jewish or Judeo-Christian deific concepts. Each is free to find the Formulae most suited to his own character and to his sense of his life-work.

*Addendum*

Verses 19, 20 and 21 of chapter XIV of the Book of Exodus are each composed of 72 Hebrew letters. If one letter is taken from each verse in turn, reading from beginning to end in the normal manner for verses 19 and 21 but reading from end to beginning for verse 20, 72 names of three letters each are revealed: the mighty and divine *Shem ha-Mephoresh*.

When, according to established custom, the terminative YH or AL is appended to each of these names, there are obtained the names of the angels of the 72 zodiacal quinances, as shown in columns 13, 14 and 15 of our table of Theurgia.

*Exodus XIV, 19, 20, 21*

19   ויסע מלאך האלהים ההלך לפני מחנה ישראל וילך
מאחריהם ויסע עמוד הענן מפניהם ויעמד מאחריהם

20   ויבא בין מחנה מצרים ובין מחנה ישראל ויהי הענן
והחשך ויאר את הלילה ולא קרב זה אל זה כל הלילה

21   ויט משה את ידו על הים ויולך יהוה את הים ברוח
קדים עזה כל הלילה וישם את הים לחרבה ויבקעו המים

# CHAPTER VI

The Twenty-two Paths and the diverse influences which give each Path a unique character.

Of seven of the Paths, each carries the influence of a Planetary Sephirah; of twelve more of the Paths, each carries the influence of a Zodiacal Sign; the remaining three Paths relate to the Elements, Air, Water, Fire. Besides these attributions, each Path has traditionally ascribed to it one of the twenty-two letters of the Hebrew alphabet.

A study of the Paths:—The Song of Praises, the twenty-two stanzas followed by their interpretation.

Table of the chief attributions which render each one of the 22 Paths unique in character.

# CHAPTER VI
## SOME DISCURSIVE REFLECTIONS ON THE PATHS*

In our illustration upon the facing page the Paths of the Tree of Life are shown. These join the Sephiroth, not indiscriminately but according to a definite pattern, their existence being contingent upon that of the Sephiroth; that is to say, the Sephiroth could be conceived of as existing without the Paths, but not the Paths without the Sephiroth.

Of the factors which compose the experience of each Path, the most obvious are the influences of the Sephiroth at its two ends. These should, indeed, always be taken into account, but they are by no means the whole story. Planetary forces, for example, are reflected in strange and asymmetrical ways throughout the Tree, although upon analysis good reason can always be found for these reflections. The Sphere of Saturn is Binah: the reflection of Saturn is on the 32nd Path,† between Malkuth and Yesod. The Sphere of Jupiter is Chesed: the reflection of Jupiter is on the 21st Path, and this is the one instance in which a planetary force is reflected into a Path adjacent to its sphere, the Path between Chesed and Netzach. The Sphere of Mars is Geburah: the reflection of

---

*Although many considerations to be found herein are pertinent to practical work and spiritual endeavour, and various allusions are necessarily made to the Serpent-Way of Return both from the initiatory point of view and the course of natural progress, this chapter is by intention a *general* examination of various aspects of the Paths as such. *Pars non est maior tota:* cf. ch. III concerning the Way of Return.

†It will be recalled that the numbering of the Twenty-two Paths begins at 11, the numbers 1 through 10 being allocated to the Sephiroth.

Mars is on the 27th Path, between Netzach and Hod. The
Sphere of the Sun is Tiphareth, but the force of the Sun
reflects into the 30th Path, between Yesod and Hod. The
Sphere of Venus is Netzach, but the lower Paths do not
receive her direct reflection, which is only found in its
fullness in the Path linking the Supernal Father and the
Supernal Mother, Chokmah and Binah. Likewise the Sphere
of Mercury is Hod, but the Path in which the power of that
winged wanderer is reflected is the 12th Path, between Binah
and Kether. The Sphere of the Moon is Yesod, and just as the
force of Saturn is reflected downwards to the Path adjoining
the Moon-sphere, so the force of the Moon is reflected
upward, to the Path from Tiphareth to Kether.

Kether and Chokmah do not reflect directly into any of
the Paths, since in human experience their distinctive forces
are translated into terms of other Sephiroth, Tiphareth and
Chesed respectively. Malkuth is represented entirely as
receiving influences, not as emanating force, and therefore
there is no Path reflecting any influence of the Earth-sphere.*

When we look to those Paths which have a zodiacal force
ascribed to them, the situation is even more complex, for each
zodiacal Sign carries the implicit character of its ruling planet,
although in a modified form: Venus manifest in Taurus is
different from Venus in Libra, for example. The ascriptions of
these Paths throw more light upon the relationship of the
Sephiroth. To take a few instances, the especial polarity of
Mars to Venus is shown by the cross-reflection, Scorpio on
the 24th Path and Libra on the 22nd. The principle of harmony
and compensation is frequently apparent: the cool
intellectualism of Virgo interposes between Jupiter and the
Sun, just as Libra between Mars and the Sun; but between
Mars and Jupiter, Warrior-King and Priest-King, the Path
reflects the royal quality of Sun-Leo.

---

* The lines 32-bis and 31-bis which appear on our Table are merely useful conventions, not representing further actual Paths, but giving space for other aspects of
the 32nd and 31st Paths.

Of the Paths ascribed to the Elements, the 11th Path is of Air, the 23rd is of Water and the 31st of Fire; again the absence of Earth is accounted for by the reason given above, concerning Malkuth.

Less immediately apparent, however, is the traditional attribution to the Paths of the twenty-two letters of the Hebrew Alphabet. It is, primarily, strange to us because we ourselves have inherited an alphabet—the Roman—from one of the most unimaginative peoples that this world has known. Many early races attached great significance to their alphabets. The Tree-Alphabet of the Celts concealed a whole mythology; the Runic Alphabet of the Norsemen, however commonplace its origin, became and remained a most potent vehicle of magick; the Hieroglyphs of Egypt, by their very nature reserved for solemn use, were also held sacred for the power of the glyphs to implement their meaning; so likewise the letters of Sanskrit; while the Ideograms of the Chinese are miniature studies in philosophy.

The Hebrew Alphabet is no exception. Originally, it is true, these twenty-two letters were convenient pictograms: the Camel, the Ox-Goad, the Fish-Hook. Centuries upon centuries of meditation, however, have deepened the associations to an intensely mystical significance. The inspiration for this is to be found in the fact that, for the people of that language, all utterance was expressed by these twenty-two letters. Furthermore, speech being produced by breath, and being the manifestation of a human spirit, it becomes a major symbol of the manifestation of God—the various meanings of *Ruach* are relevant here—and, by a further elaboration of thought, each element of speech, that is, each letter of the alphabet, becomes the symbol of an aspect of Deity. It is then reasonable to allocate these letters to the Paths of the Tree, since we are not here discussing the Ten Divine Archetypes subsisting within the Divine Mind, but the twenty-two modes in which their interwoven connotations (alternatively, their latent connotations) are

revealed to human understanding and experience: each mode
being symbolised by an uttered sound. Thus it is, for
example, that the letter Aleph (א), which represents the
unconditioned voice passing through the open mouth, is
attributed to the Eleventh Path, symbolising the first simple
Breath of Emanation, and its Yetziratic attribution is that of
the element Air. The letter Beth (ב), on the other hand,
both in name and in shape represents "a house"; it therefore
takes an appropriate place on the Twelfth Path, for Binah,
and indeed the whole of the Column of Severity, constitutes
a "house" or outward form for the energies of the Column of
Mercy, as a number of medieval representations clearly
indicate. So in the other instances, either by sound or by
shape, or both, the letters represent the deeper significances
of the Paths to which they are attached.

Another tradition enriching the symbolism of the Paths,
is that which attributes to them the twenty-two Tarot
Trumps. Here the generally accepted pattern of attributions
presents no difficulty, following as it does the plain meaning
of the cards according to their normal interpretations.

### THE SONG OF PRAISES

ת XXXII ♄

Thine is the Sign of the End, Being fulfilled
                                        Sum of existences:
Thine is the ultimate Door opened on Night's
                                        unuttered mystery:
Thine, the first hesitant step into the dark
                                        of those but latterly
                        Born to the Labyrinth!

ש XXXI △

Shining O Fire in thy strength, laughing in flames
                                        rushing to heavenward,
Sharp is thy tooth to devour all things of earth,
                                        all things transmutable,

Winning them into thine own force incorrupt,
                                 turning them hiddenly
           Back to their principles!

ר XXX ☉

Rise in thy splendour, O King! — glorious brow,
                                 gaze on thy governance
Gladdening all who behold!  Soaring as song,
                                 rule and illuminate:
Crysoleth gleaming thy crown, rise and inspire,
                                 Lion-gold, Falcon-flight,
           Joyous, ambrosial!

ק XXIX ♓

Quietly under the Moon vanishes Day's
                                 vaunted aut4omony:
Softly the voices of Night sound at our gates,
                                 stir from oblivion
Calling for sacrifice!  Lo, children are we
                                 all of one parentage:
           Go we with thanksgiving!

צ XXVIII ♒

Tzaphqiel, Bright one beyond veils of the night!
                                 Envoy and countenance
Thou of the Mother, all hail!  Thine is that far
                                 fortress of radiance
Lighting the drouth of our way:  fountain of hope,
                                 water celestial
           Deathless our thirst for it!

פ XXVII ♂

Play of the Breath and the Word, Life and the Law,
                                 counterchange intricate
Weaving the ground of our days:  this is our strength,
                                 this is our jeopardy.
Spirit oracular, tell:  knowledge and love,
                                 will they keep unity
           Or, opposed, shatter us?

ע XXVI א

Out of the wellspring of forms filling the wide
                              spheres with its fashionings
Myriad images rise, wild or serene,
                              fleshly, ethereal:
Hail, O thou Eye that hast seen all things that are,
                              Knowledge to gaze on them
            Blessing their goodliness!

ס XXV ♐

Stone of the Patriarch's dream, pillow austere
                              couching the wanderer
While between heaven and earth glorious Shapes
                              came and went ceaselessly:
Hail to thee, Gate of the Worlds, column unhewn
                              set for memorial
            Pointing the Arrow-road!

נ XXIV ♏

Nearest the heart of the seas watches the Fish,
                              shimmering, nacreous,
Moving with pulse of the tides, gliding far down
                              under their turbulence,
Crossing the fathomless caves, threading the lost
                              hulls of the argosies—
            Shadow inscrutable!

מ XXIII ▽

Mother of waters profound, dark are thy halls,
                              bitter thy fragrances:
Voices of love and of awe call thee: arise,
                              leave thou thy sorrowing!
Robe thee in web of thy waves, Mother of Life,
                              robe thee in radiance,
            Sing of thy Mysteries!

ל XXII ♎

Lash of the Winds be thou named, waking the storm,
                              stirring the hurricane,

Flailing the forests, the plains, stripping the dead
> leafage of yesteryear,
Sweeping the summer's decay!  Dance and exult,
> beauty invisible,
Terrible innocence!

## ⼂ XXI ♓

Cup that receives and bestows, generous palm
> garnering, scattering,
Thine are the bountiful rains, thine is the fount
> purpled and perilous:
Thine is dominion to cast down to the pit,
> thine to give sanctuary—
Yea, to give liberty!

## ⸲ XX ♍

Youth everlasting art thou, timeless as light
> going forth silently,
Prince of the ripening grain, hand that creates,
> changes and fecundates,
Touching the stars that they blaze, touching the vast
> whorls of the nebulae,
Siring forth galaxies!

## ⼕ XIX ♌

Twelve are the boundary-signs framing the bright
> dragon celestial,
Theli or Ouroboros, circling the world,
> serpentine, leonine:
Thee whom the Thunderer strove vainly to move,
> mighy one, shining one:
Thine be all reverence!

## ⼙ XVIII ☉

Chaos is close at our gates:  sure be the wall,
> strong be the citadel!
Now by adversity's fire wrought to endure,
> be thou our champion:

Be thou our shield of defence till, at the last,
>> Tumult shall comprehend
> Harmony manifest!

## ♐ XVII ♊

Zephyr, or Boreas wild: which is thy breath,
>> what is thy purposing?
Storm-flash or clear morning-rise, under what guise
>> hail we thy countenance?
Twain are the serpents of power, twain the august
>> Thummim of prophecy:
> Twofold thy praises be!

## ♊ XVI ♉

Votary steadfast as stone, ardent as flame,
>> stanchion of unity,
Kin to that spirit divine fixed in the sun,
>> self-spending, bountiful
Life of the fosterling worlds!  So standest thou,
>> pontifex-sacrifice,
> Changeless fidelity!

## ⊓ XV ♈

High and victorious, hail!  Scarlet-bedraped
>> windows are thronged for thee,
Thee to behold, who behold'st but to achieve,
>> victor who conquerest
But to make whole, to fulfil: judge who sees truth!
>> Hail, thou whose gonfanon
> Leads the year's pageantry!

## ⊓ XIV ♀

Doorway of vision fulfilled, bringer of dreams
>> forth to adventuring,
Sacred to thee are the red portals of dawn,
>> sacred the emerald
Gates of the jubilant spring, Mother of deeds
>> manifest, multiform—
> Mother of destiny!

ג XIII ב

Grace of the glimmering night, beautiful pale
> camel thou journeyest

Comely with bridle of pearl, cloth of most fair
> silver caparisoned:

Tracing the trackless abodes, knowing all times,
> knowing the numberless

> Seeds of the firmament!

ב XII ☿

Bearing thy truth in thy heart, opal-fire sealed
> deep and inviolate,

Over the seven-hued bridge pass to the worlds,
> share in their variance.

Hail to the voice of thy power, speaking all tongues,
> many in purposes,

> One in divinity!

א XI △

Ally of harbourless air, primrose-pale child,
> shadow-lord azurine,

Whirling the mill of the spheres, circling their course,
> tracing their vortices,

Bright as chalcedony, forth flashing then sped,
> fervid as galbanum,

> Hail, breath of origin!

These verses on the letters of the Hebrew Alphabet are
given in reverse order so as to follow the ascent of the Paths;
thus the final or 32nd Path from Malkuth to Yesod is the
first Path embarked upon by the aspirant. Carrying the
reflection of the Sephirah Binah, this Path is shadowed by
the influence of Saturn, the door opened upon the void of
night, the hesitancy of the first step. Saturn, however, is
essentially the force of Rebirth, as Yesod is of Birth; this
Path is correspondingly that of the new-born, who has come

(or as some would say, who has returned) to tread the Way.

Before proceeding, it is necessary to explain the principle upon which a number of the allusions in these verses are based: the system known as Gematria. The Hebrew letters have numerical values assigned to them as well as sounds (see Volume 3, p. 143), having been used as numerals for ordinary as well as for mystical purposes. Hence the custom arose of assessing some of the affinities of a word by finding its numeration. Sometimes an affinity is found between words or letters with exactly the same numeration, as when in our verses on Samekh there is allusion to the dream or vision of the Patriarch Jacob: the numerical value of the single letter ס is 60, but also the Hebrew word MChZH, signifying "a vision," gives the numeration 40+8+ 7+5=60. Quite often, however, an affinity is found by a more elaborate method, as in the case of Kaph, whose ordinary form has the numerical value 20, while its name in full, כף, adds up to 820, which again adds up to 10. To tally in numeration with 10, we can say that the Hebrew word for "vineyard," KRM again has for value 820, and thus 10. To tally with the numeration 500, we find that the word MY, meaning "water," has the numerical value 50, while the word ShLCh, meaning "to send" or "to let go," has the numerical value 338, which adds up to 14 and thence to 5. Much more complex exercises in numeration are also included in Gematria. Of course, if a word had a totally irrelevant meaning, it would not be introduced simply on account of a coincidence of numeration, although such a coincidence, if exact, should afford at least food for careful thought; while harmonious examples of Gematria frequently blend so completely with the rest of the symbols of the Path concerned, as to need no special mention. For these reasons, therefore, it has been considered unnecessary to give most of the examples of Gematria discovered in the construction of these verses; a few will however be selected as a matter of interest.

In the lines on ת, then, it is noteworthy that the Hebrew name of the letter Tau spelled in full, TV, gives the numeration 406, which adds to 10, the Pythagorean "Perfect Number" and sum of all things; while the Tarot symbol corresponding to the same Path is "the World" or "the Universe." ת as a single letter has the value 400, and the word for "deliverance" or "salvation," YShVOH, which is one of the attributes of Saturn, has the numeration 391, also adding to 4. By tradition, the Sign to be marked in blood on the forehead of the firstborn to save him from the Angel of Death (Exodus 12) was the Tau Cross, another form of the letter. Again, the numeration 4, simply, belongs to Daleth, the fourth letter of the alphabet, and the meaning of the word Daleth is "a door." Hence to ת, 400, is ascribed "the ultimate Door." Finally, and most significantly, we have the line "Born to the Labyrinth." The Labyrinth was an underground (and therefore Saturnian) place of trial where, after treading a dark uncertain path, one came at last face to face with Minotauros. The name Minotauros signifies Bull of Minos, that is, Bull of the Moon.

As we have pointed out in the preceding chapter, the Kerubim of Yesod are Bulls of the Moon: wonderful but of terrible power.

Thus do we see something of the fears and uncertainties awaiting the aspirant on this first progress into the unseen world by the 32nd Path. Nevertheless, it is an essential progress: this is the Path he must tread. This achieved, the Path of Fire will be open to him, the 31st Path which otherwise would but have resolved him back into the elements of his being, as fire does by nature.

The lines on ש give the magical significance of this Path. Leading from Malkuth to Hod, it is intimately connected with the Hermetic Art, that is, Alchemy. Controlled, Fire transmutes, but otherwise it "devours" all things and wins them to its own "force incorrupt," that is, to primal energy and to those principles which gave them being.

The name of the letter, ShYN, signifies "a tooth," and, written in full (not using the final form of the 〕 since one has the option in Gematria), this word gives the numerical value 360, which corresponds to the number of degrees in a complete circle. This is used to illustrate the power of fire to bring materials "full circle" back to their components. The Tarot symbol, "The Last Judgment," conveys the same meaning; but for those who are equipped to take this Path, it should signify renewal. Thus in this Path are shown qualities of all the zodiacal Signs of the Fiery Triplicity: the renewal of Aries, the devouring quality of Leo, and the transforming aspiration of Saggitarius.

Now follows the 30th Path, from Yesod to Hod. This Path, from the Moon-sphere to Hod in the World of Yetzirah, would be dim and cold, a chilling of the creative imagination by the force of the intellect, but that the full force of the Sun shines upon it. Often in considering a Path as conditioned by the Sephiroth in which it begins and ends, we shall find that some factor which is lacking or which would be thrown out of balance by those Sephiroth, has in fact been compensated by a reflected influence from another Sephirah. "Splendour" is suited both to the Sun and to the Sephirah Hod, the goal of this Path. Crysoleth, Lion and Falcon are symbols of the Sun. Of the Gematric allusions, the word RYSh, meaning "head," reverses into ShYR, meaning "song," both having the value 510; while HVD (Splendour) adds up to 15. Each of these words ultimately adds up to 6, the number of Tiphareth, whose kingly image is so strong upon this Path.

The 29th Path is another Path which would menace the traveller with the danger of disintegration had he not already encountered the forces of Yetzirah; this time it would be psychic disintegration because this Path leads to Netzach, the Sphere governing emotion and the powers of Nature. The danger is emphasised by the attribution to this Path of the zodiacal Sign of Pisces. Ruled by Jupiter, this Sign represents his fluidic rather than his celestial aspect: he is father to Venus, Goddess of the natural world, and "children are we all of one parentage." People in whose horoscope Pisces is dominant, as well as others of a sensitive psychic nature having perhaps a natural affinity with animals or with the Elemental worlds, should especially beware the renunciation of individuality here indicated. The Tarot symbol of "The Moon" pictures an eerie scene of this kind: under the light of the Moon a crayfish moves in the depths of a pool, and in the distance a domestic dog has gone forth to howl in company with a wolf, while from a tower-guarded gap a road leads away to the horizon and—whither?

Once this point has been passed, the emphasis changes. The 28th Path, bearing the letter Tzaddi, is attributed to the zodiacal Sign Aquarius and is infused with a characteristic Aquarian aspiration. This Path, running from Yesod, whose elemental affinity is Air, to Netzach, whose elemental affinity is Fire, would indeed be a parched and waterless tract but for the reflected influence therein of Binah, the Great Mother, whose symbol is the Primal Ocean. Thus, though Aquarius is in fact an Air-sign, it is also "the Water Bearer." The lines concerning this Path address Tzaphqiel, Archangel of Binah: "countenance" of the Mother by virtue of being one of her Briatic images. The letter ﬩ has the numerical value 90; the Hebrew verb meaning "to give to drink," ShQH, gives 405, adding to 9. The Tarot symbol for this Path is the Star, signifying Hope. In that picture the Star-Maiden is shown pouring streams of cool water from two pitchers. The Sphere of Saturn shines far above, beyond the Abyss; nevertheless, the hope and longing of the aspirant is unabated. Tzaddi represents "a fish-hook": it is a symbol of that attraction to the Supernals by means of hope and aspiration, which can draw one who experiences it completely out of a feeling of kinship with the material

world. Jung warns against setting forth on the quest for
complete integration before the ordinary requirements of
earthly life have been fulfilled. By a certain minority with a
special sense of vocation this warning must ever be
disregarded, but the greater part of mankind, like the
traditional Hindu householder, defer their "time of
pilgrimage" until their family and business commitments
require their presence no longer.

Now the exchange of forces of Hod and Netzach
becomes a known experience in the 27th Path, which reflects
the energies of Mars from the Sephirah Geburah. This
influence of Mars can give great strength to the relationship
of the two Sephiroth, but it does not give stability. There is a
danger of antagonism between them, and such an antagonism
would wreck the fabric of our work. Violent emotions,
therefore, or intellectual impatience, are equally warned
against upon this Path. The letter of the Hebrew Alphabet
here represented is Peh, whose name means "Mouth." From
the Mouth issue both Breath, representing the life-force
(Netzach), and Speech, representing the laws which govern
the life-force (Hod). Knowledge likewise represents Hod,
while Love in the sense of natural affection represents
Netzach. Oracular speech, again, is a combination of natural
utterance with inspired knowledge, and this is another
manifestation of Peh. Among the many gematric examples
connected with this letter we may note briefly that the
numerical value of פ is 80: "Breath" = NShMH = 395 =
17 = 8; "Precepts, Laws" = PKVDYH = 125 = 8; and "to
prophecy" = NBA = 53 = 8. The Tarot symbol upon this Path
is the Tower struck by Lightning, of which the first
significance, the threat of ruined projects, is plain. It may be
significant here that the Sword of Emanations is often shown
as a lightning-flash issuing from the *mouth* of a venerable
figure (see Revelation 1:16). The implication with regard to
the Tower would be that if true balance and harmony are not
present, power which should consecrate can only disrupt.

We now come to the series of Paths which lead to, or enter, the Sephirah Tiphareth. Here we encounter a mystery: in all cases so far considered, the Paths are taken by the initiate in reverse alphabetical order, but at this stage there is a variation, due to the fact that Tiphareth must be entered by the Arrow-Path, the direct way from Yesod. However, in this text we shall consider the Paths as they come. Our next is the Twenty-sixth Path, from Hod to Tiphareth.

The Path from Splendour to Beauty might be anticipated as an ecstatic experience, but in fact, in this Path is found the cold, earthy influence of Capricorn, the Earth-sign of Saturn. Knowledge and calculation are here, and the material aspect of things which, if developed to the exclusion of love, becomes baneful. It should be recalled that in its qliphothic, that is excessive, aspect, Hod becomes the sphere of Samael, the Tempter of Eden according to the Talmud; and the temptation offered was a way of attainment by Knowledge alone. At the same time, this desire for knowledge and for material things need not be excessive or exclusive. The letter of this Path is Ayin, whose meaning is "an Eye." We may recall the words in the first Epistle of John, "the lust of the flesh, and the lust of the eyes, and the pride of life" (I John 2:16), but, against this, our verses set the first chapter of Berashith: "And God saw everything that he had made, and behold, it was very good."

Reflected from Binah is the preoccupation upon this Path with forms, created shapes: Binah is in truth the "Wellspring of Forms." This is emphasised by a major gematric correspondence: the word OYN, which is the name of the letter, signifies an eye, but another word with identical spelling in Hebrew means "a wellspring." (Common to both Hebrew and Arabic, this second word can be traced in many Palestinian place-names such as 'Ain Karim, 'Ain es Sih, etc.) With either meaning, OYN has the numeration 780, which by addition reduces to 15 and then to 6. The verb OShH, "to do or make," has the numeration 375, which likewise reduces to 15 and then to 6. The Tarot symbol for this Path is "the Devil," generally taken to relate to material prosperity; this idea links with some already discussed. The emphasis on the trap of materialism is right, for by this Path the traveller does not rise above Yetzirah with its dangers of obsession and delusion.

To the 25th Path, that of Samekh, is attributed the zodiacal Sign Sagittarius. It is the mystical "Path of the Arrow," the direct road of true vision leading from Yesod to Tiphareth, likewise from the World of Yetzirah to the World of Briah. The shape of the letter ( ס ) is taken to represent a rough stone set up on end; its Hebrew name means "a support"; the numerical value of the single letter is 60. Connected with this by Gematria is the word MChZH, signifying "a vision," and also having the numerical value of 60; while ZKRVN, meaning "a memorial," gives 933 = 15 = 6. The Tarot symbol of this Path is named "Temperance." This can be interpreted in the light of the median position of this Path upon the Tree, and also in the light of the rulership of Sagittarius by the mild Jupiter; but the image of Temperance is of a winged angelic figure bearing the Sun-sign on her brow, and decanting a liquid from one vessel to another. The allusion seems to be to a modification in the inward nature of the initiate. It is noticeable that in the traditional Tarot designs, the vessels are held so that the poured liquid travels in a manner contrary to the physical laws of gravity; this cannot be dismissed as an accident of drawing, since it calls attention to the mystical change of plane which is to be effected when Tiphareth has been attained by the Twenty-fifth Path. The same thing is conveyed by the Archer who so often is represented as a Centaur: the horse is a major animal-symbol of Luna, and this fittingly represents the rear part of this emblem; while the forepart under the transforming power of Tiphareth is altogether human, and, gazing upwards, shoots arrows of aspiration to the Sun. Here again, then, but much more strongly, we see the transmuting force of Sagittarius which was foreshadowed in the 31st Path.

The 24th Path balances the 26th. The zodiacal Sign here is Scorpio, which is ruled by Mars; accordingly, here we have a modified reflection of the Fifth Sephirah thrown across into this Path between Netzach and Tiphareth. Nevertheless, Scorpio is a sign in the Watery Triplicity, not the Fiery; it is a strange interposition between the Spheres of Venus and of the Sun. The Hebrew letter is Nun, whose name signifies "a fish": the Tarot symbol is named "Death." It might have seemed that the Path from Netzach to the Sphere of the Sun would represent an experience of harmonious change, yet here we have the most abrupt modification of all; for the Sun is lord of times and seasons, and to the harvest must come a time of reaping: the image of Death presented by the Tarot symbol is that of the skeleton wielding a reaping-scythe. The Fish, as our verses show, is that Power which lives at the heart of the waters, which is familiar with the pulse of these vital currents, which keeps watch over the lost treasures of the deep. Just as the 26th Path can plunge the initiate into the perils of materialism, so the 24th can submit him to danger of death, for the greatest of mortal dangers is the will to die (represented by the Scorpion), and this Path will not lead him to transcend it because it will not lead him out of Yetzirah. Of the gematric correspondences of this Path, two especially are memorable. The numerical value of נ is 50. "Death" = MVT = 446 = 14 = 5. The name of the letter in full, נון , has the value 756, which reduces to 18 and then to 9. "Life" = ChY = 18, again reducing to 9.

Thus, by consideration of the 26th, 25th and 24th Paths, we learn that only the Arrow-Path, the 25th, will bring the initiate to Adepthood, to the consciousness of Tiphareth in Briah. This throws some further light upon the three Briatic images of Tiphareth: King, Sacrificed God, and Child. All three are true and valid, and he who prevails shall realise all three; but as goals of aspiration they are not equal. He who would be a King incurs the perils of צ ; he who would be a God incurs the perils of ג ; but only by the Path of ט is the goal attained. And the newborn Child shall be both a God and a King.

We pass on to consider the Paths leading to the higher Sephiroth. The next Path approached by the ascending Serpent is the Twenty-third, leading from Hod to Geburah. This Path is governed by the Element Water: the Hebrew letter is Mem, "the Waters," the Seas. Here, between Splendour and Strength, interposes the dimness, the fluctuation, the mourning of the great waters. Yet this concept of Water as an Element cannot be totally overshadowed by Saturnine Binah, even though it is shown in the Column at whose head is her Sphere: aspects of Pisces, Cancer, and of Scorpio, all of the Watery Triplicity, must be present also, just as in the 31st Path we saw the Triplicity of Fire. We have here, therefore, the selflessness of Pisces, the maternal quality of Cancer, and the brilliance and reflected fire of Scorpio. All these qualities appear in the Tarot symbol of the Hanged Man, that strangely composed and contented figure suspended head downwards over a ravine or pit. By tradition, he is suffering for a fault which is not his own; but he is more than patient; one would almost say he is in his element. This is the adaptability, the sparkle, and withal the conquering endurance, of Water.

To the Twenty-second Path are attributed the letter ל and the zodiacal Sign Libra. Libra is the airy sign ruled by Venus; here, therefore, we have a temperate and mediating influence between radiant Tiphareth and fiery Geburah. The meaning of Lamed is "an Ox-goad." Bearing in mind that the Ox is the symbol of Air (not confusing this with the zodiacal Sign Taurus which is of Earth), it follows that Lamed is not only associated with airy Libra but has itself an airy purpose.

"Lash of the Winds" is therefore a fitting title for this letter. Beauty there must be, both of Venus and of Tiphareth, though of air, invisible; but also there must be the forceful strength of Geburah. Above all there must be equilibrium, renewal; this we find in the sweeping away of the dead leaves of winter, the dried grass and dust of summer, and in the circular whirlings of the hurricane. The Tarot symbol for this Path is named Justice.

The Twenty-first Path leads from Netzach to Chesed, and directly reflects the force of Jupiter. One of the aspects of Venus is as Goddess of Fortune; and, Jupiter being the Beneficent King, it is not surprising that the Tarot symbol of this Path is the Wheel of Fortune. The alphabetical attribution is the letter Kaph, which in its ordinary form ( כ ) represents a hand cupped to receive, in its final form ( ך ) a hand with the fingers outstretched to release. This symbolism accords with the alternate rising and falling aspects of the Wheel of Fortune; it also accords with the attribution to Jupiter of the symbol of the Cup. This Cup, or goblet, must not be confused with the Cup of Binah; the Jupiterian Cup is not a sephirothic attribute, but is entirely personal to Jupiter or Zeus. These various aspects of Kaph give many interesting gematric correspondences. A few are: כף = 820 = 10,  Vineyard = KRM = 820 = 10,  Blood = DM = 604 = 10;  כ = 20, "to open, to free" = PThCh = 488 = 20; ך = 500, "to send, to let go" = ShLCh = 338 = 5.

The Twentieth Path has an Earth-sign to balance the Air-sign of the 22nd. This Sign is Mercury-Earth, that is, the zodiacal Sign Virgo. The Twentieth is the Path leading from Tiphareth to Chesed; and these factors, combined with the rulership of Mercury, emphasise Virgo's active and practical character as well as the withdrawn aspect which seems almost contradictory.

The letter attributed to this Path is Yod. This, too, has almost contradictory active and latent aspects. Part of the mystery is accounted for by the fact that this single pen-stroke, Yod ( ' ), proverbially the smallest letter in the Hebrew alphabet as its counterpart Iota is in the Greek, has the numerical valuation 10 and thus, by both Qabalistic and Pythagorean reasoning, contains the sum of all things within itself. That is only intelligible in human terms if the presence of all things is understood as being seminal. The word Yod signifies "a hand," and hence becomes the creative hand of Chokmah; the Sephirah Chokmah itself has the title "The Yod of Tetragrammaton." We thus have here a symbol which is potently male without being overtly phallic: the creative hand of the All-Father.

The Tarot symbol is the Hermit, the silent wanderer, enigmatic as the Archangel of the Annunciation, bringing the potentialities of the universe into teeming reality at all levels. Such a figure, although silent and swiftly passing, need be neither sad nor disguised by old age; it is more fitting that he should be portrayed as strong, joyous and princely, as in our verses.

The letter Teth ( ט ) represents a serpent curved into a circle. This serpent is identified as the great serpent curled about the world, whom Hebrew tradition calls Theli; to the Greeks he is Ouroborós because he is represented with his tail in his mouth as if biting it. In the Sepher Yetzirah, Theli is described as the Dragon of the Stars, set over the universe as a king enthroned; this signifies the sun's ecliptic, and hence the celestial dragon is defined by the Twelve Houses of the Zodiac. The letter Teth is attributed to the 19th Path, which spans the Tree from Geburah to Chesed, and the particular Sign of the Zodiac corresponding thereto is Leo. This equating of Leo with the Serpent of the Zodiac is interesting in connection with the fact that for some occult purposes it is necessary to consider the Zodiac as commencing from Saturn in Leo, not from Mars in Aries. It is also interesting that the Hebrew name for Leo is ARYH, which gives the

numeration 216, adding to 9, the numerical value of ‫ט‬ .
(ARYH transposed gives YRAH, "awe or reverence," which
of course has the same numeration.)

This insistent identification of Lion with Serpent
irresistibly recalls the Norse myth in which Thor is challenged
by the Giants to lift a huge cat, and fails; after which it is
revealed to him that the seeming cat is the Midgard Serpent,
"the great serpent encircling the earth." Typically for Northern skies, the cat is described as a great misty-grey being—
comprehensibly different from the golden lion of Mediterranean myth. The Norse legends are on some points a
confused medley of hearsay, and the Midgard Serpent is
elsewhere presented as the originator of worldly evil, a kind of
Serpent of Eden; we thus have no difficulty in identifying the
Midgard Serpent as representative of the lower Astral, while
Theli is emphatically representative of the higher Astral. A
most interesting correspondence here, however, is to the
Etruscan letter ⊗, equivalent to the Greek ϴ : in later texts
the Etruscan letter occurs as ⊙ , which is a recognisable Sun-
sign. The Tarot symbol for this Path is named Fortitude, a
virtue which mingles the strength and courage of Geburah
with the clemency and patience of Chesed; it is also a virtue
well suited to the contemplation of the entire span of the
Zodiac, for nobody can choose ease and success for himself
all the time, and the true Adept will not try to do so. This
Path is one of royal dignity, and the high levels which we are
contemplating put any spirit of barter out of the question.

Our initial stricture, that the purpose of this chapter is
to indicate something of the nature of the Paths in
themselves, is here enforced absolutely for the Paths yet to
be discussed. The discerning will realise why this is necessary.
The letter ‫ח‬ is attributed to the Eighteenth Path,
which runs from Geburah to Binah. Commencing from
Geburah, it is conceived in a robust and warlike spirit, yet the

Saturnian-maternal influence of Binah suggests caution and defence. These factors combine in the image of the zodiacal Sign, Cancer: the aquatic creature, the Crab, which astrologically is a feminine and maternal Sign ruled by the Moon, and whose armoured defensive shell presents a likeness both of a shield and of the Moon-disc. The name of the letter, Cheth, signifies "a fence." The Tarot symbol upon this Path is the Chariot. This is to some extent comparable to the image of the carapace of the Crab, but far more significant are the implied allusions to the myth of Phaeton and to Plato's famous metaphor of the Charioteer in the "Phaedrus."

The Seventeenth Path is that of the letter Zain, the Sword, and the zodiacal Sign Gemini. Since it is the Path from Tiphareth to Binah, from solar brilliance and beauty to saturnian and watery shadow, the duality and changefulness of Gemini are appropriate. The Sign Gemini is ruled by Mercury, the Divine Messenger; thus by this Path intuitions from the spheres of the Supernals are carried to Tiphareth. The Serpents twined about the Caduceus, the winged staff of Mercury, are two in number. Two also, by tradition, are the "Thummim" referred to in the Old Testament as divinatory objects; their origin is to be found in the two small images of Thmaa (rightness or universal order) which were worn by certain legal dignitaries in Egypt from early times. The Tarot symbol for this Path is named the Lovers. The picture thereof shows a man between two female figures, with the implication that his choice or lot will fall to one of them; these figures, variously interpreted, suggest the tradition above-mentioned, and the symbol is generally agreed to represent the need for great prudence in making an important decision.

The Sixteenth Path is that of the letter Vau, the Nail. It corresponds to the zodiacal Taurus, and is the Path between Chesed and Chokmah. Fittingly, therefore, this Path bears the Sign Taurus, which traditionally represents true priestly power. In our verses, the term Pontifex is used to denote this, since that denotes the priest as "Bridge-Builder" between the worlds. The Tarot symbol for this Path, the Hierophant, is often depicted as a Pope, but the title of Pontifex is much older than the Roman Church; it was used by the Pagan Romans, who in turn took the concept from the Etruscan magico-religious system, one of the greatly respected authentic systems of antiquity. This priestly figure inevitably has links with Tiphareth, and here we have a knot of associations which are all in their own ways important. Pontifex as Bridge-builder is called "stanchion of unity," which is associated firstly with the steadfastness of Vau as nail or pivot, secondly with the correspondence of the zodiacal Taurus with the neck in the human body. Vau has the numerical value of 6, but 6 is the number of Tiphareth. This introduces the aspect of Pontifex as sacrifice as well as sacrificer, and brings in the Bull again, this time in its Mithraic associations. In Mithraic myth, Mithras the Sun-hero is both the Slayer of the Bull, and the Bull himself. Besides this there is the feminine aspect, "Life of the fosterling worlds." Taurus is ruled by Venus but the bovine image in Netzach is that of Hathor, the Egyptian concept of the Nature-Mother as the Divine Cow nurturing all beings. Finally, it must be remarked that Taurus is in fact an Earth-sign, this again emphasising the immobility of Vau. By Gematria we find that the Hebrew verb "to be firm, established, upright," KVN, gives the numeration 726, which adds to 15 and then to 6.

The Fifteenth Path is that of the Sign Aries and the letter ה , which latter signifies "a window." It is the Path from Tiphareth to Chokmah. The Tarot symbol is "the Emperor," and the symbolism in our verses is of the kind to be expected from this series of ideas: the Sign Aries is for most purposes reckoned as the first in the succession of zodiacal signs, in our verses seen as a procession like that of an ancient Roman religious festival, when all the sacred images from the temples of the city were carried in honour; so it is with the pageant of the Zodiac, representing twelve major aspects of divine power blazoned across the sky. The one complication is that by well-established tradition, Heh is a feminine letter; much Rabbinical theory concerning the letters YHVH turns upon this. We may therefore for some purposes visualise the Victor of these lines as a female figure, the Daughter of the Father; but here a word alone suffices.

The Fourteenth Path is that which links Chokmah with Binah. It is governed by the Celestial Venus, and the Tarot symbol is The Empress. The letter attributed to this Path is Daleth, the Door; it is by the Door of this Path that the potentialities whose first energy and impetus spring forth in Chokmah, come to be formulated into intelligible concepts in Binah. This is probably all that need be said about this Path; the connotations of The Empress are entirely harmonious with it.

The Thirteenth Path is Gimel, the Camel, and the Camel is the crescent Moon. This Path runs from Tiphareth across the Abyss and to Kether; wherefore the Tarot symbol the High Priestess, whose station between the Two Pillars identifies her with this central way, holds open before her a book with the word SCIENTIA: Knowledge.

The Twelfth Path leads from Binah to Kether. This Path is the Rainbow Bridge between Primal Unity and the Wellspring of Forms, the source of all the diversity of the universe. Mortals, it is said, go under the Rainbow Bridge; only immortals may pass over it. Here it is dedicated to Mercury, the divine Winged Messenger. The letter of the alphabet is Beth, בית , which spelled in full gives the numeration 412, adding up to 7; also it is noteworthy that the name BAB-EL, which in Babylonian means "Gate of God" but in Hebrew is associated with confusion of languages, gives the numeration בבל = 34, which also adds up to 7. The Tarot symbol upon this Path is the Magician; and upon this the aspirant must reflect, no matter what his Grade or his personal station relative to the Tree. The business of the Magician is the bringing of Force into Form, and his art is under the presidency of Mercury; and some inkling of this Path, however remote, he must have: the Opal-fire in his heart.

Finally the Eleventh Path, signified by the letter Aleph and the Ox of Air, relates to that which is all-potent and which has no form. The Tarot symbol is the Fool, who steps into air because there is no other way for him to tread.

The rest is silence.

\*

## THE PATHS
### Reference Table of Major Correspondences

PATH 11
  *Position:* Between Kether and Chokmah
  *Hebrew letter:* א (Aleph)     *Influence on Path:* △ (Air)
  *God name:* Yahveh     *Archangel:* Ruachiel
  *Magical Image:* Tarot Arcanum O, The Fool
PATH 12
  *Position:* Between Kether and Binah
  *Hebrew letter:* ב (Beth)     *Influence on Path:* ☿ (Mercury)
  *God name:* Elohim Tzabaoth     *Archangel:* Mikael
  *Magical Image:* Tarot Arcanum I, Magician
PATH 13
  *Position:* Between Kether and Tiphareth
  *Hebrew letter:* ג (Gimel)     *Influence on Path:* ☽ (Moon)
  *God name:* El Chai     *Archangel:* Gebriel
  *Magical Image:* Tarot Arcanum II, High Priestess
PATH 14
  *Position:* Between Chokmah and Binah
  *Hebrew letter:* ד (Daleth)     *Influence on Path:* ♀ (Venus)
  *God name:* Yahveh Tzabaoth     *Archangel:* Haniel
  *Magical Image:* Tarot Arcanum III, The Empress

PATH 15
  *Position:* Between Chokmah and Tiphareth
  *Hebrew letter:* ה (Heh)    *Influence on Path:* ♈ (Aries)
  *God name:* Elohim Gebor    *Archangel:* Melkidael
  *Magical Image:* Tarot Arcanum IV, The Emperor
PATH 16
  *Position:* Between Chokmah and Chesed
  *Hebrew letter:* ו (Vau)    *Influence on Path:* ♉ (Taurus)
  *God name:* Yahveh Tzabaoth    *Archangel:* Asmodel
  *Magical Image:* Tarot Arcanum V, Hierophant
PATH 17
  *Position:* Between Binah and Tiphareth
  *Hebrew letter:* ז (Zain)    *Influence on Path:* ♊ (Gemini)
  *God name:* Elohim Tzabaoth    *Archangel:* Ambriel
  *Magical Image:* Tarot Arcanum VI, The Lovers
PATH 18
  *Position:* Between Binah and Geburah
  *Hebrew letter:* ח (Cheth)    *Influence on Path:* ♋ (Cancer)
  *God name:* Shaddai    *Archangel:* Moriel
  *Magical Image:* Tarot Arcanum VII, The Chariot
PATH 19
  *Position:* Between Chesed and Geburah
  *Hebrew Letter:* ט (Teth)    *Influence on Path:* ♌ (Leo)
  *God name:* Eloah    *Archangel:* Urkiel
  *Magical Image:* Tarot Arcanum VIII, Fortitude
PATH 20
  *Position:* Between Chesed and Tiphareth
  *Hebrew letter:* י (Yod)    *Influence on Path:* ♍ (Virgo)
  *God name:* Elohim Tzabaoth    *Archangel:* Hameliel
  *Magical Image:* Tarot Arcanum IX, The Hermit
PATH 21
  *Position:* Between Chokmah and Netzach
  *Hebrew letter:* כ (Kaph)    *Influence on Path:* ♃ (Jupiter)
  *God name:* El    *Archangel:* Tzadqiel
  *Magical Image:* Tarot Arcanum X, Wheel of Fortune
PATH 22
  *Position:* Between Geburah and Tiphareth
  *Hebrew letter:* ל (Lamed)    *Influence on Path:* ♎ (Libra)
  *God name:* Yahveh Tzabaoth    *Archangel:* Zoriel
  *Magical Image:* Tarot Arcanum XI, Justice

PATH 23
*Position:* Between Geburah and Hod
*Hebrew letter:* מ (Mem)    *Influence on Path:* ▽ (Water)
*God name:* El    *Archangel:* Miel
*Magical Image:* Tarot Arcanum XII, Hanged Man

PATH 24
*Position:* Between Tiphareth and Netzach
*Hebrew letter:* נ (Nun)    *Influence on Path:* ♏ (Scorpio)
*God name:* Elohim Gebor    *Archangel:* Berekiel
*Magical Image:* Tarot Arcanum XIII, Death

PATH 25
*Position:* Between Tiphareth and Yesod
*Hebrew Letter:* ס (Samekh)  *Influence on Path:* ♐ (Sagittarius)
*God name:* El    *Archangel:* Adukiel
*Magical Image:* Tarot Arcanum XIV, Temperance

PATH 26
*Position:* Between Tiphareth and Hod
*Hebrew letter:* ע (Ayin)    *Influence on Path:* ♑ (Capricorn)
*God name:* Yahveh Elohim    *Archangel:* Hanel
*Magical Image:* Tarot Arcanum XV, The Devil

PATH 27
*Position:* Between Netzach and Hod
*Hebrew letter:* פ (Peh)    *Influence on Path:* ♂ (Mars)
*God name:* Elohim Gebor    *Archangel:* Kamael
*Magical Image:* Tarot Arcanum XVI, The Tower

PATH 28
*Position:* Between Netzach and Yesod
*Hebrew letter:* צ (Tzaddi)  *Influence on Path:* ♒ (Aquarius)
*God name:* Yahu    *Archangel:* Kambriel
*Magical Image:* Tarot Arcanum XVII, The Star

PATH 29
*Position:* Between Netzach and Malkuth
*Hebrew letter:* ק (Qoph)  *Influence on Path:* ♓ (Pisces)
*God name:* El    *Archangel:* Amnitziel
*Magical Image:* Tarot Arcanum XVIII, The Moon

PATH 30
*Position:* Between Hod and Yesod
*Hebrew letter:* ר (Resh)    *Influence on Path:* ☉ (Sun)
*God name:* Eloah V'Daath    *Archangel:* Raphael
*Magical Image:* Tarot Arcanum XIX, The Sun

PATH 31
  *Position:* Between Hod and Malkuth
  *Hebrew letter:* שׁ (Shin)     *Influence on Path:* △ (Fire)
  *God name:* Elohim     *Archangel:* Ashiel
  *Magical Image:* Tarot Arcanum XX, Last Judgement
PATH 32
  *Position:* Between Yesod and Malkuth
  *Hebrew letter:* ת (Tau)     *Influence on Path:* ♄ (Saturn)
  *God name:* Yahveh Elohim     *Archangel:* Tzaphqiel
  *Magical Image:* Tarot Arcanum XXI, The Universe


  *The names and symbols associated with the Paths, in all their variety, can only suggest the rich depth of experience which they represent, or their magical potency. Those who wish to look further into the understanding and use of the Paths, with their relationships to the dream life and to the inner advancement of the individual, are directed to* Magical States of Consciousness *by Melita Denning and Osborne Phillips, published by Llewellyn. Full workings of the essential first series of Paths, from the 32nd through the 24th, are there given; and a supporting series of tapes is also available.*

# CHAPTER VII

How gods come into being: cosmic and human aspects of
   theogenesis.

Gods and archetypes. Interdependence of the god and the
   cult.

The function of great shrines and cult-centers in the formation
   and preservation of a cult, as well as in molding important
   details of a tradition. Lourdes, Sinai.

Recognizable Qabalistic patterns among the powers of Voudoun.
   The living force of the Loa. Origins of Voudoun: the
   mysterious Egyptian link with our traditions. Kindred patterns
   in Mexican religions.

The High Greetings to Celtic deities. Links acknowledged
   from ancient times between Celtic deities and gods of the
   classical world. Consequent correspondences in the planetary
   spheres. Attributions of major Celtic deities. The force of
   Celtic myth in history and tradition: mysteries of the smith;
   curious customs at old St. Paul's Cathedral, London; the
   Horned God, "St. Patrick's Purgatory and knighthood. The
   Celtic Otherworld."

Babylonian and Sumerian lore and the ancient myth of Ishtar and Tammuz. Initiatory significance of the story.

A practical aspect: general requirements of study and of magical work for making contact with a god-force which attracts the student. Study of the Qabalistic pattern and of the pantheon to which the deity belongs, as a preliminary. Serious nature of the undertaking: requirements of real worship, use of appropriate forms, and fidelity and perseverance in devotion. Establishment of a personal cult and making invocation.

## CHAPTER VII
## CHANNELS OF FORCE

Concerning the Gods, Proclus has an interesting statement in his *Elements of Theology,* Proposition CXXVI: the more nearly universal produce the more limited in nature, not by partition nor by change, nor by copulation, but by a self-generation of emanations due to an overflow of Divine energy. This is, recognisably, an account of what we should term the Emanation of the Sephiroth; it is not a complete account of the origin of the Gods as they are known to us. However, the Emanation of the Sephiroth is the beginning of the story.

To recapitulate a little, the next phase in the story is the development of man with his peculiarly fertile creative imagination. Just as man covered the walls of his caves with pictures and began shaping fragments of bone or of rock into figurines, so he began to fill the delicate Astral world about him with shapes of dominant force: Great Bison to command the bison, Great Bears to command the bears, Men to befriend him or to give commands in his name, and the Woman who was mother and bride and daughter. Man's understanding became greater; deduction fortified intuition. He imagined gods for himself, and those images too walked the Astral.

Without doubt, the fundamental quality which man has always desired in his gods is that they should hear and should be propitious to him. No cult would endure for long if this requirement did not at least seem to be fulfilled; and if the

145

cult did not endure, the god-form faded. Certain god-forms, however, were much more likely to endure than were the rest. Whether we are considering a real response from the spiritual world, or a response believed in by the devotee through a deep sense of psychological rightness, in either case the successful god-forms were those which corresponded most nearly to the unknown and unperceived Divine Archetypes in Atziluth. The reason for this is that those forms created by man which are of sufficient strength and sufficient sephirothic purity, become real channels in Briah for the corresponding Divine Forces. The initial strength of the image comes from  the sense of psychological rightness; the fact that it has also thereby achieved cosmic rightness accounts for the rest of the process.

Besides these high Briatic manifestations, there are always the astral (Yetziratic) manifestations of the same deities. These can be, and should be, true channels of the same Divine Archetype at their own level, but being Yetziratic they are much more influenced by the emotions of the greater number of devotees who are psychically active at that level. These Yetziratic manifestations are the egregores.

There are egregores of a slightly different type which can be built up by an individual magician, or by the group-consciousness of a greater number of people, with no particular reference to any Atziluthic counterpart. Such egregores are animated only by the conscious or unconscious will of their creators, and do not concern us here; their existence is merely acknowledged so as to avoid confusion.

Deific egregores of the greatest strength, and with the least tendency to deviate from their archetypal pattern, are, naturally, those which are built up at established shrines and cult-centres. At such a centre, the greater the number of devotees, the greater the strength of the egregore: the more effectively also will  any personal idiosyncrasies introduced by some of the visitors balance one another out. The human tendency to establish shrines, meeting-places at which to encounter the Gods, is thus in any case justified; but when the consideration is added, of particular places being in themselves meeting-places of the Planes, there becomes possible the establishment of shrines of unutterable mystery, such as do in fact exist in certain places upon this earth. They are material symbols of those "Gate-Sephiroth" which we have discussed: at which arriving, the traveller who is attuned to the place finds opening to him not merely a shrine, but another level of existence. The shrine need not be limited to a building: there may be no building, or a whole region may be sacred ground, as many a mountaintop has been. Where a succession of cults has obtained, the same places have often been holy to each in turn. Sometimes the new manifestation takes on distinctive features which link it strangely to a former one. The cave at Lourdes, for example, which was the site of Bernadette's uniquely remarkable series of visions, had in previous centuries been the shrine of a Goddess-cult of which the nineteenth-century girl is most unlikely to have been allowed to hear. It would perhaps be impossible to obtain exact details at the present date, but it is known that the herb which grew in the cave, and of which she ate in the course of her guided* actions, was a sacred plant in the bygone cult.

   An even more significant example occurs in the story of Moses. When he came down from Sinai with the Law, "his face shone" (Exodus 34:29). Rabbinical tradition has it that the beams of light from his countenance rose in two rays, like

---

* Guided, we should say, by a Visitant versed in Qabalistic lore. The salient points of the Visions are as follows:
   (1)  The Inspiring Breath: The Wind at the Cave-mouth.
   (2)  The Body: The Herb is partaken.
   (3)  Judgment: The Call to Repentence.
   (4)  Mercy: The Healing Spring discovered.
   (5)  Glory: The Lighted Candle left in the Cave. This links with the fact that on that final occasion, the Visitant had declared herself to be identical with a certain Concept of Perfection in the Divine Mind. Having regard to the initiatory (baptismal) significance of the ritual acts above indicated, the Qabalist must sincerely conclude that the Visitant did *not* intend thereby to boast an exclusive personal privilege.

horns; hence Michelangelo in his statue of Moses represents the prophet with horns like those of a bull. The desert and mount of Sinai were, prior to the arrival of the Israelites, sacred to the Babylonian Moon-God Sin; hence the name of the region. The crescent horns of light, then, of the transfigured Moses, were those of Sin. There might be more to consider here regarding the Moon-God in relation to the Lawgiver: the crescent-billed Thoth was the lawgiver of Egypt, while Minos, whose name marks him too as of the Moon, was likewise a renowned lawgiver, in one aspect a Judge of the Underworld. In terms of the Sephiroth, Yesod is the nearest Sephirah to Malkuth, combining the authority of the Column of Mercy with the restrictive nature of the Column of Severity. These are not points upon which we can dilate, however; we must return to our main theme, only remarking that Moses is likely to have known and to have practised the Egyptian formula of Evocation of the God-form. This would not necessarily mean that he would have been aware of the continuing manifestation when he descended the mount: "And Moses knew not that his face shone."

Other considerations besides the history of a *temenos* may affect the character of an egregore, so as to create sharply differentiated manifestations of one deity. Voudoun, for example, presents some remarkable racial and geographical variants, which form a pattern of great complexity; nevertheless, despite some overlapping of function such as is frequently found in a living system, we can state without hesitation that Voudoun is one of the great Western systems. It is capable, both for reality and for archetypal completeness, of being brought within the framework of the Qabalah; nor need it be distorted in so doing. The fundamental Archetypes are discerned in images which are so true to their respective Sephiroth that the principal Loa (Voudoun deities) correspond very closely to concepts associated with the better known Western pantheons.

We understand easily the endless rivalry between the Warrior Ogoun and Agoué of the Seas, for the hand of the exquisite Erzulie Fréda: she is a high and most delicately beautiful manifestation of Netzach, hauntingly feminine, delighting in all joy, but outpouring that all-giving love which in its superabundance turns to poignancy. Ogoun is of Geburah; Agoué is an oceanic aspect of Chesed. These three deities are all related to cosmic rather than to human life; so also are Danbalah, the Sky-Father manifest in the form of a great serpent, and Legba, who is fundamentally a Sun God. Loco, in Hod, is a characteristically Mercurial deity. He is Loco-Dé (double or twin); he is sometimes considered as the spouse of the powerful and even androgynous Ayizan who represents the Amazonian aspect of Netzach. He is primal Priest and Healer, teaching the use of herbs and of medicinal trees; he can give prophecies; he is psychopomp also, and interlocutor between Gods and men. Nevertheless, the purely magical aspect of Hod is often associated rather with Simbi, whose manifestation is the Water-snake; Simbi has fire as well as water aspects, and seems sometimes to be thought identical with, or a reflection of, the Great Serpent of the Heavens.

We have no hesitation at all, however, in identifying the Voudoun representative of Yesod: he is Guédé. Guédé is the reflection of Legba; he has those qualities as guardian of life and death, the solemn power and also the jocund sexuality, which are derived indeed from the solar force but which we know as characteristic of Yesod. Apart from this, he is also an illusionist and a sly trickster (and we know the power of Yesod to deceive); and furthermore, his power extends through the three realms of sky (thunderstorms), earth (agriculture) and the underworld, thus comprising what is in another cosmogony the domain of the Threefold Hecate.

He is also associated with a different manifestation which, however, seems to originate with a quite distinct Archetype: Baron Samedi. Guédé is sometimes even identified with Baron Samedi, although it frequently becomes clear that they are truly distinct. One does not joke with the Baron; neither does one appeal to his sense of fair play. He represents the forces of death and the grave, without any compromise except as to their manifestation. It has been suggested that the name "Samedi," which, if taken as a French word, sufficiently indicates his Saturnian nature, could instead be derived from the word "Zombie," but there are serious objections to this. The word "Zombie" is essentially a term of contempt, and its emphasis is not on the dead body as such, but on the use of it as a witless slave; it goes back to a Spanish term of contempt for persons of mixed blood, which has come down also in the grotesque appellation "Sambo." Moreover, the making of zombies is not an activity of true Voudoun, although the body-snatchers undoubtedly invoke Baron Samedi in their sorceries. While we cannot claim, therefore, that this name of the Baron is quite as simple as it appears (he is also called Baron Cimetière and Baron La Croix), yet to associate him with the Day of Saturn is so perfectly in keeping with his character that we can accept whatever circumstances have led to it, and need look no further. The Haitian system, however, is not concerned with Supernals as such, but with the immediacies of life and death; Binah, therefore, is represented by its reflection upon the Thirty-Second Path, between Malkuth and Yesod, and thus we have here the funerary associations of Baron Samedi, marking the transition between the world of physical life and the world of shadows. The confusion between him and Guédé also becomes intelligible.

Having mentioned the Paths, we have another most interesting matter to indicate. The solar deity Legba and the lunar deity Guédé are both known as Gate-keepers; the domain of each is essentially a gate between the worlds. Thus Guédé becomes patron of birth and of death; Legba, patron of these also, but principally as representing spiritual initiation. Despite the part played by other Sephiroth, therefore, Yesod and Tiphareth remain, more than any, the Gate-Sephiroth.

These parallels between the Haitian and the Qabalistic systems lead to the question, whether in the actual rites a similar resemblance is to be found. There is a resemblance if one looks deeply enough. Partly this is to be explained by the fact that any human being who has a sufficiently keen intuition of the Archetypes, is likely to discover the same truths and to found a system upon them; but in the case of Voudoun the kinship may be closer than that.

Apart from a very few European contributions (such as may be found in the Scandinavian name Fréda of the Goddess of Love, and in the Celtic name Brigitte, consort of the Guardian of Graves), Voudoun is the offspring principally of African religion and magick, and to a probably rather less extent of Caribbean religion and magick. The experts are at some points perplexed in allocating the contribution of each, for there is little disharmony between the two origins. African and Amerindian philosophies have much in common, and each has a strange natural affinity with certain elements in Christianity: particularly with that aspect of Christianity which has reference to the desire for, and the attainment of, "life more abundantly." The harmony of Caribbean and South American beliefs with those of African origin extends, sometimes startlingly, to magical instruments and articles of ritual equipment. As to the reason for these resemblances, which have led to so dynamic and vital a fusion of the two cultures in Voudoun, we see dimly sketched the outlines of a vast hypothesis.

Maya Deren, in whose book on Voudoun, *Divine Horsemen,* scholarship and sensitivity blend so outstandingly, gives what we believe to be the key to it. Writing of a certain peculiarity of Haitian seasonal celebrations, she points out that this is not typically African, unless Egypt is taken into consideration. We, for our part, emphatically do take Egypt into consideration. Throughout the age-long comings and goings of armies, of migrant tribes, of caravans bearing every sort of merchandise from one part of the African continent to another, the spread of Egyptian ideas (themselves formulated from those of ethnic groups previously absorbed into the Egyptian nation) would be a justifiable inference, even if we had no evidence; even if vestiges of Mediterranean lore had not been found in African folk-tales; even if the story of Isis and Osiris had not been depicted on the wall of a cave in Rhodesia! And some of the African ancestors of the Haitians came from territories not far south of the Sudan.

As to the Amerindian side of the story, there we touch upon conjectures indeed. We shall indicate their trend but lightly; we do not wish to be among those who bring discredit on facts by burdening them with unproven inferences. The Egyptians of old were a red-skinned race. The colour in which they depicted themselves in their murals was not chosen simply for aesthetic reasons nor from a dearth of pigments; in scenes which represent foreign visitors in Egypt, the skin-colour indicating the strangers is quite distinctive. Even to the present day, peoples known to be descended from the Egyptians, such as the Berbers, have markedly a reddish cast of skin-colour. The art of terracing, the architectural development related to this (the lintel, the upward-tapering structure with its characteristic angles of incline), a number of ritual features including the sacred rattle, the stylised and frequently profile representations of the Gods—these things we do not claim as marking any very exact or late relationship between Egyptian and Central or South American. The cultures in any case developed along their distinctive lines, moulded by their respective climates through ages of separation. In comparison of architecture, especially, caution is indicated, bearing in mind the similar latitudes of Egypt and Mexico and the tendency of early architects to base their measurements on the astronomical bearings of the site. We do say, however, that a common denominator is there, identify it who may. Thus the cult of Voudoun seems to have brought together and revivified elements so cognate and yet so long separated, that their reunited power is like the release of an arrow.

These things being so, it is not altogether strange that the Haitians have found it congenial to place the system of Voudoun under Christian presidency, both by the prayers with which the ritual meetings customarily open, and by the inevitably Christian associations of the images of saints which they employ as representations of the Loa. We do not say that this presidency is essential or even wholly suitable, but it is in plain fact the way matters have worked out in Haiti, and having regard to the historical and geographical origins of the Christian religion, we cannot be surprised. Nevertheless, Voudoun is not to be approached on terms of easy familiarity. Anyone interested in the system must first make a careful study of the works of the authorities. Further, it is not a cult for experiment. We leave aside the dangers of disaster to the dabbler; the least that could happen to him would be the experience of one such, known to us, whose consciousness, forcibly displaced from his body, spent an unhappy few hours floating against the ceiling, gazing down at his own body which lay spreadeagled on the Mambo's table, until he had sufficiently besought her forgiveness and that of the insulted Loa. Far beyond this in ethical significance is another consideration: these great Loa are living and conscious spiritual beings. In their egregores they show joy and grief; they value, as Gods have ever valued, the devotion of mankind—of fickle, weak, venal mankind. Being Gods in truth, they see beyond the daily betrayals and treacheries to the sublime heights of which man is capable, let love and loyalty and perseverance therein be but kept. Such beings are not a target for idle curiosity; they are, however, a proper subject of consideration in our study.

The Mexican deities themselves present a most interesting and complex pattern for the student who wishes to make his own researches, since in that region several systems have been superposed, and some have been developed to a vivid reality. For comparison with Guédé as a deity of the Moon-sphere, we give a short account of Tezcatlipoca. He has a smoking mirror, typifying the Astral Light, in which he can show either truth or illusion, at will: he uses this mirror to cause all manner of mischief, but his motive is fun, not malice. He is strongly inclined to the material side of existence; this makes for a continual feud between him and Quetzalcoatl, who represents the spirit and whose manifestation in the material world is the wind. Tezcatlipoca seeks human company without regard to any distinctions; he holds no condition to be essentially happier than another, since the individual's mental approach can transform either joy or misery. He takes a great interest in lovers, and one of his favourite types of joke consists in provoking sexuality. A strange detail is that in his breast he has a pair of doors, which can be opened to disclose his heart. A brave man opening these doors could grasp his heart and claim a boon from Tezcatlipoca as ransom, but a coward making the attempt would fail, and would forfeit his own life. This idea of a gate guarded by illusory terror which must be courageously surmounted, is typical of the Moon-sphere:

> Nor at the sculptured gateway pause,
>    whose mocking forms eclipse the stars:
> The base has only carven claws,
>    the gate has only shadow-bars.

It may be pointed out that the Haitian manifestations of Divinity, no matter how carefully we may trace their origins, are not precisely those of Africa nor of America. That is true, but it does not by any means invalidate their archetypal derivations: such derivations can be maintained even though their manifestations may vary widely with time and place.

We now turn to the Gods of the Celtic world.

We give our greetings to Danu.

> What child of Earth in dreaming,
>     In sleep or open-eyed,
> Has never once the gleaming
>     Of Danu's beauty spied?
> Hair in the dawn-light streaming,
>     Form in blue skies arrayed,
> The Mother whose least seeming
>     Never from heart can fade:
>
> *And thus we ask her aid.*

We give our greetings to Oenghus Og.

> With laughter, gold, and dancing flame
> Quiver the shadows of his name:
> The noonday sun around him burns
> While round his head with endless turns
> Hovering, darting, bliss to see,
> Four golden birds fly bright and free,
> One with the light wherein they bask:
>
> *Bringer of Love whose aid we ask.*

We give our greetings to Mananaan.

> Fine-fretted pearl his face, with clustered hair
>     And beard like ivy-leaves before the moon:
> In cloak of sombre blue he gazes there
>     Where sun meets ocean, dusk meets furthest dune
>     And rhythmic tides supplant all images.
> Silence is his, and wisdom deep, to bear
>     The silver trident of the answering seas.
>
> *Help us, O Guardian of the Mysteries.*

We give our greetings to Brigid.

> But who may speak of that high, calm face—
>     Dark is the hair in veils of mist—

The star-crowned head and the guessed-at grace
   Mantled in cloud to foot and wrist?
O, sure white feet on the Moon-rock stayed,
   Beauty serene of changeless brow!
Brigid, O Daughter of Night, give aid:

*Daughter of Truth, assist us now.*

In Celtic lore, besides the major deities of the cosmogony we find a great multiplicity of minor manifestations which are often, however, of considerable importance. Naturally the picture is somewhat simplified in the accounts of Celtic deities given by classical authors such as Strabo and Caesar. They inevitably tended to assimilate what they observed to what they already knew, but they wrote with keen interest and were by no means anxious to hide or to distort what was novel to them; within the bounds of their comprehension they were remarkably accurate. Caesar in particular has been criticised for his apparently too facile approximation of the principal deities of Gaul to the planetary pantheon of Rome, but it must be remembered that Rome was by no means the first cosmopolitan culture to be encountered by the Celtic peoples; indeed, they had been a great but not centralised cosmopolitan culture themselves, extending in areas from the Middle East to Ireland. James Joyce, finding his spiritual kindred in Northern Italy, was a Celt among Celts. The Gaelic language, even in the scattered parts of it now surviving, has a unity which does not always appear on paper, owing to the varying methods of representing the grammatical inflections; but in the spoken word, which is the true reality of the language, the differences fall into the background.

The second language of this widespread culture was Greek. This is a most important fact for the occult investigator, for the astral levels are strongly impregnated with it. Even in Britain, even in Wales where nothing but Gaelic might be expected, when the earlier levels are psychically investigated, the Greek language is encountered. The fact is there, though we have little evidence to impress the historian: only there is the grammatical structure of the Gaelic language itself, and in particular the verbs, in close parallel to the Greek; likewise we have the similarity in general forms of the scripts, some names such as that of the Horse Goddess Epona (which is in Greek Hippo), and the well-known words of Strabo, describing the typical urbane Briton of his time, wearing shoulder-plaid and long trousers (the wording suggests a strap under the instep) and gold-decorated belt, dignified and easy in manner, and speaking Greek with entire fluency and correctness. The Greek geographer does not express surprise that Britons should speak Greek at all—probably most of the known world of that time achieved some kind of utterance therein: but the excellence of speech does attract Strabo's comment.

To these evidential facts we add two fragments. Readers of "Lorna Doone" will recall an incident in the hero's account of his schooldays, when his classmates laugh at him for using the dialect word "goyal" for a deep dell; then an older boy intervenes, to tell them that the word is used by Homer to mean the hollow of the hand. Beside this West Country example we propose for consideration the fact that lexicographers have failed to find a derivation for the word "pixie," which in its true form as spoken (again in the West Country) is "pisky" or "pisgy." The word denotes a small, playful elemental characterised by a childlike appearance which contrasts with a general wildness, shaggy hair and pointed ears. Contrary to an opinion frequently expressed, these and other elementals have by no means departed from England, although artificial ways of life have robbed many

people of the power to see them.* One night in recent years
a traveller possessed of etheric sight observed a troop of
these little beings, romping and frolicking in the moonlight on
a stretch of grassland near Windsor. Startled to see apparently
young children out and playing at midnight, the observer
next noticed their silence; then at closer view their strangness
of form was evident. "They were a sort of bunny-children,"
said the observer afterwards, not at once associating them
with any tradition. However, these little elementals of the
countryside are certainly what would be termed in Greek
Πανισκοι, and it is this word, "Paniskoi," which we firmly
believe to be the origin of our dialect word "pisky."

We turn now to Caesar's account of the Celtic deities,
that is, principally, of the pantheon of Gaul. The previously
mentioned criticism of his account, that it approximates the
Gods of the Celts too closely to the planetary deities known
to the Romans, is in any case overstated, as we have pointed
out. It becomes almost meaningless in the light of the fact
that before Caesar's time the Celts had beyond any doubt
come to know the planetary deities of the classical world and
had made their own comparisons. Britain, particularly, had
been strongly involved in the international cult of the
"Hyperborean Apollo" centred at Delos; but the deity
chiefly honoured in Gaul and elsewhere was identified with
Hermes. Caesar states clearly that the principal deity with the
Gauls was Mercury; we say Hermes rather, not merely
because of our knowledge of the Greek association, but also
because statues have been found in which Lugh (to give this

---

* It must be added that astral beings are well known to have an ability to make an
apparent departure, while in fact only withdrawing to a lesser degree of visibility.
A Scottish lady visiting Rome a few years ago with her young son, took him to
see the Colosseum. While they walked about there, he several times asked her
what were the big black birds which he saw. From his description they were about
three times the size of domestic hens, and not a quarter as natural. Although the
mother had "the sight," she did not perceive the birds; but some time later she
mentioned the incident to a friend, and was told that the Colosseum had been
haunted by demons in the form of ravens, until St. Jerome had *banished* them,
around the year 350 A.D.! The moral for magicians is obvious.

deity his general Gaelic name, which in Welsh is Llew) is shown not only with the caduceus and other attributes common to Hermes and Mercury, but also with the tortoise which is connected particularly with the Greek story of the origin of the lyre. In other matters, however, as in the celebrations of Lughnasadh and in the myth of his death and rebirth, Lugh appears rather as a solar hero, while he has warlike aspects which almost usurp the place of the War God Teutates (Gothic Tiw). These accumulated attributions indicate a deity of great power and popularity, such as, indeed, archaeological and literary evidence alike show Lugh to have been. From the magical viewpoint, however, so complex a range of ideas need not be too far pursued. We can, theoretically, establish Lugh as representing either the solar or the mercurial force, since the numerous pantheon of the Celts provides alternatives in either case. The other conspicuous solar deity is named Grannus, whose name evidently is a masculine form of "Grian," the sun. (The antiquity of the Gaelic language is indicated by the fact that it has a feminine noun for the sun and a masculine noun for the moon, instead of reversing these genders as do most modern languages.)

Another important deity, this time entirely Irish in tradition, but like Lugh combining mercurial and solar aspects, is Oghma. He is the nominal author of the magical Ogham form of writing; he is the champion of rhetoric, and seems to have been considered to some extent as a conductor of souls; but besides these mercurial attributes, he is represented with the physical qualities of a Hercules, with whom according to Lucian he is identical. This identification would attribute Oghma to the Sun-sphere, since Hercules with his twelve labours represents the sun passing through the twelve zodiacal houses; and such an identification is further supported by the adjective sometimes applied to Oghma, "grianainech," meaning "sunlike." We may surmise a difference in emphasis according to time and place; but Apollo is a patron of the arts, and again, the souls of the dead have sometimes been said to depart in the company of the setting sun. All considered, we attribute Oghma to the Sun-sphere.

At this stage it will be convenient to tabulate the names of some of the principal Celtic divinities—not with their entire "families" as known to the archaeologists, but simply as leading representatives of the forces in question. The student will find this a useful starting-point for more detailed inquiry, as well as a basis for practical work.

| | |
|---|---|
| ♄ | Donn, Danu. Modron. |
| ♃ | Daghda (Sucellus), Taranis. Mananaan (Manawydan). |
| ♂ | Teutates (Tiw). Goivniu. |
| ☉ | Oghma, Lugh, Mabon (Maponos, Oenghus), Belen. Grannus. |
| ♀ | Maeve (Medhbh). |
| ☿ | Lugh (Llew, Lugus). |
| ☽ | Cernunnos, Brigid. Morrigan—Bave (Badhbh)—Nevain (Nemhain). |
| ⊗ | Anu, Modron. |

Donn—"the Dark One"—more literally the Brown One, is the Lord of Death essentially, but is conceived of as a benign ancestral figure calling his children home to rest. From this essential concept, he becomes sometimes a god of storms and shipwreck (seafarers may well have confused his name with the Nordic *Donner*) but also and more characteristically a protector in matters connectèd with the earth's produce, such as crops and herds—a truly Saturnian function. Danu, the goddess whose name is cognate with his, has developed along quite different lines: she is the Celestial Queen, and has become a figure of brilliance and light. If Donn is Ancestor of Men, Danu is a Mother of Gods, for the

Tuatha De Danaan are her children, including the Daghda, who himself becomes a genial Father-God; but Danu is always the young Mother, radiant and generous. Another development from the same Archetype, however, is Modron, the mysterious and aqueous aspect of Binah. Modron is chiefly characterised as mother of Mabon, the child deity of the Sun-sphere who is associated with the New Year. She has also, however, a more terrestrial aspect, the river Marne being named after her.

The Daghda is the Jupiterian Father-God, and in the Irish stories he reflects that aspect of deity which the French designate more playfully than reverently as "le bon Dieu." The symbolic attributes of the Daghda are his club and his cauldron: the club is an obvious primitive sign of power and authority, and the cauldron (not to be confused with the cauldron of rebirth) is, like the cup of Zeus or the Cornucopia, a symbol of abundance. The Daghda seems to be clearly identified with the continental Sucellus, who is a benign figure although instead of a club he bears a huge mallet. A Gaulish manifestation of Jupiter more evidently as Thunderer is Taranis; his attributes are the wheel of the heavens (which often descends to Chesed as representative of Chokmah) and the spiral thunderbolt.

Besides these celestial aspects of Jupiter, we have also the aquatic. A hint of this is indicated in the case of Sucellus, by the fact that he has as consort a River Goddess, Nantosvelta; but now we have the specifically marine deity Mananaan, whose land sanctuary and special domain is the Isle of Man. He is an aloof mysterious personage. Mananaan is the Irish form of his name; the English name is Manawydan, and although in some ways the myths differ, there seems no reasonable doubt that the two names represent one Archetype, perhaps even one archetypal image.

It may seem strange that in all this rich cosmogony of so warlike a people, only one name typically representative of

Mars should appear: that of the God of Tuesday. Even he, Teutates or Tiw, has other functions which are, generally speaking, more in evidence. He is the god of the sacred oath and of the public assembly; just as the Areopagus and the Champ-de-Mars are dedicated to the corresponding deities in their own cultures.

On the other hand, the attribution to Mars must be given also to the deity of the smiths, Goivniu. Again as in other cultures, the metal-worker has his own magical powers, for it is not only the natural tempering for victory that has to be wrought into sword or shield, spear or helmet. For this reason, some might think to ascribe Goivniu and his kind to Mercury, but the power of iron belongs to Mars, even though the smith's art has extended to less warlike matters. Many smiths have been healers; and in at least some instances in Britain, such as at Gretna and at Cockington, to the smith has been ascribed the power to solemnise marriages. It should be recalled here that Hephaestus is the true consort of Aphrodite.

The Celtic cosmogony gives us a number of solar deities, each representing some especial aspect of the Sun-sphere. Oghma is the Sun as lord of life and death, guide of souls, and bestower of the magical alphabet by which these natural qualities can be mysteriously bound. Lugh, although in the Celtic world at large he is of Mercury, yet belongs to the Sun in his initiatory capacity, as representative of Light and by virtue of his death and rebirth. Mabon is essentially the Divine Child, the reborn Sun of the New Year. For three days, we are told, he was lost and was sought by his mother Modron; then he was restored. Those three days are represented by the Celtic New Year celebration of Samhuinn, the festival of the dead (All Saints, All Souls, and the day following). During those three days, in Celtic tradition, the gates between the worlds stand open: they are no-time, and only when the gates are closed once more does the New Year begin. Another name of the Mabon is Oenghus, which (like David) means Beloved. Frequently he is called Oenghus Og, Beloved Young One, or Mac Og, Young Son.

Another solar deity associated with one of the great fire-festivals is Belen, or Bel. This name probably means "brilliant." It connects the deity at once with the festival of Bealteinne, "the Fire of Bel." He is the deity most frequently identified with Apollo, and his epithet *Atepomaros,* meaning "owning great horses," brings vividly to mind the Chariot of the Sun. Amber, too, seems to have been particularly attributed to him, and he was patron deity of many thermal springs. Finally there is Grannus, whose name appears to signify the sun-force in its simplest aspect, comparably with Sol and Helios. Nevertheless, in the third century A.D. he was known in Rome as a god of healing.

Maeve is the most truly Venusian of the strong Celtic goddesses. She is primarily a war-goddess, and in Ireland is the heroine of an epic of bloodshed and violence. In England, however, she has kindlier associations through having become the great national goddess of defence. It is for her that the hawthorn ("hedge-thorn") was named May, or May-thorn, since neither man nor beast could force a way through the dense thorns and roots of a hawthorn barricade. She became the goddess of Bealteinne, in whose honour the May Queen was crowned and the triumphal dance, interlocking mazelike in the old British fashion, was woven around the Maypole. Yet, as centuries passed, the people who did these things forgot her true identity and greatness. Her most recent name in English lore is Queen Mab of the fairies. This does not, however, detract from or efface the noble egregore of Maeve, victorious defendress of those who invoke her aright.

Of Lugh, almost enough has been said. In the Welsh story, where his name is given as Llew, the main events referred to are evidently the same as in the Irish story, though the Welsh version somewhat glosses over the fact of his death: he is wounded, and turns into an eagle. This obscuring of the sacrifice seems to indicate that Lugh was to most people in Britain, as on the Continent, a deity of the sphere of Mercury: only a certain "inner ring" would know of the solar cult.

With the Sphere of the Moon, we again come to a multiplicity of deities. The foremost is certainly the oldest: Cernunnos, the Horned One. We have referred earlier to the horned deity of the moon; this now is the form of that deity which from earliest times has been known in Britain and in Gaul. As befits a lunar deity, Cernunnos is pre-eminently a fertility god. For this reason, and also because of the great diversity of living forms in the animal world, Cernunnos is frequently represented as surrounded by animals of different species. Despite his vast antiquity, he is still a deity of great power. The witches worship him together with his consort whom they name Aradia, the Goddess of the Altar, and who is frequently called Diana. In England, he has had local cults which have persisted with amazing tenacity: at Windsor he is "Herne the Hunter" and still, from time to time, those of the clearer sight behold strange happenings in the neighbourhood of Herne's Oak. It is not generally known, but the historical fact is that in London, in the old St. Paul's Cathedral which was destroyed by the Great Fire in 1666, the annual custom was observed of offering in procession at the high altar the carcass of a male fallow-deer on the feast of the Commemoration of St. Paul, and of a female on the feast of the Conversion of St. Paul. The procession with the carcass entered the cathedral by the western door, preceded by men bearing hunting-horns; at the steps of the high altar it was met by the Dean and Chapter in full regalia, their heads crowned with garlands of roses. The carcass was at that point decapitated, the head being fixed on a spear to be borne before the cross in procession back to the western door. It should be mentioned that St. Paul's was built on the site of a

temple which the Romans dedicated to Diana—the British
name of the deity of the place is not recorded—and that in
the vicinity was one of those mazes so persistent in the
folklore of this country, and generally so reminiscent in
design of the traditional Cretan "labyrinth"—which brings us
back to our horned male deity. Again, Cernunnos is the
obscure inspiration behind the "Jack-in-the-Green," the
green-clad man adorned with leafy branches, a calf-skin upon
his shoulders, leaping and dancing through village streets; the
primeval significance of such a dance for the general
prosperity of an agricultural community needs here no
further comment.

Cernunnos has, however, a more mystical purport
besides this. Considered in its native Gaelic form, his name
is Cernowain: Horned Owain. Now, whether the name Owain
is or is not ultimately derived from the Greek *Eugenes*,
meaning "nobly-born," as some authorities would have it, is
not of major importance here, though such a derivation
would certainly be relevant to what follows. As a fertility
god, Cernunnos or Cernowain is much concerned with birth;
it is now indicated that he is also concerned with initiatory
birth.

In the north of Ireland, in the vicinity of Lough Derg,
there was accessible until modern times a great subterranean
cavern, of international fame for the strange experiences
which befell those who descended into its depths. It is a
general opinion that Dante, who was familiar with a
remarkable amount of Celtic lore, was to some extent
indebted to the repute of this cavern, or "St. Patrick's
Purgatory" as it was called, for the description of his Inferno.
Certain it is that the experience of the cavern was in the
Middle Ages considered initiatory: a man who was in other
respects fitted for knighthood was accepted as having won his
spurs if he had completed the Lough Derg pilgrimage, as it
was called. (The cavern is  no longer accessible, the church

authorities having taken fright at some scandalous reports concerning pilgrims: the entrance has therefore been filled in and a new ordeal devised, consisting of a series of flinty "penitential beds.") However, every form of initiation has its prototypic hero, the story of whose adventure forms a pattern for those who come after. In the case of the Lough Derg cavern, the prototype was named as a certain *"Miles Owain"* who arrived at the cavern, was admitted, and underwent a harrowing ordeal in its total darkness, being despaired of as lost before he at length re-emerged, a changed man. The adjective *miles* is significant, for although in classical times this word signified a foot-soldier, by the Middle Ages it meant specifically a man of knightly rank. The name of Owain chosen for the proto-hero of this initiation would still not relate it very closely to Cernunnos, but for the existence of the apparently isolated Welsh legend of Owain the Lord of the Forest who, with a stag as his herald, called all the woodland creatures to pay homage to him. In addition, the animals associated with Cernunnos have distinct initiatory associations: besides the stag, there is frequently the boar, in Celtic or Nordic associations a symbol of renewed life; also the rat, an underground and therefore chthonic symbol; and, above all, a most potent form of ram-headed serpent, peculiar to Cernunnos and highly expressive of creative energy at a spiritual level. Again, representations of Cernunnos are frequently Janus-headed; and this is a familiar device to indicate life changed and renewed, so that the face which looks to the future is not the same face which looks back upon the past. We conclude, therefore, as indeed we know to be the fact, that in Cernunnos or Cernowain we have a most ancient deity, rooted in the earth and leading powerfully into the world of the spirit.

Brigid is the most widely powerful of the Celtic goddesses. She is the power of the new moon, of the spring

of the year, and of the flowing sea. In Ireland she is most
famed, and in Britain she was Goddess of the widespread
tribe of the Brigantes. Her festival, from ancient times to the
present, is the second day of February, the Celtic Fire-
Festival of Imbolc. She has been named as a saint and new
stories have been made to accommodate her to the new
structure, but the truth of her has continued unhidden and
unchanged throughout. In Pagan times, her statue was
annually washed in sea or lake to celebrate her festival, being
conveyed ceremonially overland in a chariot or a boat; in her
association with a ship she may be compared to Isis, and in
the ceremonial ablution to Anadyomene rising from the
waves. In the Christian calendar, the second day of February
is dedicated to the Purification of the Virgin, with the feast
of St. Brigid on the day previous. In her name, she is related
also to the Nordic Frigga, who is likewise a Goddess of the
dark and watery powers; and here we have the reason for that
old tradition in the English language, that a ship should
always be referred to as "she," for a ship has so often been
termed a Brig or a Frigate. Always with candles and with
water do we greet her, the great Moon-Mother, patroness of
poetry and of all "making," and of the arts of healing.

Besides Brigid, the Celtic Triple-Goddess is also associated
with the moon. The Morrigan, whose name means "Great
Queen," appears sometimes alone, sometimes with her sister-
goddesses or other selves, Bave the Raven, and Nevain whose
name means Frenzy. In the more primitive stories, the chief
task of this triad is to mark down those doomed in battle,
comparably with the Walkyren, but in time they developed a
wider scope: it is to be suspected that they were the "three
Queens in a barge" who arrived to convey the dying Arthur
to Avalon, Morrigan herself being of course Morgan le Fay. If
that is so, she would also be the Fata Morgana of Sicily.
Again, they appear in French folklore as *les lavandières de la
nuit*. (See Appendix A.) Their activities are by no means

limited to the night hours, but time and place have sufficient strangeness to warn the prudent. In single or triple form, the Goddesses appear as women washing linen in a river or stream. A man passing by will be drawn into conversation; in the old days, he was shown that what they were washing was the astral form of his own body, dead from battle-wounds which he had not yet received. Since those times, he is safe if he does not permit the temptresses to touch him. If they do so, he is doomed; but to the man who masters them, and to women who invoke them, they are powerful allies.

The Earth-Mothers, although these again often appear as a triad, are a different matter and are wholly beneficent. Almost every important Celtic deity has a triple form, for three was the paramount number with this race before the quarterings of the compass-points and of the year—Imbolc, Bealteinne, Lughnasadh, Samhuinn—were established; the cult of the Moon-Goddesses and of the Earth-Mothers being of the ancient things, the triple forms remain especially pronounced. The Earth-Mothers represent the lower octave of Modron, since in this system as in others the identity, first or last, of the Celestial Mother with the Earth Mother is implicit. A number of ancient sculptures of the Earth-Mothers exist, showing them with grain and ripe fruit which they bring in baskets. Characteristically, they gather together and bring what other powers have ripened, for this is the proper role of Earth-forces in magical work. People who do not work according to this principle, but expect miracles of the Mothers themselves, always complain that what they gain in one way they lose in another. This is usually true, but the fault is their own and should not be ascribed to the Earth-forces.

Just as the Mothers are the lower octave of Modron, so is the Earth-Goddess Anu the lower octave of Danu. "The Paps of Anu" is the traditional name given to a pair of gently rounded hills in County Kerry. Frequently confusion arises, and Anu herself is regarded as a Celestial Mother, but none need see harm in this.

It is noticeable in Celtic legend, how often a pre-Celtic tumulus, originally intended so far as is known simply as a place of burial, becomes an entrance to the Otherworld. In the old Scottish ballad of Tam Lin, the hero says:

"There came a wind out of the north,
   A sharp wind and a snell:
A dead sleep it came over me
   And from my horse I fell,
And the Queen of Fairies she took me
   In yon green hill to dwell."

One reason for this is that the place itself usually meets the ritual requirements for such an entrance, having two upright stones with a relatively narrow space between. There is a ritual technique for making contact with various forces and deities, which employs such an entrance; we cannot deal with it here, and indeed work upon this principle is still proceeding in the Aurum Solis, for it is extremely potent and must be carried out in the most carefully protected conditions. Suffice it that if such an entrance is made, it can and will be used; such entrances occur in the natural world, sometimes as the space between two trees, sometimes as a pool which may be reputed to be "bottomless." As is well known, if such places are not magically guarded, forces most antipathetic to human life can enter. However, in the case of the tombs here mentioned, special conditions exist. In the first place, the presence there of human remains establishes a focal point of intelligibility: human contact is not necessary to the existence of the deities and other spiritual beings, but in one form or another it is often needed for the purpose of bringing these beings within the psychic perception of people seeking communication with them. We have remarked on the tradition of "Weyland's Smithy," for example. In the

Voudoun cult, there is a distinct relationship between the invocation of the Loa and the cult of the dead, although the Loa are certainly not the spirits of the departed, nor in any evident way are they connected. One recalls that the relic of a saint or martyr was until late years needed to establish a Catholic church, although that fragment may have had nothing to do with the saint of the church's dedication. This brings us to the second safeguard connected with the prehistoric tumuli above-mentioned. As burial places, they were specifically safeguarded from the entry of malignant entities by the powerful wards of early (usually Neolithic) magick. Their subsequent use as places of mystical contact, even as temples, is not surprising and is in no way to be confused with the cult of the dead as such.

These things notwithstanding, it must not be considered that human or animal remains of any kind, whether sacrificial or other, are essential to this type of contact. They are effective, but in the modern magical tradition they are superseded. An effectively charged Tessera provides the focal point, but focal point there must be.

The Celtic Otherworld, however entered, is a region of extreme beauty. Many are the stories of those who have visited it in the course of the earthly lifetime, and their witness—when they speak of it at all—is unanimous. No grief enters there with them, nor any memory of earthly care. The passing of time is unperceived; there are no changes of weather, no movement even of the air; all is gracious and joyous. As a being of that region is said in Irish myth to have described it to the hero Oisin when inviting him thither:

> "With honey drip the woodland trees
> And days on days new revels bring,
> While shining birds in music sing:
> And faint is borne upon the breeze
> In endless sleepy murmuring
> The sighing of enchanted seas.

"There all is beauty: naught uncouth
Can ever in that land abide
Where deepest peace the ages glide.
This is our dream, and this our truth:
And thou shalt reign there by my side,
The lord of all the Land of Youth!"
—*Ernest Page*

Thus we see the Celtic deities as unique and beautiful forms, but behind them we recognise the same Archetypes that we have come to know previously. So it is with all the systems that we have considered, and with many whose examination we cannot here undertake. Of the well-known Greek and Roman forms of the planetary deities, enough has doubtless been written for our purpose. If we go back to the earlier Babylonian and Sumerian forms, the same patterns are discernable. In the main, by so doing, we stand to gain little and to lose much, for the rich potential of the cosmic drama was perhaps less recognised; quite certainly, the portions of that mythology which have come down to us leave many questions unanswered. For one story, however, we must return to the eastern Mediterranean, since there only can we trace some of its implications, and the myth itself is too important, too basic to our culture to be ignored: the story which in one of its developments is that of Ishtar and Tammuz, and in another is that of Cybele and Attis.

The name Dumuzi (the Sumerian form of Tammuz: Dumu means "son") is applied to two beings, or, as it would seem, to one being with two distinct aspects: of the Deep, and of the Tree. He of the Deep is evidently the first; we discern here a relevance in the Egyptian myth of Temu, born of the primeval waters. Thence Dumuzi becomes the beloved of the Great Mother. Their relationship is a mystery, for it cannot be limited to earthly terms. In the Hymn of Eridu, where the Mother is named as Zikun (one of Ishtar's star-identities is the star Iku) it is implied that he is her parthenogenous son, born within the Great Tree. One of his Sumerian names is Dumuzi-Da, Tammuz of the Tree. In the later Adonis story he is born of the Myrrh-tree. These tree-associations bring us very near to the myth of Attis, but the link gives us no help as to origins. The earliest literary reference for Attis that we have is in the Greek poetry of Anacreon, and he introduces the story with an ambiguity which seems almost deliberate; perhaps it is indeed deliberate, and we should leave the almost-oneness of Ishtar and Dumuzi wrapped in mystery. We can recall that Dumuzi, or Attis, is always represented as an almost feminine figure, and that Ishtar in her star-aspect was regarded as male at sunrise and female at sunset; it would appear, then, that Ishtar and Dumuzi are each to be regarded as veritably the "other self" of the other.

However, in the Sumerian and Babylonian story, for various complex reasons involving jealousy in every version of the episode, the happiness together on earth of this divine couple could not last. Dumuzi was slain, and went (or returned) with the flowing rivers to the depths of the Underworld; and Ishtar wept inconsolably. This part of the story is the cause of the "women weeping for Tammuz" mentioned by Ezekiel; the great lamentations in annual celebration of this event were remarked by many. The cults of Adonis and of Attis were one in this, though there were variants in the details: one of the most significant variants was the hanging of dolls in the trees as an offering, to bring back the lost one whose presence had bestowed fertility on the land and on the herds. It is generally recognised that these dolls were a substitute for an earlier human sacrifice. Because the victim would thereby become identified with the deity, such a death had been regarded as a great honour by the members of the cult. It was, of course, regarded in quite a reverse light by those of an antagonistic religion; hence in Deuteronomy 21:24 "he that is hanged is accursed of God."

However, in the event Ishtar could only win her consort from the Underworld by descending thither to bring him back. She descended through seven infernal regions, that is to say, through the qliphothic aspect of each of the planetary powers; and at each gate she could only gain admittance by giving up a garment, but she had the victory, and brought Dumuzi back to the light.* Nevertheless, for the hold which the chthonic powers had upon him, he had to return for a part of every year. Thus his aspect as Dumuzi-Abzu, Tammuz of the Abyss, is perpetuated.

The initiatory significance of this story is tremendous. We notice, too, how the word *Abzu,* meaning the Abyss, has persisted across the languages, there being no other word for that concept. In Egypt we have it as *Abtu,* that is, *Abydos* to give it its Greek form, the great centre of the cult of Osiris. Another point which must not be overlooked, is the universality of Ishtar. She cannot be attributed simply to Venus, or to the Moon, for example. If at each of the seven gates she had a garment to give up, then all seven planetary spheres are veils of her true self. She is the Great Mother, and sephirothically she cannot be placed lower than Binah, thus to comprehend the potential of all the planetary spheres. This is confirmed by another of her names, Ama Inanna, "Heavenly Mother." Aima, from the same basic linguistic stock, is a title of Binah.

*

If a particular Pantheon attracts the student, whether one of those we have indicated or another, the lines we have set forth can be followed should he wish to establish a plan of study and investigation. At the same time, study is not Magick, and it remains in this chapter to consider the general

* Thus the Dance of the Seven Veils was an authentic and sacred dance in honour of Ishtar.

ceremonial methods by which contact can be made with the God-forces in question. These methods will subsequently be examined in greater detail.

The first essential, before the practical side can be planned, is that the student should acquire a thorough knowledge of his subject. This means a thorough knowledge of the general Qabalistic schema, as well as of the pantheon upon which he intends to work. In the early stages it is useless to concentrate upon a single deity; the related cosmogony must be thoroughly known, and as exact an idea as possible formed of the place of the chosen deity within that cosmogony. The preliminaries being completed, the next stage is that the student should begin seriously to worship the chosen deity. This is not only a matter of providing a suitable shrine, composing or finding suitable forms of address, and exploring such matters as suitable colours or incenses which will be of further value in the magical operation proper. It is also a spiritual matter of reflecting upon, attuning oneself to, deepening one's understanding of, and above all nourishing one's love for, that deity. No excuse suffices here. Not only has a free choice been made of a certain Divine Being for reasons of, presumably, a strong affinity; it must also be taken into the reckoning that this really is a Divine Being and therefore, even if the student had made no such choice and even if the Being in question were thoroughly uncongenial, the objective fact would remain that this Being was, by nature, worthy of devotion. Having made the choice, therefore, the student is to go forward without hesitation. A link has to be formed between the objective reality of that Being in the Cosmos, and the student's total psyche.

Now the magical work proper begins. If it is possible to spend some time at a historic cult-place of the deity, or at least of the pantheon, this should be done; but any such advantage would be offset if the mind were crowded with other thoughts and images. Every adjunct, physical or mental, should be conducive to the one purpose. One is to be steeped in the cult, to the exclusion of extraneous matters as far as possible. One is, in fact, to conduct a banishing within oneself before the invocation. Then the invocation is to begin, and it must be recognised from the outset that much patience and perseverence may be needed. This is not inevitably the case: if one has been aware, however dimly, of an affinity with that deity at a previous time, or if one has an exceptional aptitude for this work, then it need not be a very long time before delicate but quite distinct tokens of success are encountered. Obviously, if one is working with a cult little-used since ancient times, or with a deity with whom one has little contact, there is likely to be especial difficulty, but even this will be overcome if one works with love, and if one believes (as one should before choosing) that this deity has some particular relationship to one's magical purpose, here and now, in the hour and in the place of invocation.

# CHAPTER VIII

An essential human faculty, the power of astral creation.

Sensations impressed involuntarily upon the Astral Light by people in certain circumstances.

Ability of the conscious mind to act deliberately through the medium of astral images which have previously come into being from other causes. Ability of spiritual or elemental entities to take control of phantoms.

Typical features of unconscious astral experiences recorded by Whitman in part of "The Sleepers."

Conscious astral experiences not to be considered as a goal in themselves.

Deceptive character of the Astral Light if the conditions needed for sound magical working are not observed.

Requirements for sound magical working. The Astral Temple, necessary in some conditions, optional in others. The Correspondences: examples of their use, introducing the concept of the battery.

Principles and purposes of Color Scales. Origin and formulation of the Aurum Solis scales. The four A.S. scales themselves.

177

The magical use of color—
    In ceremonial,
    In astral travel,
    In the construction of visual images: an exercise not
        generally magically potent unless implemented by
        other working.

Movement within the Light: the occult action of vibrant
    energy, "Odic Force." Flow lines and stress lines: lines
    of formation and of destruction in the Light.

Formation of astral vehicles for higher forces. Vibration of
    Words of Power as an activating agency. Principles of
    invocation: exclusion of "correct" correspondences having
    alien associations.

The Aura. Stimulation of the Centres of Activity.

The tides:—
    Seasonal:   Tempus sementis
                Tempus messis
                Tempus consilii
                Tempus eversionis.
    Lunar (Aestus Lunae) and the Phases of the Moon.
    The Velocia, otherwise known as the Tattvas.

Planetary data needed for evocation to visible appearance.

Planetary data needed in relation to the Velocia.

Inter-relation of the individual, the Order, and the whole
    Magical Tradition in the channeling of life-forces. Central
    significance of the Solar Hero. The meeting point of the
    Great Work with the Cosmic Plan of existence. The Way
    of the Adept. The quest of the Inner Sun.

## CHAPTER VIII
## THE MAGICAL ART

The power to create is one of the essential faculties of man's spiritual nature. It is not only the artist who creates; the artist is the human being with the further faculty of translating his creations into the materials of the physical world. Everyone who is capable of thought or emotion is capable of creation in the material of the astral world—and not only is capable of such creation, but does create continually. The stronger the emotion, or the more exact the thought, correspondingly will the astral creation be stronger and more specific.

The material of the astral world is that which we term the astral light. It is more plastic than clay, and capable of finer detail than marble; but just as those materials, with which the sculptor works, are part of the fabric of the physical world itself, so the astral light which becomes moulded by our thoughts and feelings is of the fabric of the astral world. The terms World of Yetzirah, astral world, and astral light, are in fact synonymous, although each term is proper to a particular context. It will be evident that the lower levels of that world, the levels nearest to Assiah, are thronged with phantasmal forms of every description, mainly the unconsciously created productions of untrained minds, both sleeping and waking. Fortunately such productions are usually without durability, so that they incessantly fade and recede and are replaced by others; however, in abnormal conditions, such as a great natural disaster or a battle, the

179

intense emotion of one person or of a number of people can
impress upon the astral light a mental image of the event;
many "ghosts" associated with historic occurrences are built
up in that way. An image, so to call it, of this kind need not
be visual: the astral vibration "haunting" some places is
experienced as a sound, while that which lingers in other
places is experienced as an odour. The well-known
phenomenon of the "hungry grass" in Ireland is a rare
example of a strong impression affecting another sense; the
nerves of the stomach are, as a matter of fact, acutely
sensitive to emotional influences generally, as those
interested in medical matters are aware.

    Astral impressions, visual and otherwise, such as we have
here discussed, are after-images of occurrences which are past
and finished on the material level; the astral  images are
therefore in the process of receding, no matter how strongly
they may seem to persist. They are most unlikely to produce
any further effect upon earth, because no force from a higher
level is acting through them: the phantom horsemen of
Naseby are not likely to induce another battle on that site,
nor is the hungry grass likely to produce another famine.
When a higher force does act through an astral image,
however, there is a tendency for the image to project a real
effect. This, naturally, presupposes the image to be an
appropriate one for the action of such a force. Even an
untrained mind, when strongly motivated, can sometimes
find the way to a deliberate control of astral phantoms.

    A certain young man, was, through his hobby of rock-
climbing, a cause of considerable concern to his mother. She
did not allow herself to become a prey to worry, however,
until one night she had a particularly vivid and horrifying
dream in which she saw him struggling to regain his balance
upon a narrow ledge, from which he eventually fell. After
awaking from this nightmare, the mother was haunted by
the mental image; over and over she saw it in her imagination,

but the most frightful aspect of the matter was her certainty that this dream was some kind of premonition of an impending physical occurrence. It was then that she had her wonderful inspiration. The next time the memory of her dream overwhelmed her, instead of trying to dispel it she accepted it, and with great courage passively watched in her imagination the preliminary happenings. Then, at the critical moment, she exerted all her will to change the climax: to visualise her son as regaining his balance and reaching safety. Every time the mental image came back to her, she made the effort to change it in this way, until she was completely successful and the horror faded. Then, some time later, her son returned from a holiday and told her of his narrow escape from what had nearly been a fatal accident. He had reached a ledge, just as she had seen in her dream; he had lost his balance through trusting to an insecure rock, and had believed himself to be irrevocably falling over the precipice; then, as he said, a powerful gust of wind had suddenly risen to meet him, giving him just the help that he needed to regain mastery of the situation.

Concerning the source of the dream in the first place, it can be said that in those higher astral levels which project the conditions of earthly existence, changes take place before the corresponding changes are manifested on earth. This makes prophecy possible. However, because of the extreme plasticity of the astral light between that high level and the material world, and because of the variety of agencies which may be brought to bear upon the image—as was the mother's will in the episode here recounted—prophecy cannot be absolute.

With regard to the astral phantoms previously mentioned, which are in themselves only inert shadows or echoes thrown off by human minds, a complication frequently arises which causes some perplexity to investigators. It must be borne in mind that the astral light has its own inhabitants. The higher beings of the World of Yetzirah are not in question here, but it can happen that an elemental or a qliphothic entity can become associated with, and can seem to animate, an inert phantom which has no real relationship to it. The phantom of a suicide, for example, does not normally produce other suicides; yet in certain instances a succession of suicides occurring in a particular place is unquestionably instigated by a phantom activated by a qliphothic or an elemental entity. In such cases, when it is possible to arrive at the history of the first suicide in the series, this can usually be shown to result from the presence of such an entity: in the case of a qliphothic being, malicious intervention; in the case of an elemental, mere irresponsible participation in a human mood, e.g., depression, already existing. The present authors have had a number of bizarre experiences in their investigations of such matters.

This particular phenomenon, the activation of an astral phantom by a spiritual force (good or evil) is mentioned for comparison with directed magical techniques to be discussed presently. For similar reasons, we here make reference to the unconscious astral wandering of incarnate human beings: unconscious, sometimes, in the sense that the wanderer afterwards remembers nothing about it, but just as probably unconscious in the sense that he is only aware of it as a tangled dream, with no notion that a real journey has been undertaken. It is unlikely, for example, that Walt Whitman was consciously aware of astral journeying as such, yet his poem, *"The Sleepers,"* contains much that is the authentic hallmark of this, as well as much that transcends it. There we find the experience transcribed, of a great soul passing through the physical and the lower astral realms, to the pellucid spiritual perception of the higher astral. In the freedom of those regions, other natures will have other adventures. They can create problems for themselves, but only very rarely for others; because they do not move far beyond the physical world, their power of causality is proportionally limited.

To write with delight, with ecstasy of the Astral Light would not be difficult: the freedom of the blue-grey luminescence stretching into mists of illimitable distance; the initial moment of stillness which marks the meeting-place of the worlds; the drifts and vortices of vision, light, colour, music, all that the individual nature of the seer is able to perceive with response; the finding of that which one seeks (for always there should be a definite quest in such explorations) and the sense of having touched thereby one or other of the great pulses of the universe; the encounter with high radiant beings, whose very nobility stabs one's consciousness because one cannot instantly arise and follow; the hearing of words which imprint themselves on the memory, yet can never be told without paraphrase, for the purpose of language is to communicate and these words would communicate nothing to any other. To write of such experiences as if they constituted a goal to be desired for itself would be easy, and yet it would be utterly fallacious; intrinsically, the visions have no more value than a delirium, while the high utterances generally point to a perilous further way and will have worth only when one shall have travelled it. The astral world is the essential connecting link between the divine and the earthly. Macrocosmically and microcosmically it is of vital importance in magical work, but only as that connecting link.

These foregoing considerations should indicate to the student the general character of the astral light. Frequently the World of Yetzirah is described as illusory and deceptive; it is so, if the necessary conditions for sound work are not observed. If the practitioner goes only to the lower astral and creates the effects he seeks without reference to higher powers, those effects will amount only to a temporary sorcery of the type which in the Middle Ages was known as "glamour." (The activities of the Goblin Page in "The Lay of the Last Minstrel" give a good idea of the approximate scope, level, and motivation of "glamour.")

One important link between the worlds which is employed at the inception of group workings, is the Astral Temple. This is generally a reflection on the Yetziratic Plane of the physical temple as arranged for the rite: it forms an astral matrix into which flow the invoked forces.

The Astral Temple should be simple in form, but what may be termed its basic architecture need not vary from working to working. It is generally true of astral structures that the longer they are maintained in existence, the greater in fact does their durability become; apart from necessary variations of colour and symbolism, to "compose" the Temple soon requires no more than to renew consciousness of it.

For the individual, formulation of an Astral Temple is optional. The prospect of formulating one and then keeping it consciously in mind during an elaborate ritual may perhaps daunt the student. There need not, in fact, be any difficulty about this if the Astral Temple presents, as it should, as nearly as possible the same image as the physical temple. One of the main purposes of the colours and symbols common to the two is to maintain the connection between the Worlds in a manner evident to the subconscious of the magician, even though his conscious attention has many other claims upon it.

For this very reason, the ritual should lack nothing which can be woven into it of the suitable correspondences. Colour, sound, number, are all selected for this purpose, as are also the aromatics to be burned as incense. Solid matter is an intricate assembly of atoms, each atom consisting of charges of energy vibrating in certain characteristic modes. Some vibrations manifest to our senses as sound, others again as colour. Each of the selected materials, colours and sounds, therefore, conveys its especial vibration to the physical, mental and spiritual faculties of the magician, besides conditioning the ambiance itself, the watching air, the waiting astral light.

If, for   example, a rite of the Sphere of Jupiter is contemplated, it will be possible to introduce the appropriate rhythms and colours in various ways. The colour blue can be employed in a ritual garment or an altar-cover; the stone amethyst or lapis lazuli, if worn or placed upon the altar, will help to focus the force of the Sphere more powerfully. Lights may be four in number; there may be a fourfold circumambulation. There may be a battery* of four knocks. In this case we may ask ourselves, For what purpose are the Powers of the Sphere of Jupiter being invoked? Is it for balance and equity? Then the battery may be divided 2–2. Is it for prosperity? Then it may be desired to recall the Saturnian force from which the Jupiterian has proceeded, and to strike 3-1. Do we invoke the aspect of the All-Father? Then we may signify that behind the Sphere of Jupiter we are aware of the most august Paternity of Chokmah, not to be invoked but to be saluted, centrally in the battery 1-2-1. These considerations do not of course mean that during the rite itself we shall be consciously analysing the parts thereof or the reason for their inclusion; the technical details are all settled beforehand, so that when the time comes the actions need but to be carried out.†

In the case of a ritual of the Sphere of Mars, the correspondences will all relate to that Sphere. Red will be the

* A battery of knocks is often used to mark a division in ritual, the transition from one mood to another. The battery may be chosen to introduce the new mood, or else to recall the sphere of operation. Its purpose is not the mere conveyance of the total number, but includes also the significance of its parts, as exemplified in the text. Again, the effect of the rhythm is partly upon the psyche of the magician, partly also upon the astral matrix; it is, too, a signal to the unseen witnesses. In the A.S. at the end of any working soever, the battery is invariably 3-5-3. This produces two benefits, one psychological, one magical. Firstly, members become accustomed to this, and are thus not bewildered as they might be by varied concluding signals. The second benefit is that this battery totals 11, the Great Magical Number, each individual work being thus in its ending aligned with the Great Work.

† This introduces a fundamental magical principle: when once an initial Declaration of Intent has been made in the opening of a rite, concentration upon that intention is to be sedulously avoided. Attention to each element of a rite, perfecting each for its own sake in its due sequence—the speeches for their splendor, the movements for their grace, the battery for its rhythm, and so on—this, carried by the initial impetus of the Declaration, is the basis of success in ceremonial working.

colour; every weapon or other object employed can be of steel. Fivefold may be the invocation, fivefold the battery. Do we seek the inexorable advance of justice? Then five slow, equally spaced, even-toned knocks shall we strike. Do we seek the power of Mars to bring authority and order? Then we may make our battery 2-3 to bring to mind Chokmah and Binah, or 2-1-2 to signify a central Unity governing an evenly divided Plurality. The individual purpose may suggest other forms and interpretations, to suit the case. The garnet, the stone of this Sphere, may be worn centrally to a pentagonal lamen.

The importance of colour in ritual workings and in magical visualizations, with the concept of colour as an indicator of each type of force, will by now be evident. Many methods and systems of using colour are valid in magical working: the Enochian, Celtic and Ptolemaic colour systems, for instance, are rightly to be followed for workings of their own kind. The modern Qabalah however, with which we are concerned here, requires its specific grid of evaluations for the Thirty-two Paths in the Four Worlds, for in each of the Worlds, each Sephirah and Path manifests its distinctive colour vibration.

This, by the convertible cause-effect reaction which has been indicated earlier in this series, produces a most valuable instrument for the magician. If he knows the correct colour linked to a given Sephirah or Path in a certain World, then by the use of the colour he can, with the correct keys, evoke the influence of the Sphere or Path at the level required for his working; even as he can verify his results by the colour which manifests to his consciousness.

An instrument such as this must become by training and usage second nature to the magician; but, before it can be so, it must be soundly established and tested so that full reliance can be placed upon it. Accordingly, in 1965, the Aurum Solis began a program to establish the set of Colour-scales which should carry the authority of the Order. The whole work of observation and collation took approximately seven years to complete, but the resulting scales have indeed justified the work entailed in their preparation. They correspond closely to the manner in which the delicate vibrations actually manifest to the skilled perception; and at the same time—doubtless for this very reason—they place little burden upon the faculty of visualization, when it is desired to employ this.

For this purpose, therefore, an updated understanding of the spectrum was introduced as a beginning. Then a series of experimental investigations was begun, the results being checked against results obtained by different methods, and also being interpreted with regard to scientific theories of colour. Data obtained from evocations, from astral and spiritual explorations, from pendulum tests, were found to produce most interesting results when compared with traditional occult beliefs on the one hand, and an examination of wave-vibrations and colour analyses on the other.

As an example: it was found that named colour samples, intended to help seers give a material identity to their non-material perceptions, were more recognizable by them when presented as transparencies than on paper. However, the whiteness of the illumination had then to be standardized, and its brightness fixed at a degree which would not vitiate the colour, the services of photo-electric equipment being required for these purposes. As another example: in comparing pendulum readings for different, perhaps occultly-related, samples, it was found that more sensitive and meaningful measurements were obtained by comparing different cord lengths needed to obtain the same rate of oscillation, than by comparing different rates of oscillation obtained with a cord of constant length.

Here on the following pages, then, are the Aurum Solis Colour-scales:*

* The colours marked (*) cannot be exactly represented in a static form, and when visualised should be accorded movement corresponding to their descriptions. When they are painted, however, as for instance on Talismans, a static representation is needful. There are devices in the painter's art which will aid, if the magician knows them, in giving the appearance of potential movement to these colours. The Atziluthic colours, if visualised, should in every case be seen as luminous.

# ATZILUTH
## *AURUM SOLIS RADICAL SCALE*

| | |
|---|---|
| 1 | Brilliance |
| 2 | Ultra-violet |
| 3 | Dove grey |
| 4 | Lilac |
| 5 | Amber |
| 6 | Pale greenish-yellow |
| 7 | Greenish blue |
| 8 | Yellow ochre |
| 9 | Red-purple |
| 10 | Purple-brown |
| | |
| 11 | Pale lemon yellow |
| 12 | Yellow ochre |
| 13 | Red-purple |
| 14 | Greenish blue |
| 15 | Amber |
| 16 | Vermilion |
| 17 | Yellow ochre |
| 18 | Red gold |
| 19 | Pale greenish-yellow |
| 20 | Sulphur yellow |
| 21 | Lilac |
| 22 | Greenish blue |
| 23 | Dusky lilac |
| 24 | Pale olive |
| 25 | Lilac |
| 26 | Red-purple |
| 27 | Amber |
| 28 | Petunia |
| 29 | Copper red |
| 30 | Pale greenish-yellow |
| 31 | Red-amber |
| 32 | Rose pink |
| | |
| 32 bis | Matt white |
| 31 bis | Yellow flame |
| DAATH | Intense mid-purple |

# BRIAH

*AURUM SOLIS PRISMATIC SCALE*

| | |
|---|---|
| 1 | White brilliance |
| 2 | Dynamic nacreous vortex of all spectrum colours* |
| 3 | Indigo |
| 4 | Blue |
| 5 | Red |
| 6 | Yellow |
| 7 | Green |
| 8 | Orange |
| 9 | Violet |
| 10 | Citrine, olive, russet, black |
| | |
| 11 | Yellow |
| 12 | Orange |
| 13 | Violet |
| 14 | Green |
| 15 | Scarlet |
| 16 | Red-orange |
| 17 | Orange |
| 18 | Orange-yellow |
| 19 | Yellow |
| 20 | Yellow-green |
| 21 | Blue |
| 22 | Green |
| 23 | Blue |
| 24 | Blue-green |
| 25 | Blue |
| 26 | Violet |
| 27 | Red |
| 28 | Purple |
| 29 | Magenta |
| 30 | Yellow |
| 31 | Red |
| 32 | Indigo |
| | |
| 32 bis | Black, flecked white |
| 31 bis | Rich red, flecked gold |
| DAATH | Very deep purple |

# YETZIRAH
## *AURUM SOLIS CONTINGENT SCALE*

| | |
|---|---|
| 1 | Shimmering white* |
| 2 | Billowing blue-black* |
| 3 | Soft red-brown |
| 4 | Light royal blue |
| 5 | Fiery red |
| 6 | Pale golden yellow |
| 7 | Light turquoise |
| 8 | Light apricot |
| 9 | Lavender |
| 10 | Citrine, olive, russet, black, flecked gold |
| | |
| 11 | Electric blue |
| 12 | Indian yellow |
| 13 | Mist blue |
| 14 | Bright emerald green |
| 15 | Scarlet madder |
| 16 | Coral red |
| 17 | Intense lemon yellow |
| 18 | Aquamarine blue |
| 19 | Deep gold |
| 20 | Deep olive green |
| 21 | Delphinium blue |
| 22 | Intense green-blue |
| 23 | Sage green |
| 24 | Metallic prussian blue |
| 25 | Cobalt blue |
| 26 | Raw umber |
| 27 | Burnt orange |
| 28 | Grey-brown |
| 29 | Vandyke brown rayed yellow |
| 30 | Salmon pink |
| 31 | Cadmium scarlet |
| 32 | Matt black |
| | |
| 32 bis | Red, blue, yellow, flecked black |
| 31 bis | Deep clear blue, flecked gold |
| DAATH | Midnight blue |

# ASSIAH
## AURUM SOLIS ICONIC SCALE

| | |
|---|---|
| 1 | White, flecked gold |
| 2 | Black, flecked silver |
| 3 | Grey with fulvous shades |
| 4 | Nacreous green-blue merging into shell-pink* |
| 5 | Mingled pale yellow & cerise: green-blue tinge |
| 6 | Intense yellow-white, rayed scarlet |
| 7 | Luminescent greenish-white |
| 8 | Yellowish-white merging into greenish-white |
| 9 | Pale lemon yellow, flecked white |
| 10 | Seven colours in prismatic sequence |
| | |
| 11 | Cerulean |
| 12 | Deep red, brown tinge |
| 13 | Silver |
| 14 | Vivid deep green |
| 15 | Glowing crimson, flecked black |
| 16 | Rich green, flecked yellow |
| 17 | Swirling yellow & silver* |
| 18 | Shimmering blue & silver* |
| 19 | Brilliant golden yellow |
| 20 | Very dark green |
| 21 | Bluish grey |
| 22 | Deep blue merging into turquoise |
| 23 | Silver grey |
| 24 | Ice blue |
| 25 | Quivering blue radiance* |
| 26 | Grey |
| 27 | Intense fiery red |
| 28 | Yellowish grey, flecked white |
| 29 | Deep blue with swirling white* |
| 30 | Brownish yellow |
| 31 | Vermilion |
| 32 | Deep metallic black |
| | |
| 32 bis | Seven colours in prismatic sequence, flecked white |
| 31 bis | Dark translucent green, flecked crimson & gold |
| DAATH | Intense black |

There are many applications of the Colour-scales in practical working. These are too numerous, and in some cases too complex to be given here; though certain uses will be shown in Volume 3. To assist present comprehension of the Scales, however, we also give the following general observations:

1) Each Scale symbolises the forces of a particular World, and those forces can be both represented and (in the correct conditions) induced by the employment of their colours. This principle, if borne in mind, will enable the student to perceive much concerning the Colour-scales.

2) The four Scales may be taken as the signatures of the various Powers in the Four Worlds; but with regard to the World of Briah this is in a particular manner true, since here we have the archetypal Forces at their highest manifest level. Here is the reason why vestments and drapes for use in sephirothic rites are for most purposes made in the colour corresponding to the appropriate force at its Briatic level: the magician thereby places himself *en rapport* with the most potent and most stable manifest expression of that force, so that he may control and command its lower levels. Furthermore, it is to be observed that the Astral Temple correspondingly will then be visualised as adorned with the Briatic colour (and its complementary). This is because it has a twofold role: it is made to the plan and image of the earthly temple, and may in a sense be considered its reflection, but, with far greater significance, it is also a symbol of the Archetypal Temple which is the prototype and motivation for the creation of all temples and sacred buildings whatsoever, which exists as a shining vision in the World of Briah, and whose divine original is the all-encompassing body of the Star-Mother.

3) In the Colour-scales the World of Atziluth is represented by pale and muted shades. This is not by any means to imply that the Divine Mind is in itself a pale

phantom compared with the lower levels; on the contrary, it is the level of true and self-existent reality. The fate of Semele should be considered, scorched out of being by a divine force which is represented in these Scales by the colour lilac. Here, as in all else connected with the Tree, cosmic reality is not represented as it is in its own nature, but as it is accessible to the human mind.

4) The Scales are employed as keys in many works of magick and of psychism. Significant examples are:

*a*—To monitor and direct astral travel (out-of-the-body experience), and various works involving the projection of substance from the astral body. *b*—In scrying (psychic or spiritual vision, stimulated by resting the physical gaze upon a bright or dark surface). *c*—To signalize or induce changes of level in the consciousness of the magician, whether in meditation or in process of a ceremonial working. (In magical operations involving more than one person, this use of the Colour-scales can assist in raising the consciousness of all when this is required, and in returning all simultaneously when the high work is completed). *d*—To call into action the subliminal faculties of the psyche of the magician, as these may be needful at a particular point in a working. *e*—To typify, or to implement invocation of, objective non-material forces. *f*—In the formation of magical images: that is, in the art of visualizing beings according to the letters of their names.*

5) With regard to the archetypal images, the main colour employed in their construction is the Briatic colour of the Sephirah to which they correspond. To this, highlights and flashes are added of the direct complementary,† and overtones

* See Volume 3, Paper XIX, pages 129-139.

† With regard to the Briatic colours, it is sometimes asked why their complementaries are so abundantly introduced. The reply begins with the observation (p. 187) that a luminous colour is nearer to its non-material original than an opaque pigment can be. The skilled use of a complementary colour will create a "flashing" effect which, though entirely optical, produces an illusion of luminosity; and thus, through the Nephesh of the magician, the magical effectiveness of the main colour is much enhanced.

of the corresponding Atziluthic colour. Archetypal images of Geburah, for instance, have red with highlights and flashes of the complementary green; such an image being intended as a vehicle of Atziluthic force, traces of the corresponding Radical colour, amber, are added.

An archetypal image of Chesed has Briatic blue. There will be details and highlights of the direct complementary, orange, with overtones of the corresponding Atziluthic colour, lilac.

Although these images are initially built up in the Astral, the colours, character and ritual procedure make of them true Briatic channels, instruments of Atziluthic force. They should be prepared accordingly.

In this connection, it is important to observe that archetypal images should always be visualised as *luminous* beings.

6) Forms *should not* be worked out by letter correspondences for the Hebrew Divine Names; as we have pointed out, the Archetypes find direct expression in the images of the Briatic Plane.

Archangelic forms may be visualised in their sphere colours in the manner detailed for archetypal images; or their forms may be worked out according to the letter-correspondences of their names.

Yetziratic beings will have forms according to the letters of their names, or according to perceived astral images; in either case, the colours will be of the Contingent Scale.

7) The planetary colours drawn from the Sephiroth or the Paths of the Yetziratic Scale are sometimes, at particular points in certain operations, used for vestments, though not physically; the operator, at the critical stage, visualising the appropriate colour and so "covering himself with light as with a garment."

8) The Scale of Assiah is used in very advanced operations concerned with manipulation of the forces which

directly act upon the physical level. It is sometimes employed for works of evocation in which it may be desired to open a channel for manifestation on the Assiatic Plane, and is of extreme importance in relation to a certain technique mentioned in the previous chapter.

9) In the Prismatic Scale, Chokmah is "a dynamic nacreous vortex of all spectrum colours"; it is thus the active and divided state that emanates from the white brilliance of Kether. The totality of the spectrum of light is the seven colours or their synthesis, white brilliance. The synthesis of the spectrum in pigment is indigo. Pigment is colour expressed in matter and is therefore an attribute of Binah. In the spectrum of light which we are here considering, the indigo which represents Binah is in fact the shadow or negative aspect of the totality. The further emanations of the Sephiroth in Briah show forth the unfolding of the potential according to a strict pattern of relationships: the Briatic Trine manifests the three primaries, the Yetziratic Trine manifests the three secondaries.

10) In no case do we classify these Colour-scales as "objective" or "subjective." For several reasons these terms are practically meaningless in the present context, and lead to endless confusions. When it is decided that a particular World is the correct level for a particular meditation or working, the Colour-scale can be identified by name accordingly. The Scales are therefore to be used as they are needed, for the Sephiroth or the Paths in each World. This is, of course, an entirely different matter from the distinction of "masculine" and "feminine" Scales which is sometimes employed; this latter distinction is a quite valid one, and is based upon the traditional application of the letters YHVH to the Four Worlds, having nothing to do with objectivity or subjectivity.

Earlier in this chapter we have dealt with the building of images in the Astral Light. This is necessary, but image-building in itself is not enough for magical effectiveness. Daydreaming is a building of astral images, certainly, but it is generally ineffectual, though the minds of the immature continually hope for it to prove otherwise. We must therefore pass now to a consideration of *Movement within the Light.*

Movement is life; at least in the world of magical ritual it is so, and shows itself to be so in many modes. The sacred dance proclaims it, from the cosmic rapture of the dedicated dervish or shaman to the intricate spring courtship dance of the Maypole, which likewise had its cosmic dedication. The rhythm of the Ephesian krotalon or of the timbrel proclaims it, urging on the steps of Maenads dancing for Cybele or for Dionysus, of *ibaou* dancing for Hathor. With gesture and circumambulation, with vibration of voice and battery and bell, of colour and of fragrance, the magician sets in motion the subtle waves of the physical and astral levels within the temple; here too the local has reference to the cosmic, the actions stir up a current which unites within its impulse the related levels of being.

The occult action of this vibrant energy is more subtle than either sound or colour: it is that fine Movement within the Light which used to be known as Odic Force. Although a succession of other names for it have from time to time become more fashionable, yet the name of "Od" given to it by one of its pioneer investigators, Baron von Reichenbach, is linked with less misleading associations than some of the other terms. We do not customarily refer to it as Odic Force, but sometimes it is convenient to be able to use this specific name which nevertheless avoids the limitations implied by "electricity," "magnetism," or "etheric energy." Its essence, which so many observers and writers have perceived without grasping its full significance, is Movement. To halt the movement in order to search for the force, is like the action of him who brushed aside the bee while awaiting the messenger of the Goddess. To put it differently, it is like stopping the breath to search for the life. This is more than an apt simile: the breath which is both a cause and an effect in the continual movement of physical life, is filled with Odic Force, and becomes more consciously and effectively charged in the course of magical training.

Wherever there is movement—and that is everywhere throughout the manifest worlds—there is an active or latent force, however subtle. "Stress lines" and "flow lines" exist in physical matter which appears to be static. A sheet of glass may (for argument's sake) be completely uniform in texture at every point; but the designer of stained glass knows that if a piece of this glass is cut in any shape approaching an "L," and is mounted in lead as part of a panel, he can predict with almost complete certainty that this particular piece will develop a transverse crack, just to one side of the angle. Again, engineers know that no matter how uniformly a sample of metal may respond to performance tests, yet if at any point in the design of it as a machine part there is a sudden change in thickness, that point will be a focus for stresses and will most probably cause ultimate failure. Similarly every shape, animate or inanimate, has its flow lines. In glassware, these lines can be beautifully shown by placing a bowl or other article under some types of radiation; in the animal kingdom the stripes of a zebra or tiger are similarly related to the form of the creature. Plants abound in such striations, and some African sculpture shows the same concept applied to human features. All such markings, though static, bear witness to a dynamism either latent or past, and are thus comparable to the ripple marks seen on the sand of a level shore when the tide has receded.

With such flow lines and stress lines the Astral Light is filled: lines of formation and of destruction. It is for the magician to find and use them, or to change and direct them, as they may answer to his purpose; but it is only in movement that they have power. The Astral Light is by nature in continual motion; the magician is able to control and direct its movement (admitting to certain exceptions to which we shall revert with more detail later in this chapter: he does not control the Tides, he works with them).

This is the most important single secret of Art Magick. Although, as we have said, to work at this level alone would be mere "glamour," yet equally we must state that to work at the higher levels alone might be prayer, but could not be magick.

The astral substance is the essential medium of magick, and the magician will only be successful in his work if he is able to control and direct the Light: the consecration of a magical weapon, for example, will be effective only if the magician has truly locked into the substance of the weapon a "character"; that is to say, if he has conditioned the Light to a particular vibratory movement, vitalised and established by a link with the Inner Planes. This presents us with an example of the manipulation of these forces; in other instances the procedure is adapted to the occasion but must for true magical working contain the same essential elements.

It is in the Light that the magician fashions the images which are to be the channels for higher forces; his thought-waves condition the astral vibrations. Again, the key is in movement, for "thought is action" on the astral level. However, the formation of an image is not in itself magical, it is not even a work of glamour or of sorcery; such an image, if it is to be more than a transitory "thought-form," must be energized. There are many ways in which this can be brought about.

When the magician vibrates a Name of Power, he feels even his physical body tingle with the utterance. Such an utterance not only calls upon the Divine Being invoked, in an accurate and distinctive manner; the sound itself is such as to condition the Astral Light by its vibration, causing the invoked influence to "descend" into the form that the magician will have built for it beforehand. Thus the Light is receptive to influences: as it responds to the magician's willed thoughts, images are created; but this same Light when conditioned, that is, when given directed movement, becomes a vital current. Strictly speaking, Od is the dynamic aspect, whether manifesting as the aura of a living being, whether existing as an astral current or as a charge in a consecrated object, or whether manifesting as a physical phenomenon: the earth's magnetic field, magnetism, electricity, etc. To the subject of the aura we shall return presently.

The magician must control and direct the forces of the Light; he must build forms and he must cause vortices of power; he must condition the Light, changing the "frequency" by his art and molding the astral substance not only into images but into patterns of vibration and response. This is where all that he has learned of the Correspondences comes into play: by the vibration of like to like he calls the great forces into potency. Whatever his words of summons, they will include something like the main points of the Enochian invocation: "ARRISE ... MOVE ... SHEW YOURSELVES IN POWRE: and make me a strong seething, for I am of him that liveth for ever!"*

Nevertheless, in bidding the magician to use all that conduces to the operation, we must warn that a harmony, *on paper,* with the appropriate Correspondences is not a valid reason for the inclusion in the rite of an immiscible ingredient. The sole purpose of the Correspondences is by means of them to build up, both subjectively and objectively, a full concentration on the rite and on the successive acts thereof; anything which leads away from this is a misapplication of the principle involved. Under this head must be classified anything, however intrinsically beautiful, which has strongly alien associations and which therefore

* 48 Claves Angelicae, Anno 1584.

would be destructive. Certain pieces of music, in themselves apparently very suitable, come within this category on account of the associations, personal, operatic, or other, which they hold for many persons: Handel's Largo, or the Pilgrim's March from *Tannhauser,* are notable instances. Certain types of incense belong in this category also: of all sense impressions, odours are among the most evocative of memories desired or not. The ages are past when for example grains of pure frankincense were the characteristic daily offering to the Sun God. The knowledge that those grains were so offered may lead some to a passionate wish to restore the venerable custom, and anyone who faithfully aspires to this use may of course perform it privately; but because of the overwhelmingly Christian associations now attaching to its fragrance we must, for group ritual, regretfully pronounce against the use both of pure frankincense and of those adulterations of it which are sold as "church incense." Frankincense as a secondary ingredient in a properly constituted and balanced incense of Sol is however unexceptionable, and is potent in activating the Light with a vibration attuned to the solar energies.

To revert to the subject of the aura. This phenomenon, now arousing scientific interest, is a natural emanation of etheric energy, given out by any living being to an extent and in a mode commensurate with its species and vitality. To some persons this is naturally visible; others can achieve perception of the aura with practice or with the use of special equipment. In a human aura not only the health but also the prevailing mood of the individual can be discerned, as shown by the characteristic form and colours made manifest within the aura, and the general "tone" thereof, all resulting from the vibratory movements of the Light in that region. Stimulation of the Centres of Activity benefits the various levels of the psyche and also the physical body, not only in themselves, but in the balanced interaction between them.

The effect upon the astrosome is to cause an "increased radiation of etheric energy," that is, an intensified movement of the Light, which manifests in the aura. As a general point, it can be remarked that without stimulation of the Centres of Activity, the aspirant will have no personal power and, consequently, a technique requiring, for example, a balanced and concentrated radiation of force from his psyche would be of little use to him.

The development of this personal energy will also result in a general but more gradual energising of the magician's customary equipment: garments, especially the robe, will acquire an unmistakeable vibratory link with the wearer, and weapons frequently used will become similarly charged, quite apart from any ritual consecration they may have. The weapons should be wrapped in white or black silk to preserve the charge imparted by initial consecration and subsequent use. If a weapon has been successfully consecrated it cannot entirely lose its sephirothic charge merely by being left unwrapped, but it could lose an indefinite amount of vitality. The additional etheric charge imparted by frequent use would be lost in a relatively short space of time if the weapon were left uncovered between workings.

The great amount of Od which is generated by a group-working builds a very definite atmosphere in the temple, and this is extremely valuable since it acts as a unifying agent which links the brethren on the active and emotional level. This current, which would dissipate rapidly, is maintained at its maximum by virtue of the Circle and the Wards of Power which contain it within the limits of the place of working.

An aspect of the astral light which is essential to all magical work is the course of the Tides. If these are not known and taken into consideration, any attempted working becomes a matter of grave hazard; it may well be described as impossible, since the effect of a ritual can be either

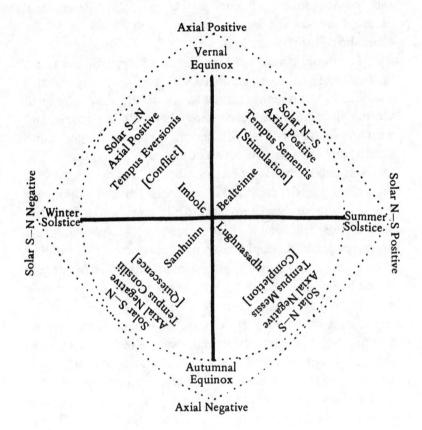

nullified or perilously reversed by performing it during the course of an inharmonious Tide. By knowing the Tides and working with them, however, the magician can powerfully implement each operation. These Tides, although effective also upon the physical plane, flow freely in the Astral Light which is both the environment and the material of the work.

The most powerful of these fluctuations, no matter what type of working is envisaged, are the Seasonal Tides. Four times do these change in the course of the year, at the time of the Solstices and Equinoxes. Thus the Tide which commences at the Vernal Equinox is the Tempus sementis; that which begins to flow at the Summer Solstice is the Tempus messis; the Tide which is brought in by the Autumnal Equinox is the Tempus consilii; and that which comes with the Bruma, or Winter Solstice, is the Tempus eversionis. During the Tempus eversionis let no works of practical magick be undertaken. Yet the personal curriculum* should be continued; and in the midst of that Tide's darkness shineth the Festival of Imbolc, the great celebration of cleansing and renewal.

*SEASONAL TIDES*
(Northern Hemisphere)

The Seasonal Tides result from two influences: the major influence being the effect of the solar particles which bombard earth's odic mantle, and the minor being the stresses set up within the odic mantle by earth's axial inclination.

*Solar influences:*

North-South: Vernal Equinox to Autumnal Equinox
South-North: Autumnal Equinox to Spring Equinox

---

* The personal curriculum would include such things as the Salutations, the Setting of the Wards (always an essential defence) the Clavis Rei Primae, meditation, etc. To be avoided would be sphere-workings, evocations, consecrations, astral travel, scrying, etc., which come under the heading of practical work.

*Influences caused by earth's 23.5° axial inclination:*

NEGATIVE
Polus a Sole declinans: Summer Solstice to Winter Solstice

POSITIVE
Polus ad Solem inclinans: Winter Solstice to Summer Solstice

From the nature of these four Tides it will be perceived that, *broadly speaking*, new works and works of commencement are appropriate to the Tempus sementis, works which should produce results on the material plane to the Tempus messis, and works which should culminate in spiritual result to the Tempus consilii; while the Tempus eversionis should be a time of withdrawal, of meditation and of fortitude. To say, as some do, that the Tempus eversionis is appropriate to works of destruction, is more than the present writers dare recommend; it would be rather like saying that the most appropriate place to set off an explosion is in a powder-magazine. Furthermore, so powerful is this Tide that trends set in motion during its course can be actually revitalised by the onset of the Tempus sementis so as to cause distorted and chaotic effects in the spring.

Apart from the precautions indicated by this fact, however, it will become evident that the significance of all the seasonal tides is continually modified by other astral currents; also vital, for instance, in connection with every working are the Aestus Lunae. The reason for their importance is given in chapter IV.

The Lunar Tides (Aestus Lunae) correspond to the phases of the moon, so that they change four times in the month. The Full Moon is the time of greatest power: the First Quarter is by nature akin to all inception and growth. The early days of the Waning Moon are not necessarily detrimental: there is a general feeling against working under the gibbous moon, but it needs only to be borne in mind that the etheric Moon-power is less than at the full. The last visible stages of the wane, however, tend to be malefic and are under the power of Hecate; while in the dark of the Moon, that is in the time between the disappearance of the Waning Moon and the manifestation of the New Moon, operations of practical magick are to be forgone.

The potency of the Lunar Tides fluctuates also from one season of the year to another. The New Moon is at its most magical in the springtime, while the "Harvest Moon" is notably the most powerful tide of the Full Moon; and not only the most powerful but the most lasting, since it may be observed that the Harvest Moon shows as a perfect disc for three successive nights instead of the customary two.

\*

"Ebb and flow of the tides of the world, silver light which quickens to growth every seed of the earth: when we walk in darkness and our eyes are turned from the light of the Sun, thine be the mirror O Threefold Goddess, which shall reflect his beams upon us!"

\*

The next series of Tides to be taken into account is also of very great importance: the Velocia. These constitute rhythmic fluctuations in the Earth's odic mantle:\* they flow from east to west.

The Velocia are traditionally known by their Sanskrit names and by the symbols which have represented them from of old time; but the fact that this knowledge has stood behind our developing Western tradition is attested

---

\* The Earth's odic mantle is to be conceived of in a double sense: that which is manifest as the aggregate of life-forces of all beings associated with this planet, which may be described as an inner aura, and the vast inorganic (though highly organised) regions of the geomagnetic field, which interpenetrates the other but also forms an outer aura estimated to extend to an average of about 80,000 miles from the Earth's surface, with immense variations due to solar influence. We have limited our observations in the text to those facts traditionally known to be of importance to the magician, and their importance cannot be over-estimated.

to, as we have pointed out elsewhere, by the symbols for
Fire and for Earth in this system. Because the West
has its own nomenclature, we call this series the "swift
ones."

The attributions of the Velocia are:

| Tattvic symbol | Tattva | Element | Elemental symbol |
|---|---|---|---|
| Indigo ovoid | Akasha | Spirit | ⊛ |
| Blue disc | Vayu | Air | △ |
| Red triangle | Tejas or Agni | Fire | △ |
| White crescent | Apas | Water | ▽ |
| Yellow square | Prithivi | Earth | ▽ |

The flow of the Velocia is reckoned from sunrise, and
the cycle is completed in two hours. The first tide in the
series is Akasha, and though each tide is said to rule for a
certain period of time, it must be realised that all these
influences exist together; each Tattva in succession, however,
has predominance over the others. So, reckoning from
sunrise, each tide, in the order Akasha, Vayu, Tejas, Apas,
Prithivi, rules for twenty-four minutes; the pattern then
repeats every two hours throughout the twenty-four. Each
Tattva has also a negative phase, but as this need never be
taken into account for our purposes, it will not be considered
here.

By a simple calculation, therefore, for any working a
harmonious Tattva may be found, according to the
correspondence between the element of that tide and the
sphere of the operation; and this concerns us deeply, for it is
essential to our work that the prevailing astral conditions be
such as will enable us to mould the light successfully into the
desired pattern of vibrations—for much sincere effort can be
wasted by working during the wrong tides—and now by
finding the harmonious tide we have this necessary condition
fulfilled:

Where Nature moulds the dew of light
To feed perfection with the same.

A rite begun in a harmonious Tattvic phase often exceeds the duration of that phase; this is no misfortune, since its commencement in the correct Tattva, with the Setting of the Wards and the appropriate invocations, will effectively provide the working with its own magical current; this, sealed within the circle, should be for the time impervious to the external tides. This may be taken as a general observation on a point which might, if misunderstood, raise endless complications in planning a ritual.

It should be mentioned that each phase of the Velocia is itself influenced by a subsidiary sequence of Akasha, Vayu, Tejas, Apas, Prithivi; however, these subsidiary influences, each lasting for four minutes and forty-eight seconds, cause only minor modifications in the essential quality of the predominant Tattva and do not at all impair its unity. Their significance is sub-elemental.

Research has indicated, however, that the flow of the Velocia is much influenced by geographical and geological peculiarities in various regions: a mountain range or a chasm can produce wild variations in their time-sequence, as also can causes which may not at once be evident, such as the presence of deep mines or of subterranean rivers. Certain localities, again, show disturbances of the force of gravity, this likewise being reflected in the flow of the Velocia: Chambery in France is one such locality, and there are many others. Where any cause of variation is present, the magician must make his own experiments and establish the local pattern, but in most regions the standard observations will be applicable.

The concept of planetary hours was dealt with in Book II. In relation to the aggregate of chosen Tides which are normally employed in the hierarchical workings of contemporary Qabalah, the influences of planetary hours are very minor: they do indeed represent real fluctuations of the Light, but their effect is so masked and influenced by the Velocia, that usually it is not possible to take them into account.* The hours vary tremendously, and it is only when they occur in combination with harmonious tides of the Velocia that they are of use in our work. For example, in a hypothetical instance where the sun rises at 7:02 on a Friday, at a time when the magical hours are sixty minutes in length, some useful combinations between 7:02 A.M. and 2:38 P.M. would be ▽ ☿ 8:14 to 8:38 A.M.; △ ☽ 9:26 to 9:50 A.M.; ▽ ♄ 10:38 to 11:02 A.M.; ✳ ☉ 1:02 to 1:26 P.M., running into △ ☉ 1:26 to 1:50 P.M.

So far we have considered the Tempora, the Aestus, the Velocia and the planetary hours. In contemporary modes of working it is unnecessary to advert always to the planetary hours, as has been pointed out, since the Velocia are so powerful upon the subtle levels; but when the hours are considered relevant, they should be coordinated as above. They may then be considered as intensifying or modifying the effects of the Velocia. The Tempora, the Aestus and the Velocia are vitally important and magical work should always be regulated according to these Tides. The magician must learn to work with and through these natural forces as a matter of course, and though in some circumstances he must of necessity work during adverse Tides, to do so is akin to running up a descending escalator: only real necessity and sure confidence will justify it. In such a case, he who has the skill and circumspection to make the best use of the available resources, may produce a *tour de force* which he might not otherwise have thought possible.

For nearly all operations, the general requisites will

---

* Their use is, however, paramount in the traditional and specialized practices of *planetary magick* properly so-called, a system which does not employ the Velocia.

suffice: the Season, the Lunar Tide, and the Velocia. Evocation to visible appearance, however, can necessitate calculations of a more complex sort. In the case of the evocation of elemental beings, for instance certain Potencies whose names are drawn from the Enochian Tablets, scarce anything more than these requirements need be taken into account:— the Tempus messis is the most suitable Seasonal Tide, as for all works needing an earthly manifestation of result; the Moon should be at the full in order to obtain maximum etheric energy, and the Tattva must correspond to the Element of the operation.

With regard to the evocation of the seventy-two Spirits of the Goetia, or those of the Heavenly Arch, there is no difficulty in finding the correct time: the relevant zodiacal Houses, with their Decans and Quinances, are already indicated, and an ephemeris will enable the exact calculation of these periods; then it is only necessary to find within the days indicated a combination of Lunar Tides and Velocia in harmony with the planetary indications. If, in addition, a suitable planetary hour is found to coincide with such a combination, this would be a strong reason for beginning the work at that time.

When the Moon has passed the full by but a day or so, so that there is little diminution of lunar force but yet it may be somewhat out of balance, one would hesitate to evoke a Spirit of Leo during the Fire Tattva, whereas to evoke a Spirit of Virgo during the Earth Tattva would present no danger.

In choosing a time for the evocation to visible appearance of Planetary Intelligences or Spirits, the Solar-Positive tides are preferable among the Seasonal Tides; that is, the Tempus sementis and the Tempus messis, and of these again the Tempus messis is to be preferred. With regard to the Planet of the working, it is necessary that this should be in the Sign of its exaltation, according to the following list:

| Planet | Exalted in House of |
|--------|---------------------|
| ♄ | ♎ |
| ♃ | ☋ |
| ♂ | ♑ |
| ☉ | ♈ |
| ♀ | ♓ |
| ☿ | ♍ |
| ☽ | ♉ |

Those who possess a knowledge of horary calculations will be able to discover particular aspects favourable or adverse to the working; we give here only the simplest basic guidance on this point. As regards the position of the Sun in the Zodiac, a Spirit of Jupiter can be evoked when the Sun is in Sagittarius, but also when the Sun is in Leo or Libra; a Spirit of Saturn, when the Sun is in Taurus or in Libra; to evoke a Spirit of Saturn with the Sun in Scorpio would be powerful but perilous. Special considerations apart, the indications are that Spirits of Venus should be evoked when the Sun is in Taurus or, failing this, in Libra; Spirits of Mercury when the Sun is in Virgo or, failing this, in Gemini; and Spirits of Mars when the Sun is in Scorpio or, failing this, in Aries. In such cases where there is a choice, the preference for this work falls to a sign of the Earthy Triplicity or at the least, of the Watery Triplicity.

Besides these considerations, a suitable time has to be fixed for the evocation with reference to the Velocia, which, again, must be harmonious to the Planet of the Working. The flow of Akasha is suitable only to spiritual works, tending away from the Earth-sphere; it is therefore unsuited to the type of working we are considering. The planetary harmonies of the other Velocia are as follows: Vayu—the Sun, the Moon; Agni—Mars, Venus; Apas—Jupiter, Mercury; Prithivi—Saturn. Finally, the Moon should be at the full as exactly as possible, maximum etheric power being required for this working, and the Astral Gate set wide; but if this is

impossible, then care being taken to obtain maximum force
in other ways, the Waxing Moon will serve.

Not alone an understanding of these exterior vibrations
is necessary to the initiate; they are but aids, albeit necessary
aids, in his work whose primary instruments are the interior
forces of the psyche. It is by commanding these that the
exterior tides are made his servants and not his masters. To
employ the Tempus eversionis as a time of meditation and
purification, for example, would be impossible to one
engulfed in depression or frustration; likewise the channelling
of the vital forces of the Tempus sementis for the
establishment of new magical works would be beyond one
who was driven by impulse or by custom to dissipate those
forces in instinctual activities. We cannot change the external
tides, nor bid them to linger beyond their season; we can and
should so command our own faculties and workings, that
we can take the help of the Tides when they are propitious to
us, without being hindered by them when they would
obstruct our work. If we begin a Work of Mars in the Tide of
Agni, then for the duration of that flow we are supported by
the Tattva; but when after twenty-four minutes Agni is
replaced by Apas, we neither give up our rite nor change its
nature. We have sealed our circle in Agni and we have fixed
our mind in the mode of Mars, and from these we swerve not
until the rite be concluded.

Thus, and in many ways, by magical working itself do
we develop and mature in the Work; and our progress is
magnified, equilibrated and reflected back to us by our
participation in the life of the Order. This, properly
understood, does not diminish individual responsibility but
enhances it. The Astral Light circulates powerfully, not
merely in the individual psyche but in the group as a
whole; the effective performance of one's part in the ritual
therefore influences the matrix which is created, not merely
for oneself but for all; and to influence the matrix is also,

inevitably, to influence to some extent the operation of the spiritual force invoked into that matrix.

This channelling of forces increases the vitality of the Order as a whole, which again contributes to the life of the magical tradition as a whole. For the life of any valid Magical Order depends upon its Inner-Plane contacts, high Beings who are by one link or another connected with the Order's particular purpose in existing; and further, it is by virtue of these Inner-Plane contacts that the Order participates in the life-current of the Western Tradition, this in turn participating in the World Tradition. Of this high fellowship, the initiate of whatever stature is according to his capacity a member; and we contemplate here not only the incarnate, but those discarnate who share in the Work of the Light.

In looking to this great pattern of interacting life-forces, we perceive a sphere beyond the range of the Astral Tides which we have defined, a sphere governed by its own spiritual Tides. We discern here the meeting-point of the Great Work with the cosmic plan of existence, and we touch upon the reason underlying the central theme of the Order's work. We have seen that even as Yesod is the Gate between the material world and the astral, so is Tiphareth the Gate between the astral and the spiritual; and therefore is the pattern of Life Renewed, which the material Sun symbolises, the pattern of cosmic life as defined for us. Therefore is the Solar Hero the chief cult-figure in the Order, defining at once the Tides of Life, Death, and Life Renewed as the spiritual current of our magical life; and the Sun-hero as him in whose footsteps we should attain to that current. For upon no other plan is the spiritual development of Western Man envisaged: Sol Invictus, Temu Heru-Khuti, entering the darkness and overcoming it, or the Mabon, the reborn Sun-child. For this cause is the Way of the Adept the way of death, entombment and rebirth to the light. For this cause, too, the Alchemical Work is the transmutation of base metal to Gold of the Sun. For the Solar Tides, when contemplated in their mystical rather than their magical aspect, become symbols of the spiritual development of the initiate. Here a general pattern cannot be given to cover all Orders: varying according to the particular cult which is followed and the particular region in which it developed, the hero meets his death in autumn or in the spring, is reborn in spring or at midwinter; in the midsummer is his full power manifest. The essential meaning drawn from the symbolism remains, however, unchanged: the spiritual levels not less than the material have their cycles and sequences, and the life of man, in its very aspiration to supersede the material world, is following a spiritual impulse which is not anti-natural, but is itself a pursuit of that which is most natural to human life. The one thing which would be anti-natural to man would be a static mode of existence with no development whatsoever, for inertia would contravene a necessary condition even of mere existence.

By all the means of development at his disposal, then— Path-workings and Sphere-workings, individual exercises and meditations besides the group rituals of the Order—the initiate has filled his psyche to overflowing with luminous and pulsating tides of life. He has followed with faithful devotion in the service of that Hero who has been placed before him as an external ideal, until in the ripeness of time he has come to share in the way of death of that Hero. With Osiris he is laid alive in the coffin, or with Maître Jacques he is stricken by the treacherous hand, or with Rhodon he is laid low by Black Dragon, or with Dumuzi he is borne down to the deep; and from that entombment, from that darkness he is called forth, to know that that which he has hitherto followed, that which has been his ideal, THAT HE IS, and more than a pseudo-earthly hero is his identity, his reality. Henceforth not merely the hero of his idealism but the deity of his adoration is within; he knows now that within the bounds of his own psyche he must evoke the ΠΡΩΤΟΣ ΚΑΛΟΣ, the Primal Beauty.

He has, in a sense, arrived at the position of Flecker's

Hajji who, having attained Mecca, has now no-wither to turn in prayer. Is he therefore to consider his personal life, with those elements of his psyche which are already known to him, as all-sufficient? In fact this is not the case, since a most important part of his psyche has not yet come into play:

"To a life beyond his life he must awaken"—

—and to a Sun beyond the sun of his everyday life. It is with Adepthood that the true magical life begins, for which all his previous achievement has been but practice and preparation; it is here, therefore, upon arising from the Tomb, that there is laid upon the Adept a sacred obligation to seek until he find that which will most completely distinguish him from even the most enlightened and advanced member of the Outer Order: the Attainment of the Knowledge and Conversation of the Holy Guardian Angel.

This quest is the one necessary work of the Minor Adept, and until he has achieved it the fulness of Adepthood is not his. This attainment is therefore of all magical works the most necessary, and it is one which the Adept must pursue by his own personal effort. The Order, having raised him to Adepthood, gives him the key for this next attainment; this he must employ in what manner and with what fervour his own nature and ingenium prompt him, until success be his. Nor is there any question here of imagined or illusory achievement; for the major result of success is to transfer his conscious awareness and to establish it upon a new basis: an interior revolution which none could, or would wish to, experience so long as ordinary intelligence and common sense held dominion in the psyche. For the new component which here comes to the fore is no longer any manifestation of conscious intellect: it is the Intuitive Mind.

The Intuitive Mind is presented as "not-self," for two

reasons. In the first place, it is no part of the conscious intelligence, and therefore it makes its appearance to the conscious mind as an alien being. Secondly, it is linked to the supernal levels of Mind: the psyche not being sealed within the physical nature of the individual, as many imagine, but extending beyond that nature and in particular reaching upward through the "fine point of the spirit" to contact with the Kether itself, besides of course the other two Supernal Sephiroth. This region of the Mind which is superior to, and outside, the conscious intelligence, we term the Intuitive Mind. It always exists, even in the psyche of persons of the most limited awareness, although in such cases it is naturally quite out of communication with the conscious mind; it can however in grave emergency sometimes communicate, even in those circumstances, through the media of the sympathetic nervous system or the instinctual subconscious. Such promptings are, in fact, what in popular language is called "intuition," although the true function of the Intuitive Mind which is our subject is a far other and grander thing. To define this, we must briefly consider the modes of knowledge.

Something may be known by instinct. This faculty is extremely limited in scope, particularly among civilised human beings. It does not comprehend general facts. A hungry man may instinctively find food and a thirsty man may instinctively take a downhill road in order to find water, but as soon as he infers "food satisfies hunger" or "water flows downhill," the matter is removed from the instinctual to the rational level.

The rational level of knowledge needs little description here. It comprises inferences from perceived facts, such as those just stated; abstract reasonings; and statements committed to memory. The vast bulk of human knowledge lies within this area.

Above this there is another mode of knowledge, of

which the conscious mind of incarnate man is not directly capable: it is the immediate perception of spiritual truth, without the process of abstraction or deduction from phenomena. This method of knowledge is limited to spiritual beings, of angelic nature or higher; and there is a region of the human psyche to which this is proper, because the human psyche, in its conscious and unconscious faculties, extends upwards and downwards through all levels of non-material being, touching both upon the divine and the demonic. (If this were not so, all religious and philosophic experience would be meaningless.) The region of the human psyche which is capable of intuiting truth directly, is therefore the Intuitive Mind. It follows from this, among other conclusions, that the Intuitive Mind clearly knows the True Will of the individual in question, even while his conscious mind may be completely deluded on that subject.

It is this Intuitive Mind which is brought into communication with the consciousness of the Adept, the time of searching being accomplished, under the title of the Holy Guardian Angel. It is Holy, being utterly apart from the mundane personality; Guardian, knowing the True Will and real abilities of the Adept, his feelings and weaknesses and all that could bring him to harm; and Angel, being purely the faculty of intuition which is by definition angelical. Nor is the Adept in any way likely to identify this Being with any part of himself; he would deny it, seeing that the Angel knows what he knows not, and often even wills what he (as he believes) wills not. Furthermore, the Adept will have encountered this Being in the Sphere of Tiphareth; and therefore to him it is an Angel of that Sphere, most greatly to be loved and revered for beauty and for wisdom. From this time forth, his magick is the work of his Angel and himself together.

Nevertheless, as he progresses further, more will become clear to him as to the exaltation of his Angel. Here begins that play of masks and shadows, of radiance and desolation, which belongs to the realm of mysticism rather than of magick. We shall not here sound it further. Plato has said that whoever loves faithfully shall at last, albeit after many lifetimes, attain the Beloved. What he has not said, and what in the many lifetimes one learns, is how shall be changed and lifted, how shall be veiled and shall reappear, ever higher and ever more luminous, the discerned identity of the Beloved!

## APPENDICES

*APPENDIX A: CONCERNING CERTAIN WOMEN.* A young Turkish Cypriot tells in circumstantial detail an adventure of his uncle, which duplicates a medieval French legend and a Celtic myth of the Triple Goddess (see Chapter VII). He proceeds to another tale, which produces a new tradition by confusing the Virgin Mary with Aphrodite in a manner well known to mythographers. But where had Ali, or his uncle, come by the previous story? Or had the uncle really seen the spectral woman by the stream?

*APPENDIX B: THE DARK NIGHT OF THE SOUL.* The ways of High Magick and of mysticism cannot completely be separated, even in the early stages, and it behoves the magical student to understand something about the Dark Night of the Soul. In its fullness, this is the experience of Binah: one of its minor reflections, therefore, is the despondency which may assail the beginner upon the Thirty-second Path. This paper offers counsel on both the sephirothic and the planetary influences involved.

*APPENDIX C: PATH-WORKING.* Some of the principles of Path-Working as conducted in the A.S. are given, with a brief account of the advanced *Leaping Formulation.* The complete text of the A.S. Working of the 31st Path follows.

219

*APPENDIX D: SUFFUMIGATIONS*. The great majority of traditional incense materials are of vegetable origin, and may be classified as gums, oils or woods. A review of historical, botanical and other lore connected with the incense materials listed, reveals a number of interesting problems in interpreting ancient recipes. A modern Celtic recipe is given, with notes on compounding, storing, choosing and burning aromatics.

*APPENDIX E: THE SWORD*. Presentation of a Qabalistic meditation. The great Qabalistic image of the descending Sword is, by a further tradition, linked with an inspiring passage in Psalm 18. This passage is here shown as relating, verse by verse, to the phases of the Sword's descent: a descent which the Psalmist, and the meditative reader, follow throughout its course, being taken up at the end to begin the Way of Return.

## APPENDIX A
### CONCERNING CERTAIN WOMEN

Ali and I were sitting outside a little cafe near Larnaca. From under the inadequate awning, we looked out over a level of rough sun-browned grass, broken here and there by saltpans over whose fierce crystalline whiteness the air quivered. As a mark of friendship, Ali had been showing me round the sights of the place; that is to say, he had conducted me all the way round the tomb of Mohammed's aunt in its modest domed shrine. The guardian of the tomb had promptly flung over my already-kerchiefed head a large, greenish and distinctly dusty veil, and had watched us with some apprehension; but my escort had worthily upheld the dignity of his thirteen years, and had further edified me by explaining that the massive sphere of stone above the tomb had originally hung miraculously in the air, but that this had so disturbed visitors that a support had now been built under it. That marvel was not, as a matter of fact, a total novelty to me. In another part of Cyprus I had happened upon a relic of the True Cross with a similar reputation, and, whichever side had started the story, it was obvious that neither Moslem nor Christian would willingly be outdone. All the same, despite this somewhat formal beginning, a curious kinship of spirit had developed between Ali and myself. During lunch we had talked of Famagusta, whither I was bound; he did not know that city, and I told him in brief the story of Othello. Somehow, beneath every difference of age and sex, nation

221

and creed, each of us had divined in the other the essential
Collector of Tales.

We now exchanged a few remarks on the extreme
contrast between this flat coastal plain and the inland hills,
when Ali, evidently meditating further confidences, took a
gulp of his orange-squash, hesitated, decided, and launched
into this narrative:

*"An uncle of mine, who lives in a village in the hills,
once had a very strange experience. It happened like this. A
friend of his was getting married in another village, and my
uncle wanted to go to the wedding, but there was no bus
that day. He would not wait until the next day, so he set
out early and walked. He has always walked a great deal, my
uncle, and he knew the way, so although it was a long
distance it did not worry him. The hills around his village are
very bare and rocky, but he thought if he started before
sunrise he could reach his friend's village before the day
became too hot. All the same, as he tramped along, he began
to be troubled by the idea that he did not know where he
was. The path was strange to him, the hills were strange to
him; he was quite lost, and wandered this way and that. He
was not afraid, but he was completely bewildered, and it
was getting late.*

*"Suddenly he came to a stream, gushing down among
the rocks. It was such beautiful cool water, my uncle would
have stopped to drink, but just then he saw a woman
kneeling at the side of the stream, washing some clothes. He
would have hurried away, for fear he might stay too long if
they began talking, but he saw she was watching him, so he
stopped, and then he thought he should go, and then he
looked at her again and she was still watching him. So he
went back and asked her, 'What do they call this place?' But
still she said nothing; she just went on smiling and looking
at him. He sat down on the ground near her, and asked, 'Who
are you?' Still she said nothing, but she put her hand in the*

*stream and then held it out to him with her palm full of water. It was in my uncle's mind that he would drink, and then he would kiss her; but just as he leaned towards her, he saw a large rock that he knew, and he knew at once where he was, and there never had been any water in that place. So he leapt up and ran down the hill; then he turned and looked back, and there was no stream and no woman."*

Ali paused, relishing my utter astonishment without knowing the reason for it. In fact, my mind was awhirl. *Les lavandières de la nuit!* What were they, or even the rumour of them, doing in a Turkish village in Cyprus? "This happened to *your uncle?*" I asked.

Ali met my eyes quite unabashed. "Yes. He told me himself. He did not make it up. My uncle does not make up stories; he can never think what to say."

"No, he did not make it up," I echoed with genuine conviction. Wherever the story had come from, Ali's uncle had not invented it; it was centuries old. The Ballad of Clerk Colville! La Belle Dame sans Merci! It so happened that a part of my business in Cyprus was to seek for traces of the medieval French community founded by the Crusaders. Apart from the documentary evidence and some buildings, to the general observer and even to the historian they seemed to have vanished without a sign of having existed. I had gleaned a few fragile wisps of evidence on the subject, but this story of Ali's was the most tantalizing so far and yet the most useless of them all. What in fact had happened? Had the uncle actually had this wierd experience in the hills—and it sounded very real—or was it a particularly vivid pipe-dream based on a story he had heard? The latter looked more probable, but where could he have heard it? Frank, Greek, Venetian, Turk: what likelihood was there of the slightest continuity between the first link and the last in that chain? There all the time, of course, was the Greek community; but this tale was not of their sort. I asked Ali

if he had ever heard of any similar incident, either as fact or
as fiction. He had not. I asked him if his uncle read a great
deal. Even the question itself hardly seemed realistic. As a
last resort, I asked him if there were any other people besides
Turks in the uncle's village. I knew beforehand that the
answer would be in the negative.

"But there is a church," added Ali helpfully. "There is
a church near the village, but nobody goes there. It is quite
old, and a bit broken. I have been inside it to look at it."

A church ... It might be one of the little Cypriot
painted churches, decorated inside and out with murals of
scriptural and traditional figures. It might be a white shallow-
domed Byzantine structure. It might ... I decided to snatch
at the moon: I took a piece of paper and rapidly sketched a
typical Burgundian church of the Middle Ages, sturdy and
barrel-vaulted. It was Ali's turn to be completely astonished.
He was, indeed, horrified. "You have been there! You know
my uncle's village; you know that church!" I tried to reassure
him. I had only made the sketch to ask him *if* the church
looked like that. So, then, it did. "Well, now we go inside. Is
this right?" I made another drawing: nave, triforium,
clerestory. He stared again. "I think you are reading my
thoughts," he said. Again I had to convince him that I was
doing no such thing; I had simply wanted to know if the
church was of a particular kind. After thinking it over, he
asked, "Is that church anything to do with the woman that
my uncle saw in the hills?"

"Yes, and no," I told him. "All I can say is, this church
was built by men who knew about that woman. I don't know
more than that. If you remember it, you may find out more
when you are older."

He reflected for a few minutes, but when he spoke again
it was on another matter. "You know so many things," he
said; "I wonder if perhaps you can tell me about another
woman? Her name is Miriam. There are many stories about
her."

I suddenly realised which particular woman named Miriam he meant. "Many stories," I agreed.

"They say she came to Cyprus," he went on. "Have you heard that? They say she walked up out of the sea . . ."

*This is a true account of my conversation with a young Turkish Cypriot. —M.D.*


**Postscript**

As mentioned on p. 167, the woman by the stream is sometimes threefold. In one such tale, if a warrior asks the "launderesses" what they are washing, they show him his own slain body. On further exploration I find this version, at least, must at some time have had a parallel in Islamic folklore: for it has been preserved in Sufi psychology, in the image of "the three washers of the dead" associated with three degrees of mystical perfection. But this does not explain away the ballad-like literalness of Ali's narrative. —M.D.

## APPENDIX B
## THE DARK NIGHT OF THE SOUL

Almost everyone has an occasional bout of depression, from whatever emotional or physical cause. When one reads books which deal with certain forms of spiritual or mystical development, however, one sometimes finds the phrase, "The Dark Night of the Soul." It is not advisable to make free with this phrase, but its meaning needs to be understood.

It first came into general use from the writings of St. John of the Cross, a Spanish Carmelite Friar of the XVI century. The deep psychological understanding which enabled him to analyse his personal experience, drew considerably upon the Moslem Arab mystics of his country, they in turn being thoroughly versed in the Greek, Hebrew and Persian explorations of inner experience. For they were all, including John himself, treating of some of the highest discernable levels of human consciousness, wherein a writer may still use the vocabulary of this or that school of thought, but the ideas expressed will transcend all boundaries. The Carmelite made in particular a detailed study of the experience of utter desolation which overwhelms the soul on entering those heights, and he called it the Dark Night. A few others have written of it from personal knowledge, but it is not an everyday experience, and the ability to write of it is even more rare;* for the Dark Night has its ecstatic as well as

---

* *Liber Liberi vel Lapidis Lazuli* of the Master Therion is here commended to the advanced student. Republished in Aleister Crowley's *The Holy Books* (Dallas: Sangreal Foundation, 1969).

227

its sorrowful aspect, and in coming to utterance the ecstatic veils the other. Nevertheless, it contains the desolation of utter loneliness and the vast bitterness of the ocean, for it is the experience of Binah. Foreshadowings there are, but the veritable Dark Night does not come in its fullness below the Abyss. It is the passion of the moth for the flame, for that supreme flame which is the Divine Spark and which in its true nature is veiled somewhat even from the Adept; but once beheld, directly yet still as Not-Self, that Spark is a totally desired absorption until the balance swings over. Hence, when anything of this experience finds words, they can but be words of love; but always there is the awareness of transcendence: the desolation and the ecstasy alike are in the supernal sphere.

One sees, therefore, the pitiful absurdity of those who know about these things without understanding them, and who openly refer their every moment of gloom to the Dark Night of the Soul. Nevertheless, like other such exaggerations, it has its element of truth: the Sphere of Binah has many reflections and minor manifestations which one may from time to time encounter upon the Way of Return, and not the least of these darkens the Thirty-second Path. The despondency and inertia which can sometimes assail even the beginner are therefore not groundless. Although depression requires firm handling, it is better to regard it with understanding also, whether the sufferer be oneself or another. This is one of the reasons why a clear distinction between other causes of depression and a possible early manifestation of the Dark Night is necessary. It is true that even ordinary forms of depression cannot usually be thrown off at a moment's notice, but we know that the cause of the trouble will easily pass: the Tides will change, or some physical malaise will disappear; perhaps, as often happens, a good night's sleep will change the viewpoint; and as soon as the victim knows assuredly that his affliction will evanish, its power over him is already broken. Similarly with the Paths: if the student who has felt himself to be oppressed by the influence of Saturn will recognise the cause for what it is, he will not imagine anything to be obscurely or permanently wrong with himself, and will find it easier to take courage and resume his work. There are moments of difficulty; there are techniques to be mastered which may need time and patience, and it is not always possible to gauge for oneself whether one is making progress; but these things need not cause depression if work and interest are maintained.

Some authors are to be criticised, who venture to write of the Dark Night and who attribute it simply to depression caused by the mystic's aversion to the conditions of material life, on his return to it after experience of inward vision. In the first place, the cause of the Dark Night is far more spiritual than that. For those who undergo it, the material world might for the time being not exist. Besides this, the sufferings of that high state, no less than its joy, characterise the period of elevation itself and not any period of latency: as, indeed, the name of the Dark Night should indicate since it distinguishes the state of desolation and the abstraction from ordinary consciousness, under the one title. It is clear, therefore, that the origin of the Dark Night is not to be sought in the material world. If these mystics could be instantly released from material life, it is not to be supposed that this would lessen the anguish of the psyche if they still could not at the same time become one with that Divinity which overpowers them and yet does not destroy. There is no reason, therefore, for the fastidious and the slothful to feel that their aversion to the world lends them any spiritual distinction; nor should the student of the Mysteries be misled into thinking he should emulate them. For most inhabitants of the material world, its phenomena are the means wh reby they should advance towards their goal; and that is a main concept of Magick itself. Courage and resolution, therefore, are the requisite qualities needed in pursuit of the Work; and these will still have their place when ultimately, after whatever labours, we come to the sublime ordeal of the true Dark Night.

## APPENDIX C
## PATH-WORKING

The following notes, which expand some ideas concerning Path-working and the further technique known as "the Leaping Formulation," are written entirely from the viewpoint of the Aurum Solis, and the method of Path-working presented here is based on a pattern that has been established in the Aurum Solis over a period of seventy-five years.

### Path-Working

For A∴ S∴ Path-working, the Bomos is always dressed in black and a single lamp is placed thereon. Incense, appropriate to the sphere at the head of the Path being worked, is burned during the later stages of the meditation: no incense is used in the early stages.

The starting-point may be a landscape or it may be a temple; in either case this is representative of the point of departure. Path-working is an entirely subjective operation: it is a "pilgrimage into the depths of mind." The temple or landscape is not designed to be a receptacle of objective forces, but serves the valuable purpose of establishing a recognisable locus to which, if necessary, the consciousness can return. In the A∴ S∴, Path-working as such is never used as a preliminary to ritual working, and the temple-forms which are used are symbolic representations only, not reflections of the physical temple. A temple-form used at

231

the opening of a Path-working is usually of very simple design, containing only the minimum of symbolism which will establish it as representative of its sphere; the "Palace" at the head of the Path, however, is usually quite elaborate, but again, is not intended to be anything more than a symbolic image.

The Working of the Thirty-second Path, as an example, may begin with a temple representative of Malkuth, or a suitably earthy landscape (see Appendix A, Volume I): the Path is then travelled, the essential quality of the Path finally blending into the symbolism of the sphere being approached. If the working is not a success, the aspirants do not enter the new sphere but are guided back to their starting-point, thus avoiding the danger of leaving unassimilated images in the mind. If the working is successful, return to the starting-point will be unnecessary, for the images become truly a part of the experience and will be assimilated without difficulty; the new "Palace" is now entered and the meditation is concluded therein.

*The Leaping Formulation*

This is based upon the principles of Path-working but is an advanced technique for the "composition of place," intended to precede ritual working. It is a high-frequency tuning-in device needing great skill on the part of the operators. Inexperienced brethren are not called upon to participate in this, neither is their presence desirable.

The Leaping Formulation invariably begins from a landscape. The group-mind of the operators moves swiftly and smoothly through the Path-symbolism into the stage of building the Astral Temple when the Sephirah at the head of the Path is attained. The temple thus built is not the symbolic representation used for Path-working, but the Astral Temple proper, which is the receptacle of the influences of the rite. It is the counterpart of the physical temple.* The ritual work now begins.

The Leaping Formulation is sometimes used for the Second Hall Initiation when the *leap* is by the 32nd Path, and for the Third Hall Initiation when it is by the 25th. Because all the Sephiroth except Yesod are approached by more than one Path, a *leap* inevitably gives a particular bias to the work, and the use of this technique is the exception rather than the rule.

### THE WORKING OF THE THIRTY-FIRST PATH
(Complete text of O.S.V. 2nd Hall Document)

*Participants are to be seated in the God-form Posture. Rhythmic Breath is to be maintained throughout.*

We stand in the warm light of a summer day, beneath a sky of intense blue. No living thing can be seen save the thorn-bushes which grow amid the harsh rocks. This is no friendly region, here is neither shade of tree nor sound of grazing herd; yet in this place, in its austerity, we may the better find that which today we seek.

Some little distance ahead of us there stands a solitary arch, built of flints by men in some past age. The keystone of the arch is of pale granite, sparkling with a myriad points of transient white fire; and carved deeply into this keystone is an emblem, the curling horns of a ram.

Why has this single arch been thus left in a wilderness of rocks and thorns? What means this mysterious emblem upon the keystone? We go forward and pass through the arch, feeling for a moment its shadow upon us.

Now we have come into an even more desolate region, a bare stony expanse; and from what cause we cannot say, the sky above us is darkened.

As we look about us, a plume of smoke arises from a fissure in the ground, to be swiftly followed by a leaping

---

* The physical temple is of course arranged, at the outset, according to the symbolism of the sphere of operation.

flame. Immediately, to the other side, a second flame leaps up; then several in rapid succession burst forth some distance before us. These flames grow to a great height, filling the sky: free and immense are they, the unshorn tresses of Fire. We look to the way by which we have come: but no retreat is possible, for flames have sprung up in that direction also.

New flames now arise, and struggle to ascend; but it seems there is not air enough to support them, and with a great sound like the beating of wings the lesser flames writhe and vanish. The tall flames also seem to strive together: they bend and entwine, they divide into tongues which blaze with yellow light, they spring up again in renewed strength and unity. Continually they roar and hiss and crackle, and seem to drum upon the air. We are caught in the midst of this fury of fire; we feel its scorching breath and are oppressed by the lack of air, but no way of escape is evident.

Now the flames commence a new movement: they bend sidelong, with a tumult of sound as if they shouted and shrieked their protest against the sudden wind that lashes them. Even above this we hear the menacing voice of storm, the majestic command of the thunder. Now the fire of the heavens replies to the fire of earth: lightning quivers and dances above the leaping flames.

The air detonates; the flames are dimmed by a brilliance which seems to tear the skies; a shaft of lightning descends directly before us, throwing the fire itself momentarily into a disregarded blackness. Even in that moment, we are aware of a change in the atmosphere about us: as the lightning fades, we see that we are indeed in the presence of one whose very gaze separates us at once from the seared and exhausted air of the material region. He is tall, of dominating appearance, with glowing countenance and with bright discerning eyes. His head is crowned with large curling ram's-horns, ivory-white and adorned with bands of steel; he wears a robe of brilliant white girdled with red gold. His aspect expresses limitless energy.

With a commanding gesture he bids us to follow him, and when he ascends swiftly into the air we find it easy to do likewise. We know that we are being taken from the domain of earthly fire, not merely to save us from it, but so that we may be shown something of its cosmic meaning.

We rise into a region which seems to be filled with cool, pure air, for we are at once refreshed; but in fact these are no longer the material elements which we experience, for led by our guide we have crossed the boundary from the material world to the astral: with the perception of the astral world we now behold that which occurs behind the veil of material phenomena. Now there flows around and before us a stream of bright scarlet light, intermingled with shimmering flashes of other hues, red-orange, blood-crimson, golden-green, sky-blue, which appear briefly, to be reabsorbed or to pass to other modes of being.

As we watch this vision of living light which swirls and undulates ceaselessly, we become aware of fleeting and phantasmal forms, flashing likewise within that tide of supramundane Flame. Shapes of tall trees shimmer awhile in the changeful vision, trees vast of trunk or strangely plumed of leafage; animal forms appear too, semblances of armoured fish, fanged and flightless birds, dragon-like reptiles. Here appears a noble stag with slender limbs and towering antlers, challenging and dominant until a wave of the flashing stream brightens and swirls, and the shape vanishes; there is the supple shape of a lion which crouches as if to stalk its prey, seemingly invincible, a marvel of lithe muscle armed with steely claws and with elongated canine teeth like downward-stabbing tusks. Again the current shifts and flashes, and the lion disappears. Human forms, too, are seen, massive or refined of limb and feature: some bear the aspect of the warrior, some of the thinker, some of the craftsman; women too, maternal, amazonian or meretricious. All appear but briefly, to be swiftly engulfed in the tide of astral fire.

We are saddened with an irresistible melancholy by this

showing of the transitory nature of all life-forms!—nothing flourishes for ever, nothing endures!—but then, in other parts of the current, we behold new and different forms emerging, in like measure as the old disappeared. We see new animal forms, but fewer; new human forms, and more numerous. We see the new briefly prospering in their particular modes, until they in their turn are consumed by the stream: but now, instead of being merely saddened, we watch to see where they shall reappear and in what changed aspects. Furthermore, among these many fleeting forms we glimpse some few which are strangely familiar to us, whose life-experience we seem to have known from within. For each one of us the tale of this succession of lives will be different, but slowly its pattern will become clear to us: we also who watch this changing tide of shining flame which is the current of natural life, we also are part of it; we likewise shall pass and be reabsorbed; yet elsewhere, changed but not destroyed, we shall reappear to continue our course. There is strength in this knowledge—strength, and the will to endure.*

Led by our stately and indomitable guide, we move forward through the scintillating current which surrounds us. The astral fire still swirls and darts forth from time to time its long pulsing flashes of radiance, and as we become more closely united to its subtle nature we detect in it not only movement and colour, but also sound: scarcely perceptible but wholly harmonious chords, answering to the coruscations of the light, impinge upon our consciousness. Those vibrations which at first only manifested to us as colour, now make themselves known as sound also; but whereas the colours had appeared to be sometimes discordant in their brightness, yet now that the vibrations manifest in some measure as sound, our spiritual

---

* This Path, the 31st, inculcates the Stoic philosophy as exemplified by Heraclitus, and is intellectual in conclusion; the "opposite" Path, the 29th, inculcates the philosophy of Epicurus. Both express truth; neither can contain the whole truth; each is in any case below Tiphareth.

perception begins to grasp their essential harmony, the intellectual significance beyond the simply astral.

The musical quality of the rhythm increases. It does not at first give the impression of an actual melody, so much as of a series of harmonies, drifting cadences, broken lilting snatches, brought into unity by a grand and sonorous descant; then an undertone of melody becomes distinguishable and gradually develops, swelling into an austere and measured chorus of sound which answers, meets, interweaves with the descant, then fitfully sinks to a near-silence while huge chords take its place. Then the sublime melody is resumed.

This music is not altogether that of the human voice, nor of any recognisable instrument; for it is the direct effect of that which every voice and instrument attempts, that is, a simultaneous stress wrought in the atmosphere and in the sphere of mind: here we have the audible rush and leap and pulsating radiance of the essential nature of fire, that fire which visibly still courses around us. But not yet have we come to the heart of it.

Fire shining and quivering, fire flashing with life and running its course through the universe! Vital, ever-changing fire: coruscating, singing, triumphant fire!

We have risen above the surface of the flowing astral fire, and the choiring flame-voices sound ever more clearly and jubilantly; we are ascending into the realm of spiritual fire, which the astral but mirrors. This is ecstasy, stark and yet glorious. This is the life of fire, assimilating all things to itself yet totally denuded, even of material form. Thus live the Gods! Are we then as they, we who are thus uplifted? We look to our guide. He, who has proceeded ahead of us, shines altogether as a flame of whiteness; we behold neither the ram's horns with which he is crowned, nor the bright robe which envelops him. Higher yet we rise: that which seems like air around us is filled with bright and rippling sparkles, and holds an intensely dry heat. We become aware of a throng of beings therein, a throng scarcely perceptible even to our new consciousness, beings of a nature more entirely spiritual than we have previously encountered. The united gaze of great brilliant eyes is fixed silently upon us as we pass through their ranks. We are to be in some unknown manner put to the test, proved by the fire.

We ascend still higher. Hotter and brighter, more scintillating is the atmosphere in which we move. A sensation like thirst assails us, but it is not a thirst for water: it is a craving for shade, for the least vestige of shadow to which to direct our movement. There is none. We are encompassed by a world composed entirely of sparkling radiance; if we advance further we must also go further into it. There is no other possibility. And still the eyes await the outcome.

That which must be endured, let it be accepted with a good will; for we cannot avoid the pain, but by reluctance we might fail to assimilate the potential of the experience.

A ripple of heat, like a breath from a furnace, flashes scarlet and silver as it runs onward across and through us without hindrance; then another and another wave of fire follows it. We feel strangely lightened, emotionless and liberated from fear by the touch of this spiritual flame, even though its fiery nature oppresses all our powers of sensation and leaves us arid, unutterably void of every opposite quality. The intellectual vision, however, is intensified. We comprehend why this purgation of every emotion is at this time needful, since we are to behold something of the eternal ordering of things, and emotion is in its very essence turbulent and chaotic. We are upon the verge of many perceptions; and still we are surveyed by the high pure eyes of the winged watchers. A burst of sheet-lightning expands around the luminous form of our guide who still goes star-like before us. He turns: in the fading of the flash we see his arms raised in benediction and farewell; then he is gone from us.

Another wave of fire meets us: this time, of blazing whiteness sparkling into flame-orange. We are absorbed into it, we are transformed to very flame; we feel and behold only that intense radiance until we reach the essential heart of it—

Blackness: icy, intense cold and blackness.

It strikes and benumbs.

There is nothing, nothing even to endure. We wait passively, until at last, released from the ice-heart of the flame, we find a dewy mist drawn down upon us. We move forward upon our path, but we now behold only shadowy shapes veiled by the moist and gentle vapour. The mist thickens to actual drops: we are walking through falling water, through water that swirls about our feet. Now before us a waterfall crashes and cascades in the dim uncertain light. We pass through the force of the torrent to find ourselves standing on the rocky floor of a large cavern.* A faint luminescence filters through the waterfall behind us; the smooth stone of the cavern walls is variegated, translucent white and orange with veinings of black. We proceed into the depths of the cave: as we go, the sound of the waterfall which at first is loud in our ears, gradually recedes until we hear it only as a faint murmur.

As we reach the end of the cavern, where a shaft of light shines from above, we see worn steps ascending, cut into the living rock. We climb the steps; eight are they in number, and when we have reached the topmost we find ourselves on the threshold of a sacred place: we are about to enter a temple which now opens before us.

As we enter and walk across the expanse of the black lustrous floor, our eyes are drawn to the far end of the chamber. We pass between the two pillars, Machetes and Nomothetes, into the very centre of this temple whose walls are of translucent stone, of the appearance of carnelian.

---

* Here incense is placed on the coals.

Before us is that which first drew our gaze: a great curtain, silvery and iridescent, with the gentle play of unnumbered colors upon its surface. It moves and shimmers, magnifying every least stirring, and seeming almost alive in its ceaseless quivering. Upon it is depicted the Caduceus, the staff of Hermes entwined with the twin Serpents, the White and the Black. Before the curtain stands the Bomos, draped in glowing flame-orange, and upon it a smoking censer and the mystical Tessera.* To the south of the Bomos is the Banner of the New Life;† above us, suspended from the high ceiling, burns a single lamp, symbol of the Eternal Flame. We salute the East.

Stillness pervades the temple, with a sense of calm expectancy. We have come through ascending flame and through falling water, and we have arrived at this quietness. We comprehend that where all is ordered in just measure, there is balance and stillness; nor is this the stillness of an inert mass, but rather it is a vibrant and living quality, the equipoise of force against force. As a man stands upright, he appears to be balanced without effort; yet the interplay of tendon and muscle is continuous to maintain him thus. So does the Caduceus, which is in one sense an image of Man, show us Serpent entwined with Serpent, pinion balancing pinion, and symmetry ruling all. Thus in the realm of Mind are opposites to be balanced, for in their balance do the multiplicity of qualities compose a true unity, even as the man with all his diversity of corporeal parts and qualities of mind and of spirit, is yet one individual. Again: not only the final totality is one, but the initial totality is one. In the material world all things are intricately wrought of one fundamental Energy; likewise the astral stream of life-forces

* See Book V.

† White Octogram enclosing yellow Octagon with red Equal-armed Cross in centre, all on black field.

continues through phases of change and of becoming, while upon the spiritual level all has come from one unity and shall return thither. Knowing this, we can regard no extreme as ultimate, for all shall be balanced and counterpoised in the totality. This also do we acknowledge in the sign of the Caduceus: for these truths are of the dominion of Reason, which is of Mercury.

*A battery of 3-5-3 is given by the director to signify the conclusion of the working, and to re-centre the consciousness of the participants on the objective level.*

## APPENDIX D
## SUFFUMIGATIONS

♄   Myrrh, Asafoetida, Violet Leaves, Jet,
    Guaiacwood (Lignum Vitae), Oil of Violet, Poppy.

♃   Nutmeg, Cedarwood and its Oil, Pine-gum,
    Olive Oil, Juniper.

♂   Opoponax, Aloes-wood, Tobacco, Oil of Nicotiana,
    Dragon's-blood.

☉   Cinnamon, Vanilla, Laurel,
    Heliotropin, Olibanum.

♀   Red Storax, Benzoin, Amber, Roses, Verbena,
    Saffron, Red Sandalwood, Coral, Ambergris.

☿   Mastic, Lavender, Fennel, Yellow Sandalwood,
    Aniseed and the Oils of all these.
    Styrax (Liquid Storax), Spikenard ( ☿/Psychopompos).

☽   Camphor, Galbanum, Almond, Hazel, all Lilies,
    Bay, Jasmine, Aromatic seeds.

⊗   Dittany of Crete, all Fruit-woods.

The short list of aromatics given above, provides a working
guide to incense materials under their planetary attributions.
Some few of these materials are partly or wholly of non-
vegetable origin: ambergris is of animal origin, coral may be
variously described as animal or mineral, while jet and amber

243

244 THE SWORD AND THE SERPENT

can be considered as minerals of vegetable origin. However, the great majority of all incense materials are of the vegetable kingdom, and appear in our list as gums, oils or woods. A few are simply dried leaves or other parts of green plants, such as seeds or roots; but in fact not many herbs are suitable to be used in incense, however sweetly they may smell when fresh or dried, for when burned they tend to a uniform odour of scorched hay.

The true incense gums have a long history, although this is not always easy to decipher. In Genesis 43:11, listed among the materials which the brethren of Joseph took into Egypt to trade for wheat, we find mentioned storax and stacte, as well as terebinth trees whose wood is full of a fragrant oil. We cannot take for granted that these materials were intended for use as incense. The name of storax is employed for two gums, one of which is otherwise known as stacte; therefore, since stacte is also named here, we can suppose that the storax in question is the other kind of storax, which is better called by its Greek name of styrax to avoid the confusion. Styrax is a greyish syrupy liquid, a balsam in fact, obtained from the tree or shrub *Liquidambar orientalis*. It grows in various parts of Asia Minor but not in Egypt, and the ancient Egyptians valued it as an ingredient in perfumes and sometimes for use in mummification. It has been found by analysis in the embalming materials and perfume-jars from Egyptian tombs. In our list it is attributed to Mercury, having, along with the exceedingly rare and precious spikenard, a special reference to Hermes Psycho-pompos. The arts of the physician, the perfumer, the incense-blender and the embalmer were closely related in early times, for the same aromatics were used by each. A few drops of tincture of benzoin on a lump of sugar provided a homely remedy for a cough into the early years of this century, usually without any known reference to its attribution to Mercury, ruler of Taurus, the zodiacal sign which corresponds to the throat in the human body. Again, through the ages the antiseptic and healing properties of powdered myrrh made it renowned as a dressing for wounds, which only went out of fashion in the nineteenth century when the use of the sword began to wane. The attribution of myrrh is to Saturn, both its name and its bitterness associating it with the Mother-Ocean; but also in this curative association we see the restrictive influence of Saturn turned to good purpose in stanching the flow of blood.

The violet plant, represented in our list both by the leaves and by the aromatic oil, is representative of Binah not only for its night-darkness but also for the concealment of the fragrant blossoms. Of the poppy and its high symbolism we have treated elsewhere. Another material attributed to Saturn, however, is the malodorous asafoetida, which in the Middle Ages had a great reputation for banishing demons; but when fresh it is unfortunately liable to banish anyone else who comes within range of it. It is one of the torments with which, in the Grimoires, recalcitrant spirits are frequently threatened.

The list given for Jupiter is relatively simple, depending as it does upon the various trees associated with the Father-God in the lands from Lebanon to the North. Oak-wood is not to be recommended as an incense ingredient because of its acrid smoke; but the fine qualities of cedarwood and of its oil are extremely suitable for this purpose. Cedarwood is, besides, a traditional emblem of immortality and of incorruptibility. Nutmeg is in some old documents referred to as nut-mace, and this illustrates the confusion which has so frequently existed between different aromatics. Olive oil is included in our list because it has a pleasant and distinctive fragrance; the olive tree has Jupiterian associations because it is an emblem of peace, and because of its dedication to Pallas Athene. In Eastern Mediterranean lands, olive leaves are sometimes burned in a small bowl by the peasants, as a sweet suffumigation to welcome guests. To pine-gum we shall refer again presently; it is one of the few incense materials which can be gathered in northern regions, and is accordingly prized by us.

Of the incenses of Mars, the resin known as dragon's blood is remarkable for its deep red colour as well as for the pungent, spicy odour which it emits while burning. It is strongly Martian in character and is frequently burned without any admixture in appropriate rites. Opoponax, a finer and scarcer gum, has similar qualities with a higher dignity and solemnity of character. It may be startling to find tobacco and the fragrant oil of nicotiana (which comes from a different plant) in a list of incenses, but they have the necessary qualification: a fragrance which is released by burning. Tobacco does not, seemingly, represent the more aggressive aspects of Mars, but rather its more genial and fraternal associations; nevertheless the subtle irritant which it contains should not be forgotten.

Highly interesting in this section of the list is the aromatic substance named as aloes-wood. Here a confusion of names such as has already been mentioned, offers us a convenient solution to a practical difficulty. One of the finest incenses of the ancient world, bitter yet attractively fragrant, rather like myrrh or saffron but richer, was that known as aloes. It was pressed from the leaves of a rare plant of the order *Liliaceae,* whose chief source, perhaps the only source, was the island of Socotra. Like many other incense ingredients, it also had medicinal uses, and these uses are equally well served by two more plentiful and cheaper gums of related species, Barbados aloes and Cape aloes. However, neither of these can be used as a substitute ingredient in incense: when burned, they both smell thoroughly unpleasant. Unfortunately, to use the true Socotrine aloes is out of the question: it would not only be fabulously expensive, but in fact we have not for a long time seen even

a mention of it as a marketed commodity. There is, nevertheless, an alternative of quite respectable antiquity, a
material named as aloes in recipes dating at any rate from
before the Christian era. This is a kind of fragrant wood, with
a smell not unlike that of Socotrine aloes, but sweeter and
less pungent; the tree grows in parts of India, and the wood
was introduced into Europe by Arab traders. Sometimes it
is known as eagle-wood, perhaps from a peculiar feather-like
mottling which appears in the grain, or perhaps from a Latin
misapprehension of its Arabic name, *agallocha*. The wood of
this tree, or of a closely related tree which grows in China,
is fairly plentiful; so that in any incense recipe which calls
for aloes, one should without hesitation use eagle-wood.
Further experiment is not to be recommended: both the
Indian and the Chinese species of the tree are quite safe,
but another close relative is the deadly manchineel tree.

Cinnamon is without doubt the pre-eminent incense
of the Sun. Burned upon glowing charcoal, without addition
of any other ingredient, it emits a pure, fiery, not over-sweet
spice odour which relates it at once to the quality of the sun's
beams. Throughout ages, the chief place as a solar incense has
been given to olibanum, which is the gum of true frankincense—as such it was used in Egypt, Greece and Rome—but
inevitably, in succession to those cultures, the churches have
taken to themselves the use of frankincense so that now, by
reason of that association, all magical virtue is gone from the
gum and we have no hesitation in according the first rank
to cinnamon. Vanilla and laurel (*not* variegated laurel) are
good solar aromatics with tradition to recommend them,
and besides these there is heliotropin, which has accrued to
the solar list by a somewhat complex misunderstanding, but
which now fulfills a useful purpose there. This white
crystalline powder is the solid form of the essential oil of
the little sweet-scented plant which is known as heliotrope,
or "cherry pie." The crystals have an odour somewhat like

vanilla or bitter almonds, but when they are burned this odour becomes more pungent. The plant is called heliotrope because the intense lilac blossoms are heliotrope-coloured, that is, the colour of heliotropes or sun-stones. Sun-stones are stones which were much prized by navigators in ancient times, because even on a clouded day they would turn pink when pointed in the direction of the sun; this is due to a peculiarity of the stone in refracting light from its surface. The Greek name for that stone was Heliotropos, the Sun-seeker. Nevertheless, it is a fact that the essential oil of the plant smells very much like vanilla, which is a true Sun-incense. The world of magick is full of such happenings, where the causes seem altogether fortuitous, but the conclusions triumphantly hold good all the same.

Among the incense materials of Venus, many evidently have been chosen principally for their sweet and sensuous quality, but here too we find three notable marine substances: amber, coral and ambergris. The first of these is a form of pine-resin which has fallen into the sea, most frequently on the Baltic shores where the forests grow to the edge of cliffs or of beaches; from thence the drops of amber may drift for considerable distances, becoming more or less fossilised by the action of the sea-water. Amber gathered for use as incense is not the mature and completely hardened resin which is used to make necklaces; for incense we need "young" amber, which is very much softer and which, on being burned, still gives forth a recognisable odour of pine-oil. Coral, on the other hand, when added to incenses is used solely on account of its attribution to Venus, for it has practically no smell, pleasant or otherwise, and is not in itself combustible; but the delicate white or pink colour of some of its species, together with its origin beneath the waves, associate it so strongly with Anadyomene that is is often used in this way.

Ambergris, by contrast again, is by no means a beautiful

material, but burns readily and has an odour of penetrating sweetness; it is usually diluted in the form of a tincture, of which only a few drops are added to an incense mixture, else it would be overpowering.

Medicinal herbs belong to Mercury, and among these lavender and fennel are notable for their fragrance. Mastic is a true gum, with a peculiarly delicate and fugitive odour; it thus has been traditionally dedicated to the winged Mercury. His other aspect, as conductor of departing souls, we have already mentioned in connection with styrax and with spikenard.

Camphor is a gum of the Moon, both for the purity of its fragrance and for its translucent whiteness. Bay is a dainty and highly aromatic form of laurel; and as laurel is sacred to Sol, so is bay to Luna. Almond and hazel are woods of the Moon, the latter especially for its employment by the "dowser" or diviner. Aromatic seeds belong to this Sphere for their association with its generative qualities, but also because this is the Gate of the Astral World, wherein are to be found the seeds of those events which later blossom in manifestation upon earth. Oil of jasmine, however, has to do with the Gate of the Astral in another way. It is used in rites of projection of the consciousness. In treating of the Moon, the Triple Goddess too is always to be remembered, and here the lilies come to the fore; these typical Moon-plants have all their parts in threes, three or six petals, stems of triangular section, leaves in whorls of three.

Galbanum is a native of Persia. It does not come from a woody plant, but from a group of species of the order *Umbelliferae*, the same order to which our little cow-parsley belongs. Other members of that same order give us such diverse products as angelica (when you eat pieces of its candied green stems on your iced cake, you can reflect that now no demon will come near you) and the European hemlock, the most notable poison-plant of antiquity, a decoction of which gained a perpetual mention in history by taking Socrates out of this world. The chief producer of galbanum is the plant *Peucedanum galbaniflorum;* and the earliest reference to the gum itself is again biblical, but this time in the first indisputable list of ingredients for use as a sacred fumigant (Exodus 30:34): "The Lord said to Moses, Take aromatic substances, stacte and onycha, galbanum of a good odour, and the clearest frankincense, equal parts..." In this passage, we find that a non-aromatic mineral, salt, is to be mixed with the ingredients. The purifying and preservative properties of salt had already been accorded a symbolic value; and it was in order to represent or even to induce these qualities on the spiritual level, that the salt was to be added to the other ingredients.

The Sphere of Earth has its own incense-plant, dittany of Crete. It is employed in Evocations to Visible Appearance, and in similar rites, on account of the heavy exhalations given off by the leaves; the fresher the plant, the better. It is supported by the fruit-woods, on account of their association with Demeter.

In the great temples of various lands, blended incenses of an extraordinary complexity came to be used. A famous Egyptian recipe for an incense known as *kyphi* is found in a rather late papyrus. It names a number of ingredients, some open to more than one interpretation after the manner of the examples we have given.

Another very complex incense undoubtedly was that used at the Temple at Jerusalem. We have a recipe which is claimed to be ancient; whether it is or not, the original was undoubtedly just as complex. Our recipe contains benzoin, cascarilla, balsam of tolu, orris, cloves, cinnamon, rose-blossoms, lavender, mace, yellow sandalwood, briarwood, lilies of the valley, vervain, star anise, myrrh, Indian frankincense, Arabian frankincense, potassium nitrate (that is saltpetre, added merely to improve combustibility), powdered gold, powdered mint, melilot flowers, orange-blossom, bay leaves, juniper berries, patchouli, borax, amber, Sumatra benzoin, white sugar (!), Chinese myrrh, and a number of floral essences: rose, jasmine, violet, mignonette, bergamot, musk, oil of cloves, all to be added in liquid form in small quantity.

Conspicuous among all this is the powdered gold. Here again, as with the Exodus recipe, we have a non-aromatic mineral added to the mixture, from fairly obvious motives: to make a costlier and worthier offering, to emphasise the regal aspect of the deity, and to represent the corporate nature of the community making the offering—for as blood is to the body of the individual, so gold is, or was, to the body of the community.

Something has been said of difficulties which arise in interpreting ancient recipes. Two further examples are here given, because they are typical of recurring forms of difficulty. The first is a confusion which is found in recipes of all ages, from ancient times to the present; it involves the two Greek words *nitron* and *natron.*

Nitron means simply nitre, that is, saltpetre, otherwise known as potassium nitrate. As in the recipe already cited, saltpetre is frequently added to materials which do not burn easily or steadily, to induce a more ready and regular combustion. Nitron is of no use in any process to do with embalming. Natron, on the other hand, is soda as it occurs in the natural state: usually washing-soda with a certain admixture of sodium bicarbonate. The Egyptians used it extensively in embalming. It is of no use whatever in incense, and any sort of soda when placed upon a fire produces unpleasant fumes, probably extinguishing the fire. Yet these two materials are frequently confused, not only in modern translations, but even in quite old Latin or Greek versions of various recipes. One has to use one's judgment, according to the purpose of the recipe.

Another difficulty in tracing the identity of incense materials, is that even a pictorial representation may not be of great help unless one knows the probabilities. For example, Queen Hatshepsut, somewhere about the year 1500 B.C., sent off an expedition to the Land of Punt. The expedition duly returned, laden with products of that country, whose location we are not told. Among the treasures are enumerated a quantity of aromatic trees; and these are represented on the walls of the queen's mortuary chapel at Deir el Bahri. They seem to be of two kinds, one with leaves and one without; but apart from this detail, they are too conventionalised in the usual Egyptian manner to convey very much. They could, however, be myrrh-trees. Nevertheless, the outcome of this mystery is very interesting, since there is a species of frankincense tree which never has more than rudimentary leaves, and this tree grows in Somaliland. Myrrh also grows in Somaliland, and many Egyptologists, for this and other reasons, are now accepting the hypothesis that Somaliland was the legendary Land of Punt.

Great is the fascination of research in the incense-lore of the past; however, the requirements of the present age also call forth their own studies. Voudoun has its own especial suffumigations. For Celtic rites, we have an incense of fine fragrance which is entirely without Oriental ingredients, but which burns long and steadily as is required for a magical rite:

| | |
|---|---|
| Dried lavender flowers | 20 g |
| Dried red rosebuds | 20 g |
| Saffron | 5 g |
| Pine gum | 50 g |
| Powdered orris (Florentine iris) | as required |
| | |
| Oil of lavender | 10 drops |
| Oil of roses | 10 drops |
| Oil of anise | 15 drops |

To compound this incense, a particular technique is

required, owing to the semi-fluid and highly adhesive condition of fresh pine-gum. Before proceeding with the other ingredients, the pine-gum is first blended with the powdered orris-root until it forms a mass of crumbling granules which, if not subjected to undue pressure, can be handled without inconvenience. (The same technique is advisable for recipes containing styrax, another semi-liquid resin.) The pine-gum, thus treated, can be thoroughly blended with the dry ingredients, among which it will form small grains. Finally the essential oils are added, the mixture being turned over and divided with a spatula, so that each of the oils will be distributed through the mass. Fine division for this purpose is not necessary, as the oils are in any case extremely pervasive. The mixture should be allowed to stand for about twenty-four hours in a cool place, to blend before use.

With regard to the oil of anise, it may be remarked that the solidifying or "freezing" temperature of this liquid is at just about a temperate room temperature, so that at such a temperature one is never sure whether one will find the bottle full of a clear colourless liquid or a somewhat milky-looking solid which looks rather like candle-wax. The smell of aniseed is unmistakeable in either case, but for convenience in handling, if the oil happens to have solidified, it is advisable to warm it gently by placing the bottle in warm water for a few minutes.

For short periods, mixed incenses undoubtedly improve by being allowed to stand so that the ingredients may blend thoroughly. For longer storage, however, it is advisable to keep the ingredients separate from one another so that they may be freshly mixed shortly before use. Stale aromatics are useless. To preserve a stock of incense ingredients, they should be kept in tightly sealed jars in a cool, dark, dry place. Refrigeration is bad for liquid materials, and with regard to others it may defeat its own purpose by causing condensation as soon as the material is removed from the store. Gums or resins should require little attention beyond this, though some need stirring occasionally to prevent their granules from uniting into a single mass inside the jar. Dried woods, and herbal materials such as rosebuds, benefit by the addition of small sachets of a neutral dehydrating agent, such as is sometimes used among photographic materials; the dehydrating agent should never, of course, be placed loose with the ingredients, as its accidental inclusion in the mixture would be most objectionable.

For blending incenses, a certain minimum of equipment is needed, to which other items may be added as desired. Basic are the pestle and mortar, a marble or glass slab and a spatula for blending, a small chemical balance and some droppers for oils and essences (several are desirable so that they can be used for different aromatics in succession, without the operator either contaminating his stocks or having to interrupt the compounding to cleanse the dropper).

To clean the equipment after use, surgical spirit followed by mild soap and warm water should be adequate.

It should not be taken always for granted that incenses must be blended; examples of incenses made of a single substance have been mentioned, cinnamon for example or olibanum, and this point is worthy of emphasis. When a blend is made of several materials, however, it is desirable from the practical viewpoint to select from the various classes of material—a gum or resin, a wood, an herb, an oil—not necessarily one of each, but a balanced selection which will burn well and not too rapidly. A sufficient variety of materials is included in our list to permit a harmonious choice. It is generally requisite to keep entirely to one planetary attribution, but (as in our Celtic incense) a balanced range of attributions is occasionally to be preferred.

Many other materials exist which are used in incense but which we have not included: Burgundy pitch for instance, which is a useful extender, but which lacks character and can be unpleasant if it becomes dominant; and such ingredients as mace, cloves, cassia, to which no objection whatever is made, but which are such everyday substances that the student will have no difficulty in making his own experiments with them.

For the actual burning of incense, we use two types of thurible: a swinging censer, and a standing incense-pot. In each case, the incense is sprinkled upon a cake of glowing charcoal which stands upon a bed of sand in the thurible. Some people use charcoal impregnated with saltpetre for ease in lighting, but the fumes can be obnoxious in an enclosed space, and in any case may be inimical to the rite; we therefore prefer as a general rule to pour a little white spirit on the charcoal. When ignited after this treatment, it flares; after a moment the flame is to be blown out, when the charcoal will remain glowing upon the hot sand.

To familiarise oneself with the exquisite incense-materials and with their correspondences is a most interesting part of the traditional magical studies. It becomes a true alchemy, in which the substances are realised as participating in the qualities which they represent: qualities to which the operator gives a mode of expression through this medium.

## THE SWORD IN THE 18th PSALM

Qabalistic tradition links the descent of the Sword in its successive phases with the mystical and allusive words of Psalm 18, verses 8-16. The Hebrew letters shown on the diagram of the Sword (page 34) are a mnemonic for this text, each pair comprising the first and last letters of the verse attributed to a specific phase of the downward flashing course of the Sword.

Here, then, the meditative reader follows the course of the Sword from the inconceivable heights, through the mighty influences of the spheres, to the region of Earth—whence he is caught up again at once upon the Way of Return.

At the close of this sequence of verses, having traced the path of the Sword from Kether to Malkuth, the psalmist declares: "He drew me out of many waters". For there are many waters, many aspects of water. Water as a symbol of affliction and grief occurs in several psalms, but in others water is a symbol of cleansing and healing, of life preserved and renewed. It is also a symbol of birth; in this context of the Sphere of Malkuth it calls to mind particularly that great "bringing forth from the waters" described in Genesis 1,9: "And Elohim said, Let the waters under the heaven be gathered together unto one place, and let the dry land appear: and it was so".

This whole series of verses from Psalm 18 is replete with references and sidelights of Qabalistic significance of many levels, which the student will have delight in exploring. Such exploration is itself a magical act; the words of the psalm themselves open the mind by practical experience, to the ways of Qabalistic thought. More than that, this traditionally revered passage is of the nature of a talisman: it carries a potently rewarding contact with the influences of numberless minds of magically and mystically trained Qabalists who have meditated

257

upon it through the centuries. To enter into this meditation, to share in continuing this tradition, is to enter progressively into a high communion with those minds, with their knowledge, their wisdom and their power.

The arrangement of material is as follows:

1. עו There went up a smoke out of his nostrils, and fire out of his mouth devoured: coals were kindled by it.

*(The first phase of the Sword arises in Kether and flashes to Chockmah.)*

2. וו He bowed the heavens also, and came down: and darkness was under his feet.

*(The second phase of the Sword issues from Chokmah and flashes to Binah.)*

3. הו And he rode upon a Kerub and did fly: yea, he did swoop down upon the wings of the wind.

*(The third phase of the Sword issues from Binah and flashes to Chesed.)*

4. יﬦ He made darkness his secret place, his pavilion round about him; dark waters and thick clouds of the skies.

*(The fourth phase of the Sword issues from Chesed and flashes to Geburah.)*

5. ﬦש From the splendor that proclaimed him, there passed through his thick clouds hailstones and coals of fire.

*(The fifth phase of the Sword issues from Geburah and flashes to Tiphareth.)*

6. שו YHVH also thundered in the heavens, and ELION gave forth his voice; hailstones and coals of fire.

*(The sixth phase of the Sword issues from Tiphareth and flashes to Netzach.)*

7. וﬦ Yea, he sent out his arrows, and scattered them; he shot out lightnings and discomfited them.

*(The seventh phase of the Sword issues from Netzach and flashes to Hod.)*

8. וַ And the channels of waters were seen, and the foundations of the world were revealed, at thy rebuke, O YHVH, at the blast of the breath of thy nostrils.

*(The eighth phase of the Sword issues from Hod and flashes to Yesod.)*

9. יָם He sent from the heights, he took me, he drew me out of many waters.

*(The ninth phase of the Sword issues from Yesod and resolves in Malkuth.)*

# Book IV
## The Triumph of Light

For

*BUNTIE WILLS*

a token of friendship and esteem

*Light and life shall be drawn at last to the radiance of one
star, and that star shall mount to the unshadowed height.*

# CONTENTS

*DIAGRAMS*

## PREFACE

The Western Mystery Tradition has its own psychology, which now, with the publication by Llewellyn of the present volume, receives the name of *Psychosophy:* it is not simply a modern study of the psyche in living man—although that is comprehended—but it is also the understanding thereof, directed to the purposes of man's esoteric progress, and perceived in the light of the historic traditions and researches of the Mystery Schools and of the high philosophers who have formulated Western spiritual culture.

The limits of this book permit only an exposition of the main plan of Psychosophy, indicating chiefly the relationship between the components of the psyche and the Qabalistic system of its intensified evolution upon the Way of Return. The general ground of psychological knowledge which this study assumes, is that which can be gained from the researches of modern psychology, and from the works of Carl Jung in particular. Certain of his hypotheses differ, it is true, in some respects from those of the Aurum Solis: but then the purpose of his work was different also. Of our veneration for his work and our indebtedness to it, little need be said: it will be evident, we trust, at many points, and we have commended his published volumes to the serious attention of our students. Furthermore, the student who desires aid in self-knowledge before proceeding to advanced magical work, will probably find his greatest rapport with the therapeutic and analytical methods of the Jungian school.

We must give some account here of a main divergence in Psychosophy from Jung's conclusions. This difference is in the psychosophical view of the relative structure of the male and female psyche. According to Jung, the characteristic psyche of the male has a masculine conscious personality, which is influenced to a greater or less extent by a subordinate female component, largely unconscious, known as the Anima. The characteristic psyche of the female, on the other hand, has a feminine conscious personality, influenced to a greater or less extent by a subordinate masculine component, also largely unconscious, the Animus. (One of the most usual needs in therapy is to detach these great psychic factors from false associations in the "personal unconscious," and to identify them as high and potent archetypal forces, which they are.) The conventional Jungian viewpoint has it that these variations constitute two distinct types of human psyche: the male type which has (besides other components of course) a conscious personality and the Anima, as against the female type which has (besides its other components) a conscious personality and the Animus. Thus the female type of psyche has no Anima, the male type no Animus.

*We see the convenience of this distinction from the clinical and empirical viewpoint of therapy, since naturally the male component in the psyche has a different functioning as a subsidiary factor in a female personality, from that which it would have when identified with the consciousness as it is in a male personality.* For magical and mystical purposes, however, the artificial division of the human race into two groups, each with a separate and distinct type of psyche, is unacceptable.

For one thing, one sees that in a human being (of whichever physical sex) the true personality can as a psychic fact be centred anywhere between the two extremes of sexual polarity: it would go beyond the scope of this work to discuss the multiple physical and psychic factors causing the various sexual orientations, but hardly anyone is even approximately "purely" male or female in the conscious personality, while the unconscious (and therefore usually projected) polarity varies accordingly. Further upon this point, we see that in the changing conditions of life in our culture, male and female with increasing frequency exchange characteristics of personality, in a way which would be impossible if the psyche of each was inherently of a fixed and separate nature. Another consideration which is of great importance to both the magical and the mystical tradition, is the teaching that as the psyche evolves towards maturity it must reach an equipoise of characteristics so that the Opposites of male and female may be completely reconciled. The Jungian view of "integration" as an objective harmonises completely with this occult doctrine, which through Christian and Gnostic sources has become recognised as an essential part of the Western Tradition: but if a difference between the male psyche and that of the female were a fundamental part of human nature, then the perfecting of human nature would surely necessitate the heightening of that difference, not its reconciliation. We see, indeed, in therapeutic work concerned with bringing an immature psyche to full adult development, for instance, how the initial confusion of childhood may need to be dispelled and the polarities established: but none the less, the ultimate goal for the mature personality is to bring both polarities into consciousness and so to resolve them.

Again, and of vital importance from the occult viewpoint, endless difficulties would be raised with regard to reincarnation, in those cases where a person demonstrates unmistakeable memories of a lifetime spent in a body of the opposite sex to the present one.

Most important to Psychosophy however are the

implications which concern the central Column of the diagram of the Tree. It is well known that both Anima and Animus can exercise a strong inspirational influence in the psyche, according to its development. It has often been thought in non-magical psychology that these two archetypal forces carry the inspirational character in their own right. This is not the case. In the chapters of this book, something will be found concerning the descent of the Intuitive Mind in the psyche of the Adept. The Intuitive Mind is associated essentially with the Column of Equilibrium. In the psyche which is not yet ready for this development, but which is in its measure maturing, the Intuitive Mind is not perceived as a distinct psychic entity, but its hidden influence is confused with the character of Anima or of Animus as Muse or as Hero, and may be projected therewith.

In this book, to avoid cumbersome sentences, the Aspirant and the Adept have generally been accorded the masculine pronoun only. It must be pointed out here that the psychosophical system applies to male and female alike: unless the context directly refers to the male only, therefore, "man" is the human race, and the pronoun "he" is intended as the common gender.

—*M. Denning*

*In all the Histories given in this volume, both in the text or in Appendix B, the names of the subjects have been changed, and none need think that any of the quick or the dead who bear those names are intended. Where necessary, attendant circumstances have been changed, or else care has been taken that through lapse of time or other causes, the events related can harm nobody. At the same time, nothing concerning the essential psychological or occult aspects of the histories has been falsified.*

**Part I**

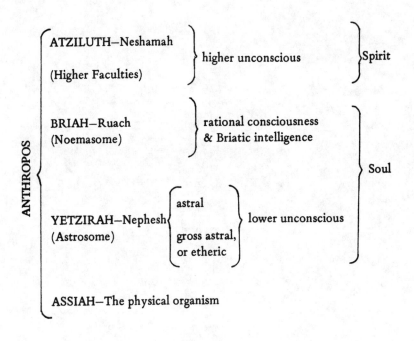

ANTHROPOS

ATZILUTH—psychoessential principles

BRIAH—noetically-directed principles and energy-complexes

YETZIRAH—energy complex (energy bodies)

ASSIAH—sub-atomic, atomic and molecular patterns

## CHAPTER I

The magician's understanding of psychosophy should be
fostered by:
  A good grasp of general psychology, with emphasis on
  the works of Carl Jung.
  A deep study of the special development of certain aspects
  of psychology in relation to magical practice.

An antagonism sometimes assumed between psychology and
  magick. Such an opposition is not necessary but tends to
  arise from two causes:
  The sceptical attitude of many writers on psychology and
  particularly on psychiatry.
  The fear of disillusionment which leads some occultists to
  avoid psychological studies.
The student is counselled to avoid barren reading but not to
  shun aspects of truth.

The psyche as comprising soul and spirit.
  The physical contribution to mind-stuff. Some aspects of
  heredity. The "evidence of the senses" and its liability
  to error.
  The Nephesh, its powers and limitations.
  The Ruach as conscious centre of the personality: its dual
  function, as rational ruler of the Nephesh and as
  instrument of the higher faculties.

A case of untrained astral travel cited to illustrate the work
   of various levels of the psyche.

*Noteworthy points in the case:*
Successful reliance upon unconscious lower faculties, e.g.,
   in direction finding.
Indistinct recollection of implanted knowledge (traffic lights)
   without ability to bring over further details from the brain.
Discovery of the ability to pass material barriers.
Discovery of the reality of psychic barriers.
Power of the mind and the higher astral to pass where the
   lower astral cannot.
Power of healing by the psychic faculties.
Experience of "snap-back" into the physical body on approach-
   ing close to it.

*CHAPTER I*

*THE LOWER SELF*

Human life, in its illimitable variety, is made up of an intricate series of relationships between physical and non-physical factors. Magick, considered in its own right, is an art of humanly directed and highly specialised interaction between physical and non-physical factors. Some understanding of the basic principles of human life is thus essential to the practice of magick: and the greater the understanding the more exactly, other considerations being equal, can the art be directed. A comprehension of general psychology is therefore of great value to the magician: and besides this, there are also certain specialised aspects of psychology which have to be examined in relation to magical practice. (The magical structures and techniques themselves are to be examined in Volume 3 of this series.) It is strongly to be recommended that besides the present work, the student should acquaint himself with some books on general psychological subject-matter. Textbooks on experimental psychology give a grasp of the basic psychosomatic principles: while of works based on the clinical aspects of psychology, one or two of Freud's pioneer studies should be read for the sake of an historical perspective of the subject, and the volumes of Carl Jung are most highly recommended: some at least of these last should form a part of the student's permanent library. Some later writers, of the Jungian school particularly, highly merit attention but this must depend upon the student's personal inclination and available time.

An objection is sometimes raised by occultists who consider that psychology is inimical to the practice of magick, and that a study of the subject may destroy or at least diminish the power of the magician. This objection generally rests upon a double basis, neither aspect of which contains any real cause for anxiety, but each is entitled to our comment. In the first place, there is the sceptical attitude of certain writers, of the Freudian school particularly. Such writers, in attempting to explain any type of magick, invariably create an impression of having explained it away: it is also to be remarked that they ultimately create an impression of having explained away everything else in human life, except possibly a subconscious inclination to incest. This view is inevitably somewhat depressing, and an intensive course of such books is certainly not recommended. Their initial impetus is to be found in the works of Sigmund Freud himself, and we ask the student to peruse some of these if only for the purpose of seeing the roots of the concept in question and its mode of development: he may also chance upon authors of this persuasion in his general reading, and it is better to be familiar with their viewpoint than to be taken unawares by it. They can generally be recognised by their "nothing but" attitude, with which they tend to mar writings which might otherwise have considerable sociological and philosophic value. Magick, for instance, they frequently dismiss as a protest of the underprivileged. Now, that is quite an interesting hypothesis: it also applies perhaps to most forms of human endeavour, since childhood for example is by nature an underprivileged condition unless the child is "spoilt" and therefore strives for nothing: while among adults, even the rich and successful can feel, and frequently do justly feel, that their inner life ought to receive some especial attention to compensate for years of neglect. As a full explanation of magick, however, the hypothesis is inadequate because it takes no account of the actual working of magick: clearly such a writer either does not believe in magick as an objective reality, or imagines that given a sufficient motive, the rest follows spontaneously. Besides the fact that the "nothing but" attitude is inherent in Freudian thought, it must be borne in mind that an author who writes on psychology with a clinical or mainly clinical background, quite rightly bases his contribution to psychological knowledge upon his own first-hand observations: and among his patients he is not likely in the course of a lifetime to meet with many real magicians, though he will have daydreamers aplenty. One or two such books therefore, although to be taken with reserve, can be a useful cathartic even to the serious student of magick. An examination of motives is all to the good.

The other root of the objection raised by some occultists to a study of psychology, is a belief, sometimes based on personal experience or observation, that such knowledge can cause an actual loss of magical power. Here again, a distinction needs to be made. The mere reading of books, in itself, does little or nothing unless there is an inner response to those books. The truth behind the objection is to be found in a sense of loss sometimes experienced by recipients of psychiatric or psychotherapeutic treatment, occasionally even by readers simply of books written from a clinical viewpoint, when the subject's contact with the clinical aspect results in a hidden motivation being brought to consciousness and losing its driving power thereby, or a fascination being resolved into its components and thus disappearing. This type of disillusionment, of course, is not suffered only by students of the occult. A man may suddenly become profoundly aware in the midst of his courtship, that a characteristic which he finds particularly endearing in his girl may have had a significance for the deeper levels of his mind quite other than that which has appeared on the surface. A church worker may discover that his (or her) devout activities are an outcome of something quite other than religious conviction. In each case a potent motivation is lost. What happens next is entirely a question of the particular case. The disenchanted one may simply breathe a sigh of relief and set out to make up lost time in the ordinary affairs of life: or the sense of deprivation may be acute enough to initiate a search for a substitute interest: or, quite frequently, it will only be a matter of recovering from the shock, allowing his motives to readjust, and then continuing as before. In the case of the student of occultism, as with the others, if he finds that his fervour has been based entirely upon a false motivation, it is better for him to be cured of it and to depart, than to remain in his delusion: while if he be drawn to magick as his true way of life, the disappearance of an irrational factor may indeed rob him of a means of drawing energy from the personal unconscious, but this loss may be a necessary step in his life before he can learn to draw consciously upon the true sources.

Further on the subject of real or imaginary antagonism between psychology and parapsychology, it is of course true that prejudices exist on both sides, but fortunately these are only the personal idiosyncrasies of the people concerned. It must be stressed that although as has been mentioned, the traditional Freudian attitude is excessively reductive and sceptical, by no means all psychiatrists have preserved this tendency: the progressives among them are distinguished by a truly scientific willingness to follow the evidence wherever it leads, while some of the most notable are doing work which would hitherto have been considered entirely within the domain of occultism. Among psychotherapists of other schools the open attitude is the most frequent. Telepathy is an established fact, other forms of ESP are the subject of continual investigation in a number of countries, notably in Russia for example: and from the recognition of these forces to recognition of their controlled direction is but a step. The existence of non-material entities originating outside the human psyche is perhaps more difficult to establish, but at least the principle is becoming recognised here, that evidence of a standard which would be considered reliable for the existence of a living material entity should be taken on its own merits, neither more nor less, for the non-material, and should not be ruled out on mere *a priori* grounds of presumed impossibility. What is needed here in the dialogue between occultists and psychiatrists is just such a complete acceptance of facts, without any premature building of hypotheses thereon. As long as each party merely states in simple truth "This is my experience . . ." much fruitful work on a highly complex subject is possible. This at once opens the door to serious investigations as to the nature of that world in which the psyche participates: or as we should say (bearing in mind the different levels both in the objective universe and in our experience of it) the nature, not of that world but of those worlds.

The term *psyche,* in its modern sense, signifies the total non-material component in the individual human personality, and comprises both the level of the personal conscious mind and those levels which, whether normally or otherwise, lie outside the personal consciousness. Those other levels are in Freudian terminology referred to as "subconscious," a word which creates certain possibilities of misunderstanding: we prefer the Jungian term "unconscious," with the warning however that even this epithet needs to be understood in its specialised sense. Of the contents of the unconscious, the conscious mind is totally unaware: as soon as some factor of that contents is perceived, that factor is coming into consciousness: that is to say, into the conscious mind. There is no reason to assume, however, that the "unconscious" is unconscious in itself at its own level: any more than we

should assume our next-door neighbour to be lying in a
coma just because we cannot hear him moving around. He
is probably very busy about his own concerns: and so is
the "unconscious" part of the psyche.

The "unconscious" levels comprise not only the regions
of the psyche which are nearer to the material and instinctual
than is the conscious mind, but also other regions further
away from it: by a familiar and convenient metaphor, we
refer to the former as lower, to the latter as higher. This
accords with much traditional symbolism: however, in some
contexts it will be found more apposite to refer to the
material and "lower" levels of the personality as "outer," the
more spiritual as "inner," this again agreeing with an
accepted usage.

Within the psyche we distinguish, in the first place, two
great divisions: that which is frequently referred to as the
Soul, comprising the unified animation of the physical body,
with the instinctual and emotional nature, besides the mind
which is characterised by the rational understanding: and
that which is frequently referred to as the Spirit, comprising
the higher aspirational and vital principles, with the Higher
Genius or Divine Spark which is the transcendental essence of
the individual. The Soul therefore, besides animating the
body, is the vehicle and instrument of the Spirit: it thus has
a most important role in the development and enrichment of
the personality, and indeed most of the life-experience of
the individual unfolds within its ranges. The lower unconscious is a part of it. Events which may have been completely
forgotten by the conscious mind, such as the great venture
of birth itself, here imprint their influence, as well as other
contents which are unknown to the conscious mind and may
never become known to it.

The question here arises, of inherited patterns of temperament and of behaviour. This is extremely debatable
ground. It is well known, for example, that children may

reproduce mannerisms of relatives they have never seen: such factors are conspicuous in early life but frequently tend to disappear as other influences, and the child's own emerging personality, take control. The causes for this are various. A father, for instance, may suddenly realise that his young son's first efforts to walk unaided are just like Old Uncle So-and-So. The cause here may be entirely physical, a family tendency to underdevelopment of a minor tendon, or so forth: or again, the father, who of course has never seen himself walking, may himself have unconsciously imitated Old Uncle So-and-So, to be mimicked in turn by the child. Where the cause of an action is manifestly not entirely physical, unconscious telepathic communication between parent and child, or frequently grandparent and child, is to be suspected, before any question of inherited memory arises: nevertheless, inherited memories do appear to exist and in some cases would seem to be the most probable explanation of a phenomenon. Two examples will suffice to show the difference in emphasis.

A certain man who went out to the Far East as a young soldier in World War II, underwent such physical and mental agonies in the jungle and subsequently as a prisoner of war, that he eventually arrived home in a state of breakdown. After some years he had so far recovered as to have established himself in a satisfactory position to marry: but the horror of his past experiences still beset him to the extent that everything associated with those experiences was a closed subject: he would not discuss it with his bride, save to express a wish that their children should be brought up as absolute pacifists, and might never so much as know what part he had taken in the past conflict. However, their first child was a highly-strung and acutely intelligent little boy who from his second year began to show a keen interest in precisely the forbidden range of topics. The father, it should be mentioned, had a particular fear of talking in his sleep about his war-time sufferings, and had therefore ensured that, from birth, Paul should sleep in a room which would be out of earshot of any such utterances: the mother declared that in fact her husband talked but little in his sleep and even less that was intelligible, although he would occasionally awaken with an inarticulate nightmare cry. However, despite all precautions, the child's talk was all of war and, strangely, not of death but of capture, and of the hardships and sufferings of prisoners. With seemingly uncanny art he seized upon any chance remark dropped by child or adult, any partly-heard story, any picture in a paper or on television, which would help to build up his store of information: so that by the time he was seven years old, his father said bitterly, Paul knew almost as much about Japanese P.O.W. camps as if he had been born in one. Thereafter however, it is pleasant to be able to add that the obsession slowly faded, and with little assistance the boy took to the more usual interests of an intelligent youngster.

In this episode we see several factors at work. Although clearly the child obtained much of the material for his phantasy through ordinary channels, it does seem probable that his initial, and continued, impulse in that direction arose from a real telepathic link with his father: this being the more likely because of the powerful repression of the subject-matter in the psyche of the father, as evinced, for example, by his dread of talking in his sleep. As with an electrical circuit, the creation of a resistance of this type can build up a tremendously powerful charge. Again, it is almost inevitable that both parents helped unwittingly to foster Paul's interest by refusing to discuss the stories and television programmes in question, while they would, presumably, have discussed stories and pictures with other subject-matter: nevertheless both parents felt that the questions which their young son asked on those matters, and the inferences he drew, were occasionally quite beyond his age and quite beyond his level of intelligence on other subjects: "You could only suppose," said his mother, "that some part of his mind knew the answer already, to make him able to ask the question." In none of this, however interesting it is from the viewpoint of telepathy and of a child's suggestibility, is there any indication that Paul actually *inherited* either his inclination to the subject-matter, or any actual knowledge of it, from his father. Had he done so, he would presumably have inherited the negative attitude also: whereas in fact, until attaining the age of reason the boy not only showed a marked unconscious rapport with the repressed levels of his father's mind, but also, by his very positive curiosity, acted as a kind of safety-valve to them.

We turn now to our second example. Here we have the case of another intelligent and highly-strung child, in this instance a little girl born and reared in the midst of a large English town, and dominated until about her seventh year by a nightmare horror of wolves. Janice was fond of animals and had a number of picture-books showing lions, tigers, elephants, and even bears, which she loved, besides the more gentle creatures: but pictures of anything even resembling a wolf upset her at once. They were so like the things in her bad dream, she explained.

This bad dream she had, apparently, only experienced twice in its entirety, but it had so terrified her that for weeks together she would try in vain not to go to sleep, for fear of dreaming it anew.

In her dream, it was always winter-time: the trees were bare and there was thick snow on the ground. She was out in the open country, in a horse-drawn wheelless vehicle, going forward at a steady pace. Then she became aware of *them* in the distance: there were a number of them, and they looked black against the snow. The horses would have fled with her, but she had to check them: this was part of the horror of it, she knew exactly what she must do but not why she must do it. She had to go slowly, to make sure *they* had seen her. Then she could let the horses gallop, but what a race it was! Nearer and nearer they came. She saw ahead of her a high wall, with tall stone gateposts like part of a castle: between them was a strong wooden gate. As the horses reached the gate, it opened sufficiently to let them and the vehicle pass through: then the gate was slammed shut, and the men on the wall struck down the pursuers. That was the way the dream ended the first time Janice remembered dreaming it, a little before her third birthday: the next time, a few months later, she had awakened before the final slam of the gate, and the hideous question in her mind ever since had been, would it be closed soon enough? On the third occasion when she could clearly recall having the dream, when she was six (there had been one or two intervening nightmares about wolves, but she was not sure exactly of the subject-matter,) a kind of division had arisen in her mind about the wheelless vehicle, of which she had apparently taken no notice before: but now, part of her mind was dismayed that the vehicle in which she must escape had no wheels, and tried, so to speak, to add wheels to it: whereas another part of her mind said that it was right as it was. This conflict apparently awakened her, again without seeing a safe ending to the adventure: and her only experience of the dream after that was fragmentary, the dread having shifted now to the question of whether the gate would open at all.

The intriguing fact about Janice's dream was that, quite unknown to her and to her parents, what she had described was in substance a traditional Polish method of decoying wolves. In reality, of course, the decoy in the sleigh would have been a bold huntsman, not a little girl: the child's terror at this unsuitable dream-experience is more than understandable. On inquiry, it transpired that her father, although of mixed European descent and born in France, was partly Polish. The question remained, why out of all the varied possibilities of his ancestral past, should his young daughter have acquired this one particular wolf-episode? It was already established that she herself had had no very frightening experience with wolves or large dogs. Had the father perhaps had such an experience?

The father, a man of exceptionally powerful build, bared his shoulder by way of answer. There, deeply scarring the muscles, were the healed lacerations of great canine teeth. "Janice has never seen this," he commented. The story of that scar, he went on to explain, was the story of the one occasion when he remembered being thoroughly terrified. As a boy, he had lived with his parents and brothers and sisters at their home in a village of northern France, where his father had kept a huge and savage mastiff to guard his property. This creature was kept chained in a yard by day, and the other children would go nowhere near it: but, explained the speaker, it had been his custom, whenever his father was absent, to show off his bravado and agility by going into the yard and baiting the mastiff, leaping away just beyond the reach of the chain as the powerful animal rushed at him. One day he enraged the mastiff to such a frenzy that, straining forward, it pulled the end of the chain from the masonry: and before the lad could grapple with it (as he would even then have done) his heel slipped in the mire, and, falling, he was seized by the shoulder and shaken as a terrier would shake a rat. Had not one of his brothers, who had looked on, found sufficient presence of mind to run to a neighbour for help, the speaker felt quite sure that he would never have survived to have either a wife or a daughter.

Little doubt remained but that this experience of her father's, a few years before his marriage, was in some way linked with Janice's strange dream. Certainly, here, an inherited memory seems genuinely to be involved, but in

an indirect manner. It is to be noticed that Janice apparently
picked up nothing of her father's personal experience, save
perhaps for the one vital but problematic factor, that of
slipping quickly enough out of reach of the canine assailant.*
It looks, then, as if the memory was not inherited by the
daughter, so truly as by the father: but that it had never
reached his conscious mind, active though it may have been
in the unconscious. (What was it, in reality, that had driven
him to bait the mastiff?) From his unconscious mind, where
it had become charged with the horror of his savaging by the
huge creature, Janice had apparently taken by telepathy the
ancestral memory of the wolf-baiting, and had brought it
to consciousness in her dream.

We cannot linger upon these matters, but to remark that
they seem to bring us almost as near as human experience
might be expected to lead, to the building-up in the remote
past of inherited instincts in the Nephesh, the animal mind.
To the civilised human being there is always something of a
shock, of distaste, in these stories, for the realisation which
they carry of those levels: nevertheless, our instinctual part
is a veritable portion of the natural world, and therein lies
not only its justification in existing, but its necessity to us.
We need this as a tree needs its roots, although, like the roots,
the instinctual nature is for the most part kept out of sight.

The lower part of the soul may be described as bounded
at its lower limit by its contact with the physical body, and
most notably with the autonomic nervous system: at its
upper limit, by the impingement of the rational mind upon
the emotions. The region of the psyche thus demarcated is
characterised in Qabalistic terminology by the name
Nephesh, while the rational mind (which is still comprised

* Students of Jung will doubtless take particular note of the change from the
single mastiff of the father's experience, to the pack of wolves in the daughter's
dream. This quite valid observation does not detract from the historical accuracy
of her dream: however, it may perhaps contribute to explaining her attunement
to that particular aspect of the matter. It is clearly quite useless to speculate as
to what Janice might have dreamed if she had been a boy!

within the soul as part of the lower nature of man) is the *Ruach*. Since the Nephesh is the seed-ground of the conscious emotions as well as of the unconscious impulses whether instinctual or other, it tends to a continual fluctuation, influenced by both physical and mental variations. This fluctuation is a principal characteristic of the Nephesh, and is to a greater or less extent passed on by it to the adjacent regions. For example: the rational mind may gather from some other source, information which produces an emotional reaction: this emotion, acting through the Nephesh, affects the physical body to a greater or less degree, causing changes in glandular secretions, in rate of breathing and of pulse, and so on, these in turn causing other reactions. Or again: a bodily condition may be produced by entirely physical causes, such as cold, indigestion, or fatigue: this condition can act through the Nephesh to affect the emotions, producing a depressed state which may manifest in the consciousness as a vague sadness or even as an irrational fear: the mind, disturbed by this emotional prompting, may then rationalise it by reflecting upon previously-ignored problems or difficulties, or, more practically, may think upon means of taking the physical organism from the initial causes of distress, or of removing those causes themselves.

It is not necessary for this process that the emotion concerned should attain any very evolved state: not necessarily beyond the domain of the Nephesh, that is. The sensory data produced by the nerves, and coded (as we may say) by the brain, need only be realised by the Nephesh as being unpleasant in intensity, for immediate reactions to take place at both physical and rational levels. The rational mind may question the data further: and it is of interest to the student that this examination, unless additional information is brought in by other means, is not always successful. There may simply be inadequate information from the brain, as in the case of a toothache, when the sufferer either cannot identify the aching tooth or is totally mistaken about it ("referred pain"): or errors of this kind may be due to a natural complication of the nervous system, as with the tricephalous nerve for example: the sufferer may feel the symptoms of an upset stomach as if the gastric nerve had been thereby disturbed, and, on reflection, may even think he can identify the offending article of diet, probably a food against which he has some degree of emotional bias: whereas the message that his consciousness ought to have received may be that he has strained his eyes, the *optic* nerve being the affected branch of the tricephalous. These everyday examples, which could be indefinitely multiplied, should indicate that the "plain evidence of the senses" is not always as plain as it seems, and all possible supporting indications are to be desired where objective certainty is the important consideration. Furthermore, the physical body and its senses are adaptable to a fairly wide range of conditions: this adaptability, which is an excellent quality in itself, makes it impossible for us at the same time to regard the body as reliable measuring instrument. It can easily be shown how an unaltered electric light, for instance, which appears quite dim when we come into its range from a bright room or from full sunshine, can be painfully bright if it is suddenly switched on when we have been for some time in total darkness. Divers and others who keep the ears covered for any length of time, experience an abnormal acuity of hearing on return to the world of sound: by contrast, the ability of the town-dweller to ignore an increasing volume of noise, gradually causes a degree of actual physical deafness. Similarly, it is instructive as regards sense-evidence to place before us three bowls of water, one as hot as can comfortably be borne, the second completely cold, and the third moderately warm. We keep one hand in the cold basin and one in the hot, for two or three minutes, then we plunge both into the warm. It becomes immediately difficult to believe that all the water in that basin is of even temperature, for the cold hand feels it as hot and the hot hand feels it to be cold.

The close link between the Nephesh and the physical body is manifested in many ways, from variations in physical posture (including facial expression) following the emotional direction, to the restless pacing of the anxious or the spontaneous leaping and dancing of the enraptured. Commonly, the rational mind, the Ruach, is also caught in this connecting link, so that it can be said that one sees what the person in question is thinking. In some sports and games this is a well-known weakness: in fencing one watches the eyes of the opponent for warning of his next action, since by the time a movement of arm or hand is perceptible it is too late to parry or to take advantage: the experienced fencer therefore trains his mind to act as independently as possible of the emotions, so that no intention may reveal itself until the very moment when the muscles are to be directed to a given attack. A similar reason produces the mask-like face of the card-player. This detachment of the mind brings a just sense of achievement: nevertheless it should be but a useful exercise, and should be compensated for in other ways: the real perfection of natural man is most nearly expressed when the physical body, the Nephesh, and the Ruach act in harmony, reason and the higher emotions directing, the instinctual nature exulting in, the physical body manifesting and completing an athletic feat or an aesthetically conceived dance (see Volume 3 concerning *the Dance as instrument of Magick.*) In such activities is the Nephesh in particular exalted, for their fluid and changeful movements reflect its own nature. It will need little prompting in the matter of movements most suited to the magical purpose, for it is the seat of those faculties which are frequently called psychic.

Besides its indispensable role as the representative of the instincts by means of the emotions, the interpreter of the physical body and the doorkeeper of the astral world, the

Nephesh has also the defects of those qualities. The psychic researcher knows that for every true phenomenon which merits public telling, there may be a dozen or more others, equally well authenticated, over which he prefers to pass in silence. The Nephesh can produce beauty and horror, it is true: but it can also combine the crudest sentimentality with bawdiness and melodrama. Such episodes in psychic life may offend the critical taste which is dominated by the Ruach: nevertheless, they occur, and a true account of the sphere of the Nephesh must contain at least this passing reference to them.

The Ruach is rational and logical: it comprises also the more highly organised emotions, with the faculty of moral judgment: it can work with the filing-system of the brain, it can deduce from basic principles, but it does not comprise in its scope the higher qualities of spiritual organisation and perspective which have given rise to such phrases as "godlike intellect." It is an essential part of the psyche as is the Nephesh: it guards and complements that and the physical body, directing them in their work in conjunction with itself as the foundation and instrument of the higher faculties. It is the conscious centre of the personality in civilised man, and as such corresponds to the "Ego" of psychology. The chief characteristic of the Ruach is its power of reflection, of self-regarding: it can consider the activity of every other component in the psyche or in the material body of the organism so far as it is aware of them. It cannot however adequately consider its own activity while in its primal state, since only the Briatic intelligence or awareness, which yet sleeps, would enable it to do so.*

---

* Neither can the Ruach-consciousness (Ego-consciousness) be aware, while in its primal state, of the World of Briah, even though that world is properly its own habitation. This is the fundamental paradox of human nature. The Ruach's awareness of the astral world is gained by its contacts with the Nephesh substance: its awareness of the material world is gained by its contact with the physical body through the link of the Nephesh: but at the Briatic level the

To deny self-awareness absolutely to the Nephesh is difficult, for we have to account for the evidently deliberate jokes sometimes contrived by it in dreams, just as we cannot deny the evidence for deliberate but completely spontaneous clowning occasionally, on the part of domestic animals. The explanation may be the intrusion of a certain Ruach-element, which appears in dreams not only as humour but as a critical interpolation, as in Janice's dream when the thought intruded that her vehicle "ought to" have wheels. In domestic animals it may be supposed that a trace of Ruach-element has to some extent developed to compensate the dulling of their instincts, but this again is only possible if we suppose some rudimentary Ruach-faculty to be present even in wild animals. This we can only gauge when they are confronted with a man-made situation for which their instincts do not provide. The ability to cope with non-instinctual problems does show certain boundaries which of course vary with species, age, sex and other circumstances. Cars and trains, to an unsophisticated animal (whether wild or domestic,) do not seem dangerous, presumably because the smells and sounds of machinery are not registered in the instinctual catalogue of warnings. Cows, at the passing of a train, will notoriously begin running in the same direction as the train: they are evincing merely the herd instinct: while many creatures, from partridges to lions, can be approached by car without at all alarming them. Nobody, on the other hand, who has seen a wild stallion unpicking a complex knot with his teeth, or a semi-wild bull carefully feeling with one horn for the latch of a gate, will easily be convinced that no element of

Nephesh neither is present nor can normally avail. Until the attainment of Briatic consciousness, which is one consequence of the descent of the Intuitive Mind, the Ruach remains "turned inward" at the Briatic level, although it is "turned outward" through the Nephesh as regards the Yetziratic and Assiatic Worlds. (The Intuitive Mind can occasionally communicate through the Nephesh, as in the case of rare premonitions, and as also in the case of dreams of archetypal images: but these occurrences cannot be considered as the norm.)

reasoning exists in the minds of those creatures. We can of course object that they are merely adapting their instincts, which would lead the former to castrate, the latter to disembowel, an adversary: but that which adapts instinct is a form of reason, just as it is reason fully-fledged which has developed all the skills of the human hand. However, here we must leave animal psychology for it is no proper part of our study.

The Ruach, then, is bounded at its one extremity by the Nephesh which it to some degree interpenetrates, and at its other extremity by the domain of the higher faculties to which it should be receptive. That it often fails to be receptive to those faculties, besides over-dominating the Nephesh, does not signify that it should therefore be deposed from its function: the Ruach is from every aspect an indispensable part of our total organisation. It must both control the Nephesh, and work with it and (in everyday life) through it. Part of the work of the Ruach, in reading and interpreting the records of the physical brain, is still the subject of considerable research. As is well known, the ability of the brain-cells to record knowledge does not, in itself, constitute intelligence although a good stock of knowledge is an obvious advantage. A useful study in psychology can be made of the various factors which inhibit the availability of knowledge when it is present: for, as we have indicated, between the Ruach and the physical brain is necessarily interposed the Nephesh as animating force, as unconscious instinctual activator of the brain-processes, as guide to the Ruach that it is "on the right track," as we say: but wherever the Nephesh is present the possibility of subrational loading occurs, and this loading may be totally oblivious of the main requirements of the case as seen by the Ruach or even by the organism as a whole. Thus, for instance, a boy with a keen visual sense may have to be told in his schooldays that he must not solve certain problems by geometry, but must work them out in algebra. In after life he may find himself in a situation where the swift solution of just such a problem could be of vital importance. The Nephesh, however, could in some personalities still block this process by taking on the bygone voice of the teacher, with "You must work this out by algebra." Or again: the Ruach in examining a problem may perceive that a certain factor would present an advantage. The Nephesh, guided by tiredness or inertia, may influence the Ruach to halt the examination at that point, so that the corresponding disadvantages are not considered. This is a frequent cause of "unintelligent" human behaviour, particularly in the following which is given to alleged panaceas in the political world. What is generally termed intelligence, then, is dependent upon the freedom of the Ruach, and also upon its capacity for swift and accurate performance in gathering relevant material from sense impressions and from brain-stored data. In the former requirement we see the need of the Ruach to act independently of the Nephesh: in the latter, the need for the close co-operation of the two faculties. It becomes apparent as we proceed that this delicate balance is not achieved between Nephesh and Ruach alone: some degree of awareness at least of the higher faculties is essential.

It is at this juncture appropriate to examine an example which illustrates to some extent the interrelation of Ruach, Nephesh, and brain. The subject, Laura, was an unmarried woman of higher than average I.Q., but with a strongly emotional nature, who without any occult training had been an occasional "astral traveller" from childhood: she had in some instances been seen by percipients of only moderate sensitivity, who had the impression that she wore a trailing pale-coloured dress. She had also a slight history of physical sleep-walking in her late teens. Besides these experiences, she had at the time of examination begun Helionic* travelling, which was in process of superceding the Hecatean.† It does not appear that she had ever had any conscious technique for

*See Vol. 3, concerning primary techniques of Nephesh and Ruach projection.
†Ibid.

leaving the body, which according to her sister lay in an almost cataleptic and unwakeable sleep meanwhile: she had to wait for occasions when, for unknown reasons, she "found herself outside," as she put it, and then she simply decided where she would go and what she would do. Nothing in connection with these adventures had ever frightened her, nor had she ever experienced any difficulty in returning to her body afterwards. It must be added that she was thoroughly accustomed to life in a large town, and was in the usual style of commercial employment.

On the occasion in question, which was during her twenty-seventh year, she awakened one night to find herself apparently walking along the street near her home. Several circumstances convinced her that she was not dreaming: there was, to some extent, the mere fact that she questioned the matter, although she did not consider this to be an infallible test: then, the fact which had first caught her attention, that she heard no sound of her own footsteps as she moved forward. Besides this, she felt no slightest impact of air upon her skin: and again—a rather curious point—there was the fact that she felt it to be a certain definite time during the night, perhaps an hour after midnight, which would make it about two and a half hours since she had gone to bed. In dreams, she commented, it might seem like daytime or like night-time, but it never seemed to be a certain time which could be related to the hour at which one had gone to bed. Apart from these matters however, she felt, although she did not explore the situation in any detail, that she was quite her usual self. What, now, (she had wondered) should she take this opportunity to do? She called to mind a man with whom she worked: he suffered from some form of heart trouble, but although she liked and respected him she knew little about him, for he was rather unusually quiet and reserved. She knew he lived in the next town, perhaps ten miles away. She resolved to go and see whether she could do anything to help his state of health. The fact that she did not know his address did not trouble her: she knew in any case the way to the general area, and resolved that when she arrived there she would "think of where he was and just go there," as she put it.

Up to this point—that is, up to her actual setting out on this astral journey—her description of her mental processes seems normal, in the general sense of the word: only through knowing her usual style and manner does one perceive that it is all rather too naive to be truly natural: as if, even to bring the episode back to recollection some years afterwards, she had had to put into abeyance a considerable part of her habitual vitality and discursiveness. No comment on this was however made at the time: and without interruption she continued her account.

About half a mile from her home, she had to cross a main road. It was a wide arterial road and at most hours of day or night there would be some traffic upon it, frequently a considerable amount: but at that moment it was deserted. She considered crossing its bare expanse: but although she hesitated for some time, the traffic signals remained at green. She did not know what to do. Would she be visible to the driver of a vehicle? Would a vehicle be visible to her? She no longer felt quite sure. What would happen if a vehicle, perhaps invisible to her, were to strike her in her present state? She stood by the traffic lights, trying to work this out from basic principles and slowly realising that her "brain was not working:" then, despairing of an answer and feeling that she was wasting valuable time, she summoned up her courage and went forward across the road.

Her narrative contains nothing further to our purpose until we find her standing outside a tall detached house in which, she realised, her friend lived. She hesitated between trying to ascend to an open window, or going to the front door: then she decided on the side door, because "people often leave their side doors unlocked." She found the door and was about to turn the handle when suddenly she remembered that whether it might be locked or unlocked, her hands would have no physical strength. Again she stood in a dejected state of indecision for some time until, slowly, the answer came to her: since she was "out without her body," the door could present no barrier to her: she had but to go boldly onward, willing herself to be inside the house, and inside she would be. After a moment she realised that she had passed the threshold and was now in the kitchen. Several people, she felt, were in the house: she accordingly fixed her mind on the personality of her friend, succeeded in singling out the particular feeling of his presence, and followed it as it became stronger, into the next room, up the stairs, and to another closed door. Once more, taught by experience, she thought to advance without hindrance: but this time, despite her struggles, she could not at once succeed. She deliberately considered in her mind the intended work of healing which was her purpose there: then she redoubled her efforts to get in. At last she succeeded, but, as she puts it, "it was like going through a fine-mesh sieve." She crossed the room (observing a bedside lamp which she afterwards described accurately) to look at the person lying in the bed. Compelling herself to see beneath the surface, she arrived at a conclusion as to the nature of the infirmity and then carried out her work of healing. Of her return home, she stated that she remembered only the moment when she was standing at her own bedside, looking down at her unconscious body. Then, as she leaned over it, to quote her own words once more, "One moment I was looking downwards, and then there was a sort of click and I found I was staring up at the ceiling from the bed where I lay." The next morning at work her friend thanked her for *what she had done*, and told her it was the first morning for some months that he had been able to start the day without digitalin: there was later evidence too of the reality of the improvement in his condition.

Laura's account, then, gives us as direct an insight as possible into the levels of experience where the mind must operate without the physical brain. With regard to the limited descriptive ability previously remarked, Laura was asked when her story was completed, why she had felt it necessary to speak in this way. She replied that she had spoken as she had felt the time of the occurrence, because she wanted to be certain of adding nothing. Her thinking had been very simple during that experience, because she had felt rather as if she had been partially stunned: "If I could have been hit on the head without feeling any pain or discomfort from it, I think I should have felt as I did while I was out of my body. It was like a sort of keeping on coming back into reality."

In other words, Laura felt her sense of continuity to be mildly impaired, as in slight concussion. This is of some interest as cases are recorded of other persons, differing from Laura in that they were not known to be recurrent astral travellers, but citing their sole experience of detached consciousness as being the consequence of a fall, of delirium (e.g. in malaria), or of comparable circumstances. Enquiry failed to show any comparable history in Laura's case, however: she and both her parents enjoyed robust health, and none of her experiences of extracorporeal awareness had been associated with any illness, accident, or drug. In all cases she had simply gone to bed as usual, without even a premonition of what was going to occur. It can therefore be confidently put forward that the "concussed" state of mind which she describes was an effect, and not a cause, of the separation of her consciousness from her body.

We perceive her mind, then, seeking but not finding access to its familiar brain-index: as a matter of psychological interest, we notice that being deprived of that material, the inculcated veto upon crossing the road in defiance of the traffic-signals asserts a considerably greater authority than it would over her normal mode of thought. Ordinarily, her practical sense would certainly not have hesitated before

crossing a manifestly empty road regardless of the signals:
but in her projected state, the authority of the traffic-lights
had to be rationalised, so that she even forgot that she was
now *less* vulnerable to physical harm than in her physical
body. Again, we have her hesitation as to how to enter the
house. It is evident, apart from any other aspect of the matter, that excepting the slight and barely-perceived amnesic
sensations, Laura's consciousness in her astral body does not
strike her as being very different from the everyday situation
in her physical body.

Something very different takes place when she attempts
to enter her friend's room. It is a well-known fact that the
development of the higher faculties gives a resistant quality
to the aura which enables it to repulse alien astral visitants:
rarely indeed, however, can an account of the matter be se-
cured from the viewpoint of the repulsed visitant. It is noteworthy that the boundary of the psychic barrier is identified
in this particular instance—probably accurately—with the obstacle of the material door.* But Laura's presence is not
Hecatean but Helionic; and her reaction to the difficulty is
most interesting. One of the valuable features of her story is
her total lack, both at the time of the experience and at the
time when she recorded it, of any occult training or knowledge. Here, then, she stands outside the door, with all her attributes (save for her material organism) of her complete spiritual, emotional and instinctual personality. Spontaneously
she fortifies her powers by making what we should term a
solemn declaration of her magical purpose. Her purpose is to
heal: it is tacitly made plain by her declaration that she has
not come to injure or to seduce by her intrusion. Quite probably, even apart from the effect of her declaration upon the
developed intuitive powers of the man she was approaching,

---

* Similarly in other circumstances, humanly-appointed barriers and egresses are
effective beyond the material level. The acceptance by non-material entities and
by psychic forces of material barriers which they could by their nature traverse,
is a frequent characteristic of such phenomena.

this deliberate recollection of her motives was necessary to release her own powers. We have seen how she hesitated to cross an empty road in defiance of the traffic regulations: the ordinary convention against entering the bedroom of a man whom she respected, may well have made part of her difficulty in passing the threshold. At all events, we are told that having declared her purpose she was, with a further struggle, admitted.

Her purpose of healing fulfilled, it seems that her return home was unconscious or, more probably, was simply at once forgotten on her return to bodily consciousness (as being presumably uneventful until the moment before she re-entered her physical body.) Such a sustained effort as this night's work would have been very tiring to an untrained and only slightly experienced practitioner.

However, we should now return to develop our account of the lower levels of the psyche with their relationship and interaction. While it is possible for the high faculties of the psyche to act through the unconscious regions of the Nephesh, this is inadequate and undesirable for the magician: such action, being unperceived by the rational mind, cannot be consciously controlled, and furthermore to encourage this development tends to place the Nephesh itself in dominion over the whole personality. The rightful vehicle of the higher faculties is the Ruach: this again, if it avoids that purpose (and the conscious reason has a very real resistance against owning its subordination to any authority) then, so far from maintaining its ascendancy over the Nephesh, it imperceptibly loses that natural dignity. Beautiful though the world of the Nephesh undeniably is, and inexhaustibly mysterious, yet it cannot be allowed to govern the entire life of one who has set foot upon the Way of Return. It must be allowed due place, both for its rightful development and for the pleasure and refreshment of the whole entity: also, for the student, so that by practical experience its character may be known:

but its direction is contrary to the current of evolution, contrary to the way of integration: therefore to place oneself entirely beneath its domination would, for most of those who have gained some knowledge of the occult, be to negate the purpose of incarnation and would be contrary to the following of the True Will. The warning here is primarily directed to those who might submerge themselves in the attraction of the elemental spheres, or who might pursue a similar fascination by means of drugs: but there is also danger to the magical life in the completely "respectable" but vapid and aimless standards followed by the many through lack of occult understanding. The magical student cannot accept their norms. Such lives are governed by merely instinctual and mass-emotional impulses to a far greater extent than is generally realised: not of course that the Ruach is inoperative in them, but because, carrying nothing of the higher faculties, it fails of its purpose: whereas the magician, the poet and the artist, whom society regards with suspicion as living in the world of dreams, must, if they are to bring their works to fulfilment, direct and rule their dream-world by the higher faculties acting through the Ruach, as the charioteer guides his team.

# CHAPTER II

As the physical body is part of the material world and is subject to its conditions, so the Nephesh is part of the Astral Light and is subject to the conditions of the astral world.

Terms relating to the Nephesh or Astrosome. Distinction between its two levels as separating in projection or at death. The Centres of Activity. The Aura.

The Ruach or Noemasome. The emotions. The whole person involved in formulating a judgment. Unity is desirable: confusion of levels is if possible to be avoided.
>    Examples of a dream blending true prophecy with illusion.
>    Example of clairvoyance blending astral perception with involvement of the physical nervous system.

The action of Ruach and Nephesh in influencing the psyche and the physical body of another person:—
in healing,
in cursing,
in love-charms.

As bearing upon such influences, the philosophy of Avicenna in the eleventh century: also the experiments of Professor

Vasiliev in the twentieth century.

Some considerations on the Astral and Mental Bodies as affected by death.

## CHAPTER II
## THE ASTRAL AND MENTAL BODIES

Incarnate Man exists on all four planes of the universe simultaneously, although his degree of awareness is limited by his condition. The physical body is of the stuff of the World of Assiah, and is subject to the conditions of life and of existence in that world: it comes into being, it rises to maturity, it sinks into death and passes away. It is capable of reproducing its like: it also combines in itself all those senses and faculties by which man is ordinarily able to create or to bring about changes in the phenomena of the World of Assiah. As is well known, in psychosomatic conditions the physical body is influenced, sometimes to a considerable extent, by non-material factors: while there are many ways also in which the physical body can in turn affect the functions of the Nephesh, and even of the Ruach.

The Nephesh, being a part of the Astral Light, is often referred to as the astral body, or Astrosome: sometimes it is called the etheric body, while by some schools of thought the term "etheric" is reserved to that lower region of the Nephesh which we prefer to designate as the "gross astral," and which is immediately linked to the physical body. This distinction is useful when describing the state of the psyche in projection for instance or at death, for then certainly a division occurs between the two levels of the astral body: the term "Splitting the Moon" applied by other schools to the process in projection indicates a recognition that the parts thus separated are not intrinsically separate, but both comprise that level of the psyche which pertains to the astral world or "Moon-sphere" generally. Apart from the phenomena of projection and of death, however, the astrosome functions as one whole, its levels interpenetrating to an extent which varies from individual to individual and from time to time.* The astrosome is rightly considered to be a "body," since it corresponds to the physical even to the most minute detail, and also since it is one of those parts of the total personality which act as a vehicle to the higher faculties. The astrosome has, however, certain distinctive characteristics of its own. In it, and corresponding for the most part to neural and glandular centres of the physical body, are to be found those Centres of Activity, the principal of which we shall discuss further in Chapter V. Those principal centres, however, are by no means the only ones existing within the astral body, which, when these centres are viewed clairvoyantly, can have as a whole very much the appearance of a complex railway junction at night, ablaze with signal-lights of different colours and of widely varying intensity, with here and there the reflection of one or more of these colours upon a connecting line. Despite the changeable character of the Nephesh, the astral substance thereof being in a continual state of fluctuation (in response to emotional stimuli, the influence of bodily health, or spiritual exercises, for example), it has in respect of its main features the stability of the physical body at least. Associated with the astral body is the aura (cf. Book III, pp. 200-201), an emanation of energy from the total personality which is radiated by the astral body: it

---

*The level of consciousness, which for practical purposes marks the boundary between the domains of Ruach and Nephesh in any given person at any given moment, is in fact widely variable: consciousness can plunge deep with habituated introspection, while on the other hand the whole emotional area of the Nephesh is as subject to the power of the unconscious as the dried-out sea-land of Limna to the power of the ocean-goddess Dictynna (for which see Euripides, *Hippolytus.)*

is technically referred to as the *Beta force-field*, its physical counterpart being the electrical aura or *Alpha force-field*, which is radiated by the physical organism. Many phenomena commonly held to be of psychic origin are in fact produced by the electrical aura: the truly psychic faculties have their seat in the Nephesh. In this series, the term "aura" is used to designate the *Beta force-field*. Like the Nephesh itself, the aura is responsive to every influence from whatever level originating. When the psyche is infused with energy of a high spiritual vibration, the aura (or the *argyraigis*, to give it its esoteric title in this circumstance) becomes a protective barrier which effectively excludes all external Yetziratic forces of a lower vibration than its own. However, at the will of the magician, the sphere of sensation is attuned to, and can admit, external influences of the Yetziratic world.

A characteristic of the astral in projection, is the "cord" which unites it to the gross astral, that part of the Nephesh which must continue in immediate contact with the physical body if the latter is to continue living.

In projection, the link is maintained, although it may not be noticed, especially when the distance between physical body and astral presence causes a considerable attenuation of the cord. Some proportion of the substance of the gross astral itself frequently participates in projection: where this is excessive, "astral bleeding" results (vide Vol. 3).

The mental sheath, the Noemasome, when this is perceived, tends to the outward appearance of the subject but has a particular luminescence, varying in degree with the individual. It is not usually termed a "body," for the Ruach is supposed by the majority of people to be the "true self" which is carried by the material and astral vehicles: but it

participates in bodily form by virtue of its causal relationship,* through the Nephesh, to the physical body, also by
virtue of those finer levels of the Nephesh which are practically assimilated to it. The psyche is not a system of harshly-
defined boundaries.

Particularly difficult to define is a boundary between
Ruach and Nephesh with regard to those highly evolved
emotions which, in their achievement, belong clearly to the
domain of the Ruach but which nevertheless take origin in
the unconscious regions of the Nephesh. Among such
problematical subject-matter we find the great loves and the
aesthetic creations of mankind, as well as such morally-toned
emotions as anger or compassion. It must not of course be
forgotten that regardless of what we may conclude as to
the origin of all these things, it is a total person who enter-
tains or manifests them, not a part of that person's psyche or
material body. It is Hippolytus, not his tongue or his heart
(despite his protests,) who swears to Phaedra that her secret
will be respected: likewise it was the total personality of
Renoir which produced Renoir's paintings, and not merely
a piece, albeit an important piece, of his anatomy: despite
his highly cogent answer to Modigliani on the question.
However, an understanding of motives, and of structures
within the psyche, is of great importance to the magician,
to help him determine whether a particular work should be
carried out at all, and, if so, by what means at what level
it may most effectively be fulfilled: also for the greater

* The primal involutionary formation of the human psyche is from an impulse of
the Yechidah in the Divine Mind, projecting thence in turn the Chiah, the
Neshamah, the Ruach, and from the Ruach the Nephesh and finally the physical
body as vehicle of incarnation; for which reason the Schoolmen used to say that
the soul is the "form," i.e., the pattern or prototype, of the body. It is therefore
found that when involution gives place to evolution and the human organism
seeks its spiritual fulfilment, certain primal patterns show themselves as being
"built in" from the beginning. We see the instinctual level of the Nephesh in part
stimulating, in part reinforced by, the physical reactions of nerve and gland: we
see the emotional level developing from the instincts but at the same time
developing into the pre-existing higher level of the Nephesh: and so with the
Ruach. Then the Ruach under the influence of the dimly-perceived Neshamah
should develop further.

purpose of enabling him to see the place of that work and of every work in the plan of his particular present lifetime, with, if possible, some light also on the place of his lifetime in his cosmic development.

As great a clarity as possible, also, is to be desired in order to avoid that confusion of persons and of levels to which the works of the Nephesh are especially prone, even when, (to take one example) a prediction which is fundamentally true and beyond the scope of mere coincidence is produced through its faculties. The creative imagination may be unwittingly engaged, mingling truth with phantasy, or again, the nervous system may be entangled with the faculties of the Nephesh so that what is mentally and imaginatively perceived is likely to be physically experienced also. All these confusions are symptomatic of a lack of training and of comprehension, and therefore are so characteristic of the lower levels of "psychic experience" that a plethora of examples is available: however two are selected as illustrating various related questions. One concerns a prophetic dream, sufficiently detailed and exact to rule out any possibility of coincidence, but differing materially as between the dream and the fulfilment.

Henry W. in his student days became strongly attracted to a young girl of vivid personality and appearance, who was just embarking on a secretarial career. Two of Sylvia's qualities, however, frightened him: her emotional intensity, and her possessiveness. On this account he determined that he must at any cost break his infatuation, and, as soon as an opportunity offered, he went abroad for a few years. During that time, fresh scenes and new faces, and, be it added, a new love-affair, so occupied him that he gave scarcely a conscious thought to the object of his previous obsession: but one night, shortly before his intended return, he had a singularly clear and detailed dream about her. In his dream, he was walking along a street, when unexpectedly

Sylvia came to meet him. She was wearing a garment of a
type and colour he had never associated with her: an elegant
and very low-necked housecoat of blue watered silk, with a
long, full skirt. Her blonde hair, which he remembered as
short, now hung to her shoulders. He was delighted to see
her and they engaged in a happy conversation about his
travels, until suddenly a young boy, seemingly about ten
years old, not resembling anyone known to the dreamer,
also appeared and said to Henry, "If you really knew her,
you would have nothing to do with her." Henry asked the
reason, and the boy replied distinctly "She is living as the
mistress of her former employer." Thereupon, in the dream,
Henry turned to Sylvia and asked if this were true. She did
not reply. He tried to force her to speak: in the end he
seized her throat and demanded an answer. She sank limply
to the pavement, and he realised that he had killed her. From
this frightful dream he awoke shuddering, to find that a
violent thunderstorm was in progress: the lightning had in
fact struck several tiles from the roof of his house, just above
the room in which he lay. On reflection, he was inclined to
attribute his dream entirely to the storm: but a short time
later, having the opportunity to discuss the matter with a
friend who was experienced in the Jungian system, he recounted the whole affair. It was not difficult to attribute
the various elements of the dream in the accepted manner:
a young, attractive and demonstrative girl, setting forth
into the world, was sure to cause some suppressed anxiety,
not to say jealousy, to her friends and admirers, while the
role ascribed by the dream to the employer was not only
a melodramatic commonplace, it was also very considerably
that of the archetypal chieftain. The unfamiliar garment
worn in the dream by Sylvia was also found to be significant:
it was blue, and it was *watered* silk, and it was of a fashion
which revealed much of the shoulders and bust while
completely hiding the legs: this and her long hair identified

her as a mermaid, a siren, and the mermaid-character represented exactly those qualities which Henry had previously
feared in her: changeful passions, and possessiveness. Furthermore, this identification undeniably accounted sufficiently
for Henry's infatuation: he had unconsciously accepted the
figure of Sylvia to represent the Anima in his psyche, and this
was the sea-aspect of the Anima as the Great Mother. The
boy in the dream was a figure of the *puer aeternus,* frequently enough seen in dreams and needing no further
elucidation: here, a childish figure of shocked innocence,
having no deliberate intention of the tragedy which resulted
from his words. As to that tragedy, which was mere fiction,
it held one aspect of importance: Henry, always a studious
young man, must take care that his resentment of the
symbolic Sylvia did not develop into a resentment of his
rational intellect against the inspirational Anima. All this,
Henry felt, exactly fitted the case: and having committed
his dream to paper for the purpose of that discussion, he now
practically forgot it.

After some months, he returned home and having re-
established himself, one day he was overcome by an impulse
to ring up the office where Sylvia had worked and to ask for
her. A girl's voice answered, "She doesn't work here now, but
I can give you a number which will find her most evenings."
So Henry renewed contact with Sylvia and they arranged a
meeting.

He saw her coming along the street somewhat as in his
dream, but she was wearing a smart black outfit, while her
hair, though she had indeed grown it long, was fashionably
piled up on top of her head. After they had exchanged
greetings, she invited him home for a cup of coffee and took
him to a comfortable flat. Presently, having heard the main
points of his news, she settled him in front of the television
with some fresh coffee, and went off to change from her
outdoor clothes. Henry spent most of the time staring in

astonishment round the room itself, with its ponderous
furniture and book-lined walls: but this can have done little
to lessen his profound sense of shock when at length Sylvia
came back into the room, with her hair hanging in loose
waves to her shoulders, and her slim form clad in the identical low-necked full-skirted housecoat of blue moiré which
he had seen in his dream. His subsequent account of the
matter was that he could not accept it: he kept thinking that
if he looked at the garment in a different way he would find
that the colour, or the shape, or the fabric was really unlike
his dream: but try as he might, he could not persuade himself
that any difference existed. It was the identical garment.

Despite his preoccupation, they found much to talk
about until suddenly Sylvia glanced at the clock. "Henry,
I've something to tell you. This isn't really my flat: I gave
up my flat because I spent so little time there. I—"

"You are living as the mistress of your former
employer," Henry heard his own voice saying in a curiously
automatic manner.

"What a funny stilted way of putting it! How did you
find out? I suppose the girls at the office know, after all.
Are you furious Henry? Please don't be—"

Henry was not furious. He experienced nothing of the
rage which had possessed him in his dream: he simply felt
rather sick, bewildered and helpless. In any case, before he
could formulate any suitable response, the door opened
and a well-groomed middle-aged man came in. Sylvia hastily
introduced them. "Ah, Henry: Sylvia's old playmate!" said
the newcomer, extending a cordial hand. "I've heard so very
much about you! What has she given you to drink? Coffee?
We must put that right . . ."

Henry never visited there again, and never again saw
Sylvia: but at least nobody murdered anyone, so the most
vivid and dramatic incident in his dream remained unfulfilled.
It is interesting that the fact of so many details in his dream

proving to be prophetic, did not in the least diminish the reality of the interpretation given to him earlier. The persistence of his attraction to Sylvia indicates that she was for him, in some way, a true Anima-image. And it was the Sylvia with whom he had this strange affinity, who had presumably chosen the blue moiré because she felt it was "right" for her. The large skirt and revealed bust are as characteristic of the Goddess as is the Mermaid-figure; as witness both Minoan and Celtic examples. Nevertheless, it was certainly through the unconscious levels of the Nephesh that the true message was conveyed to Henry's awareness: one symptom of this is the "funny, stilted" words on which Sylvia remarked. The Nephesh is often characterised by old-fasioned and even ritualistic forms of expression: it continually reminds us in one way or another of its links, through the collective unconscious, with the entire past history of our race: even of our world. As to the high feminine component in the psyche, the Anima, it is to be remarked that Henry in fact did not lose its "inspirational" quality by his final break with Sylvia. In this connection we may here point out that although many Jungians regard the inspirational role as belonging intrinsically to the Anima (or to the Animus in the female-type development of the psyche) there is more to be said on this matter which we shall give when treating of the higher faculties. Meanwhile, reverting to Henry's dream, we surmise that the death of Sylvia in that dream foretold the deposition of her image from its place as representative of the Anima. We may also surmise in the violence of the dream a certain degree of rebellion on the part of a suppressed aggressive instinct, in compensation for the certainty that in real life the highly civilised and intellectually developed young man would react quite differently. However, despite these evident subjective factors (including the boy-figure as messenger from the unconscious to the conscious worlds, like a youthful Hermes, and also including the minor confusions which need not be reiterated) the essentially prophetic quality of the dream remains. It is indeed possible that the great storm which was in progress may have been an immediate cause of this moment of insight, just as a physical shock can give rise to a period of astral projection. Who knows, indeed, how fractional may have been the displacement of the elements by which Henry escaped death when the lightning struck the tiles from the roof over his head?—or how great may have been the shock thereof to his extended aura?

We turn now to the waking experiences of Mrs. D., a natural clairvoyant who retired a number of years ago but whose abilities and limitations were alike most interesting. A few biographical details may be considered relevant as indicating the closeness to nature and the powerfully moving energies which are often associated with this type of psychism.

Mrs. D. was born in a village of one of the more remote districts of Wales. She was to some extent psychic from childhood, but this was not remarked as anything very unusual in her community, and she worked, grew up, and in due course went courting like all the other girls. The manner of her courtship was, however, perhaps a little unusual even in that region. The wild mountains surrounding the village were the traditional and accepted place for lovers' meetings, and wandering there, she and her young man one day found a beautiful and little-known waterfall which they at once claimed as "theirs." Beside the pool at the foot of the fall were piled a great quantity of boulders, carried down by the torrent at some earlier time: and this hardy couple, instead of merely lying in the sun like Kingsley's young lovers "deep in fern on Airlie Beacon," spent their courtship days gathering the boulders (and thus scattering a numerous colony of spiders, who must have dwelt there long without disturbance) to build a cottage close to the fall, fitting the stones together without mortar in the immemorial manner of their people. This cottage, to which they gave a Welsh name meaning "Spiders' Castle," became their home when they were married, and as their family increased they simply added to the building. Even there, her days filled with the work of housekeeping and cooking in absolutely primitive conditions, Mrs. D. began to be sought out for advice and for word of the future. When, however, the children were all grown and she herself became a widow, she began to heed the invitation of some of her kindred, and an inner conviction that she would prosper so. She packed her few possessions, leaving "Spiders' Castle" to its previous denizens, and departed for the English Midlands. There, on the outskirts of an industrial town, a few well-judged ventures enabled her to establish herself in a few years as a clairvoyant of increasing repute. Even in this she chose nothing stylish: her ostensible method was simple teacup-reading. A little investigation, however, was enough to show that the way in which Mrs. D. used a teacup, was much closer to crystal-gazing than to the rule-of-thumb methods of many of her kind. The tea-leaves, which she noticed only at the beginning of a reading, acted as a starting-point for her visual imagination: the intensity of her vision rapidly became hallucinatory, so that she would declare without hesitation that the scenes and persons which she described could be seen inside the teacup. She expected her sitters to be able to see them too, and any hesitation or expression of doubt would make her so excited that the continuation of the sitting was threatened. Nevertheless, the accuracy and detail of her predictions was often of a very high level. For instance, one day when she was just beginning to be known, she received a visit from a young man who was wearing country tweeds and a bowler hat, and who asked for a reading. It scarcely needed any special talent to tell his profession, and when she declared that he was a detective he began to take his leave, feeling that his purpose had been frustrated. "Sit down again," said

Mrs. D: "You are at the beginning of your career, and this. is your first plain-clothes job. I believe you want to help people, and I can tell you one or two things. "She proceeded with the reading, until suddenly a darkness descended upon her and instead of seeing what should happen she felt as if some part of her consciousness were living it. "I am in a wood, at night," she said. "I am waiting for someone—for some men who mean to break into a large house nearby. I am listening for the least sound—Oh! Someone has seized me from behind: he is hitting me on the head but I have hold of him also. I am shouting for help and I hear other men running away: the one who has me struggles to be free also, but I hang on and I keep shouting while he hits me. Oh, the pain in my head!—but I must not let go, I must not let go! And then help comes: I am safe!" She opened her eyes and looked in a dazed fashion at her visitor. "That's all I can tell you: but you will remember when the time comes, *you must not let go.*"

It befell exactly as she had described it: the young detective almost thought himself overcome by the assailant in the woods, but Mrs. D's words came back to him and he hung on despite the shower of vicious blows upon his head. He was promoted, as his courage deserved: and Mrs. D. received a much-prized letter which certified that she was no "fortune-teller," but a true clairvoyant.

One of the most interesting features in her work, was her liability, as illustrated in this episode, to become affected by physical pain associated with the matter which she had to tell. Hardly ever (she said) was this a pain which the visitor had at the time: it was either a pain which that person would have in the future, or quite often it was one which someone near to that person was already suffering. "Come to me with rheumatism, headache, toothache, anything you please," she used to say: "but if you have someone at home suffering from anything of that sort, then please stay away, or I shall have to suffer it too!" One of the characteristics which she thus unconsciously demonstrated, was the extremely gross astral level at which her clairvoyance operated, being intimately linked with the physical nervous system: also a peculiarity which is somewhat akin to that found in standard ESP testing: where a number of subjects give habitually the next card which will be turned up, or the one immediately past, when the object of the exercise is that they shall name the card which is turned up currently. It is as if that which is actually present is used by the unconscious motivation only as a hurdle, or as a stepping-stone to what is beyond. The story of the detective's teacup reading is here given almost verbatim from Mrs. D's personal reminiscences, but has to some extent been checked independently: it is, in any case, completely consistent with all that could be known of this extraordinary woman. Our own investigator made no attempt to deceive her and "sat in" at some of her readings, which were informal to a degree, most of her visitors being people from the neighbouring industrial area. An interesting sequence of events took place a few years before Mrs. D's retirement: one day she confided in our investigator, "I think I shall have to pack this business up soon, it's affecting my heart. Have you ever heard of teacup-reading doing harm to a person's heart?" Being assured quite to the contrary, she continued "I don't know what it is, then, but I can't stand much more of it. It always happens when I'm doing a reading: not every reading, and not every day: but four or five times a week, I'll be just in the middle of a reading, and seeing such nice peaceful things quite likely, when suddenly— bang!—it's like a great crash without hearing it: everything goes dark and I don't feel I'm sitting there any more, I seem to be falling into a huge blackness: I think I lose con- sciousness for a moment. Then I struggle back, and there

I am in my chair and not a minute has passed: but it's so horrible that I dread it, and the worst of it is that it comes without warning."

It sounded sufficiently like a heart affliction to prompt our investigator to recommend Mrs. D. to take medical advice; but a mystified G.P. found this sexagenarian, who had in her time borne nine children without medical aid, to be an almost incredibly healthy woman for her age. He could only advise a month's holiday: this she took, and had no attacks during that time. As soon as she resumed the readings, however, they returned: but only for a short while. One night a vast explosion at one of the factories shook the entire district: windows were smashed by the blast to a considerable distance. The casualties, fatal and otherwise, were numbered in hundreds: almost all were male, as the night shift was then working. Mrs. D's "heart attacks" ceased forthwith: the readings which she had been doing when they occurred, had all been for the womenfolk of the men involved in the explosion. Nevertheless, the experience had certainly unnerved her considerably: she could not forget the possibility that something similar might happen again. After a couple of years she took out all her savings from under a loose floorboard, and bought herself a cottage in her native land, more comfortable than Spiders' Castle. (We cannot give the full details of her horoscope, but her natal Sun was in Leo, with Cancer ascendant, a strong Neptune in Aries, Uranus in Leo: particulars which may interest the astrologically-minded.)

It is not only in studying clairvoyance of this type that we encounter the involuntary transfer of physical sensations from one person to another. Untrained or improperly trained "healers" are especially prone to it, some of them actually cherishing a mistaken belief that their participation in the sufferer's "conditions" is a proof of the efficacy of their work. In point of fact it proves nothing, although it does indicate a probability that contact upon a low astral level has been established. As not even a headache is quantitative, the fact that the "healer" endures a certain amount of it does not necessarily reduce the pain of the original sufferer by a single pang: although the astral contact itself, which in these cases is signalised by the transfer, may for various reasons cause real alleviation. It should be made clear to all such operators that the transfer of symptoms in this way is both unnecessary and highly undesirable: that it points to a faulty technique whereby the personal energies of the operator mingle with those of the beneficiary, and if such work is undertaken, a proper method is needed which provides for the transformation of all energies entering or leaving the psyche, together with their adequate replenishment from higher sources. The principles involved will be made clear in Volume 3 of the present series. When the level of the operation is raised in this manner, the benefit to the recipient will frequently be much increased, while the painful and exhausting effects upon the operator should completely cease. The subject of psychic healing is an extremely complex one, the methods of different operators showing a considerable variation and involving widely differing principles: it is mentioned here chiefly for its bearing upon other matters. If, for example, a sufferer can without volition be the cause of physical symptoms to a careless healer, or, even at a distance, to the untrained clairvoyant, then what is the likelihood that a human being or a discarnate entity could, with intention, cause changes by non-material means, in the psyche of another?

This is a question of great importance in the history of magical psychology, having been under debate from the Middle Ages at the least. We may take, so as to clarify the exact scope of the debate, the question of solemnly-imposed curses: a form of influence which the medievals in fact discussed extensively. To put the matter in general terms: A,

having a real or imagined grievance against B, solemnly
declares, with or without attendant ritual acts, that B shall
either die or suffer some injury or loss, in an appointed
manner or within an appointed time. B, in a number of
instances, dies or suffers as declared by A: either because
(1) B was going to die or suffer thus in any case, and A,
perhaps "beside himself" in an access of anger or grief,
foresaw the fact: or (2) B consciously knew of A's declaration and behaved accordingly through an unconscious process
of inner acceptance, or, (3) A's words or ritual acts were in
themselves potent to affect B's mental, astral or physical
body without his conscious knowledge: it is convenient to
include under this head also the possibility of any discarnate
force acting on A's behalf. There is another possibility,
(4) that of pure coincidence, in which A's declaration is in
no way causal to B's subsequent corresponding behaviour,
nor is the future fact of B's behaviour in any way causal to
A's declaration.

All these four possibilities can likewise be applied,
*mutato mutandis,* to that other favourite department of
perennial sorcery, the love-charm; but here a fifth possibility
comes in, to complicate matters still further:— A, having
performed without B's knowledge a rite to gain the affections
of B, may quite unconsciously begin to behave towards B
with so much increased self-confidence and subtle assumption of intimacy as to gain a favourable response, sufficient
to set the desired progress spiralling to its achievement.
Therefore, although both the curse and the love-charm are
examples of what the medievals meant by "fascination,"
the former gives us a more clear-cut picture of the setting for
possibility (3), which is the true subject of our question. An
actual example will not be adduced, because in any given
case a detailed knowledge of the facts is needed to rule out
the possibilities (1), (2) and (4). We will only comment
further on these possibilities, to point out that in maintaining

an attitude of healthy scepticism against too easy an acceptance of (3), the investigator must beware of going to the
other extreme and applying (1) or (4) where these involve
wild improbability. (2) both needs and deserves most careful
consideration, because even where B does as a fact know of
A's declaration, the effect which this knowledge *alone* may
produce will vary tremendously according to the physical
and emotional constitution of B. In some cases a sense of
guilt on B's part may lead to A's declaration being seized
upon as suggesting a suitable form of self-punishment: but
here again caution is necessary in the interpretation, as the
matter upon which B has an inner sense of guilt, may not be
at all the matter which gave rise to A's anger. "Pathological
confessions," especially to murder, are a well-known phenomenon: those who make them are generally written off
as publicity-seekers, but some at least are simply seeking
punishment. These people may have committed unknown
crimes, but just as probably their sense of guilt has been
developed falsely, e.g. by unwilling or sadistic parents or
teachers, thus producing a sub-rational "complex." The
same possibility obtains when a person complies with the
terms of a curse. Nevertheless, from whatever cause, this
inner compliance can produce astonishing phenomena.

All these points being carefully considered, we are still
left with a residue of well-attested instances which seem
to illustrate so clearly our possibility (3), and to rule out the
others, that the only argument which can be, and which
sometimes has been, raised in contradiction is an *a priori*
argument that such influence is impossible. This argument
has resulted in a debate through the centuries.

Here we must introduce a medieval thinker of the first
magnitude, to whom we shall later make reference in connection with far higher matters than our present subject: the
Persian Ibn Sina, known in European scholarship as Avicenna.
Born in 980 A.D., he was a practising physician at the age of

sixteen and thereafter made philosophy the pre-eminent
concern of his brilliant and eventful life. He studied the
Greek philosophers extensively, basing much of his personal
work upon the Neo-Platonists, but developing their ideas,
partly in the light of Islamic schools (among which, notably,
the Persian, wherein Neo-Platonist and Manichaean concepts
had already before his time formed an amalgam never to be
completely assimilated to any exoteric creed, whether
Moslem, Jewish or Christian) and partly in the transmuting
flame of his own genius. The proposition of Proclus, concerning the catena of emanations of Divine Energy, progressively
more limited in nature as each emanation is further from the
source,* reappears in Avicenna with certain additions: here
it is ten "Intelligences" which emanate, differing from one
another, not in nature since all  are divine, but in kind, in
consequence of the diminution of "simplicity" as the catena
develops away from the primal Unity: thus the second
emanation partakes of the character of duality, the third of
triplicity, the fourth of quaternity and so on. That in
Avicenna those emanations are perceived to be ten in number, is most probably in its origin a debt to Pythagoras. It
becomes amply evident that Avicenna is one of the fathers
of the Western System; however, we should give consideration to his ideas, as to those of any thinker, for their
intrinsic worth and not merely for any authority attaching
to them: the historical background is of interest as showing
the level and the quality of the thought to be anticipated.

In his "Sixth Book of Natural Matters" (Sextus
Naturalium), section 4 chapter 4, Avicenna points out that
the soul is more enduring and of a higher order than the body
by virtue of its spiritual nature, being thereby akin to those
spiritual principles by which matter is in the normal course
of events formed and changed. The power which the soul

*See Book III, page 145.

thus exercises over matter is not limited to the body which it inhabits.

This passage is a favourite with later writers because of its possible relevance to mineral transmutation, which is in fact one of its simpler applications: but where the material to be worked upon is the body of another living person, B, it just as evidently follows from Avicenna's words that the "soul" (and spirit) of B are likewise by nature free to keep and protect their particular earthly frame from harm caused by A's intervention: that is to say, provided there is no inner cause which inhibits that defence, such as the "guilt-complex" which we have mentioned previously. The full force of Avicenna's evaluation of the respective dynamism and passivity of soul and body cannot however be appreciated without some knowledge of his metaphysical view of the natures of spirit and matter. He sees the existent universe as a gradation of existences from the total actuality of pure undifferentiated Spirit, to the total potentiality of primal undifferentiated Matter, with every kind of spiritual entity, living being, and inanimate material at their respective stages between the two. The total potentiality of primal undifferentiated Matter, since it is conceived of as being as yet inchoate, without impress of any specific purpose, Avicenna considers as "evil:" thus accomodating, and at the same time disarming of any moral implication, the notion of the evil nature of matter* which he had inherited perhaps from the Persian Manichees, (as well as from Plotinus who again is careful to attach no suggestion of turpitude to the material universe.) It gives however a real sense of hierarchy to his gradation of existences, allowing of no doubt that any entity which is by nature more material than another, must thereby be at least implicitly subservient to that other.

---

* Very much as Freud describes the undirected sexuality of an infant as "polymorphous perverse" without intending moral censure thereby. It becomes apparent that any undirected force is seen as partaking of the nature of chaos, and therefore as "evil," i.e., inimical to personal or social organisation.

This view of the universe was at once, and rightly, perceived as an important enunciation of the magical philosophy. Consequently, it came in for a great deal of attack from ecclesiastical quarters in the thirteenth and fourteenth centuries, when the Church was for various reasons determined to stamp out all belief in the possibility of material transmutation. The chief ally of the Church in this campaign as champion of ignorance, was naturally the arrogant rational mind, the unenlightened Ruach of the ignorant, jubilant as it has so often been to deny the possibility of anything which it cannot of its own nature dominate. Truth, however, has a way of triumphing through the very means which are invoked against it, and the truth concerning the powers of the human soul and spirit has nothing to fear from scientific investigation provided this be scientific in full sincerity. Professor Vasiliev of the University of Leningrad, in the period between the two World Wars, conducted a research programme on the transmissibility of thought, under most strict laboratory conditions which provided even for the screening-out of the transmitted thought had it been due to any subtle form of electromagnetism (or radioactivity for that matter, since leaden chambers, airtight and electrically earthed, were used.) He found that under these conditions it was possible for the recipient not only to become accurately aware of the transmitted thought within minutes or seconds of its transmission, without even being informed beforehand that the transmission was to be made at that time, but also to react to commands thus transmitted, e.g. to fall asleep or to awaken: and that at the distance, in some tests, between Leningrad and Sebastopol. It is quite evident that Professor Vasiliev conducted these researches with complete integrity and impartiality, and furthermore that he had no apparent motive for wishing the outcome of his work to be what it was: since the findings of his great research programme, which had initially received official encouragement from the Soviet Government, were in the event relegated by that Government for some twenty years in the interest of materialism, until other matters of policy fortunately prompted their publication.

Returning to our question on the communication of thoughts, of images, of commands, we may glance here at a remaining aspect of the matter, which stands out if we compare Vasiliev's findings with Avicenna's. To employ terms which we have already defined, does Ruach speak to Ruach, or does the Ruach of the communicator "send a message" which is received by the Nephesh of the recipient, and which then "rises" as an *isolated* impression from the deeps of the lower unconscious into rational awareness? Or does the Ruach of the communicator work through its own Nephesh to reach the Nephesh of the recipient, with the results aforesaid? The last-mentioned is the most usual state of affairs: the higher faculty does direct the lower, but its own associated lower faculty rather than another person's.* (From private experimental work, the authors have ascertained that at least in some cases, the Ruach of the communicator influences its own Nephesh which in turn produces an effect in the *Alpha force-field* by means of the autonomic nervous system. The "message" is then transmitted to the *Alpha force-field* of B, whence it affects the autonomic nervous system of B, and is received as authentic sense-data by the Nephesh [and thence the Ruach] of B. This elucidates some of the mechanism of cases in which, in common occult parlance, a curse "bounces:–" because the communication rebounds at the level at which it is operating, it is not the Ruach of A which receives the repurcussion, but his probably more vulnerable Nephesh, or again, his *Alpha force-field* and nervous systems.† ) It can be presumed that in such

---

* An impression received directly by the Nephesh from an external source does not necessarily "rise" into consciousness, but may cause a focus of disturbance at the level of entry, giving rise to nightmares or obsessional ideas.
† Autonomic and cerebro-spinal.

matters as sending to sleep or awakening the recipient, as
in Vasiliev's experiments, the command conveyed thus to
B's Nephesh need not in fact penetrate to his Ruach before
being put into effect, as such activities are not necessarily
controlled by the conscious mind. Evidently the conscious
mind *can* normally intervene: this however would not be
likely in the experimental conditions, as the recipient, being
a willing participator in the research programme, would have
no motive to inhibit his Nephesh from obeying any command
of the sort which it might receive. Avicenna's hierarchy of
being is thus maintained here: a hierarchy which is, we may
observe, suggested in principle at least by Hamlet's words
concerning the Ghost:—

> "Why, what should be the fear?
> I do not set my life at a pin's fee:
> And for my soul, what can it do to that,
> Being a thing immortal as itself? . . . "

This clearly does not equate exactly with our terminology: for "life" in this context we must suppose the
physical body is intended and perhaps the astrosome as
animating it: for "soul" we would substitute the noemasome
and the higher faculties. Nevertheless, the main principle
comes out clearly, that inter-personal psychic influence
cannot involve the higher levels without their assent. What
must be added to Avicenna's concept, however, is that while
the noemasome can undoubtedly command the lower levels,
it is also undeniably accustomed to receive data from them.
Thus the Nephesh receives data from the nervous system, and
the Ruach receives data from the Nephesh.

From these assembled facts, sufficient evidence can
easily be deduced to show how a person can in conducive
circumstances be led to fulfil the terms of a curse which
may never be known to his conscious mind. This does not

preclude a degree of insight, as indicated in our possibility (1), on the part of the person who lays the curse, as to the weak points in the emotional "armour" of the victim: weaknesses caused by unconscious states of health, or by acceptance of occupational dangers, or of course by guilt. Blessings, certainly, are equally adhesive if applied with equal care and suitability: but adverse effects are usually the more noticed, even as it is most commonly the bad news which makes the headlines.

The quotation from Hamlet brings us to another topic, the separation of the lower parts of the psyche at death. This subject, to receive adequate treatment, would at least require some account of the higher faculties: nevertheless there are important aspects of the matter which belong essentially to our consideration of the lower faculties. Many thinkers and observers have generalised upon this subject far too much: hence a great measure of their disagreement.

At death* the gross astral can in some cases be reassimilated by the astral (we are not in this passage discussing what occurs when the higher faculties are sufficiently developed, as in the Adept, to assimilate to themselves the lower parts of the psyche), though more usually astral and gross astral are sundered. In the latter case there are several possibilities:— the gross astral complex may become (i) dissociated completely from the physical corpse, or (ii) it may remain linked to the corpse.† In both (i) and (ii) the gross astral will eventually "dissolve" into the currents of astral being,§ the unifying and vitalising force being withdrawn from it, but the gross astral complex is capable of independent— though blind—existence, for a longer or shorter period before

* The full details of what can occur at death and after are not entered upon in the present work, because the range of possibilities is too wide to admit of an adequate treatment.
† (ii) is more common than (i).
§ Granting certain exceptions where the gross astral may be fastened upon by an astral entity as a "habitation," and thus perpetuated by an alien force for a period perhaps of centuries.

dissolution occurs. In (ii), however, while it continues in existence, the gross astral will reflect the state of the corpse: *of itself*, it will remain "within" the body. In (i), the gross astral complex will, as it were, drift, but will have no volition. (iii) The deceased may, through erroneous ideas or a particularly strong tenacity to the material levels, or through a desire to communicate with the living, seek to retain his link with the gross astral. (iv) Where the deceased was in life dominated by the emotional and instinctual nature, the astral, after the sundering of the gross astral, may nevertheless in some instances retain a stronger affinity for the discarded lower Nephesh than for the Ruach. In such cases the astral may form a subrational reattachment to the gross astral, not involving the ineffectual Ruach.

As regards communication with reference to (iii), we must suppose that the evolution of our deceased subject has not reached the stage of mental awareness (for although no rules are to be made for those who have attained Briatic consciousness, at the same time it is improbable that they would seek to communicate in this manner.) Consequently, the Ruach of our subject is functioning through the fine astral material of his Nephesh, and he has awareness of the astral world. The illicit desire to communicate by means of the gross astral results usually from the failure of the intended recipients to recognise his higher vibrations:— but whatever the motive, the results can be most unpleasant if (iii) occurs with (ii)—witness the case of *the scholarly man* below. Communication is, of course, probably quite frequently achieved by personalities of this general level of development, without recourse to the discarded gross astral.

It is interesting at this point to note that the work of *necromancy* requires a freshly-buried corpse: the reason for this is that there is a greater chance of (iii) in conjunction with (ii) occurring with a fresh cadaver than with a long-buried corpse. But even if (ii) applies, necromancy will be unsuccessful if (iii) does not, and no amount of coercion or of sorcery can compel (iii) if the deceased has sundered the links.

Where (iii) occurs with (i), or even with (ii), there is no permanent harm done if the deceased strives to maintain the links, motivated only by good: a successfully conveyed message, or a blessing conveyed to the living and acknowledged by them, are usually all that is sought: but where (iii) occurs with (i) or with (ii) for reasons such as tenacity to the material levels, real harm may occur both to the deceased and to the living. When the lower psyche reverses its evolution, it cuts itself off from the sources of cosmic life: it thus finds itself to be suffering from spiritual starvation, and in an attempt to replenish itself it will turn to astral vampirism, just as in physical starvation human beings will sometimes turn to cannibalism.

Sometimes, unfortunately, where (iii) occurs with (ii), the deceased may have an indirect awareness of the corpse.

In extreme and rare instances where conditions (iii) and (ii) obtain, the personal consciousness of the deceased may be linked to the corpse itself: details of this subject are forbidden by the A.S. to be published, being too repugnant to human nature, and, as touching upon "the undead," contrary to the general weal.

Yet there are many shades of grey, and two general examples of the subject we are considering may be given from the experience of innocent people.

In one case a scholarly man solemnly engaged himself by a promise of a frequent type, but made this time to his children, that if personal survival were a fact, he would if possible return after his death to let them know. At intervals after his demise, the young man and young woman were appalled by fleeting visions of him, evidently eager to impart his news, and apparently quite unaware that he was manifesting in the guise of a progressively decaying corpse. All

that was needed however (though this required some heroism
on the part of the young people) was to convince him that
his message had been lovingly received and understood, and
that he ought now to depart for higher realms.

The other case, equally harrowing in its implications,
concerns a bereaved mother who, some time after seeing her
only son's embalmed body laid in the grave in due form both
religious and civic, began to be disturbed by dreams in which
his likeness appeared and said to her, "I cannot rest, I am
lying in water." So frequent did these troubled dreams
become that at last the grave was opened, and it was found
that a spring had broken through from the subsoil of the
cemetery. In this instance it should be pointed out that as
it was a dream-figure which had been seen recurrently by the
mother, her mind adding remembered qualities of speech and
movement, there is no real evidence here that the son's
consciousness was involved in the episode: the dreams much
more likely represent the communication of Nephesh to
Nephesh. Nevertheless, the fact remains that an undesirable
link between the son's astral and his corpse-bound gross
astral existed. This is not a plea for better burial conditions,
it is a plea for cremation: which is a sure means of destroying
not only the corpse itself, but also—when the quite usual
condition (ii) obtains—that most gross region of the Nephesh
which is likewise discarded at death by the Ruach and its fine
astral vehicle, and of course by the higher faculties.

It need hardly be added that on ample evidence as well
as reason, this in no way impairs the discarnate personality.*
A very interesting fact is observable with regard to the
reincarnation of persons whose previous bodies were cremated: they retain memories of the lifetimes concerned, and
in some cases show physical resemblances to their former
"selves," no less often—we would say from observed in-

* Nor can it cause any suffering, save in the rare case of the "undead," whether
cremated within days, or centuries, of death.

stances—than persons whose remains were buried. It should be recalled that out of that minority of human beings who retain clear and veritable memories of past incarnations, only a small proportion again, show any conspicuous physical resemblance to one of their previous bodies: but of the few startling instances of likeness which we have encountered, some have borne a living resemblance to a body which is known to have been cremated at the end of its history, just as some have resembled past "selves" whose final chapter had closed with a traditional burial. This suggests that the area of the psyche which carries this resemblance is by no means the most gross: a hypothesis which is further borne out by the fact that the incarnation most closely resembled is not always the most recent one. The whole subject is as complex as is the psyche itself: but we must add that there are indications that a marked development, mystical, magical or both, can cause almost a continuity of identity even when the new life occurs in quite different circumstances of heredity and environment from the old. This is in accordance with what we should theoretically expect: for where such a development is present, it causes an increased communication of the physical and Nephesh-qualities of the personality to the noemasome, and hence the more complete preservation of those qualities. At the same time it must be stated that no experience however mundane and unremarkable, or however traumatic and rejected, is ever truly lost: and those who can consciously recall no past splendours, joys, or sorrows, possess just as surely, stored in the "vast caverns" of the psyche, a history which goes back to the commencement of life on this planet.

Nor is conscious memory, though most desirable, an essential condition of the continuation of one's work. One may have longed to be able to follow out a particular development in scholarship, in science or in the arts: when circumstances are more propitious one will assuredly do so.

One may have sought, apparently without hope, for some other particular fulfilment in one's life: in another life one will assuredly find it. Especially we must emphasise that even to have set foot briefly upon the Way of Return is to guarantee that in some subsequent life one will renew that quest: in a hundred subsequent lives if need be shall that Way be pursued.*

---

* For that matter, the discarnate interval between earthly lives has its special opportunities: too many spend that time wandering in impenetrable mists, or basking in some self-made paradise, or striving vainly to find return to the remembered earth-ways, or wrapped in nightmares of past ills wrought or suffered. But incarnate life remains the truer school of the evolving spirit.

## CHAPTER III

That which is frequently termed the "spirit" in the human psyche is the Higher Self considered as a unity.

The rational faculty:— not the highest function of the Ruach, but of great importance in co-ordinating the other mental and bodily faculties, and in assessing the data they present to it.

The first awakening of the Ruach to the higher faculties; signalised by its increased perceptiveness of, and sensitivity to, the archetypal images as exemplified in the material universe.

The Platonist tradition of idealistic love, and its especial relationship to this stage of development of the Ruach. To Plotinus, as to Plato, the misery or bliss of the personality as a whole depends upon the right direction of the Ruach.

"Courtly love:" the influence of the medieval cult traced to our own day. The cult of the Unattainable: a natural stage in the progress of the psyche, and likewise in the historical unfolding of Psychosophy. Its esoteric significance. Perils of too swift an ascent to the imageless heights.

Psychological and initiatory bases of true progress. The rational faculty transcended. The experience of Omar Khayyam: the Angel and the Wine.

## CHAPTER III
## THE HIGHER SELF

The Higher Self, considered in the first instance as a unity, gives meaning and co-ordination to the faculties of the psyche. In one sense, it can be understood as forming a trine with Ruach and Nephesh, completing and crowning their work: in this context the word *Neshamah* would be applied to the Higher Self as a whole. If Nephesh and Ruach together form the soul with its subrational and rational faculties, the Higher Self constitutes what is frequently referred to as the spirit. Here we make reference again to the Four Worlds: for as the conjunction of all things is in man, so the Worlds are represented in his nature, and so correspondingly he exists in all Four Worlds. The Ruach participates in the World of Briah: its knowledge of the astral and material worlds is gained entirely through the Nephesh and through the brain-consciousness, while, equally, it is in itself incapable of knowing directly anything of the World of Atziluth.* Until the higher faculties are to some extent brought into communication with its consciousness, the exercise of pure reason may seem to it the highest function of which the psyche is capable: hence the antagonistic scepticism of the traditional type of "intellectual" when the intuitive faculty comes under discussion. So low a limit however cannot be set to the true nature of the Ruach: it should from its place in the structure of the psyche be a vehicle to the higher

*Cf. footnote concerning Ruach-consciousness (Ego-consciousness), pages 288 and 289.

faculties, even when its knowledge of them amounts only to
a confused awareness of the existence of "something beyond." This confusion is, indeed, characteristic of Neshamah-
awareness before the mystical experience of the higher
faculties comes to the Ruach. For this reason, without such
experience, the highest awareness which the Ruach can have
of the Archetypes subsisting in the Divine Mind, is through
their images and from conclusions intellectually deduced
therefrom. This is not said for the purpose of belittling the
understanding at that stage: there is, for instance, nothing
in Dante's *Commedia*—not even in the ultimate heights of
the *Paradiso*—which exceeds the bounds of what is possible
with a tremendous poetic (not mystical) perception, and of
course with a peculiar concurrence of the emotional nature
and of the physical brain. Furthermore, in the initiatory plan,
this first opening of the intellect to the influence of the
Neshamah is implicit in the entrance into the degree of Minor
Adept which at once sets the initiate quite apart from those
who know nothing higher than the Ruach's rational function,
and of course miles apart from those who are guided by the
external doctrines and the blind faith of a formal religion.
Such an initiate is of the company of "le persone accorte,"
the wise or perceptive, of whom Michelangelo writes

> A quel pietoso fonte onde siam tutti
> S'assembra ogni beltà che qua si vede,
> Piu ch'altra cosa, alle persone accorte:
> Ne altro saggio abbiam ne altri frutti
> Del cielo in terra . . .

For such persons see in "every visible beauty" an archetypal likeness, bringing to their minds the unseen and sacred
fount which is the Divine Mind: and the perception of this
likeness, says the initiate* who is still altogether an artist

---

* That Michelangelo was in his youth a member of an occult group which derived
its authority from an elder group of which Dante had been a member, is demonstrable to the occult student of medieval and Renaissance Florentine literature.

without direct mystical experience, is "the only taste and the only fruit we have of heaven on earth." The meaning of these lines recurs in precis in Keats'

> "Beauty is Truth, truth beauty, — that is all
> Ye know on earth, and all ye need to know."

Keats, indeed, brings the essence of this situation far more clearly to the surface. We are not saying that Keats necessarily took his thought here directly from the Tuscan sonnet, although that is possible: he may, as some have suggested, have been guided by eighteenth-century German cogitations upon the theme, or he may simply have formulated his concept out of the general ambience of Renaissance Platonism to which he was so apt a disciple. We are saying that in the intrinsic content of the lines themselves, the meaning of the quotation from Keats coincides with and penetrates the meaning of Michelangelo's lines, and thus gives us an almost clinical presentation of the philosophic and psychological position we are at this moment examining. Beauty and Truth are not only different concepts existing at the ordinary level: they form with Goodness the three principles inherited from Neo-Platonist thought as characteristic of the Divine levels of being, and this Keats will have known, if only as intellectual fact. To comprehend the real distinction of these attributes does not belong however—as Keats sensitively perceives—to that consciousness which we should describe as "below the Abyss" and which he describes as "on earth."

While the metaphysical view of the universe presented by Plotinus, for example, is not sephirothic, it is by no means out of harmony with the Qabalistic system. Besides recognising the existence of four Worlds, he indicates, conformably also with Pythagorean doctrine, the existence of parts of the microcosm to correspond with these. In the exterior universe, the two Worlds between that of Nous (Atziluth) and that of

Matter are those of Soul: the Higher Soul, proceeding from
Nous and illumined by it, and the Lower Soul which is the
Anima Mundi, otherwise "Nature" (in the Renaissance
sense), from which proceeds in turn the material universe. In
the human body and psyche, according to Plotinus, three of
the four parts cannot change their correspondences: the
highest part of the psyche, the spirit, is in Nous and cannot
leave that World: it cannot be said to "belong" to the particular individual who represents it in the lower Worlds, for
it participates eternally in the Divine Mind no matter what
at any given time may be the condition of the lower psyche
which it has emanated: needless to say, the lower psyche
may be totally unconscious of that participation. The physical body is likewise inseparably part of the material world,
while the instinctual and emotional nature is part of the
"lower soul" of the universe. What can change, says Plotinus,
is the affinity of that part of the human psyche which
corresponds to the "higher soul." (In other words, what
we should call the rational mind.) This can tend downwards
towards matter with the instinctual nature, or it can aspire
towards the spirit. The misery or bliss of the personality as
a whole depends upon this choice. Thus far Plotinus.

Now we know that the Ruach is in fact the one part
of the psyche which is capable of self-determination of this
kind, and that any advance to be made by the personality
is dependent upon right decisions being made by the Ruach.
It is the Ruach which has to take control of the Nephesh and
of the physical body, and to govern these with understanding
as well as with reason: and in order to fulfil even this
function aright, the Ruach has to accept the guidance of the
Neshamah, insofar as this is presented to it. The individual
of course does not generally recognise consciously what is
occurring, but we can say that at this stage the Ruach seeks
for guiding principles which are shown forth at the Briatic
level in a mode which it can accept. The chief of these

guiding principles is that of Beauty: that principle which in the Neo-Platonist system is the essential character of the World of Nous, and which in our system is seen to have a particular affinity with the perception of the Ruach by reason of its Tipharic nature. (Vide Part I, Chapter V.)

One great gift to the Western world with especial relevance to this stage of awareness, is the whole literature of elevated romantic love, poised as it were between the utterances of instinctual attachment on the one hand and those of religious mysticism on the other. Indeed the gulf between this kind of love and the instinctual sort is so marked, that it has through the centuries been understood by its special devotees as a vital intermediate stage in the development of the psyche. Seen from this standpoint, the hero-cults are but special examples, pointing the way for the lover (and shall we not use that superb word-coinage of the child Marjorie Fleming, to add, the loveress?) to make his or her own cult of devotion, the cult of that especial Other in whose whole personality the devotee most finds divinity mirrored. This is both the mainspring of Platonism and a natural development in the aspirations of the developing psyche. A tremendous transference of levels exists in this type of love, but it is not of the same kind as the confusions which beset the uninitiate: that is to say it is not a matter of the Nephesh seeking what it needs in a symbol or a substitute reality, as occurs in neurotic manifestations: here it is primarily the Ruach which is dazzled by the as yet unidentified content of the Neshamah, even though the lower faculties may involve themselves in the turmoil as is their wont. Furthermore, there is not at this level the same element of substitution involved: a human being, or any being for that matter, is no mere symbol of or substitute for divinity, but is the representative and receptacle of some aspect thereof: and is at this stage a rightful object of adoration, provided only that that being represents a true aspiration of the adorer. Hence

all the remarkable and prayer-like "You" songs which are
so popular in our own age, and which address the beloved as
the sun, as a star, or as mirrored by every loveliness in the
world: while from the poetry of past centuries, the devotee
may choose any number of similar utterances differently
expressed, and may wonder, over and over, by what marvel
another mind has put forth so exactly his own truest
aspirations.

To interpret this kind of poetry as the sublimation of
a sexual impulse is to lose sight of the fact that here is a
phenomenon in its own right which has quite another origin
within the psyche. It loses sight also of such historical facts
as Dante's ordinary life as husband and father quite independently of his sustained glorification of the deceased
Beatrice, and the frequency, well known to psychological
observers, of the happy and successful marriage of a subject
to another person than his or her lifelong-acknowledged
"soul-mate." The perception that there is a love which is
in its essence not of a sexual nature (although of course,
given the opportunity, the instincts will try to follow the
lead of the mind, even as in certain cases the elevation of
the Ruach can lead to physical levitation) was seized upon
by the great medieval discovery of "courtly love" which
gave a mystical and even occult inspiration to so much
Troubadour and Minnesinger utterance. Rome pinpointed
the cult as a "heresy:" it was, indeed, not a heresy but rather
a separate religion sprung from Greece and Persia and
nurtured in the high civilisation of Provence (hence the
"courtly" associations): and, though little of any formal
aspects of the cult have come down to us, so much having
been obliterated in the hideous destruction wrought by the
"Albigensian Crusade,"* yet that which comes of a natural

---

* The Albigensian Martyrs, nos confrères de Provence, by no means stand alone
as victims of the ignorance and violence of Christendom. (See *The Misery of
Christianity*, by Joachim Kahl.)

phase of development in the psyche can never be totally lost. The Church of Rome destroyed the Singers: the Song was beyond its power.

The cult of the Unattainable is not only for young lovers playing with melancholy: it is also for the physically fulfilled who rediscover in one another the high dignity of spiritual beings: but its great exponents, voicing the aspirations felt by so many others, have ever been those who, whether outwardly lamenting or frankly glorying in their high calling, have celebrated a love which they have in truth no intention of fulfilling on any earthly level, and who have preferred that their circumstances should not permit of this. For the longing expressed therein is not in truth for a mundane partner, but for a deity. Here we could quote in support of this statement any number of verses in every language of Europe, so easily for centuries have poets greater and lesser fallen in with this viewpoint until they have made of it a convention, needing the most precise ear to tell the true devotee from the lip-server: more effectively perhaps we can point out the work of an apparent enemy of the cult, the poet of the domestic and Christian, the pedestrian, the occasionally bathetic, but none the less a true poet and thus acutely perceptive: Coventry Patmore. One of his main tenets is that the fortunate lover has as much to celebrate in poetry as the unfortunate: a happy marriage gave him the opportunity to explore this hypothesis by direct experience, and indeed he has been called "the poet of matrimony." However, in one of his most notable poems he analyses the inspiration derived from his love for his wife, and in particular the continual self-renewal of that inspiration: and he comes to the inescapable point that beyond all the shared intimacies, shared parenthood, day-to-day domesticity, there remains the unassailable and in truth unapproachable Otherness of her inner self. It is this, he perceives, which is the real object of his love: and this, of course, there is no

possible means of possessing. In this moment of insight
Patmore is revealed as a devotee of the Unattainable just as
surely as Dante, or as the lover of the sadistic (i.e., of the
genealogy of De Sade) and elusive Laura de Noves.

In truth, any love which engages the higher faculties,
or which is called forth by the higher self of the beloved, is
in that measure unattainable, and is also in that measure
deathless. This statement may at first glance seem unrealistic
to those who have attained a point in life where they can
look back upon perhaps a series of such loves from childhood
onwards: but upon consideration it can be seen, firstly, that
no person ever really "takes the place of" another in one's
deepest affections, since to love presupposes an appreciation
of the beloved as a unique and unrepeatable individual: and
secondly, that no love is ever really "lost" or ever really
forgotten.

To say that no love is ever really lost, that nobody ever
really loves in vain, seems perhaps a difficult proposition but
it is none the less completely true. At some level or other, an
attraction is always mutual: it does not always manifest
equally on both sides, or there may be serious obstacles
arising from the outward circumstances or the inner aspirations of one or both parties. To overcome such obstacles at
all costs may lead to happiness as in the case of Elizabeth
Barrett and Robert Browning, or to tragedy as in the case of
Abelard and Heloise: but even if the attempt is never made or
is in fact impossible to make, and even if the crowning
experience in the lifetime of one is but an episode in the
lifetime of the other, still these variations make but little
difference when viewed in the light of an everlasting affinity.
Nor can we limit our observations to one lifetime. We have
to bring into consideration the dismay of the magical student
who has written verses of unique adoration to the great love
of the present lifetime, only to find in exploring a past
incarnation that remarkably similar verses were written by

the former self to an entirely different love. For it is not always even remotely likely that the present object of affection was also the earlier one, and the tendency to believe them identical, when it is not simply an attempt to evade an awkward self-revelation, can be caused by an honest mistake: as sometimes regrettably occurs also within the context of a single lifetime, to a person just awakening from sleep. How does all this square with our philosophy?—for here will serve no mere

> " —it was in another country,
> And besides the wench is dead."

The fact is, that the psyche has a far greater capacity for love than is generally attributed to it: and while there remains any possibility that a change may occur in the dominant aspect of the psyche (as happens progressively during the developments of a lifetime, and as may happen even more startlingly from one incarnation to another, for one is never *altogether* the same person twice) there must be also a bringing into play by the new dominant aspect of its own affinities and loves. The former dominant aspects do not however go out of existence. "An old flame never dies:" the minds of elderly men and women often reach out to the childhood sweetheart, even across a lifetime filled with human relationships of all kinds: nor is this strange, for the idealism of youthful love is all-giving and often engages the higher faculties, even though unknowingly, in a manner not so easily repeated when the instinctual nature has fully developed, or when the ego has put forth its "outer bark" of caution and self-interest.

We do not mean in these paragraphs to imply that even those attractions which are entirely biological or odic in origin, will be given the status of immortal loves. While in one sense it is true that whatever touches the psyche has its place in the record, yet the imprint of such relationships is generally so slight as to be negligible, and whether their purpose be fulfilled or not, when their season is past they disappear to all practical purposes. It is however also true that a real love may be discovered by means of an initial attraction of this kind, or again that an affinity which is in its first impulse spiritual may be disguised by the haste of the instinctual nature to follow in the wake of the higher faculties.

What is certain is a tendency on the part of human beings to aspire to and desire an imperishable love, so that many persons persuade themselves that each successive attraction is of that nature. The reason for this aspiration is that the Neshamah, although rightfully corresponding to the World of Atziluth, nevertheless, while still only confusedly perceived by the conscious mind, casts a reflection downward into the Briatic world of archetypal images. It thus comes about that the conscious mind to some extent identifies itself with the Briatic image of that one of the Supernals which manifests in the same sex as the main tone of the psyche (usually the sex of the physical body), while an image seen as "other," which cannot be assimilated in this manner, becomes an object of love. The true object of love, however, is still at this stage not consciously perceived, and any human being who in a sufficient degree corresponds thereto will become the surrogate object of an idealistic, projected devotion which is almost worship: this adoration can only terminate if the human object thereof breaks the identification with the ideal, either deliberately (as a wise teacher may do) or by an act inappropriate to the ideal (as in our account of Henry and Sylvia): or if, as the lover ascends the Way of Return, the surrogate is replaced by one nearer to the divine—or by the Divine outright. But that is not yet in our account of the matter.

How spiritual or otherwise may be the total expression of a love of this kind, will depend upon the right order and control previously established by the Ruach of the lover over the Nephesh. This is the essential meaning of the speech attributed to Stesichorus in the *Phaedrus* of Plato, a speech which tells much of the soul's quest for a love corresponding to one or another Divine Archetype not consciously remembered, besides recounting the famous allegory of the Charioteer. The self-identification with an archetypal image likewise has its perils, but in antiquity this self-identification was chiefly taken notice of in the controlled conditions of the Mystery Religions, where every care was taken to prevent the chief danger: that is, the self-attribution of deity to the lower levels of the psyche rather than to the higher. The alternative peril, however, though in the nature of things more rare, could not always be prevented: the premature break-through of the Ruach of a devotee to the spiritual realities behind the archetypal images, with resulting insanity. This danger is incurred when from one motive or another the Briatic level of a cult is rejected by the aspiring faculty of the devotee, at a stage before a true contact has been made with the intuitive faculty which alone could guide him safely in the terrible experience of the imageless heights, but after it has become impossible for him to withdraw from that which appals him. The result is the disintegration of his rational personality: a disintegration surely symbolised by the dismemberment of King Pentheus (in Euripides' *Bacchae*) and his thus becoming despite himself a presentment of that Dionysus whose cult he had rejected: a madness represented in the *Attis* of Catullus, which does not recount the original myth of the deity but rather the experience of a devotee who has gone so far in that cult as to have performed the self-emasculation which irrevocably sealed him to the God and the Goddess, and who then by a reassertion of the ego sought to withdraw where no withdrawal was possible:* or an insanity which the modern age has seen in the fate of Nietzsche. As a friend of the Dionysian Richard Wagner, Nietzsche could sustain his philosophy even though his intellect perceived the ideal of aesthetic beauty to be but a "mid-region," a roof as it were built into the psyche to shield man's perception from the terrors of the skies: but to know inwardly such a truth is already to have transcended it, and the powerful intellect subsequently carried the ego-consciousness of Nietzsche onward to contemplations in which, with no intuited spiritual reality to sustain it, it could only wreak its own destruction. The concept of God or of the Gods, Nietzsche declared in the Prologue to "Thus Spake Zarathustra," must be swept away as frustrating man's creativity: but this achieved, the archetypal images gone, where was creativity itself? The Atziluthic Archetypes themselves were utterly beyond him. This Prometheus leaped to snatch fire from heaven, only to lose it in the void. "The night returned in double gloom," and in that darkness closed his earthly days.

Such examples as these, known to Western man in different ages of his history, have bred that caution which gives us the utterances of Michelangelo and of John Keats which we have quoted in the beginning of this chapter: a caution which is no different from that of the Chorus in the *Bacchae* seeking happiness rather than illumination, and not very different from Catullus' heartfelt *Procul a mea . . .*

---

*A translation of this poem is given as Appendix A of the present book: not merely on account of its mention here in the text, but chiefly because this poem is itself an initiation of pity and terror, in which Catullus makes from the material of a cult deeply embedded in both the higher and the lower unconscious, a vivid experience in which the reader can share. It does in fact carry the mind further into the contemplation of divinity than the level discussed in this chapter, for here we catch a glimpse of a holy, ancient and inexorable Power to which any attribution of goodness or of beauty is irrelevant: although to other devotees in other circumstances the Mother has shown herself as all beauty and goodness. Of the personal devotion of Catullus to the Gods, sufficient evidence appears plainly in his poems, perhaps especially in his *Siqua recordanti:* for Catullus as a probable initiate of the Mysteries, a good study is *L'Ultimo Catullo* by Enzo V. Marmorale (E.S.I., Naples 1957.)

*domo* in the closing lines of the Attis poem. In the modern Mysteries the danger of catastrophe is practically obliterated by the task which confronts the Minor Adept as soon as the gate to the full faculties of the Ruach has been opened to him. That which gives and governs the intuitive faculty must be sought while still Goodness and Beauty and Truth fill his heaven: so, beneath them or beyond them, his consciousness shall not go unguided. Meanwhile the Neshamah, which is Aspiration, rules his thoughts and deeds.

At this stage of development the Neshamah is symbolically considered as all-encompassing or central to that heaven, as if a new noonday sun stood in his sky. Here opens that phase which Edward Carpenter records to its culmination, man's divinisation by love of the divine in man. Thought and perception are illuminated, not as yet by direct spiritual apprehension but by the joyful certainty that all which is manifest is indeed transcendent in significance. Verities perhaps long known become charged with a new sense of discovery, owing to the heightening of consciousness and the impingement of reflections from the supernal energies. This is the region of artistic and poetic inspiration, in which even the simplest perceptions can become charged with a potent intensity which compels first projection and then assimilation: upon analysis, it becomes apparent that the mainspring of this compelling quality is in fact love, recognisable as such in its effects although its true direction is as yet concealed. Such experience, although dynamic, is not destructive to peace of mind, if the understanding plays its part. That to which he aspires and must aspire, in symbol and in image surrounds him. Yet, too, struggle is one of the essential conditions, for his aspiration must be unfaltering. Material things are in themselves lawful to him, for he is still an incarnate being: they are also for his rightful use as symbols and as sacraments of his aspiration: what is forbidden to him is to go back upon his tracks and to prefer the

symbol before that which it represents. Here in the Sphere
of Tiphareth he is committed to the quest which shall fulfil
his Adepthood, committed as surely as the flames of fire are
committed to rise upward, or the tendrils of a young vine
to reach out for support: and it is a quest which may take
many years before its fulfilment. For all those years is he
beneath the rule of the Neshamah, whose law is Goodness,
Beauty and Truth.

But the reflections originating from the Neshamah are
in their own way just as hallucinogenic as the reflections sent
up into Ruach-consciousness by the Nephesh. This fact can,
in some cases, lead into various complications. For instance,
although it is requisite for the true development of the
subject that the principal forces imaged into the Ruach at
this stage of development should be presentments by the
Neshamah of the Supernal Sephiroth, they are not always
such in fact, and may be linked with, or overwhelmed by,
unsuitable material transmitted upwards from the unconscious regions of the Nephesh. Thus in Wagner's Tannhauser,
we find that Wolfram, whose Star of Love is an earthly
woman in whom he sees the projected image of the Supernal
Mother, typifies the Adept following the right way of spiritual progress; while Tannhauser, equally an Adept, and
following no human symbol but the Goddess herself manifest in the Sephirah Netzach, is shown as all but destroyed by
his choice. The appeal of a story of this type to medieval
minstrelsy is evident, even in its mere prototypes: less
popular, but of equal importance, would be the contrasting
picture of an Adept being lured back into Hod. Even the love
of truth itself can be a snare if it degenerates into an insatiable hunger to know, to know and to know, never feeling
that one has learned enough to look higher.

Before the Ruach participates in the angelical nature,
such diverse catastrophes as those of the Nietzsches, the
Tannhausers, the Fausts of this world, are a very present

danger. Now herein is a crisis, the resolution of which can only be a certainty where the aspirant is a disciple of one who has attained to full Adepthood, one who is capable of seeing certain matters very clearly. Verily, many lone aspirants triumph: a far greater number fail the test. Further, the integrity of many Orders breaks down completely at this point: these are the cults which are ruled by "Hierophants of the Lesser Mysteries," who are themselves but novices in the realm of Adepthood: that their students are raised to a form of Adepthood is indisputable, but the process ends here. Even so, the inner greatness of a disciple may need only this impetus to realise itself and to go forward to full attainment.

Where an Order is governed by full Adepts, there is a living force which can raise to the Sphere of Beauty in truth, which ensures that the deed of the soul is in response to the stimulus of the spirit: this is no mere gold which tinctures gold, it is the living power of the Lapis Philosophorum itself. The aspirant has experienced the reality of the Way, and in the New Life the dangers are obliterated: until the fulfilment of the Solar quest he is beneath the rule of the Neshamah and he has a touchstone for that which he seeks. He is told, "Pursue the Magical Arts, but above all Seek! You are released from your allegiance to this Order. Go or remain with us as you shall fulfil the Quest which is yours alone."

It will be evident to the reader that the exoteric matters which we have been considering in this chapter are but a natural counterpart of the esoteric fulfilment, the guided and equilibriated Way of the Adept. The fervours and ecstasies of the Adept's quest however are those of attainment, not of the unattainable. Thus we have Omar Khayyam describing how he

"Divorced old barren Reason from my Bed,
And took the Daughter of the Vine to Spouse."

For his "fruitful Grape" is of no literal vintage, but symbolises the source of Dionysian ecstasy: and the Daughter of the
Vine is that Aspiration which should visit every sojourner
in the Sphere of Tiphareth. But this "new Marriage," he tells
us, was "long since;" elsewhere in his verses he mentions
himself as having sat "on the Throne of Saturn," so it appears
that his occult progress had been carried very considerably
further: even though the plan of initiation in the Ismaili
Order to which he belonged was not exactly the same in its
grades and its elaborate organisation as the forms prevalent
in the West. That Order became notorious for the political
murders carried out by the drugged fanatics who formed its
outer guard (the *hashishiyy,* or Assassins) though it is
evident, both from the writings of Omar Khayyam and from
what we know of the inner teachings from other sources, that
the Order itself was neither orthodox Moslem nor essentially
political in nature: indeed, other Ismaili Orders are known to
have been entirely mystical and peaceable. Again, it is known
that in the Order of Assassins great care was taken to segre-
gate the various grades, on account of the changes in philosophy which went progressively with the initiations: so that
there are several reasons for supposing that a man of Omar's
intellect and character was never brought into contact with
the brutal and repellent aspects of the organisation. Nevertheless, it is certain that if he had wanted to praise in his
verses the use of hashish or of any drug that was used in that
milieu, he could quite openly have done so: instead he chose
to praise wine, which was not used and the very naming of
which was regarded askance. It is quite clear therefore, that
if he does not mean wine itself he must be using its name
as a cover for something, and that something is not another
drug. An examination of the verses brings out the meaning
of the symbol distinctly. Islam, as a dogmatic religion,
leaves no room in the lives of its devotees for a private
intuition of things divine: all must go by rule and by rote.

Islam also forbids, on the material level, the use of the intoxicating ferment of the grape. Wine, therefore, in such an association of ideas, becomes a fitting symbol for the divine and non-material intoxication, the intuition which transcends reason and leaves dogma standing. Omar, the mathematician and astronomer, has enough of exact calculations and reasonings in his professional life: for his vision of divinity he desires something altogether different. This symbolism being understood, the "Angel Shape" which appears, bringing new abundance of the precious fluid to the philosopher, is well recognised by us.

At the same time, despite the idyllic contentment which Omar commends and the deep appreciation shown throughout his quatrains (their sequence means nothing, they are chosen at random from the collection of a lifetime) for the world of beauty and for the company of his friend, still we find him as cautious of his happiness as are the maidens of the *Bacchae,* or as a dweller in an oasis who is careful always to look towards its centre, and not to sit facing the desert. Nevertheless, he knows what is out there: the Waste of Annihilation and the Dawn of Nothing. What is the cause of this melancholy?—initial temperament, or defective training, or that desolation inevitably tasted by those who stay the course, the Dark Night of the Soul?—when spiritual intuition, having attained to dazzling certitude, is suddenly withdrawn, and in the dusk the Angel Shape does not appear? It could be any of these, probably all of them in some measure. The seasoning of scepticism which many occult Orders impart in their training to counteract any tendency to credulity and superstition, was considerably exceeded by the Assassins. This apart however, the quatrains contain much of that fair region of the Nightingale and the Rose, the Vine, and the Beloved, which has imaged deathless beauty to the mind of the West, for an age and an age.

For into a Europe dominated by feudal politics and church dogma a new lyricism, that of Provence, brought a fresh vision of life's potential of joy and beauty; a vision fortified by a philosophy which owed nothing to faith or creed. It came from the Arab and Persian worlds: not the Arabia and Persia of Islam, but from the wide perceptions of those great freethinkers—Avicenna's name particularly must again be inscribed here—whose understanding was nurtured on the treasured writings of Greek philosophers, on the far-circulating Tao of the further East, and on the Hermetic and magical wisdom of Alexandria: many of the main elements of the Qabalah itself. The mystical commitment of the lover to the beloved, the adoration of the nightingale for the rose, the longed-for draught of immortality—all the reiterated symbols and images, inevitably carrying hints of their deeper meaning, flowed into the hungry European consciousness with the full force of a poignant certainty that life could indeed be re-fashioned "nearer to the heart's desire".

So, truly, it is re-fashioned; for the inner purport of the symbols is to show the destiny of the adept, and thus, soon or late, of every being.

## CHAPTER IV

The Higher Self considered as a trine; initially from the involutionary standpoint as devolving from its first principle, the "Kether" of the psyche:

Origin of the individual in the Divine Mind: the *Yechidah*, all-potent towards its own eventual fulfilment, not to be confused with (or regarded as belonging to) the evolving "lower personality."

The second emanation of the Higher Self: the *Chiah*, or Higher Vital Principle.

The third emanation of the Higher Self: the *Neshamah*, or Formative Principle.

The psychological functions of Chiah and Neshamah as Animus and Anima.

The confused reflection sent forth by the Neshamah into the world of Briah as the first intimation of the Higher Self, carrying the influences of Chiah and Yechidah mingled with its own characteristic influence. Possible effect of complexes in the Nephesh, to distort or to cause incorrect attribution of these downward reflections of the Supernal Archetypes.

The Holy Guardian Angel as the messenger of the Yechidah, emerging by the hidden gate of Daath, to manifest as a being of Tiphareth to the Adept in due course. The Intuitive Mind, which completes the action of the Ruach by linking it with the supernal faculties. This development related to the philosophy of Avicenna.

The Adept's further progress: the Abyss. The choice of supernal Paths: the direct apotheosis of the Ipsissimus, or the patient maturing of the Magister Templi.

## CHAPTER IV
## THE TRINE OF SPIRIT

In treating of the component parts of the psyche from a practical viewpoint, it is logical to follow the order of evolution. This immediately gives the subject-matter a human relevance, but it has one disadvantage: each level in turn of the psyche must inevitably seem to depend upon the level below it, whereas, to give a true picture of the psyche as it is in itself, each level should be shown as having emerged from the one above it. With regard to the lower levels of the psyche, no particular harm is done by limiting ourselves to the evolutionary view: by this abridgement we may regard the story as a continuation from that of man's physical evolution, the psychological phase culminating in individuation at the level of Ruach-consciousness: but in considering the higher levels, although it is still useful to relate these to the progress of the individual, still no intelligible account of the matter can be given without bringing into the reckoning the involutionary activity of these levels, as it is in the psyche's highest realisation.

The Yechidah, the inmost principle of the psyche, cannot be conceived of as "belonging" to the personality: its correspondence is to Kether, being that initial unity from which the psyche devolves: it is the perfect and deathless *idea* of the particular individual in potential in the Divine Mind, although the idea of the same individual in extension in the

Divine Mind of course partakes of all ten Atziluthic
Sephiroth.* In no person can we say that any of these ten
"Voices" is lacking at the Atziluthic level, however devoid of
some corresponding quality the earthly manifestation of that
person may be. The Kether of that divine plan of the individual, however, similarly to every Kether-aspect has a
transcendent quality of its own, its total potentiality, its
perpetual "becoming."

We must emphasise the complete otherness of the
Yechidah from a personality sent forth by it: and when that
personality considers itself as identified with a particular
incarnation in which it is currently manifest, the Yechidah
must seem altogether alien.

In the order of involution, the Yechidah emanates the
Chiah, or Higher Vital Principle, the Animus or masculine
aspect of the Spirit: the Neshamah, or Formative Principle,
the Anima or feminine aspect of Spirit, is emanated as the
third of the Supernal Trine, all corresponding thus far to
the sephirothic pattern.

These Supernal functions of the psyche, however, are
not in their true nature known to the Adept even when he
comes forth from the Vault and sets under feet the Bronze
Cross of the Four Elements. That force which emanates from
the Yechidah becomes in its next modality the Chiah, and,
transmitted thence, in its third modality becomes the
Neshamah: the Neshamah thus corresponds to Binah, which
in its essential nature the Neshamah represents within the
Atziluthic trine of the psyche. The Neshamah casts a reflection downward, through the microcosmic Daath, into the
Briatic level of the psyche: the Neshamah, however, does not
appear thus clearly from without, but as a confused, inchoate
influence, wherein are the forces of the spirit, the influences
of the Three mingled in the light of the Neshamah.† (Just as

* Concerning this, see Chapter following.
† For obvious reasons, human language has achieved little facility upon this
theme: the student must consider the meaning of each reference to the Neshamah
as it occurs in its place.

the Sephiroth must be considered, not only according to the diagram of the Tree of Life, but as objective realities, each modality being universal, so, similarly, the student must consider the aspects of the spirit, not as "left" or "right" according to the diagram—valuable as that glyph is—but as intensities of being. We may say of these "inner" modalities that Neshamah is the "outermost" of the three principles of the spirit.)

Daath is the Gate by which the triune light of the Neshamah shines out, and Daath is situated in the Abyss: but as yet the Adept does not see the Gate itself, nor shall he see it until to him it is a Gate indeed and his matured consciousness may enter thereby.

The Supernal Powers are three: two are their Briatic images: the Woman and the Man. (To Kether is assigned no image in the modern Qabalah.) The predominantly male of soul who identify with the Man shall love the archetypal Woman, the predominantly female of soul who identify with the Woman shall love the archetypal Man. Or they may love a human being in the likeness of the image, and shall learn deeply by that experience. There is a third image which must here be mentioned, the Child, but the Child is not yet seen: nevertheless its existence and position are indisputable and vital facts of the psyche: it is neither image nor Archetype.*

Those in whom male and female are balanced, and who generally tend most to the Way of the Mystic, will love equally the Woman and the Man, finding these in the whole human race as does Whitman for instance, or exemplified in especial but paired loves: as he whom we call Shakespeare loved the Fair Man and the Dark Lady, or as Michelangelo loved Tommaso de' Cavalieri and Vittoria Colonna.

These are the generalities of the images of the Images:

* This is the mystery, cosmic and microcosmic, which is named of the *Blue Lotus*. It is traditionally said that Daath, the Invisible Sephirah, has no image, but rather is it that in Daath is the *Image Invisible*. Even thus is the function of Daath, to stand between the imageless Archetypes and the archetypal images, and the root of the Blue Lotus is deep in the Abyss.

yet more subtle modes are there in which they may win their
devotees. For the Chiah is not only to be interpreted as Male,
but sometimes as Elder: and then the corresponding polarity,
the Neshamah, will represent the Younger. If the Chiah is the
religious power, the Neshamah is the temporal; if the Chiah is
the leader, the Neshamah is the follower. Thus do these two
Supernals divide between them all the pairs of opposites, so
that sex is far from being the only determinant which may
validly lead the subject to identify himself or herself with one
or the other polarity and to find the complementary polarity
imaged in another person who is thus seen as the beloved
one. In the psyche, however, there is a complication. The
Anima has a strong affinity with the gross astral level of the
Nephesh, as the Animus has with the lower, Nephesh-tinged
Ruach: the Ruach may therefore at that level be considered
as the inferior masculine component in the psyche, the lower
Nephesh as the inferior feminine.

If however the Nephesh of an individual is not correctly
oriented, its influence upon the Ruach and its reflection of
the Neshamah will alike be impaired, thus interfering with
the development of the psyche at every stage.

That deep level of racial and archetypal egregores, which
is touched in part by the Nephesh of every psyche however
unconsciously, is termed the Collective Unconscious of the
human race. This "deep" level, which exists in the Anima
Mundi, Yetzirah, comprises in the first instance the common
Collective Unconscious of the whole human race and second-
arily the distinct cultural and ancestral archetypal egregores
of its subdivisions. It must not be confused with the Higher
Collective Unconscious, which is touched by the Briatic
Intelligence and the Neshamah of every psyche. The egregores of the Lower Collective Unconscious can, if sufficiently
pure, attune the Nephesh to the Higher Collective Unconscious, and the Nephesh is in its fashion capable of influencing the Ruach: but in right progress the principal factor
is the attunement of the Ruach to the Higher Collective

Unconscious. It must rule and not be ruled by the lower worlds, while being itself receptive to the higher.

There is also for each individual a more superficial unconscious level which is correspondingly called the Personal Unconscious. This level is likely to be peopled by distorted or spurious egregores, the result of conflict-situations in the personal life and representing the "complexes" of clinical psychology. These parasitic phantoms, created by the psyche within itself, occur to some extent in a great majority of human beings who come well within the range of normality: this majority being that vast group of people who could be defined as being of "neurotic type" without being actually neurotic, and who, also, for the most part have had no psychological or occult training, nor experience of psychiatric or psychotherapeutic treatment. To put this to the test: one of the most common symptoms of neurotic tendency is an irrational fear, and how many people do we meet who have not such a fear, either of a harmless situation or of a harmless creature? At the same time, by far the greater number of such instances need cause no resulting injustice or cruelty to the objects of the irrational aversion. It must also be mentioned here, that any such symptoms do NOT constitute an invitation to the amateur therapist.

Distorted egregores formed by complexes in the personal unconscious draw the Nephesh ever further out of harmony with the egregores of the Lower Collective Unconscious (with which they may be confused or whose place they may usurp) and thereby with the Higher Collective Unconscious also. In the evolving personality of the Adept, a progressive purification of the Nephesh takes place: the Nephesh thus becomes a true mirror of the Higher Collective Unconscious.

On the other hand, a great degree of freedom from complexes can be caused by various factors:— by a very healthy and well-balanced personality, by training, or by

certain psychotic tendencies, which, again, may be encompassed well within the limits of normality, and it is only
instances within the range of normality that we are here
considering. In all these cases, it is likely that the lack of
complex-material will be offset by dreams etc., with a
content of archetypal material associated with the Lower
Collective Unconscious. It is to be remarked that a tendency
to give practical effect to their interest in the occult seems
especially frequent in the last-mentioned group as among
the very well-balanced.* The reason for this more direct
access to the Lower Collective Unconscious would appear,
as far as the mildly psychotic are concerned, to be that the
usual worries and stresses which build up complexes in
average neurotic-type people, mean little to this type whose
personality stands to some extent upon a different basis and
which has a private scale of values: this sometimes means that
even those unwarrantable interferences which parents (and
indeed teachers) frequently feel entitled to make in the
individual development of a child, outside the requirements
of ordinary good behaviour, will be shed "like water off a
duck's back" by such a personality from the beginning. Apart
from certain negative qualities, such as a lack of compassion
which is not due to abnormal selfishness so much as to a
genuine inability to understand the commonplace anxieties
of others, it can be difficult to distinguish these individuals
from exceptionally highly evolved persons who have a
perception of the true presentments of the Neshamah, or
from those with a history of previous training. An interesting
character-study in this regard is that of the Prophet Jonah
as depicted in the Old Testament. The hero of that strange
book can certainly be classified as belonging to one of the
minority-groups we have been discussing, so that the same
is probably true of the unknown author. The episode of the

* In contrast to people of markedly neurotic tendency, who are often drawn to
the passive forms of psychism.

gourd-vine, and the speech (not at all characteristic of Biblical writings generally) in which God expresses concern not only for the people but for the animals of Nineveh, can be contrasted with the behaviour of Jonah in the great sea-storm: not simply his "inconsiderateness," but the mere fact that he *could* lie down and sleep serenely in a situation where, after all, he was humanly speaking in as much danger of death as those who criticised him. (The student who looks into this question is not required to swallow the whale.)

Members of these minority groups, both the psychotic-type normal and the highly-developed, as well as those, of course, who by past training of some kind have already passed the early stages of occult progress, frequently show a distinctive characteristic in common when they begin those exercises which create a temporary division in the psyche: they are not troubled by the entity which in many systems of occult training is called the Watcher, or the Lower Watcher, at the Threshold. The reason for this is quite simple: this Watcher is not in fact a valid archetypal egregore, either objective or subjective, but represents simply the action of that which the Freudians call the Super-Ego, confronting the subject with a self-image likely to overwhelm him with those feelings of guilt and of anxiety concerning his unworthiness or inadequacy, which the neurotic type does tend to thrust down below the level of consciousness and so to accumulate from an early age. The absence of this Super-Ego, and consequently of this Lower Watcher, is also typical of another group which can be particularly mentioned, although generally they could be classed with the advanced to a greater or less extent:— those who have had from birth or from childhood a definite memory of a past incarnation. This, we have found, means that no matter how dominating or critical the parents in the present incarnation may have been, their authority never will have had quite that absolute and all-pervading quality which would otherwise characterise it. Even the slightest awareness on the child's part of a personal existence not shared by them, can act in exactly the same way as a hole in a vessel which is being subjected to an exhaustion-pump.

The foregoing comments indicate the need for screening out the contents of the personal unconscious during training before the higher levels are attempted, that the associations of a complex may not be attached to an image which should be archetypal: an error which could have grave results. Much of this screening is effected by the training process itself: but where this does not suffice, or where it can be seen that it will not suffice, it may be the aspirant himself who has to be screened out of the Order. A Magical Order is not the place for psychotherapeutic treatment, even though magical work carefully directed can help a person to act out a complex and to replace it by an appropriate and potent affirmation, and any form of mental or emotional disturbance falling beyond the range of normality must, by the rule of the A∴ S∴, be rigorously excluded for the sake both of the subject and of the existing members of the Order. In the light of our references in this work to Plato, Ficino, Shakespeare, Michelangelo, Omar Khayyam, Walt Whitman, surely we scarcely need point out that the Order does not commit the common mistake of attributing normality only to heterosexuals. Neurosis, certainly, can afflict people of any sexual type. We agree that a man who is fundamentally heterosexual is manifesting neurosis if, for instance, owing to an unconscious fear of women for whatever reason, he believes himself to be strictly homophile: but then likewise the man who is congenitally and thus normally homophile becomes neurotic if, having developed for whatever reason a fear, penetrating to the unconscious levels, of males as objects of love, he believes himself to be heterosexual. This means, inevitably, that when a true homophile has changed his attitude as a result of shock-treatment for example, he is not truly "cured" but simply conditioned like any unfortunate laboratory animal, and is now in reality suffering from an artificially and cruelly induced neurosis.

It is also true that many homosexuals whether male or female who are genuinely so by temperament, and not as a result of neurosis, do in fact become highly neurotic through the circumstances of rejection and persecution in which they frequently find themselves, even in some cases from childhood. The A∴ S∴ would have to exclude these people from membership, simply as sufferers from neurosis: it can however and does add its voice to the call for a more enlightened public opinion to end their ostracism. At the same time it must be stated that the Order emphatically does not share the opinion which has been expressed by a number of Platonists, that love between members of the same sex is intrinsically "superior" to love between opposite sexes. It is certainly not that, any more than intrinsically inferior. What is in any case true, is that love is not love unless it engages the complementary supernal principles: for the rest, as Jung very plainly points out in *The Structure and Dynamics of the Psyche,* sex and age are two of the "modalities" influencing human behaviour, but in neither does the psychic fact always correspond to the anatomical fact.

Whichever way a person initially leans, it must be borne in mind that the ultimate ideal is for every human being to be psychically androgynous. That is one of the great lessons of life, and those who are not yet ready to learn it in the occult schools must at least learn it to some extent in the ordinary experiences of life. The man who courts a girl, makes her wishes his law: at that time she is his "lord and master," as the men of the Middle Ages and of the Renaissance did not shrink from saying. The wife who would lean wholly upon her husband in material things, must be his inspirer in the things of the spirit: otherwise she is a vampire, and their partnership may end in psychic and perhaps even material bankruptcy. The father's authority must be tempered by tenderness and understanding: the mother must be a tower of strength to her sons and to her daughters alike.

The magician may be hermit and celibate, yet all these things and more he must know in his heart for truth: that the spiritual realities underlying the patterns may be found in his soul by the Powers.

Thus, then, having overcome the World of the Elements, does the Adept stand equilibriated in Tiphareth. In that equilibrium he must set forth upon the greatest magical adventure which has yet befallen him, to win the knowledge and conversation of the Holy Guardian Angel, otherwise called his holy Genius. Equilibrium is vitally necessary to him in this quest, for the fulfilment which he seeks will not come about unless in accordance with the aphorism, "As above, so below." One of the most general certainties which man has held concerning Angels, that is, messengers of and from the Divine, is that they are sexless beings, not inclining to one sex more than to the other. It is true that in ancient times angelic beings were often represented as male to symbolise the creative power carried by their messages, while in modern times they have most often been represented as female, probably for reasons of sentiment rather than of philosophy.* Nevertheless, the knowledge that they should be sexless is still in evidence. This must be emphasised in our account of the essential concept of the angelic being here in question, though it should be obvious that this does not preclude the Holy Guardian of any person in particular from manifesting to that person in a male form or in a female form as may be suitable.

The Holy Guardian Angel is a beam transmitted from

---

* Art of Mediterranean origin, probably influenced by the classical concept of the Genius, has most often represented angelic figures as male. Germanic art, probably influenced by the tradition of the Filgia (Anima), has most often represented angelic figures as female. Goya's frightful "angels," which are women in ecclesiastical vestments, are but caricatures of both traditions.

the imageless Yechidah, when the Adept has attained a sufficient ripeness, outwards through the Chiah and Neshamah
(in a sense the Mother has always been pregnant with this
force, and now this fact takes precedence over her impregna-
tion by the Father:*) and thence projected through the
still-concealed Daath-Gate which, however, gives to that
beam its own likeness, not visual but exaltedly intellectual,
as Child.†

Forth, then, from the mysteries of that Supernal region
which even in symbolic representation defies dimension,
issues this Being of living light and love whom the Adept,
and he alone, is to know as his Angel.§ Of such a meeting
what can be written?—but it takes place in the Sphere of
Tiphareth, and little by little it unfolds the fulfilment of
that sphere. Gradually does he come to understand that what

* This awesome process in the Supernal nucleus of the psyche is almost beyond
description. Mythology itself here scarcely takes the tension between fact and
symbol. In the Tree of Life, the Path of Mercury (the Divine Messenger, often oc-
cultly considered as androgynous) is the Path between Binah and Kether. Arche-
typally, the Mother is pregnant by that which she is to bear, this of course postu-
lates the impregnator as being in some sense pre-existent. The myth of Myrrha
gives us an aspect of the story, Cinyras the Sacred King representing the God even
as Myrrha's Son does, and Aphrodite being the Goddess even as Myrrha is: behind
this story stands the great myth of Ishtar and her Son-Spouse Dumuzi, who again
is of parthenogenous birth and so by implication pre-existing. Dante dares to give
us another fragment of the picture, in "Vergine madre, figlia del tuo figlio."
† Child but not infant, neither male nor female.
§ In the Portal Ceremony, which precedes the Adeptus Minor Initiation proper, the
aspirant, in the knowledge of the secret arcanum of the 25th Path (vide Ch. VI, Book III),
stands upon the threshold of the Greater Mysteries symbolically as newborn Child. He
parts the Veil: the revelation is his own mirrored reflection. He may well believe that he
comprehends instantly the meaning of this: that all which he has to learn, and every further
experience, is comprised within that inescapable enigma, himself. Nor is that a false
interpretation: yet it is trivial beside the reality which awaits him. His mirror-image
represents far more than the duplication of his ordinary consciousness. He must eventually
come face to face with his glorious guardian and yet his twin Self, whom, through whatever
effort, he must emulate, and with whom he must work—this is the inner message as new
born Child gazes upon symbolic image. Newborn Child he is, for in the mysteries which he
is yet to enter upon, and of which the Portal Ceremony is but a partial foreshadowing, he is
to follow the inexorable course of Sol Invictus, "hero and hero's God," but an intimation is
given to him that there is a space between day and day: not yet is he that Child of Tiphareth in
whom King and God are integrated, that child who is to seek until he finds that which is
named the Holy Guardian Angel. Subsequently, in the Adeptus Minor ceremony itself, his
child's sunrise, his King's noon, his God's sunset, lead to the terrible sojourn in the
Darkness: but with the rising of a new Star, the former symbolism of the Portal gives place
to deathless reality. The triumphant, beauteous Child of Tiphareth stands forth:—he it is who
is commanded to Seek!

he perceives is not the Universal Plan, but only that fragment of it which represents his own life-work: he could not perform it alone, but neither will this be expected of him.

Regardless of what we have said of the origin of this Being, the Adept's experience here is of an Angel of Tiphareth: for he is bounded by the Sphere of his attainment. Here, characteristically of Tiphareth, is all brought to harmony: or rather, with his new perception the Adept sees the underlying harmony, which is a greater and more potent condition than mere equilibrium, ever subsisting between higher and lower, between the things of Mercy also and the things of Severity.

The Intuitive Mind is the key to that mystery of Man, which has so disturbed Western thought for upwards of two thousand years. One of the remarkable features in the development of Western religions and philosophies, has been the gradual realisation of the existence, at an advanced point in individual evolution, of a gap or chasm across which the advancing consciousness cannot pass unaided: a point at which its hitherto repetitive methods of overcoming obstacles will not suffice. Certainly this gap corresponds to a real state of things in the psyche's inner experience: the surprising thing is that the Western Mysteries alone appear to have taken full cognisance of it. Plato gives no intimation of any later crisis awaiting those who leave the dark cavern of illusion and begin their progress into the light, but the initiatory cults some few centuries after his time begin to be full of it, if only by the implications of their very existence. In exoteric Christianity the place of the missing factor in the psyche has largely been taken by "Divine Grace," an unsatisfactory attempt to solve the problem since the various Christian theologians have never reached an agreement on the paradox that in order to seek grace one must already have it: but there has been a tendency on the part of Christian Qabalists to try to accommodate these

doctrines. An early example of this is to be found in the only
real disagreement, apparently, which ever occurred between
Marsilio Ficino and Pico della Mirandola in the fifteenth
century. Ficino, as a dedicated Platonist, had no idea of the
existence of the Abyss but was proposing a continuous
ascent from material life to the divine by a "stair" of increas-
ingly elevated loves, when his Qabalist friend Pico apprised
him of the obstacle. Pico, however, besides being a Qabalist
was from beginning to end a Christian, and put forward
"Divine Grace" as the necessary assistance: Ficino eventually
accepted this view, and wrote his later works conformably
with it: in his circumstances he had little choice. Nevertheless, it was a clumsy compromise: although the Reality which
is named in occult doctrine as the Holy Guardian Angel is
the same which underlies the pale abstraction, Grace, which
is put forward with so little understanding by the Churches.

This should be compared with the findings of Avicenna
with regard to the "Tenth Intelligence," the last of the
Emanations in his system. This in one aspect represents what
we should call the Sephirah Malkuth: however, the philosophic understanding of the Sephiroth was only at that time
barely entering upon its course of formulation into the
scheme of exact concepts which we at present know. Further
confusion existed because the distinction of the Four Worlds
appears not to have reached Avicenna, although the writings
of Orientius, Bishop of Auch (c. 400-450) who seems to have
been of Spanish origin, and of Salomon Ibn Gabirol, known
as Avicebron (born at Malaga, c. 1020) bear witness to the
existence of that doctrine, in the Iberian Peninsula at least:
while four levels of the psyche—intuitive, rational, imaginative and perceptive—had been recognised by the Pythagoreans.
In view of Avicenna's apparent lack of these formulations, so
that he was almost entirely limited to introspection for his
interpretation of the Emanations, it is not surprising that he
sometimes confused the levels, sometimes over-identified the

cosmic with the psychological, and also amalgamated in some
points the functions which in our system are attributed to
Malkuth and to Binah. To the Tenth Emanation, therefore,
he attributes the function of the Neshamah, that is, of what
he calls the Active Intellect.

His philosophic explanation of the distinction between
the Active Intellect and the natural human consciousness
(which he terms the Receptive or Passive Intellect) is founded
in his concept, upon which we have previously remarked, of
the negative, "potential" quality of Matter, as contrasted to
the positive, "active" quality of Spirit. He sees the lower
nature of Man, the body of course more extremely than the
soul, as belonging to the world of potentiality only. The soul
may indeed rise towards Spirit, but has no means of transfer-
ring itself into the mode of existence of Spirit, since the
latter comes from the Divine and thus partakes of the nature
of pure Deed or Act. (It is noteworthy that in everyday
speech we refer to something as *act*ual when we mean that
which certainly exists now, as against that which has only a
potentiality of existing.) Avicenna observes that however
high the natural human consciousness may soar up from basic
principles, it lacks within itself the capacity to grasp the
purely "abstract:" in parenthesis, the word "abstract" itself
is a product of this inability, since it presupposes a labour of
arriving at the essential by peeling off or *abstracting* the
phenomena associated with it, and by deduction, which is
not the direct method by which the Intuitive Mind perceives
a truth at the spiritual level. So in Avicenna's philosophy the
Active Intellect must irradiate the Receptive Intellect to
complete the nature of Man.

Man in his lower consciousness is unable to apprehend
directly the Atziluthic noumena, the pure Archetypes,
without the assistance of his Intuitive Mind. This, then, is a
problem to which no merely exoteric solution either in
religion or philosophy is possible.

The descent of the Intuitive Mind is into that level of the Ruach which is named the Briatic Intelligence.* The Light and Love of the Angel stirs the Waters of the Pool of the Five Porches: the Briatic intelligence awakens, and the Adept sees his Angel. (The epiphany of the Angel will be unique to the Briatic level of each individual psyche.† ) In response to the stimulus of the Angel, the Ruach grows to its fullness and the Adept learns to control and direct his new faculty. Many things, now, he will perceive "through the unknown, re-membered gate" of Briatic consciousness, but the Ruach even in its highest development remains incapable of intuiting truth directly. This is but one aspect of the matter, however, when the Adept, in the company of his Angel, grows from his child-state to maturity, when "realisation of selfhood" is induced by the Holy Guardian, the Not-Self. Of the dialogue between intuition and rationality, ah, who may tell?

Henceforth the Angel will be with the Adept: but the Adept is warned to look to a certain matter which is implicit in this writing. Upon this nothing further shall be said.

Now, the mind of the Adept will not, as we have said, be universalised, but it will be vastly expanded and inspired. Again, this quality of inspiration is proper to the Sphere of Tiphareth, which is the reason why that Sphere must be attained before the fullness of inspiration can be sought: but the fullness of inspiration is not found even in Tiphareth until one's Angel is one's Dionysus. Under this inspiration the Adept develops, until at last he knows the Gate of Daath wellnigh as his Angel knows it.

---

* As has been indicated, it is possible in an emergency for the Intuitive Mind in the Supernal levels of the psyche to bypass the conscious mind where this is not amenable to "higher" influences, and to communicate with the Nephesh, whose gross astral level can communicate with the autonomic ("sympathetic") nervous system. This communication is by means of the Neshamah-Nephesh affinity afore-mentioned. In such instances the recipient may react instinctively to the com-munication, which thus remains itself below conscious level, or the disturbance may be brought into consciousness to become a matter for rational consideration. In either case, the communication lacks such a detailed intellectual content as would be received into the Ruach by an Adept: the explanation of this is obvious.
† The Adept will of course keep the Feast of the Epiphany!

It must be understood here that we are describing in
few words a process in spiritual development which may take
years or lifetimes to accomplish. This cannot be otherwise.
Just as it can be said of the new Adeptus Minor that he is
committed to the quest for his Holy Guardian Angel, without
reference to the fact that many years may pass before that
quest is fulfilled, so do we look from the attainment of the
Knowledge and Conversation, to the crisis of the Abyss
which, again, may be any number of years distant. To
venture the Abyss is a decision which, in truth, no being can
make for the Adept. It may be incarnations distant: but the
commitment is implicit, and whither his destiny carries him
he will go.

A further choice is made by the Adept who thus enters
the Abyss. He may ascend directly by the Thirteenth Path to
Kether, to merge gloriously into Divinity, as Ipsissimus. Such
a choice does not result in a loss of individuality, but rather
a fulfilment of it, as the word *Ipsissimus* signifies: for who
could be more truly *himself* than he who completely and
deliberately plunges all that he is into the Yechidah, that
pure Idea of himself, which throughout all the vicissitudes
of his existence has awaited him, a living and perfect flame
of unutterable brilliance in the Divine Mind of which it is
a part?

The alternative choice for him who enters the Abyss is
to pass thence to Binah: thus he is once again and in a
different mode new-born. In the Sphere of Binah, as a
Magister Templi, he experiences the full depth of the Dark
Night of the Soul. The Neshamah, to which his consciousness
is here united, admits him to the experience of Binah alone:
and this is Binah not as the Bright Fertile Mother, for in
isolation she is the Dark Sterile Mother. Again there is
something of an allegory to be found in the "Lament of
Attis," for the Sphere of the Mother is also the Sphere of
Saturn-Chronos, and a part of its experience is that of the

complete magical ineffectuality and dependence which are symbolised by the emasculation. Comparably with the poem, too, there is utter desolation here, but there is also high ecstasy. The Angel indeed is still with him, most near to him, though not always perceptibly: also that which was before seen as Beauty and Goodness is now seen as stark Holiness, to the confusion of utterance but not of love. In that ultimate analysis, one loves a Being, not this or that attribute.

The negative aspects of this picture are restored to their true balance and brightness only when Binah is united to Chokmah, in peace and power: that is, when the Magister Templi becomes the Magus. In the consciousness of the Chiah, his is the mind now in truth of the all-potent Father and of the Bright Fertile Mother: he is the Right Hand and the Left Hand both upheld in the Gesture of the Calyx: and above and between them shines the Illimitable Brilliance of the Primal Glory.

# CHAPTER V

The Composite Tree and its correspondence to the parts of the pysche. The "Neshamah of the Sword": the Ten Sephiroth in the spirit from which the complete plan of the individual is developed downwards through the Worlds.

Correspondences of the Sephiroth, considered as upon the Composite Tree, to the parts of the psyche (Malkuth here being represented by the physical body). Indication of various terms used to express the functions and inter-relationships of those parts within the individual.

Impossibility of showing the descent of the Intuitive Mind in a diagram of this type.

The Gate Sephiroth and their correspondence to the Centers of Activity. The problem of Hod and Netzach; the problem of representing modalities of living existence by a diagram.

The six principal Centers of Activity described.

The Flemish "Annunciation", a work showing deeply occult significations and great richness of symbolism.

*The points (by no means exhaustive) noted in relation to this picture:*
   Red Pillar and White Arch.
   The linen basket, allusion to the "white work" of alchemy.
   The lamp of the Quintessence.

Occult significance of the monogram which is commonly
rendered as IHS.

Three stages of mystical development shown by the
progressive floor patterns, the third showing the
Star of Regeneration supporting the foot of the Angel.

## CHAPTER V
## EPILOGUE TO PART I

From the foregoing chapters on the various parts of the human psyche, something will have become apparent regarding the attribution of the psyche together with the physical body to the Four Worlds of the Holy Qabalah. The Yechidah, Chiah and Neshamah belong to the World of Atziluth; the Ruach belongs to the World of Briah; the Nephesh to the World of Yetzirah; and the physical body to Assiah.

The pattern of the Composite Tree as applied to the psyche is of paramount value, for it indicates the evolutionary development of the psyche, and to attempt an explanation of man without taking the "composite" interpretation into account would be plainly impossible. Nevertheless, considered alone, this pattern would give a false picture and would result in the same errors being made concerning the psyche as have been made concerning the Worlds by so many.

If the psyche is studied only from the "composite" viewpoint, the spirit of man must be seen as comprising only the Supernal Sephiroth, but in fact the spirit is the totality of the Holy Emanations, the complete Atziluthic microcosm, the total archetypal reality of man. In this context we sometimes use the term NShMH HChRB, the *Neshamah of the Sword*, or again, *psychoessential principles:* these terms are applied, in the involutionary sense, to the totality of the spirit as comprising the "Supernal Neshamah" and the Sephiroth from Chesed to Malkuth. In each of the Four

371

Worlds the relevant level of man is represented by a complete
world of the Ten Sephiroth.

The NShMH HChRB does not, however, enter directly
into our consideration of the Way of Return, being the
involutionary "deed" of the spirit (and this book is concerned with evolutionary progress on the Way of Return).
From the evolutionary viewpoint then, which is based on
the Composite Tree, we say that the spirit is triune—
Yechidah, Chiah and Neshamah—and from the evolutionary
viewpoint this is quite correct. When treating of the
evolutionary patterns of the psyche, the involutionary
completeness of Homo Quadruplex is inevitably left in
the background: we maintain it none the less.

The following diagram is of great importance in
studying the evolutionary plan of the psyche:—

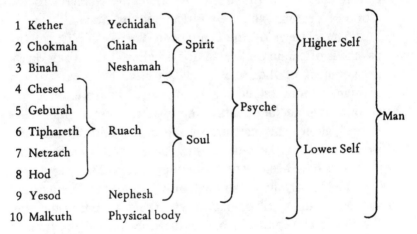

This diagram cannot take into account the supremely
important development, the descent of the Intuitive Mind,
which is described in the foregoing chapters. Much of the
general imagery associated with this has been conveyed in
the text of Chapters III and IV and elsewhere. It need hardly
be said that the matter itself has to a limited extent become

known even to people who, having no formal occult training, have not been known as Adepts, but who have been of genius or near-genius status. Often however they have not known what was occurring although their new intuition has told them the essence of it: Gerard Manley Hopkins illustrates this very clearly by his poem "The fine delight that fathers thought . . ." The true Adept, again, has had no doubt of that which he experienced in attaining the Knowledge and Conversation: but an analysis of the occurrence in psychological terms for the benefit of the student has been lacking.

If the formulation in our table is compared with the configuration of the Trines of the Composite Tree, the only difficulty found will be with regard to Hod and Netzach, whose influences we have indicated as coming within the domain of the Ruach, the Gate-Sephirah of which is Tiphareth, while in the scheme in Book III they are shown in trine with Yesod.

This difficulty, in fact, accurately reflects a problem which experience repeatedly encounters in human development: for as we have indicated, the boundary-line between Nephesh and Ruach is by no means clearly defined. The work of the Ruach, besides its function as vehicle of the higher faculties, is to bring the emotions and the subliminal data into right order and use, not to repress them nor to leave them to an autonomous existence. (The student must beware of taking the diagram literally: it is but a partial and static representation of the truths intended, a symbolic conformation. The true sense of this matter will be seen quite easily.)

The special affinities existing between the Gate-Sephiroth of the Composite Tree and the levels of Man are as follows:—

This leads us on to a consideration of the Centres of Activity which exist in the astrosome. The Magical Tradition of the West affirms six *Principal Centres*, of which five correspond to the Gate-Sephiroth. These are known as:—

  a) CORONA FLAMMAE

  b) UNCIA COELI

  c) FLOS ABYSMI

  d) ORBIS SOLIS

  e) CORNUA LUNAE

  f) INSTITA SPLENDENS

*Corona Flammae.* This is the Kether-centre of the psyche, its site being located above the crown of the head of the physical body: the Corona of spiritually developed persons being easily perceived by those with etheric vision, gave rise to the representation of the "nimbus" or "halo" in medieval religious art. Although the Corona Flammae as thus perceived, or as visualised in various magical exercises, is but a part of the World of Yetzirah, yet there is a most powerful correspondence between this astral Centre and the Yechidah. It is thus that true and vital energy is drawn down into the psyche through the Corona Flammae for magical purposes.

*Uncia Coeli.* Although it is without a Central Column sephirothic connotation, this Centre, which is situated in the midst of the brow, is of great significance, its function in the psyche being reflected in the Byzantine mystical tradition, as witness the distinct and careful demarcation of the "square inch" on the brow of a number of Christos-figures which are well known to experts in

Byzantine art.* It is imperative, in the conscious rousing of *all* the Gate-centres, that the power from the Corona Flammae be resolved and intensified by the Uncia Coelia before passing to the centres upon its subsequent course. Usually, in exercises designed to awaken the Gate-centres, the Uncia Coeli is ignored: this omission is emphatically condemned by the present writers. A great deal of confusion has existed between the functions of this Centre and of the one following: a confusion which should be most carefully avoided by the student, because the Uncia Coeli has a correspondence to the Neshamah and the Flos Abysmi to Daath, and to confuse the Centres will lead inevitably to a foolish confusion between Daath and the Neshamah.

*Flos Abysmi.* The Daath-centre, located in the throat, is an integral function of the psyche in its own right. It symbolises the transitional state, situate in the vast Abyss which sunders Noumena and Phenomena.

*Orbis Solis.* In some older presentations of the Western tradition, the astral Centre representing the Sun-sphere was directly associated with the great nerve-centre situated in

---

*A particular development of the esoteric tradition which is of the highest importance must here be brought to the attention of the serious student who wishes to research the historical ramifications of the Western mystery tradition: it concerns a system of mystical philosophy which has had a profound influence in the West, but which has escaped the attention of so very many.

This system, arising from a fusion of older traditions of the Eastern Mediterranean with material from the timeless and well-nigh sectless mysticism of the monasteries, Sinai, St. Sabas, the Hesychasts, permeated with its developing symbolism the sombre mosaics and paintings of Byzantine art. It appears in the insignia, the ritual, and the architecture of the medieval Order of the Knights Templar. It inspired the design of the Baptistery at Florence: it guided the hand of Giotto (1270–1337) to depict the *House of Sacrifice* as the Temple in his frescoes (cf. Book II, "Mathematical Symbolism"): it likewise guided that unknown Flemish painter whose masterpiece, the Annunciation, is shown in this volume. It appears in much of the guild-work in all the arts of medieval Europe, and was handed on thence to the Renaissance Platonists: notably its veiled influence is signalled by its symbolism in the work of that great philosophic luminary Marsilio Ficino. Not, indeed, by the mere occurrence of the mystical symbols, but by their use in a significant context, must the student trace this vital substratum of the Western magical tradition, which is characterised by the Eightfold Star, and whose key-word is Regeneration: a regeneration not dependent upon creed or sacraments, but upon the understanding and application of unchanging spiritual laws.

the upper abdomen, and the physical nerve-centre itself was accordingly named the solar plexus. Modern understanding however has perceived this so-called solar plexus to be intrinsically involved with the lower emotional nature, so as to be entirely unsuited to symbolise the Ruach as the Sun-centre must do. In the modern tradition therefore the Orbis Solis is located in the breast as relating to the heart. This region, identified by the whole modern tradition of Western thought as the seat of the nobler emotions and aspirations, is well suited to represent that function of the psyche which mediates between the higher and lower faculties.

*Cornua Lunae*. This, the Moon-centre of the psyche, is located in the genitals. Besides being in fact a part of the astrosome, as are all the Centres as here contemplated, the Cornua Lunae has its own especial correspondence to the Nephesh. Even a cursory enquiry into sexual psychology will reveal that this is by no means a simple matter of instinctual motivation alone, but is laden with the utmost elaborations of phantasy, and thus conspicuously pertains to the World of Yetzirah. If the Uncia Coeli (see above) is omitted, there is a particular tendency to imbalance in the Cornua Lunae, due to the fact that of all the Centres the Cornua Lunae is the one whose actual correspondence is to the astral world in which the Centres are aroused. The affinity between Neshamah and Nephesh thus becomes an essential balancing factor, that the lower may be equilibriated by the higher: and here we have one of the reasons why the inclusion of the Uncia Coeli is essential (the student may care to reflect that this is, in one aspect, the marking of the Signum Tau upon the "forehead" of the *House of Sacrifice*).

*Instita Splendens.* Although in the astrosome each foot has its own Centre of Activity located in the instep, for the purposes of visualisation when the feet are together the

Instita Splendens is one Centre shared by both feet. This is
the Malkuth-centre of the psyche, and has a correspondence
to sensory-consciousness. It thus represents the contact of
the psyche with the earth-forces, and for effective magical
development should always be considered as well-defined
and beneficent.

———

To conclude Part I of this study, we can turn to a
remarkable assembly of symbols shown in a beautiful and
in some respects unique painting executed in the early XVI
century by an unknown artist of the Flemish school (see
the frontispiece of this Volume 2.) The painting is now in
the Fitzwilliam Museum at Cambridge. The fine degree of
preservation of this picture is in itself unusual, and bears
witness to its having been handed down by a series of owners,
perhaps the members of an occult fraternity, who were well
aware of its remarkable significance. To a casual glance it
appears to be simply a devotional representation of the
Annunciation, one of the most frequent subjects in European
art up to modern times. Even on that level however, it would
be evident that the artist was thoroughly versed in the
appropriate symbolism, and had the skill and taste to apply
it in a far from banal manner. For example: there arose in
medieval times a custom of representing in such a scene two
pillars, one for the Angel and one for the Virgin: not to look
any further for the origins of this, it may be pointed out that
in the subterranean chapel shown in Nazareth (in Crusading
times as today) as the place of the Annunciation, there are in
fact two pillars, originally from an older edifice, framing the
altar: popular tradition early attached to these the names of
"the Angel's Pillar" and "the Virgin's Pillar," the next
development being that a rumour arose of a treasure
concealed in the Virgin's Pillar: whereupon some medieval
robbers removed a portion of the solid stone thereof to see

for themselves. With such a starting-point of partly conscious, partly unconscious symbolism, it is not surprising that although the Angel's Pillar remained in artistic tradition a single pillar, the Virgin's Pillar came to be represented as something which was in itself dual, an arch or a porch. At the same time, alchemical influences came into the matter, and so it came about that in some of the more recondite examples the Angel's Pillar was shown as red (for the male principle, Red Rose) while the Virgin's Pillar or arch was white (for the female principle, White Rose, the *Anima Mundi* who had to be redeemed from bondage.) A very simple example of this tradition is a small painting by the Sienese painter Duccio (c. 1255 - 1318) in the National Gallery, London: the Angel stands by a red pillar, the Virgin within a light architectural structure, white in hue. Now we see what subtle use our unknown Flemish artist has made of this tradition: for behind the head of the Angel appears a slender red column, while, by means of perspective, the Virgin is seated just within the area of a white-arched doorway. Were this all, we might think it an accident: but beside her stands a basket with a piece of white linen, as if to be taken for washing: a clear allusion to the "women's work," the "white work" of alchemy. The redemption of White Rose (who is, as a main interpretation, the lower principle in man) is highly relevant here. Furthermore, above her hangs the five-flamed lamp of the Quintessence. And lest the initiate should still need reassuring that he is not looking at an ordinary Christian presentment of this Mystery, let him look at the girdle of the Virgin, most conspicuously tied with a curious knot which is unmistakeably the central member of the traditional Girdle of Isis.

Another piece of symbolism appears in the foreground of the picture, a device which through the centuries so many have used without understanding that by itself it could not be taken to determine anything. On the vase which holds the

lily-spray is that mysterious monogram, I ℏ S which has
been variously interpreted as standing for *Iesous-Hireus-
Soter,* or for *In Hoc Signo,* but of which every interpretation
makes it evident, by sheer lameness, that the symbol came
first, the explanation after. Essentially, the central letter in
this monogram is what looks like a letter "h" with a cross-
beam intersecting the upright.* This central sign thus
becomes in itself a representation of "the Cross upon the
Mount," which has a number of interpretations older than
Christianity: but in the present design its most likely
significance seems to be that of the "World-Axis" or
balance-beam, set up at the point regarded as the earth's
navel. This is not however the feature of the monogram most
interesting to us. We can at once recognise, from whatever
origins the image came, the Cross upon the Mount as forming
the central object in those Calvary-groups so often situated
upon the "rood-screen" in churches, where in medieval
times it was very usual to paint upon the ceiling directly
over the group a rosette containing this same monogram. In
fact, this monogram represents that group. On the one side
of the axis-cross we have the letter I. We are told that the
male figure on one side of the Cross is John, the female
figure on the other side is Mary. There is no difficulty in
identifying the letter I as standing for the male figure,
therefore. But though the I can stand for John (Iohannes)
the letter S can hardly stand for Mary in any language.

It can, however, stand for *Sophia.*

We have then on the one side the Greek letter Iota
which is the same in sound and in signification as the
Hebrew Yod, the active and all-spiritual male force: and on
the other side the letter Sigma which stands for Sophia, the

---

* This central sign is unlikely to represent the sound of "h". To try to interpret
it as a letter or to guess what word it might signify, is impossible without knowing
the time and place of the monogram's origin, but it seems certain to come out of
some form of Greek Cursive script: several Cyrillic letters of various traditions
resemble it closely. The modern capitalised form I.H.S. is therefore without
authority.

passive and all-potential female form representing his antithesis and counterpart. Did our artist know what he was
inscribing upon that exquisite vase? We cannot be sure: but
if we look at the white-robed dynamic figure of the Angel
with his Wand of Power, and at the meditative dark-robed
Virgin with her book, the implications hidden in the
monogram are repeated. This Virgin, with the secateurs on
the floor at her feet, is discernably related to Durer's
Saturnian 'Melancholia" of some years earlier.

There are a multitude of remarkable features in the
painting, many of which will be immediately obvious: but
this Annunciation yields three main interpretations,
Christian, alchemic and psychosophical. The psychosophical
symbolism (hail to our unknown brother!) is twofold. One
aspect of this last we shall now briefly consider: the other
aspect is left to the discerning.

There is nothing new in looking for cryptic meanings
in floor-patterns. William of Malmesbury, describing the Lady
Chapel at Glastonbury Abbey in his own time, states that
the floor-pattern conveyed a mystery which might not
otherwise be uttered. He does not impart to us either the
mystery or the floor-pattern: but what we have here may
not be very different from that lost work.

The first pattern, nearest the door, is a simple checker-
board, dark and light. This pattern, still a favourite in the
Middle East and the West for dedicated buildings of all
kinds, represents virginal balance and repose. The following
words indicate something of its significance: —

OMNIS GLORIA EIUS FILIAE REGIS AB INTUS,
IN FIMBRIIS AUREIS
CIRCUMAMICTA VARIETATIBUS.

The second pattern is much more individuated. The
dark and light tiles have been arranged to form octagons:

closed areas each with its guarded centre. The octagon is a symbol of developed personality, but it is not intended that this should be for ever kept in isolation: complete in its defence as far as the outer world is concerned, it is open at its centre for development from the inner levels, comparably to the symbolism of the octagonal font which represents the inner shrine of the transformed self.

The third pattern has a further rearrangement and enrichment. Here we have the eight-pointed Star, "the Glorious Star of Regeneration," in a form not very different from that used by the Aurum Solis. If we reconstruct what can be seen of it in the painting, we have:—

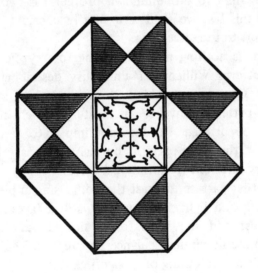

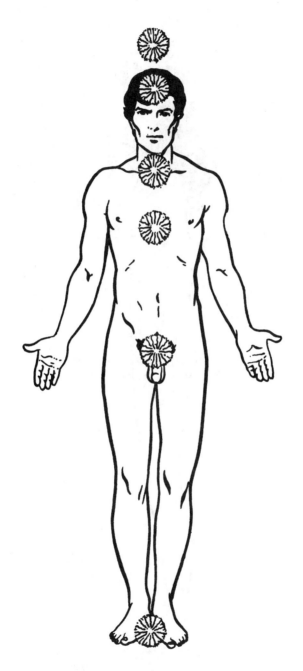

**THE SIX PSYCHIC CENTERS**

*See pages 375-378*

**THE SIX PSYCHIC CENTERS**
See pages 375-378

*Part II*

*CHAPTER I*

Provenance of psychological knowledge. Psychology and Psychosophy.

Advantage to the magician in utilizing both Qabalistic and clinical approaches to knowledge.

The conscious mind seen as limited by the bounds of the higher and the lower unconscious. Two keys to progress in extending our sphere of effectiveness—goodwill and careful work.

Application of these keys to relationships with others, likewise to the relationship of one's consciousness with different levels of one's own being.

Some aspects of the Nephesh illustrated by facts of psychic experience. Tangible evidence from the reactions of the physical body.

Good effect of assurance given to the lower self of the value attached to its work.

Stimulating results of a sense of novelty and adventure. The director's duty when the aspirant is attending routine meetings.

Misguided treatment of persons of psychic ability: over-frequent testing by researchers, over-frequent consultation of professional clairvoyants by clients.

Evidence for the separate functioning and different abilities of mind and brain.

The nature of the instincts: origins of man's innate inclination to Magick.

## CHAPTER I
## THE SUBRATIONAL FOUNDATION

The history of modern psychology is too well known to need repetition here. The great names associated with its development, beginning with that of Sigmund Freud as the originator of the development, have been those of physicians: as a consequence, much of the basic research and the resultant findings have been derived from the observation of the mentally or emotionally sick, and have been oriented to the cure or alleviation of their condition. This has led to much criticism which however is by no means so justifiable now as it was in the earlier days. Social psychology and industrial psychology, for instance, are two considerable branches of psychological research whose subjects, one might almost say by definition, come within the range of normality, since the abilities to earn a livelihood and to form human relationships are generally considered as primary, though of course not infallible, signs of the normality of an individual. Furthermore, in the main stem of psychological investigation, the name of Carl Jung is associated with a lifetime of profound study and interpretation of human cultures of different eras and worldwide provenance, directed to an understanding of the fundamental nature of mankind and thus the establishment of a norm by which the deviation or otherwise of the allegedly sick could be evaluated. His especial interest, the traditions of Gnosticism, was concerned with a way of wholeness certainly allied to the teachings of the Qabalah, although so far as can be determined none of the Gnostic sects presented a comprehensively universal system in the manner of the Holy Qabalah itself. Thus the bases of the study of the psyche have been extended by its various contributors to comprise ancient and abstruse philosophies and likewise the daily life of twentieth-century man.

Nevertheless, the main impetus and emphasis of psychological research does admittedly remain, for the world at large, in that field in which it originated: the field of mental and emotional sickness. This is, again, no condemnation of the work for general reference: the human psyche, like the human body, has a certain inherent character which shows itself as underlying all possible deformities or distortions, and, properly interpreted, these distortions of the psyche can but shed light upon its nature and possibilities, and the manner of its vital processes. The experience of the physician has been invaluable in the formulation of modern psychology, not only for the obviously necessary tracing-out of the relationship of the psyche with the physical body and their linking in the glandular and nervous systems, but also in a more subtle kind of experienced analogy-drawing whose scope has not yet been adequately explored: for certain it is that allowing for the different "fabric" of the psyche and of the material body, close and significant parallels exist between the processes by which each attempts to secure its health and survival. An eruption upon the skin, or the occurrence of nightmares, indicate the attempt of the body or of the psyche to cast out something incompatible, whether intruding from without or generated within: while in both body and psyche there is also a tendency, when an undesirable intrusion cannot be ejected, to try to render it harmless by isolating it, building an impervious wall around it. Thus the muscular tissues immure for instance an embedded bullet, or the unconscious immures a traumatic experience. These are simple examples, but they are very typical of the action, both of the lower unconscious level of the individual psyche, and of the life-force generally: precisely the same reactions, with regard to intrusions regarded as ejectable and as non-ejectable, can be seen in the communal actions of a hive of bees.

With regard to the instinctual and the lower emotional levels of the psyche, clinical observation and inference has made contributions of great depth and value. For the magician, however, their scope and the scope even of psychic investigators and parapsychologists, is but ancillary. He cannot look to their work for anything more than concurrent evidence: nor indeed does he need anything more than that. His own approach to the study of the psyche is different from theirs: he has a different objective, and he has a different starting-point from both psychic investigator and psychiatrist or psychotherapist. The starting-point of the magician has been his Chamber of Art: he too has a specimen psyche for investigation—his own—but by definition it must be in a reasonable state of health, his quest being not so much its healing as its progress and its perfecting. Furthermore, he has what his exoteric counterpart has never yet had: a blueprint to aid his work, nothing less than the glorious vision of the universe and of the psyche in their perfection, which has been built up through long centuries by the illuminati. That the findings of the modern exoteric psychiatrists agree as well as they do with the high wisdom which is accessible to the magician, constitutes in itself great evidence for the profundity and integrity of their work.

This being the case, the magician would be ill-advised to ignore their hard-won truths. As in a graph, the points strictly necessary to plot a line or a curve can well be supplemented by other points to confirm it: and where these points have been obtained independently by a different discipline and from a

separate source, the result is a deep enrichment of understanding. Besides, it is not, ultimately, only for the benefit
of the magician that the findings of the psychologists and
of the Qabalists should be co-ordinated. The greater the
measure of relevant truth available to the healer, the more
effective the healing is likely to be. He who places a fractured
limb in what appears to be the most natural position, and
who carefully applies splints and bandages, does something
certainly towards its satisfactory setting: but he who knows
exactly the anatomy of the limb as it ought to be when
whole, and who performs his work accordingly, will
predictably produce a much more satisfactory result. This has
a parallel of prime importance in the guidance of the psyche:
and the study of the modern Qabalah and the psychosophy
of the Aurum Solis is therefore most solemnly urged upon
the attention of all who are concerned in that field of work.

Nevertheless, this present study, although based fully
upon principles of psychosophy which are of universal application in the human psyche, is oriented altogether to the
training of the magical student, and to his understanding of
the psychological factors involved in his training.

The aspirant newly embarking upon his training, as we
have indicated, stands between two vast areas of unconsciousness, or rather, areas of whose content his ordinary awareness is unconscious:—the Upper (or Inner) Unconscious, and
the Lower (or Outer). The Lower (or Outer) Unconscious is
closely involved with the instincts and with the physical
nervous system, or rather systems. The aim of the student
from the beginning must be to bring more psychic material
into consciousness. Very little, however, can be achieved by
unaided determination. Determination is essential to success,
but it is not determination of the type which runs its head
against closed doors: it must be an extreme tenacity fortified
by patience and goodwill. Goodwill is by no means the same
thing as weakness or indulgence: but it does enable us to

make allies of those parts of the psyche (and indeed the physical body) which through their intrinsic nature or through our personal inexperience we cannot directly command. Even where we do command, goodwill should not be forgotten. This applies also in different ways, of course, to our dealings with our fellow humans and with the Powers.

There is nothing sentimental about this, in fact the reverse. As an example: the student of Magick who has also to earn his living, will find the time that he formerly gave to his friends curtailed to a lesser or greater extent, depending upon the stage and the intensity of his training. The friends may raise an objection to this, but he must be ruled by what he knows himself to be doing, and not by what they imagine him to be doing. In reality, one glance of his mind towards them, directed with goodwill, can do more for them (and progressively so as he advances upon the Path) than hours of idle talk which might only dissipate their energies and his own. Similarly, and especially during performance of the Exercises, a friendly impulse directed to the faculties involved will be of considerable assistance. (But never send pity, whether to oneself or to another: pity is poison.) It is worth while to remember that by suitable devices, forms of activity which ostensibly are not at all magical have been turned into something very like magick by people of all sorts. In instructions for body-building exercises, for example, the student is frequently advised to perform his exercises in front of a mirror. This is partly so that he may "ensure the correct posture," and partly again so that he may "be encouraged by observing his improvement," but what is not so generally pointed out is that the muscles and other bodily tissues do actually respond to being held in conscious attention, so that the student who "encourages" them in this way stands to receive more benefit from his efforts than someone who gives them nothing but conscientious thoroughness. In the world of feminine beauty, too, the dressing-mirror is not merely an adjunct to vanity but an instrument of art: relaxation and vibrancy, animation and poise, being allied qualities in the face and figure which are brought fully to life in this way. If attention can do so much for even the physical body, which shares strongly in the inertia of Assiah, what can it not do for the astral body in both its finer and denser levels!

Consequently, when the magical exercises are performed, care should certainly be taken that every posture and gesture is carried out exactly as directed, and this observation can be made the opportunity to give a moment's greeting, so to speak, to limbs and trunk as these are involved: but also the purpose of the exercise, and the inner faculties which are directed towards that purpose, should receive from our consciousness an attitude of encouragement and confidence. The effect of well-performed exercises can be greatly enhanced thereby.

In this directing of attention to the various parts of the body, the feet should not be omitted. When the student is instructed to visualise light as descending to the ground between the feet, this means the ground between the feet and not a vague region below the knees. To perform this visual-isation correctly it is necessary to be conscious of the feet themselves. Tall people often have more difficulty than short people in this respect, and one sees that instead of the easy self-confidence which might be anticipated from their extra inches, they often display a shy hesitancy in comparison to the brisk practicality of their shorter colleagues. There are several psychological reasons for this, but there is much to commend the saying, "You can have your head in the clouds, but keep your feet firmly on the ground." Whatever type one's physique may be, awareness of the feet is necessary to the psychic well-being which is the basis of magical work. The feet, like the hands and the face, are so responsive to every vibration of the psyche as to present an index of the character of the individual: as is known not only to the tarsomantist of the East, but also to the old cobbler of the West, who comes to understand a remarkable amount about his clients from the way their shoes are worn. Yet the feet are given little attention by many who should appreciate their occult importance. Often, when the psyche throws off a condition which is causing useless distress—a worry, perhaps, or a fear concerning some matter in which we are powerless to act effectively, and would do better to occupy ourselves with other things—the feet are completely left out of the liberating process, and remain entangled in a miasma of depression. It is well to make a practice, perhaps nightly, of directing a moment's goodwill to each foot, its physical parts and its astral centre, at the same time mentally shedding from the feet any residue of the day's petty worries and frustrations.

One of the greatest aids in securing the co-operation of the Nephesh and of the autonomic nervous system, is to let them know that their work is valued and taken seriously. The magical diary is, from the beginning, an excellent means of doing this. Nothing, of course, would be gained by writing of one's performance of the magical exercises in glowing terms which the facts would belie: a true and just assessment must be made, but can be made in complete frankness and confidence because the entire purpose is to assist one's progress. When the work is well done, the ego should not take all the credit to itself: the other faculties thrive on the confidence that their contribution is duly appreciated and faithfully recorded. As the magical diary progresses from the disciplined jottings of the beginner to the full record of the more advanced magician, the reality of the help thus gained will be found.

Another very important aspect of this encouragement of the Nephesh-faculties is the renewal of a sense of novelty and adventure. In a magical Order, the responsibility for this lies largely with the person directing the aspirant: but the student working alone must take it as a personal charge. In the nature of things, to maintain an even level of interest is impossible, and if the attempt is made it will be found that more and more effort is needed, so that the search for novelty becomes first unhealthy and then impossible: there must therefore be ebb and flow, but the introduction of fresh interest and new lines of approach is essential, particularly during periods when perseverance in an unchanged exercise is called for. The circumstances of meditation may be varied, a different and perhaps highly effective tone in the magical voice may be sought and found, a few days of recapitulation on previous work may be planned, both for the sake of revision and to avoid staleness on the current work: a variation in incense or lighting in the Chamber of Art may lead to valuable discoveries in interpretation. The reason for creating such renewals of interest is to be found in the nature both of the Nephesh and of the nervous and glandular activity of the physical vehicle: for while the conscious intellect of the student is expected to maintain an adult level of application to the Work without a continual experience of new stimuli, it must be recognised that the lower unconscious levels, prior to their integration in the acceptance of the True Will, are likely to evince just about as much capacity for sustained attention to an unvarying object, as a young child or an animal might have. This would be a predictable fact on philosophic grounds alone: but besides that, there is an abundance of evidence drawn from the psychic research of many investigators, which points to the same conclusion: likewise an investigation carried out by the A.S., bringing in other relevant material, can appropriately be quoted at this point.

There is a well-recognised factor in all types of psychic experimentation under standard conditions, which brings about a certain pattern in the results: no matter what the initial level of performance of a given subject, provided it be

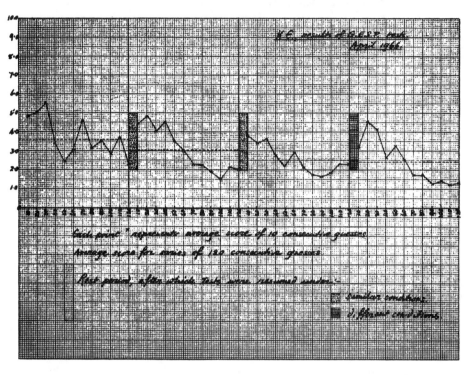

*General ESP Tests*

noticeably different from chance level,* there is a marked
tendency over a run of tests for the average to approach and
sometimes to reach chance level, that is to say, to reach the
proportion of correct answers which could be expected from
random guessing. The same pattern is repeated over a series
of runs, so that the graph of test results shown on p. 397 may
be regarded as typical.

Although our true concern is with Magick and not
with clairvoyance, telepathy, or other forms of simple
extra-sensory perception, yet the data provided by research
into those subjects is extremely helpful for the insight which
it gives into the functioning of the lower psychic faculties,
which form a vital link in our chain no matter how elevated
our ultimate purpose may be. In order to gather information
on the non-magical experience of these levels, the A.S. at
one time carried out an enquiry, the subjects taking part
being attested clairvoyants of both sexes, of professional
standing. These gifted subjects were not only asked to
co-operate in certain tests, they were also asked questions
relating to their preferred conditions of work, and similar
matters. There were a few conspicuous differences here, from
the results gained by testing non-professional subjects: in
particular, the effects of "tiredness," so noticeable in our
graph, were more delayed in manifestation in the profession-
als, although, as the enquiry revealed, this same difficulty
beset them in other forms. Contrary to popular belief, it was
found that the majority of them did not regard personal
knowledge concerning a client to be any special advantage,
indeed it was frequently seen as the reverse: it would cause
embarrassment, and beyond this it would hinder the action
of the psychic faculty in a way which the subjects generally
did not understand: the fact being that the Ruach would

---

*Some subjects may show a psychic faculty which is certainly genuine, but which reveals itself
by giving *wrong* answers more consistently than mere random guessing would do. The cause
of this is in the unconscious processes, the circumstances of the test itself probably being in
some way adverse to the subject.

thereby be brought into play, when it would better have been stilled so as to allow greater freedom of action to the Nephesh. (It did however help, usually, to know certain general details, not only of the client but of any absent person involved in the client's questions: sex, age, marital status, the very indices that any counsellor would need in order to make a reasonable picture of the material presented: a few psychics however denied that they even wished to be told this much.) This dislike of being "spoon-fed" agrees with what we know of the Nephesh: it tallies for instance with the key discovery of the twentieth-century theatre, that a setting which merely suggests an appropriate theme to the imagination, endows a play with a far livelier reality than that achieved by the painstaking "realism" of the Victorian stage. For these reasons, we must beware of explaining exclusively by "tiredness" the well-established fact that although a psychic will often upon first meeting a new client give one or more startlingly unequivocal predictions, which are afterwards exactly fulfilled, nothing up to that standard is ever again given to the same person. Our team of subjects in this investigation did however state that the stream of new and varied personalities was an important stimulus in their work: regular clients had to be dissuaded from returning at over-frequent intervals,* and a few had found for themselves the error of allowing the clairvoyant-client relationship to become a personal friendship. A friendly and informal acquaintanceship seemed to be the ideal.

Something, evidently, was expected of the clients also: the psychics described their corresponding reactions to "vibrant" or to "depressing" types, while the person with a

---

* A basis was here established for the old superstition that it is "unlucky" to consult a psychic more than once in a day(!). The dissipation of astral energy by both parties can be considerable: and just as it is possible to "talk out" a cause of worry in some cases, so it seems likely that the astral motivation of a desired objective can be unwittingly "talked out" in the same way, especially with experienced psychic perception focussed upon it. The A.S. regards the use of divination in general with extreme reserve.

definite problem was greatly preferred to one who had merely come out of curiosity, or in hopes that the clairvoyant would be able to "see something" for the future in an existence in which the client had made no effort to create the least likelihood of interest.

These details are given as being of confirmatory interest: they all agree with what we should expect of the action of the Nephesh and of the movement of the Astral Light. Parallel situations and reactions occur in various human relationships: in the world of education, again, we find the desirability of an easy but not familiar relationship between teacher and pupil: here too, freshness and originality are of major importance in the presentation of the material. Furthermore it is a known fact that in the first term of the scholastic year, from September to December—three or four months at most —after the long summer vacation, half of the year's intended curriculum must be covered, or it is doubtful whether the year will successfully achieve the whole. The action of the Nephesh as intermediary between Ruach and brain is the key to the process of learning. The most unforgettable lessons are those learned with the greatest involvement of the subrational channels. Intelligence rather than learning is the function of the Ruach: the more intelligent individual usually learns better than the less intelligent from having stronger and more cogent motivation to do so, from organising the subrational faculties more capably, and from linking new with previously learned material more effectively: but he is still dependent to a great extent upon the subrational faculties and the physical brain for the real work of learning. The I.Q. of the "absent-minded professor" is as high as it was in his keen student days, but from various causes both physical and emotional, the subrational faculties are no longer giving the appropriate support to the rational ones.

Here incidentally we have a portion of the evidence for the separate existence of the mind from the physical organism.* The observable fact that intelligence does not deteriorate with the learning ability of the elderly is of great significance: but so is a minor demonstration of the same type, which has been experienced by anyone who has tried to continue work on a problem late at night, when the body is thoroughly tired. Although the brain in that state is quite unable to process ideas or to supply the necessary factual details, the mind may still wish to go on grappling with the problem, and can perhaps see in a vague manner the general lines along which a solution might be found.

In another, but related category, is the experience of an interesting group, people who when placed under general anaesthesia are occasionally forced into a state of projected consciousness. Enquiry usually reveals that they have had other indications of awakening psychic faculties, although perhaps only slightly or a long time previously. Quite often such a person before the operation expresses a dislike of general anaesthesia, or assures the attendants that it will be of "no use." It is, of course, a matter of normal medical ethics not to discuss subsequently anything which a patient may have done or experienced while under anaesthesia, but in this case the attendants' reticence has another motive besides: —prudence lest a factor which is not within their control may be interpreted unfairly to the discredit of the anaesthetist or of the team as a whole. The patient, therefore, if he is considerate, will not try to compel them to discuss the occurrence: a consideration which the "layman" would do well to show generally to people whom he knows to be bound by an especial code or creed. A typical form is that the patient, effectively anaesthetized and for all practical purposes unconscious, "sees" the operation and subsequently describes it with considerable accuracy, but sometimes from a visual angle which is not that of his head. This occurrence

* For other aspects of this subject see Paper XII, Volume 3.

is not explicable by telepathy: for one thing, the patient will competently describe instruments, etc., without being able to name them, and, for another, the viewpoint is sometimes stated precisely as being "between" two of the persons present, or "above" the operating table. No sensation of pain is reported. It is, in fact, a true instance of projected consciousness: but we cite it here, simply for its contributory evidence of the separability of mind and brain.

Some observations which go further along these lines have been made with regard to the "feeble-minded." These people primarily show an extremely poor co-ordination of the physical systems, so that whatever intelligence they may have can have little possibility of showing to advantage: nevertheless it has been found that in many cases, persevering and unprejudiced care can bring out signs of more intelligence than they had been supposed to possess. Even among those who have been placed in mental hospitals as imbeciles or as idiots, this has been observed: and the comments of a psychiatrist who worked for many years at a large mental hospital in the South of England have a particular value.

Dr. J. had begun his professional career as a complete materialist: conformably with this attitude, he believed the psyche to have no real existence except as an aggregate of nervous and glandular reactions interpreted by the brain, in an organism conditioned entirely by heredity and by personal experience. Over the years, he had among his hospital patients a number of congenital idiots who had been brought to the hospital from, generally, thoroughly unsatisfactory home circumstances. The visits to the hospital of the parents and siblings of these patients gave Dr. J. an opportunity to observe and interview the relatives also, and thus he was easily able to confirm that in the great majority of such cases the family as a whole was of low intelligence, so that even had the patients themselves escaped idiocy, nobody could have predicted for them any normal degree of mental development. These unfortunates passed their days in an impenetrable apathy, and in the nature of their general maladjustment usually lived to no great age. One of the heralding symptoms of approaching death, however, as Dr. J. repeatedly observed, was an awakening of mature intelligence. It seemed as if the apathy had been broken by a hope, by an awareness of impending release. (But, he asked himself, a release of *what?*) Nor was this all. Putting the highest interpretation that he reasonably could upon the change, he would have expected in all the circumstances that this newly-dawned intellect would appear as a *tabula rasa*, a virgin faculty devoid alike of concepts and training: instead he perceived, and this repeatedly, a rational mind fully formed, cogent in reasoning, and showing a spiritual elevation and withal a refinement totally inexplicable in terms of the life-experience of these persons. After this manifestation however, death invariably and rapidly supervened.

There was no element of doubt whatsoever in these observations of Dr. J. He considered from every aspect of his knowledge the phenomena which he had witnessed: he could produce materialistic hypotheses to account tentatively for many of the facts, but the development and maturity in these cases of what we should call the Ruach did not admit of any such explanation. At the risk of being considered "fanciful," he had to conclude that during the lifetime of the individual, the mind had been (as he expressed it) elsewhere, receiving, he supposed, from some unknown source a training suitable to its true capacity.

\*　　\*　　\*　　\*

The Nephesh and the physical body compose for the Ruach a vehicle subject to laws and limitations which are in part alien to the Ruach itself. If the personality is to be integrated, as it must be for successful magical training, the lower faculties cannot be allowed to dominate the scene, thus leaving the higher faculties unmanifest and inarticulate, as is frequently advocated by a kind of pseudo-mysticism nowadays. A degree of asceticism is most desirable in the early training, although it must be clearly understood that this is not asceticism for its own sake, nor for the accumulation of "merit." The breaking of old habits which have been formed at random, is most favourable to the formation of new ones which are chosen of true purpose: the Nephesh is taught to look for guidance to the Ruach, and the Ruach in turn becomes accustomed to take heed for the true benefit of the Nephesh.

The instincts in themselves form the motivation of the lowest level of the Nephesh, linked directly to the physical organism. To glance briefly at some of them as they occur in ordinary life, and at their relationship to the emotions, will clarify their position and nature. There are an indefinite number of instincts, for in many ways they are closely inter-related.

There is the *instinct of flight*, which underlies the emotion of fear: if we could always run away when prompted by the instinct of flight, we might never consciously feel fear. A schoolmaster, walking one night along a deserted road with his mind on his daily cares, suddenly took a most agile leap sideways and as a result found himself standing on one foot in the middle of the way. Looking about to see what had caused this extraordinary occurrence, he saw on the lamplit pavement a short length of rope, coiled so that it looked at first glance very like a snake. In his state of abstracted consciousness, instinct had evidently taken control: he had felt no fear, and did not even consciously perceive the rope until he turned round and noticed it. Since he had responded at once to the impulse to leap out of harm's way, fear would have been super-fluous: similarly, there are people who probably have never known any feeling of temptation, since no such feeling emerges to the consciousness of one who yields to every impulse. In truth, emotion of any sort must be conscious, or it is not emotion. Psychiatrists have written concerning "subconscious jealousy," for instance, but no such thing exists: there is a subconscious (or unconscious) urge to possess or to dominate a love-object completely, and there is a subconscious (unconscious) impulse to destroy and/or to identify with an interloper: if the synthesis of these drives comes into consciousness as an unfulfilled desire, we then have the emotion of jealousy.

Related to the instinct of flight is the *instinct of pugnacity:* both are brought into fulfilment through an activation of the suprarenal glands, and whether the outcome is flight or pugnacity is very much a matter of individual conditioning and self-confidence, factors which again bring other hormones into the matter. The instinct of pugnacity, likewise, is not in itself an emotion. If an extremely pugnacious individual is provoked, he will lash out at his adversary faster than thought or feeling, and not until he sees the other lying perhaps unconscious, will he realise what he has done: from beginning to end he may experience no emotion whatever. The less pugnacious individual, similarly provoked, will not at once lash out: he will, however, feel an intense emotion of anger.

The fact that the same remarks apply, *mutatis mutandis,* to the *sex instinct,* is almost too obvious to need comment. People often cannot think of any reason why they jumped into bed with a particular partner, for whom they feel no emotion whatever. It is useless to consider what might have happened if they had been prevented from so doing. From instances in which such rash action was prevented, it seems about a fifty-fifty chance whether they would thank their

stars for the escape, or decide that they were seriously in
love. Again, instinct must not be confused here with conditioning. The "grow-up-and-get-married-and-have-a-family"
syndrome is so inwoven in our social system, that for people
to follow out this pattern without either real thought or deep
emotion must not be laid entirely at the door of instinct:
particularly since, in the commercial world, the best jobs and
chances of promotion are usually available only to young
married men of whom the employer can feel "sure."
Nevertheless, a great deal of instinct is involved in the matter,
although, we repeat, unconsciously. The man who enjoys a
strip-show or a "girlie" magazine is not acting upon instinct:
he is revelling in a pleasure-pain ambivalence which arises
from the frustrated stirring of an instinct. Many women claim
not to be interested in pictures of attractive males: this is
very probably true, since in the feminine development of the
psyche the more typical level of sexual motivation is at the
truly instinctual and therefore unconscious level. We have
pointed out in another connection the relationship between
Anima and Nephesh, between Animus and Ruach:* the
present topic likewise pertains to those relationships.
Especially with regard to the unevolved type of woman, one
sees this repeatedly. A group of young girls come along the
road, seemingly engrossed in their conversation together. A
group of boys come from the other direction. The boys are
at once consciously aware of the girls as objects of interest.
The girls take no notice: but almost invariably, just as the
two groups pass each other, all the girls simultaneously will
produce a peculiar high-pitched provocative giggle, for no
matter what ostensible reason. It is unmistakeable. They are
not being deliberately "sly" or "teasing," they are acting
from pure instinct. This explains the mystery which has
always perplexed the male sex, of the strange mixture in

* Cf. Part I, Ch. IV.

many women of provocativeness and frigidity. If it is understood that the provocativeness of the more typical woman is likely to be wholly unconscious, or almost wholly, and that her unresponsiveness is often a result of that same unconsciousness of instinct, the mystery is less alarming. Her unconscious instinct, after all, is necessary to her passivity. A whole barricade of social pretence which has been built up from the Middle Ages to the nineteenth century, to the effect that women were more "shockable" than men and that sexually suggestive subject-matter must therefore not be mentioned in their hearing (by which pretence they also were conditioned, if possible, to believe it themselves) was created to disguise and to keep secret this fact, of woman's unconscious and therefore irresponsible sexual motivation, and high suggestibility. That same unconsciousness of the sexual level is also the cause, however, of the "Barbara Allen" type of happening, in which a girl dismisses a lover, only to realise too late her real attachment to him: in such a case the attraction only rises to consciousness as an emotion of love when the object of the attraction is no longer present, that is, when the instinct is frustrated. Of course the same sort of experience can befall a man, particularly one who from a strict early training or from pride has thrust his emotional life abnormally into unconsciousness: it belongs far more, however, to the "average" woman. Her greater insistence on love and sentiment in sexual relationships, too, is based on the fact that the truly sexual element in her own motivation is, in the main, unknown to her.

None of this applies, to anything approaching the same extent, to women of more intellectual, or "Eros-type" temperament (Ruach-Animus dominant.) Such women are far more complex beings than the simply feminine woman, who as a biological entity need have little conscious idea of what she is about. These more complex and in some sense more "masculine" women are of extremely varied types,

from the "steel-true, blade-straight" woman who chooses her
man as much as he chooses her, and loves him consciously
and loyally, to the skilful artist who works not in marble nor
upon canvas but upon her own person to create a wonder of
seductive grace, studying what instinct no longer tells her of
that which will charm the most. However, no class of human
beings is all sweetness and light, and among these complex
and sexually awakened types of women we find also, for
example, the nymphomaniac: for when her exaggerated
manifestation of instinct is due to psychological causes, she is
frequently searching for a form of Animus-type, active self-
expression in sex which she is not likely to find.

The *parental instinct* is quite a separate thing from the
sex instinct, but is, again, in its basic form unconscious.
Parents may be well aware of love for their children, of
course: but that is not the same as the mere instinct to
produce and to care for the offspring. A number of parents,
in fact, are carried along entirely by instinct until the
children are old enough to be discovered as friends: the age at
which this can happen depending upon the characters of the
parties concerned. The trouble with instincts of this kind is
that although they may become excessive they can still
remain at the unconscious level, so that a mother or father
when accused of over-possessiveness will look within for
some conscious emotion of the sort, and, finding none, will
deny the accusation outright. Many references are made by
psychological writers to the maternal instinct, scarcely any to
the paternal, yet the latter is just as real: and, since the male
in particular has an instinctual urge to govern not merely
his own progeny but a tribe, "paternalism" is apt to reveal
itself in all walks of life with results which are sometimes
excellent, sometimes lamentable.

*The creative instinct* is often claimed as an impulse
specifically human: in a certain sense this is true. Many
creatures create something: a honeycomb, a nest, a burrow, a

cocoon, a cobweb: one can tell the species of the creature from the style of its work. Frequently this instinct is related directly to the reproductive pattern: birds build their nests, annually in most cases, as a receptacle for their eggs: a domestic cat will make a nest in the straw, dry leaves, or newspapers for the birth of her kittens, treading the material down to make a hollow of the right size and shape: the elaborate structures created by bees, wasps, ants, over many generations, are likewise for the purpose principally of the continuance of the species. The cocoons of the silk-moth and of many other insects are made when the creatures are about to undergo their own vital transformation from larva to adult. The elaborate beaver-colony, a marvel of animal craftsmanship, is designed with a view to both breeding and hibernation. In the whole animal world there is nothing comparable with the endless spate and variety of human creativity, which in most of its manifestations cannot be called instinctive: yet instinctive in its origins it seems indeed to be, and we may ask whether it is not in some way involved with the reproductive instinct, as in the nest-builders, with the self-preservative instinct as in the cocoon-builders and hibernators, or with the predatory instinct as in the spiders.

To arrive at some clarity on this, we go back as nearly as we can to the physical origins of the human race. Middle Palaeolithic man was capable of crude creative art. The cave-paintings of Late Palaeolithic man were lifelike impressions of animals, coloured with pigments which in some instances have lasted freshly until today: he carved animal-heads and small images on bits of bone, and these too have that living breathing quality. We recall in contrast that penetrating remark of old Cosimo de' Medici, "Every painter paints himself:" a comment amply endorsed by modern psychology. We would wish to know, therefore, what, so far as we can discover, are early man's first individualised pictures of Man?

The Mother and the Hunter both have very early representations, although featureless and without individuality. There is no representation of the Artist as such, but there is a striking image of perhaps even greater interest than that would be. In the cavern of Trois-Frères in the Pyrenees, is the famous figure of the nude and masked "Sorcerer" occupied in his ritual dance. Other very early representations of human males also clearly represent masked and magical figures. This certainly was hunting-magick, there being plenty of evidence to maintain that observation: but it was indisputably magick none the less, dance-magick, and doll-sorcery with images of beasts of the chase as the objects of action. It would seem that these techniques are well-nigh as old as the human race.

From the viewpoint of our study of the instincts, all this is paramount. Some occurrence, some circumstance, some unconscious perception, stirs the physical and psychic energy of this creature we call Man. According to the general nature of the stimulus, nerve-centres and glands take up the released energy and use it to produce the chemical materials which at once precipitate an instinctive reaction to the occurrence or circumstance. If it is possible instantly to pursue, kill, rape or flee from the outer cause of the disturbance as appropriate, we need not suppose the consciousness of primitive man to be much involved in the incident. Sometimes however the appropriate action proves to be impossible, and then emotion is generated and the matter needs to be pondered upon. Man learns by his mistakes. However, in the matter of the chase it is too important, for reasons both of food and of communal safety, to let success and failure come as chance may hap. A surge of energy follows in the form of the creative instinct: and behold! —as this creative instinct comes into the conscious mind, it takes form as the will to do magick. The form which this magick takes, in the event, is the germ of a form which

even today is one of the most notable: the drama
representing the desired outcome.

This impulse, to make assurance doubly sure in any
important matter by magical means, can attach itself to any
instinct or aspiration possible to the human mind, or to any
combination of instincts or aspirations. The creative instinct
which gives rise to it can therefore be identified now as a
specifically human instinct, born of an awareness that by the
nature of man's psyche he is not always to take life as he
finds it, nor only to contend by material means. This
perception, however, presupposes a standard by which to
judge what should be done, and to establish such a standard
it is necessary to have a conscious objective in view. Without
this safeguard, almost everyone whether deliberately or not
would in effect be aiming for an earthly immortality without
toil, age, or suffering of any kind. Such an objective is either
unattainable, in which case it is a false and delusory goal, or
if we posit it as attainable we must confess that its fulfilment
before the spiritual evolution of the individual is complete,
would effectively block most means of progress. If however
the advancement of our personal evolution is taken as the
objective, this purpose rather than the spontaneous promptings of the instinctual nature will determine our wishes. That
is the meaning of the statement, that asceticism is to be seen
as a means, not as an end in itself. For the fulfilment of
an evolution, we can accept as reasonable the obstacles to
be overcome and the trials to be endured in pursuit of
the Work: but also, we can accept the alleviations which
are ours to claim for the Work's sake. To say, "I wish never
to have a day's ill-health in all my life," would be foolishness:
but to say, "I will not catch cold this winter because it
would hinder my magical programme," is valid. That,
however, is but a slight example: the vital aspect of the
matter is that when once the student has set foot upon the
path of High Magick, he is never until the ultimate moment

of his identification with the Yechidah left without a
conscious "next objective" to gain. It is by a tacit acceptance
of the Work in its entirety that magical training becomes
possible.

*CHAPTER II*


True spirituality does not oppose the healthy development
of the ego; but a false spirituality can cause the personality
to transfer the natural authority of the Ruach to the
Nephesh.

The role of true spirituality, that is of the influence of the
Higher Self, is to guide the Ruach into its inheritance. The
medieval story of Valentine and Orson viewed as an
allegory.

The long and persevering preparation of the Ruach before the
Hero-Angel can bring it to its completion.

Vital factors in this preparation:— self-awareness, and the
making of well-judged decisions on the problems posed
by life. Magical training and practice as preparation.
Flexibility and initiative encouraged by the A.S. in the
working of the personal magical programme.

Memories of past lives as an aid in recognising the continued
"common denominator" of the personality through its
various changes and masquerades.

The vital importance of *relevance* in moving into the new life.
Old viewpoints do not need to be painfully given up; they
are found simply to fade from significance before the new
vision.

413

Truth perceived with a faculty "not human but divine".

Adepthood, "the vindication of the balanced personality in its entirety".

## CHAPTER II
### THE EGO AND SELF-AWARENESS

All too often, the ego is the "Ugly Duckling" of the psyche. A misguided but fanatically enthusiastic spirituality has repeatedly set up an ideal of "selflessness" in the pursuit of which the normal individual cannot hope to compete with the gravely neurotic, who is lauded (and exploited) by organizations of every type. In education of the conventional sort, even the developing ego of the child is still snubbed and repressed at every opportunity, often by teachers who find it easier to misapply Christian doctrine than to answer questions which go beyond their text-book. Then, in consequence, the pendulum swings to the other extreme: the false spirituality is overthrown and the repressed psyche turbulently asserts its right to live. Such a movement is afoot in the present time: but still it is not the ego, the rational mind, which is thereby accorded the victory. Popular outcry does not acclaim the Ruach, but the Nephesh. Two centuries, after all, are little time in the history of man: and our present insurgents against authority are still symbolised in their attitude by those Sans-Culottes of Paris who tore the cross from the altar in the name of Reason and then—also in the name of "Reason"—enthroned a harlot there. The Nephesh must not thus dominate the Ruach. The feminine principle when redeemed from the bondage of matter shall be enthroned indeed, but the throne of the Ruach is reserved for another, or all is flung into chaos. There is a true spirituality, which is not imposed from without as the false is, but which is found within, and which does not seek to destroy the ego, but to lead it into its rightful inheritance. This it is the work of magick and of psychosophy to establish.

There is a fable which was widely known and well loved in the Middle Ages, and which continued to be retold and printed with strange woodcut illustrations, and to be sold in the form of chapbooks by peddlers at fairs and markets, to be read over and over by young and old alike, until the eighteenth century, when, significantly, it went out of favour: apparently people no longer found in it a personal "message." One obscure printing of it is recorded in the nineteenth century, but even that was in a different age from ours and now the tale is quite unknown except to a few antiquarians. It is time, however, to tell it again: the story of Valentine and Orson.

Orson must originally have had a different name, for the one by which we know him is simply *ourson*, bear-cub. Valentine and he were twin sons of an Emperor, but when they were babies they were one day put out in a garden adjoining a large forest, and presently it was realised that Orson had disappeared. He had in fact been carried off into the forest by a she-bear which had lost a cub, but nobody saw this occurrence. After a fruitless search he was mourned as lost, and Valentine was brought up as the sole heir. Meanwhile Orson grew up among the bears, to live as a "wild man of the woods."

"Wild men of the woods" were a congenial concept to the medieval imagination: it is very possible, on several counts, that something of quite material existence helped in some instances to build up the image, but still it remains from the psychological viewpoint more important that the medieval mind cherished the concept, perhaps finding pleasure in self-identification with the idea of men who had thus escaped the meshes of feudal life, even at the forfeit of food, shelter and human society. The "wild man" is not represented as a gregarious being in the traditional tales. So the old woodcuts show Orson as a typical ' wild man," covered with rough hair, barefooted, and carrying a primitive club.

Valentine, however, had never fully accepted the belief of his brother's death, and, having reached manhood, set forth in search of him. He had no idea where to seek, but took the road through the forest at a venture. It was a long and lonely road, and he was not out of it by nightfall: resting there for the night, he was set upon by a large and fierce bear.

Before he could slay or be slain, however, a strange cry rang out from a thicket: and there emerged a Wild Man, who spoke to the bear in a manner which it understood, and pacified it. Of course, the Wild Man was Orson. Slowly the two brothers perceived their mutual likeness: and Orson was carried back to princedom by his twin.

The first unkown teller of this fable, which varies somewhat from version to version, probably had no consciousness that he was creating an allegory, nor would many of his medieval readers have consciously perceived this: yet it is undoubtedly the allegorical quality which accounts for the mystically-attuned mind's deep relish for it. Orson represents for us the human psyche plunged into the harsh and challenging conditions of material life. He lives as the beasts his neighbours live: save that he wields a club, little distinguishes him from them. Yet, did he but know it, he is a Prince, and the son of an Emperor. In the forest he grows to maturity, that is, his Ruach-consciousness develops. His twin brother, in other words his Holy "Genius" or "Guardian Angel," comes to him in due time: the name Valentine is generally taken to mean Strong One, or Hero, with a connotation also of good health: the "Whole" One. The incident with the bear is interesting. It gives Orson the requisite opportunity to transcend his environment: spontaneously he comes to meet his twin, he exercises authority over the bear and is obeyed. To have by experience learned the language of the forest is but an additional advantage to him. His Ruach is able to control and to direct the animal nature in accordance with a higher motivation: by this means he earns recognition of his own high sonship, and is taken by his Hero-brother back to their true home.

Essentially, it is the work of the Ruach, and the crucial choice made by the Ruach, which makes this ultimate reintegration possible. That often-maligned faculty, the ego-consciousness, precisely because it is the central and conscious mind of the psyche, has to perform the double task, both of exercising a firm but benign authority over the Nephesh, and of becoming itself receptive to the Intuitive Mind. Thus in the work of the Ruach are the higher and lower levels each given expression in consciousness.

Although in one view of the matter the meeting of the Ruach-consciousness with the Intuitive Mind is rightly and necessarily presented as a single act taking place in a given moment of time, yet it is also true to say in this case as in many others, an effect which appears as sudden will in reality have been a considerable time preparing. All the faculties concerned have been present from the beginning, and the requisite harmony between them has been assured step by step. Without a certain degree of this harmony the aspirant would not have been a sane human being, without a higher degree of it he could not have been able to perform the magical work thus far: while the practice of the work itself must have carried the development to an even further degree of harmony. Perseverance and meditation are essential: but especially that particular form of "meditation" known as Experience in the Work, which may take many years to build up in the psyche, and which confers as nothing else can the harmonious interaction of the parts thereof with each other and with the body. Two factors must here be mentioned, which help to insure against those insurgences of the Nephesh which can imperil a design of this kind: one is the search for the True Will, the other is the high degree of flexibility and initiative encouraged by the A∴S∴ in the working of the personal magical programme.

On the use of this latitude, no advice can be given except to develop as much self-knowledge and honesty with oneself as possible: also to maintain a certain willingness for new experiences. Self-knowledge is not at all the same thing as destructive self-criticism, and a confident spontaneity is of such great value that it is generally worth making a few mistakes, even painful mistakes, to achieve it. If the Ruach is to fulfil its task as guardian of the psyche, it must know the particular psyche of which it is guardian. Life sets everyone a series of problems, and the "right" solution for one would not necessarily be right for another: all these things have a bearing upon the manner in which the True Will is to be followed out. Above all, worry about the past is one of the most sterile and therefore one of the most poisonous causes of psychic distress ever discovered. The magician should remember that no matter at what point he finds himself on the circumference of a metaphoric circle, nor by what causes he came to be at that point, there is always a possible radius from that point directly to the centre.

Where major errors have been made—errors, that is to say, as regards the progress of the person concerned, but not always from his conscious viewpoint—experience shows that the unconscious levels of the psyche will often stop at nothing to rectify these. The cutting short of an incarnation is one of their methods where no other solution presents itself: we are not here referring to suicide, which does not admit of generalisations, but death from "accidental causes" or from disease. Of course in such cases it is not humanly possible to say that if the problem had been absent, the disease or accident would not have occurred: we can say only that in certain known cases, where persons have been trapped in a false position from which no normal escape was possible, and where the particular viewpoint made it impossible to render the dilemma irrelevant, a previously unsuspected disease has been seen to develop with surprising swiftness, and to prove fatal despite good initial hopes of recovery. Since these disasters were apparently the result of hopelessness of reaching something seen as the true life-goal, which in almost all cases had been rendered unattainable by the subject's own hesitancy or "wrong" previous choice, the undesirability of making decisions entirely by impulse is evident: in such cases, where death supervenes, one can only conclude that a wiser choice must be made by the subject in a future incarnation, but obviously it is generally preferable that the Ruach should be able to prevent this hazard. For the charioteer to throw the reins upon the necks of the horses is to bring all to disaster.

Magick is a wonderful aid in maintaining the ever-changing balance of the psyche. Meditation, study, devotion to the Gods, development of the psyche, the making of a magical instrument or of some requisite for the Chamber of Art, the devising or the spontaneous deed of a ritual to declare one's purpose or one's need, one's exultation or the sheer joy of life, of the day, the night, the season, one's paean to the Snake or to the Goat: all these things deepen and enrich that inner life which brings true self-awareness. The psyche will find its own time and will take its own route to the goal: but the more intimately united within itself it is, the less danger of false choices or erroneous judgments on major issues. The less danger also, of making major issues out of minor ones. For the magician, so far from fleeing from life and from reality, as some critics are fond of suggesting, has in truth mingled his own life with the life and reality of all worlds, has seen the kinship of his own being with the immensities of the stars and with the blind stirrings of amoebae, has held strange communings with Dryad and Naiad, has raised his soul to the Divinity of his worship and has made his individuality an inwoven part of ritual dance or mime. Unchanged in nature is his human heart: but how expanded in understanding and how liberated from former habits of mind! He takes his present-day self seriously indeed, but not tragically: for perhaps he recalls how tragic was the love of one captured as a slave by the Moors, or how ardent was the faith of one who lived as a monk on an island now lost beneath the waters of the Seine. Rose-leaves and leaves of Bay: these things are faded and vanished, with a thousand more which for a time filled his heaven but now are gone: the storm the oak has riven, yet here he himself still is, whole in being and alert in consciousness: but this he knows, whatever else there be, and through whatever chequered worlds he range—he shall go forward until that long day's ending when, his cycle of evolution completed, he shall return with bliss into his Source. With such knowledge, not merely intellectually accepted but realised as true by the whole psyche, asceticism is not needed to loosen the hold of outer things: the material world can no longer dominate, although wholly or in detail it can be loved.

There is no loss of personality in this. Now, when selfhood seems like a garment most casually worn, it has reached a new and potent reality. No longer is there a striving for self-expression, or a careful maintaining of the equilibrium of the faculties: there is but a natural flowing-forth of the individuality. It is of this mystical state that Ficino writes, At first be careful to be careful, then be careful to be careless: at last be careless even about that. He refers in these words only to the attitude concerning oneself, not to the attitude to externals. In inner matters, the Ruach is centred entirely upon that which is beyond itself. The psyche is ready for its Visitant.

We have mentioned the recollection of past lives, which frequently takes place to a certain extent in this period of preparation, but there are also many persons for whom no very detailed awareness of such memories is possible until after the Descent of the Holy Guardian Angel. No adamantine rules can be made about the sequence of such phenomena, which varies from one individual to another in accordance with many different circumstances. It is however certain that after the Descent, and consequent upon it, a great expansion of consciousness will be experienced in numerous ways. It is not merely an enlightenment as to past, present or future events which is in question here, but far more significantly it is a direct apprehension of the underlying causes of these things: a clarifying of that intricate linking together of acts and motives which governs both that which the Adept is, and that which he is to become. For the Descent is by no means the end of the evolutionary process: it marks, on the contrary, the beginning of a great acceleration thereof.

In the presence of the Angel and in the magical works performed with his aid there is an ever-renewed sense of wonder. The Adept walks in a world made new, a world which seems a shrine especially framed for that presence: it is characterised by a particular sense of release, of holiday, which has nothing whatever to do with the occupation or otherwise of the outer man. The outer self indeed may be more occupied, and more responsibly occupied, than ever before: this is irrelevant to the state of the psyche, or rather, of those inner regions of the psyche which now irradiate the whole life.

The sense of wonder is inseparable from the experience of the Intuitive Mind. To consider this fact, and the significance of it, is in itself a worthwhile reflection for all. Even short of the Intuitive Mind, there is open to everyone the possibility of contemplating all phenomena encountered in the course of living, with the receptive eye of wonder. Mostly we do not do so, or have not done so from childhood; the receptive or truly objective eye having been progressively withdrawn as the "affective," emotionally-toned and subjective tendency supplants it. The adult, in a state of mind compounded of fear and laziness, thinks most usually with mental "counters" instead of with allusions to reality, and the habit spreads from topic to topic of the mind, until only the hobby (if there is one) is spared as a window upon the universe. In the past decades a number of writers and visual artists have tried to combat this parching and destroying attitude, to restore the perception of reality to life, by the unfamiliar approach or by the use of peculiar techniques: we are still too close to the movement to evaluate it effectively in brief, but it seems there are three things which must be said of it. There has been an overall stimulating effect, a challenge to re-think and to re-evaluate, which has spread like a circular ripple from this movement and which is in itself productive of much good. The movement itself however, as distinct from this gentle outward-spreading wave, has underestimated the human tendency to shrink away from shock, to reject innovation or frequently to be quite honestly unable to assimilate it: much in the movement has thereby failed of its purpose. And thirdly, too few of the participants in the movement, when it comes to the point, have had anything but their own viscera to offer to the multitude.

To give more than that, the Artist must be also the Adept. For the truth still holds, that "every painter paints himself:" and in this manner also every writer writes, or musician composes: and how therefore can he present a universe who has not a universe?

From the Descent of the Holy Guardian Angel forward, then, the Adept "has a universe:" that is, although in one sense his psychological motivations continue to spring from

the individual which he is, yet also there is a door open upon
another motivation which is without the limitations of time
and place. In a very exact sense of the word, he
*comprehends:* but also, because the reflective power of the
ego-consciousness is aware of this comprehension, the
personal criteria of values and of proportion insensibly
change in adjustment to it. Yet it remains evident that this
new comprehension does not destroy the sense of wonder,
but quite the reverse: neither has the Adept, usually, any
inhuman sense of immediate access to the treasury of ideas.
The Ruach does not seize upon, and vaunt itself upon, the
advent of the Intuitive Mind, because from the beginning it
perceives that Mind as a Being altogether distinct from itself:
and also because it glimpses in that Mind a vastness of range
and scope which verifies that sense of difference. The Ruach
has found a "leader" whose authority it can have no wish to
dispute, though the decisions made by the Angel are not
always those which the ego-consciousness would have chosen
unaided. On occasion they may be diametrically opposed to
positions which the Adept has maintained for years, and
momentarily from force of habit he thinks to hold back: but
the realisation comes that the motive for holding to the old
position no longer has relevance: the old sanctions do not
intrinsically command obedience, but neither now is there
any personal need to set them at defiance.

Because of the new comprehension, a distinctive
attitude of mind tends to manifest itself, subject of course to
the individual character of the Adept: a reviewing of
knowledge already familiar, for the sake of the new vistas
opened up therein, and for the delight of knowing in reality
that which had been known only in token previously. It is in
truth as if, in the adult state and with full consciousness and
memory, the Adept had entered into a new incarnation.
Certain and most true it is, that without that great irradiation
of spirit by the Intuitive Mind, none is fully the Adept. Man

in himself—that is, without the knowledge and conversation of the Holy Guardian Angel—is totally incapable of attaining to the direct intuitive comprehension of even the least thing. He may form a philosophic estimate or a scientific estimate of the nature of anything which interests him, but ultimately what he knows is not the thing itself, but the concept of it which he has built up in his own mind; and the discrepancies and false associations involved therein may be numerous. The Adept however, in and through the mind of his Genius, begins to know and perceive things as they are. That is not to say that he knows all things suddenly in this way, nor indeed that he knows all things—his human mind and brain are still finite—but it does supremely mean that that which he knows of any thing in the intuitive mode, is altogether objectively of that thing, and is cleanly free from any "affect" or personal association or prejudice with which he might previously have endowed it. In the accepted terms of psychology, *participation mystique* is at an end, or at least is in a rapid decline: our Adept is still a Minor Adept and the completion of this release still belongs to the Sphere of Tiphareth. When it is complete however, no matter what power he may exercise over external things, they will have none magically over him.* After that, and only after that, he will be free to proceed towards his liberation from inward bonds, just as prior to the treatment of bodily injury it is frequently necessary to safeguard the patient from potential causes of further harm.

The unclouded perception of reality is however a sovereign good in itself. In alchemical terms, we see that here the regeneration of Red Rose—the Ruach—and the redemption of White Rose—the Nephesh—are in this same act

---

* We are asked, What about incense? What about colours, sounds and rhythms of the ritual? Will these no longer "work" for the Adept? Of course they will work *for* him: as he wills. He still has a human body and Nephesh, he still has the built-in lines of association which he has carefully created in years of magical experience. But these things are his instruments, not his masters.

achieved. "This it is which Philosophie dreameth of:" but of which philosophy in itself can only dream without means of attainment: thus far has philosophy accompanied the Adept, but from this point he must proceed with Magick alone. Even the most perceptive of philosophies can only reason "about it and about:" for as Plato has indicated, a faculty not human but divine is needed for the apprehension of truth. This then is that which is signified by the union of thé Roses, the Red and the White mingling in the Golden: whose budding and opening shows forth the unique integration of the personality, the Beauty of Tiphareth.

Adepthood is, from the psychological viewpoint, the vindication of the balanced personality in its entirety. It answers to the whole paradox of man's nature, which must revere and yet be self-sufficing, must be integrated yet must find its expression at many levels. All worlds indeed are comprised in man's nature, but only with the Descent of the Holy Guardian Angel can he begin with true comprehension to explore them. This presence, and this illumination, are the boons sought in the *Hymn to All the Gods*:

> *Hear me, great Lords of Freedom!*
>
> *Grant me by knowledge of the holy writings, by dispersal of the night which encircles me, a high and true perception: that I may truly know the incorruptible God, and the man that I am. . . .*

## CHAPTER III

The unique destiny of each individual. Expansion of awareness desirable, so that the deeper trends of the psyche may become known to the conscious mind.

Interplay of forces at conscious and unconscious levels, resulting in a continual re-balancing of Ruach and Nephesh. The gradual and harmonious nature of this process: living with relation to the higher faculties involves no assumption of false attitudes and no sense of deprivation. Possible sources of inner conflict can be perceived and avoided by the Nephesh without coming into consciousness.

The True Will should be followed with all perseverance, but without repression of any faculty.

The discovery of the Divinity Within. Solitude:— heaven or hell, according as the inner presence has been discerned or not.

The concept of the Abyss.

Importance of the pre-entheist stage of development, when the love-object is seen as quite separate and other, whether human or divine. The great spiritual training imparted by love, whether of one or of many beings.

Inner realization of the harmony of the levels of being. "The Key and the Lock".

Concerning the true and ultimate Beloved.

## CHAPTER III
## LOWER AND HIGHER UNCONSCIOUS
## AND THE TRUE WILL

Every planet has its orbit, and every star its station. To know, and to know with realisation, that his nature extends from the spiritual heights to the spiritual depths, is not sufficient for any human being. This range, whether realised or no, is the range of every human being: yet each one is unique, not only subjectively in his own experience of himself, but objectively. No two, even though they be twins, even though we may posit them to have come by exactly the same ways in the labyrinth of the ages, can have exactly the same destiny, for each one has an individual bias which will cause even identical circumstances to be interpreted differently. Certain broad classifications there are, which enable us to consider these differences in general terms and to discuss them intelligibly, yet those classifications themselves are relative and admit of wide variations in their application. People are more or less introvert, more or less extrovert, more or less spontaneously concerned with intellectual aspects, more or less concerned with emotional aspects. The level of consciousness varies within all types. Some, again, adhere to the traditional, some seek out the new. There are innumerable factors which make each one exactly what he is (or what she is) and nobody can say that any one of these factors "ought" to be different, or that one temperament is intrinsically better than another. The healthy extrovert can be singularly insensitive: the innately religious can be

singularly lazy. It may be required that one should adapt
oneself somewhat—and adaptability is another very variable
quality—or it may be more appropriate to find scope for
one's particular idiosyncracies. Diabetics are frequently good
organisers: while firms which process quantities of
colour-films, necessarily in total darkness, employ large
numbers of blind people who go about their work in
complete confidence where a sighted person would be lost
and bewildered. The catalogue would be unending of the
varieties of human experience and capability even on the
ordinary level: in terms of the higher or more inward
faculties when these are awakened, it is no longer a question
only of a different assortment of varying characteristics, but
of a unique fire and brilliance.

To live with reference to the higher faculties, as we have
seen, is a mode of existence which begins with awareness of
the Neshamah. It is beyond the conscious control of man to
dictate in what manner the Neshamah shall manifest to him.
Magical or mystical initiation can hasten the time of that
event, although the content and richness of the experience
will still largely depend upon the inner preparedness of the
initiate himself. In a magical Order, the previous training of
the adept will have been directed to ensuring that this inner
preparedness for the new development is as complete as
possible. This is not to suggest that the relationship of Ruach
and Nephesh will never at any later time undergo further
adjustment: in truth, readjustments are made continually
throughout life, and each day's happenings and each night's
dreams bring into action new aspects of the one function or
the other. Within the Nephesh itself, in the shadows remote
from ordinary knowledge, an endless interchange of material
goes on between the personal and the impersonal, as also an
interplay between the psychic and the physical. The criterion
is not a cessation of these activities but an absence of any
implication of major crisis therein: the general maturity and

adaptability of the psyche are the best guarantees of this security. It is not a question of the objective magnitude of any matter which comes up for revision: there can be no objective standard in such matters, for it is precisely the inner attitude of the person concerned which allocates relative importance here. To give an example: a member of the A.S. who was by profession a legal psychiatrist had, with the expansion of his scholarship and interests, come to a personal realisation that he could no longer with either sincerity or peace of mind consider himself as contained within the framework of the religion in which he had been born and reared: he came of a strict Jewish family. Accordingly he broke away, apparently without regret, from that faith itself and from all the customs associated therewith: and for several years no signs of difficulty presented themselves. Then, from no immediately conscious motive, or at least from none which seemed to him to be of any intrinsically great intellectual or emotional force, he felt impelled to become a vegetarian. There was absolutely no reason why he should not take to vegetarianism if he wanted to do so, but his doubly trained mind found something at once worth enquiry in the seeming absence of adequate motivation. Only a brief examination was needed to bring to light an escape proposed by the Nephesh from an unconscious dilemma. The desire of liberation from a restriction which had become pointless, had prompted a deliberate breakaway from all Jewish customs, so that pork must be to him as any other meat: but a veto imposed by training and example still gave him an aversion to eating pork. If, however, he yielded to this aversion in its original form, he would feel that he was betraying his True Will: so the Nephesh now presented the aversion under a new guise, proposing that he should give up eating every kind of meat, pork thus no longer having to be considered as a special category. (This is in agreement with what has been observed with regard to many people who have broken away from one religion or another which imposes dietary restrictions: quite often an adherence to the dietary restriction is the most difficult bond to sever, because of its imposition in such cases as a conditioning upon the instinctual level, inaccessible therefore to intellectual argument.) Having perceived this stratagem, by which the Nephesh had presented him with the solution of a conflict before he had been aware of the existence of the conflict itself, he laughed delightedly at the whole matter: after all, as he said, it was his spiritual capacity, not his gastric capacity, which he aspired to enlarge. This minor incident, however, could easily have been seen as a major crisis, and thus could have been made into one, by a less mature or less balanced personality. By a humourless insistence upon the will to freedom, a real repression could have been forced upon the Nephesh, culminating as a neurosis which might have manifested as (for instance) a gastric affliction.

The establishment of the entheist conviction, the realisation of the inmost light of divinity illumining the psyche, is a development of prime importance in the progress of the magician: but if it is to be of any worth whatsoever to him, if indeed it is not to do harm, it must be entirely sincere. The day of that revelation is better somewhat delayed than in any manner falsified. To search for the God Within before that deity is ready to be found, is to unsettle one's external focus and to find nothing within which is worthy of worship. It is also to incur the possible horror to which some temperaments are liable, of finding within an unintelligible and inhuman Chaos of gibbering and amorphous solitude, of turbulent and life-swallowing obscurity: the Abyss. The peril and horror into which one inward glance can cast the psyche in some individuals, may seem incredible to the student until he recalls the extent to which many people are appalled at the prospect of being thrown upon their inner resources, the stark fear of solitude which is common even to many adults, the strict limitations which are placed by law upon solitary confinement even as a penalty. With the paradox of unreason, people have killed themselves from no other cause than solitude, from the fact that by lack of some outward thing to hold their attention they have been virtually compelled to look within. To such people, "within" is Hell. Totally unevolved man is not affected by this danger, for he cannot discern even the existence of the Abyss: man evolved to, or approaching, the level of the Minor Adept, either knowingly or by unperceived inner development, has overcome this dread. For these reasons, a traditional saying has it that he who can abide in solitude is either a wild beast or a god. This saying must have puzzled many "natural solitaries" who have not seen themselves as belonging to either category: but one who is progressing by spiritual evolution independently of magical initiation, may well find that the period corresponding to the experience of the Vault necessitates months, years, or a lifetime spent as a solitary before the personality can emerge with its new values equiposed and its new orientation established.

The Abyss is a reality in the awareness of Western man, at least in his evolved awareness. Recognition is found elsewhere of the peculiar qualities of solitude, or of the psychic disintegration which may come about upon release from the control of the conscious mind: the essentials of the matter can be traced in many regions of the world. It is an instance of an inner reality which has been given name and formulation from the existence of symbols in the outer world to which it can be related: an example of one of the very facts which we have been considering, that human consciousness in itself can work only by abstraction, only by relating the unknown to the known in some manner. We may then have the curiosity to ask, what has been the especial distinguishing feature in the outer life of Western man during the development of his culture, to awaken a collective awareness of this awesome frontier in the psyche, this perilous chasm sundering the human mode of being from the divine?

Human language is notoriously deficient in words referring primarily to spiritual realities. These realities therefore are represented generally by figures of speech, which usually supply the only possible mode of communicating anything about the matter intended, and which therefore gain such wide acceptance that their metaphorical or allegorical nature is forgotten. We may validly infer that it was only by contemplation of the phenomena of the outer world that man became aware that something in his inner experience could be imaged thereby, and thus given a name and an identity. The mystical marriage, the caverns of the Unconscious, are examples of this usage.

This is true also of the Abyss. To consider this we must glance briefly at the Middle Eastern regions and the concepts which evolved there before ever the Qabalistic system was defined. The Qabalah has formulated and brought together all these concepts into an exact pattern of relationships: in the earlier structures we shall inevitably find, from the Qabalistic viewpoint, an overlapping of aspects of being.*

The word Abyss itself tells us much. Sumerian myth gives us *Abzu,* the Water-Deep. To many whose religious experience was interwoven with that myth, the Water-Deep would have been represented by the Persian Gulf: not a very abysmal expanse of water, nothing in depth compared to the Caspian for instance, but an intelligible source of fear to the surrounding peoples when one contemplates their low-lying territories and recalls the succession of flood-stories in the early traditions. That might have sufficed in itself to fix the

* Third Hall Initiates of the Aurum Solis are referred to the study, *Qabalistic origins in Sumeria.*

idea of the dread water-region in the Western mind: it is known from innumerable modern clinical examples how regularly water, whether oceanic or other, presents itself as an image of the unconscious. The pathological hand-washing of the guilty, so accurately portrayed in "Macbeth," is for instance an attempted relegation of a remembered fact to unconsciousness; but here in the Water-Deep we have something whose action, not controlled or desired, could and sometimes did obliterate man's works and man himself inexorably. The concept and its implications change from one culture to another. In Egypt upon the Nile we find *Abtu* (Abydos), the centre of the Osirian cult, associated it is true with inundations of fertile and beneficent aspect, but also the scene of the mythological death—in one version the drowning—of the deity, and his subsequent restoration: a drama whose mystical application in course of time completely replaced its agricultural connotations. The Hebrew concept of "tehom," the Water-Deep as primal chaos, mingled with and reinforced the other concept of the Water-Deep as overwhelming flood. In Greek and in Latin, the name of Abzu was perpetuated—*Abyssos, Abyssus, Abysmus*—since the folk-speech of everyday had no alternative word for it.

Of the great archetypal images whose existence is recognised by Jungian psychology, it is quite evident to anyone familiar with their character that these are to some extent represented by normal elements of human experience, as well as manifesting modalities in the Collective Unconscious and, as we should say, the Divine Mind also. In fact, so apparent are their earthly counterparts that some psychological writers of Freudian persuasion, on account of their own materialist outlook have attempted to discount Jung's findings as to the Collective Unconscious, and to state that there is no indication except that a personal and particular concept of, for example, the Mother in both loving and stern aspects, exists in each individual human mind. Now the generality of human experience, not excluding clinical experience, indicates quite frequently that the archetypal reality does exist beyond the earthly reality, and that people do sometimes have dreams or associated ideas in which a figure apparently representing an earthly parent or partner takes on connotations or performs actions which belong not at all to the known person, but to an Archetype. Nevertheless, the fact that those writers can put forward such an argument, does underline the circumstance that every Archetype of which we have cognisance, has a counterpart in outward and earthly life. It could not be otherwise. Until the Intuitive Mind is contacted, the human mind can work only by abstraction, recognising the unknown by some analogy with the known.

That being so, it is surely extremely rash of certain other writers to attempt to deal in an altogether negative and hidebound manner with the question of discarnate spiritual beings: one sees it quite often put forward by such writers that no possible reality can be ascribed to discarnate beings save as the projection of autonomous complexes from the unconscious of the seers. Of course people can and do have autonomous complexes, they can and do sometimes have illusions resulting therefrom: but such illusions prove nothing. They can, if anything, be taken to suggest at least the tradition of something existing for the psyche to mimic, and one might cogently ask how the tradition first arose: this likewise proves nothing, but it is a more positive and philosophic attitude than the other. Nobody can validly base a disbelief in the objective existence of spiritual entities, upon the fact that a certain known neurotic imagines that they tap him on the shoulder: nor upon the fact that he (the sceptic) has never had any comparable experience.

As regards practical attitudes, in fairness to the

psychiatrist we must allow that these can be a different matter from the purely philosophic approach. Numbers of people every year see or hear something, for at least once in their lifetime, which the conventional norm of civilised belief would reject, but they do not generally take their experience to a psychiatrist. The person who does so, is seeking help either on that score or on some other: it is thus reasonable to begin from an assumption that any deviation from the conventional norm which that person manifests, *may be* a symptom of his trouble. There is also the undeniable fact, that a person with untrained psychic perception will tend to be aware only of influences or presences belonging to one spiritual level: these will thus inevitably show a general character which is typical of the seer. Finally, there is also the distinct possibility with the untrained, that objective spiritual realities of one kind or another may have been perceived, but subjective psychic contents will mingle therewith: this may mean that the subjective contents supervene because a situation has been created in which they can gain a hearing, or again it may mean something very much more grave: when through repression a complex has developed into an autonomous "splinter personality," it is occasionally observable that an alien entity takes possession of the "splinter," informing it with an energy which it did not have of itself. The psychiatrist may in such cases diagnose correctly the cause of the first development of the complex: in cases which have produced mere poltergeist phenomena, treatment of the neurosis is likely to be successful, but in other cases this cannot be done because actual insanity develops, or sometimes death occurs from obscure forms of blood-poisoning. From the occult viewpoint, the diagnosis with regard to the original autonomous complex is acceptable, while the poltergeist activities, where these develop, frequently indicate an unconscious alliance with elemental forces: but the more serious consequences above indicated would result from invasion of the "splinter" by a force of Qliphothic or even of human origin.

It should be pointed out that while in his earlier writings Carl Jung maintained the conventional psychiatric attitude that all experiences of seeming discarnate presences are to be assumed to be manifestations of autonomous complexes, the experience of a lifetime led him away from that opinion. While never making any incautious assumptions, he added notes, as may be perceived for instance in his "Structure and Dynamics of the Psyche," to indicate that a purely psychological explanation of such experiences would not always be adequate.

The position of the magician in this matter is entirely different. He is not a psychiatrist working from the outside of the question and trying to find the causes of another person's unsought experience. The magician is concerned with his own experiences and, unlike the psychiatrist's patient, he knows exactly why he has them. The magician is not at the mercy of chance visitations: he selects, he invokes, he dismisses. As long as these three functions hold good, he has no cause to suspect any kinship between the spiritual beings known to him, and the illusory manifestations experienced by the psychically unstable.

This is one of the reasons, apart from the other obviously good ones, why the student is frequently reminded to observe balance in his various magical operations, so that a reality of choice may be established. It must be borne in mind that to choose consistently even that which is uncongenial to the conscious bias of the personality, may be no safeguard against illusion in the results since a repressed unconscious attitude may be diametrically opposed to the conscious one. The best guarantee both of objectivity and of balanced development in training is to follow out a programme which has been pre-arranged to avoid one-sidedness. It is a good thing to look back over the magical record occasionally to see that the effects of the work have always corresponded to the intentions in this matter.

This avoidance of bias in no way precludes the search for the True Will. The True Will relates to a high level, and to have broadened one's functioning potential in magick must be advantageous, whatever the True Will may ultimately direct as the Work. The True Will must be sought from the beginning of magical training: the Holy Guardian Angel will in due course ratify (or otherwise) one's identification of the True Will, but to postpone the effort to find it until the Angel comes would show an unsuitable degree either of presumption or of diffidence. The natural faculties must be used and reinforced meanwhile.

At this point an important distinction must be made, which will indicate the whole difference between what we call the "higher" and the "lower" unconscious. Of the fundamentally unsatisfactory connotations of "higher" and "lower" we have treated elsewhere, but those terms remain in some ways the most convenient for connecting with other people's modes of thought. As to the undesirability of autonomous complexes in the lower unconscious, psychosophy is completely in agreement with the findings of psychology: such undiscovered contents can do untold harm in ordinary life, and although magical practice is in fact therapeutic, its initial activation of them might in some cases lead to results suited only to a far more primitive type of society. The best that we can say, therefore, for complexes in the lower unconscious, is that mild examples can be tolerated. With regard to the higher unconscious however, it will be perceived that a small group of frankly autonomous elements is here more than tolerated, is alluded to with something like veneration. This distinction is of the first importance, and indicates the reason why the higher unconscious itself must be carefully distinguished from the lower.

It is no part of the task, whether of therapy or of

training, to psychologise a person away from the ideals which inspire him. From childhood onward, we see that the individual who is too soon self-reliant will only reach a certain level of development and of proficiency, and will there rest, considerably below the level of his true potential. In magical training this is especially true, because magical training should represent so great an increase in the attainable potential. Spiritual narcissism (not to mention the ordinary narcissism which is sometimes seen in would-be occultists) is no basis for true magick. Therefore it is not for those who guide the aspirant in his development, to forestall that projection of the Neshamah upon the outer world, which causes us to seem to find our higher self in something external, whether man or woman or the cult of a God: or in all three for some. In this exchange with the outer reality, we link the inner unconscious reality to our conscious mind. Through love for that which is projected, with love for that which receives the projection, we learn it gradually, we rehearse it over and over to ourselves, assimilating it to our consciousness until the likeness of the love-object to the inner faculty appears to be exhausted, when the projection is withdrawn to await an opportunity of completing the process. Thus may we worship at several different shrines, whether divine or human, until the compass-needle of the personality finds its true setting. When sufficient of the content of the Higher Unconscious has been brought into consciousness in this way, projection will cease: that is to say, although one may still *love* external beings or an external cult, one is no longer compulsively bound to them: one is no longer *in love* with them. The final state of being "in love," that proper to the Minor Adept, is reserved for that which the conscious mind can never assimilate, to that which is not a matter of projection upon any external being or cult: that which is perceptible to the psyche as a completely autonomous spiritual entity, not in any sense "belonging" to the ego: the Holy Guardian Angel, the Intuitive Mind.

The process of assimilation to consciousness necessarily relates only to that which can first be projected by the unconscious, that is to say the consciousness assimilates through projection only that which is strictly of the psyche itself. Therefore, to have experienced the Anima is not to have known the experience of the Sephirah Binah, and to have experienced the Animus is not to have known the experience of Chokmah. Nevertheless, the high dignity of this development is not to be underestimated. By whatever means have been most suited to the total individuality of the Adept, all obstructions and obscurities in the lower and in the higher regions of the psyche have been brought into equilibrium or have been related to consciousness. A modicum of shadow, certainly, remains: the roots need darkness in which to draw nutriment, while the branches have their natural foliage: but here in the plenitude of the Tipharic realisation, with the coming of the Angel, we have the clear crystal tree of Eridu, from the inmost of whose trunk there shines forth like flame the presence of Tammuz, the Treasure in the midst of the Pillar. And the crystal root descends to the deep: and its branches veiled in leafage reach up to the stars.*

This, one may say, is the description of a truly beautiful and mystical state of being: but why, or how, is it Adepthood?

An individuality thus balanced and poised, if conceived of in the abstract, seems indeed to be without tension, without volition save to its inmost Summit: but considered as an actuality, this is by no means the whole story. It would certainly be possible for one without magical aspiration to proceed entirely in mysticism from this point, extended and

---

* The Magical Powers (so-called) of Tiphareth are named as two, and these correspond to the coming forth of the Adept and the subsequent Attainment of the Knowledge and Conversation. In the Pagan Qabalistic tradition the powers are *The Adept's Step,* otherwise called *The Mysteries of the Bronze Cross,* and *The Vision of the Life within the Tree.* Patefacta patefacienda.

aware, so to put it, in all directions equally: like the figure of the *Stella Regenerationis* itself. However, here the Magical Memory comes into play. Now that all the barriers of the personal unconscious are down, at least to the extent that that which is within can be listened to freely by introspection with no prejudice, the vast impulses which have brought the Adept into incarnation begin to make themselves understood. This is a matter for slow unfolding: for not only are the caverns of Memory fathomless indeed, but also the Holy Guardian Angel will direct the Adept's wanderings therein as may be best suited to his ultimate purpose, and this purpose is not immediately declared. The Angel's rulings may seem arbitrary, but there is no gainsaying them and gradually the point towards which the pattern is being drawn together will become clear. It makes little difference whether life has gone according to the Adept's conscious wishes or not: whether his decisions have hitherto rested in his own hands or have been directed largely by the will of others. So surely can each circumstance be employed to bring into perspective a true portrait of the Adept which must be acknowledged as just, that it will seem as if every accident, every mischance must have been planned towards this purpose. Perhaps it was so: the Angel's hand has guided him for longer than was guessed! To say this would make the Angel responsible for some strange happenings, and the Adept is not at once told. Nevertheless, there is the pattern, not fully clear (as it shall not be for longer yet) but sufficiently so for the Adept to apprehend the precise taste of the personality of *who* looked into the Mirror.

Paradoxical though it may seem, therefore, it is not left to his conscious mind alone to decide the precise nature of his True Will. In passing through the death and rebirth of the Tiphanic initiation, he now sees, he has gained a greater selfhood, but a self whose exact nature he could not truly know until informed of it by the Intuitive Mind. This is in a way the strangest paradox of all. Man's inability in his ordinary ego-consciousness to apprehend directly the nature of any external thing, is a philosophic commonplace: he now realises that whatever he may previously have thought or felt concerning himself, he could not before the Descent of the Angel fully apprehend even his own nature. The Ruach unaided has the power of self-regarding and of self-reflection, but not of self-intuition. Now therefore he sees for the first time that the way by which he has come was as individual as the coffin of Osiris, made precisely to his measure and to no other's: and the gate of his aspiration, the way of his True Will, is likewise narrow and unique. Freedom, however, he has, as great as any man ever had: since for what has man through the ages striven and laboured, prayed and dealt violence, plotted and pillaged and wept and scourged himself, but for this one shining prize, the freedom to be what he essentially is?

So far has our Adept come upon the Way of Return, however, that he perceives another thing. Mere being does not suffice. A clod of earth is what it is: a snowflake is what it is, while it is. For that which is divine within his nature, and which is progressively infusing his nature, Being must be Doing. To a God, to be is to do; and that which by nature he is, his deeds, or rather the continuous deed which is his life, must express.

Thus it is that the Adept has become the Philosophers' Stone, *Lapis Philosophorum,* which is also *Filius Philosophorum,* the Grand Hermetic Androgyne: that which transmutes whatever can fitly receive it, even inert Saturnian lead, to the sun-gold of Tiphareth. But more than this, the manner in which he fulfils his transmutations, all that he does in the world, will be himself expressed: not by deliberate act or contrivance to imitate himself, (which would be vain and worthless) but because he does nothing but what is rightly his to do: and does continually.

Conformably with this, a new aspect of the Magical Link presents itself. It is not now a question, as for example in the consecration of a Magical Weapon, of creating a channel simply within the activated Astral Light and calling down the appropriate Divine Force, linking oneself with the operation by performing it and by certain acts therein. The Adept who carries out any comparable operations, on whatever level, is himself the channel by which the Divine Force descends and is directed to the purpose of the operation. This is in itself an incomparably more potent procedure, besides being immediately and implicitly linked with the Adept's Will and Work. Nor is there need for him to identify himself explicitly with an appropriate facet of his individuality, for all that he does is linked to his individuality as a whole, each modality and element therein being brought into action as required. At the same time, it is understood that the operation is in furtherance of his True Will, or as an Adept he would not be performing it.

It is in Adepthood and in the progress thereof that the principle comes to be plainly exemplified, that the external Universe and the human psyche, Macrocosm and Microcosm, stand in relation to one another as the lock and the key. The nearer to its complete perfection the psyche is brought, the more perfectly it images in miniature the Spiritual Universe as a whole: and the more perfectly the Adept perceives the interrelation of that Universe and his True Will. The modalities of the two Sephiroth Geburah and Chesed are in due time brought successively within the domain of the Ruach when this has been illumined by the Intuitive Mind. It is to be remarked how without this illumination, many thinkers have been at a loss to explain how the functions of these two Sephiroth do not annul one another; the manifestation of the Will, and the further intuitive perception of its place in the universal plan, provide a clue to the complementary nature of these Spheres.

Of the Sephiroth beyond the Abyss and their correspondence to the inmost region of the psyche, something has been said earlier in this volume. The Yechidah does not belong to the psyche, but the psyche to it, and it to the Divine Mind. The confusion presented by the mixture of terminology, "highest" and "inmost," is in itself so significant, and perhaps so inseparable from any account of these matters, as to merit further comment. As the passage from one state to another on the Way of Return is experienced, numerous personal accounts both magical and mystical in context make it clear that this progress may indifferently be described as "upward," "inward," or as both together. In reflection and meditation upon the psyche, "inward" proves to be by far the more meaningful expression, of more value both to the student and to the devotee of the Divinity Within. On the other hand, if one is explaining matters with the aid of a diagram of the Tree of Life, or if one has (as most students have, and should have) a diagram of the Tree upon the wall, then "upward" is the obvious term to use when bringing into consideration the relationship of the parts of the psyche to the Sephiroth. But man is the microcosm, the "small universe," and within his being are the tides and rhythms of the cosmos, the ego-consciousness not stationary but continually moving, now peripherally, now considerably "further in." It is very desirable, up to a point, to indicate the relationship of the psyche to the Tree, and the reality of the agreement is also significant as vindicating the viewpoint of psychosophy. Nevertheless, one should grow beyond that point. It is not at all desirable to go on picturing the parts of the psyche as corresponding to a series of discs on a diagram.

The great central Light which blazes with undying radiance, the sounds and splendours, images of things beautiful and hideous, things present and things remembered,

human countenances, signs, formulae, the dim region of
dreams partly remembered or never consciously known,
sense-perception of touch and odour and taste, the impulses
of nerve and cell, the walls of material flesh and bone. This
too is in its way a mere stylised presentation, but if it helps
to break the spell of the diagrammatic representation it serves
a good and refreshing purpose. Roman and medieval thought
divided mankind into planetary types: one person would be
described as martial, another as jovial, or saturnine, and so
on. There is more truth in saying that all the types are
present in each human being, one or another preponderating
not only with individual temperament but also to some
extent according to mood and circumstances. We each of us
know more intimately than any words or images can present
them, the very feel and savour of these modalities. All this
and far more is comprised in Microcosmos, and each level of
this entity corresponds to its own level in the outer universe
of existence: this is the Key to the Lock.

The correspondence of Key and Lock is inherent, and in
the spiritual development of man is assuredly to be realised
soon or late: nevertheless, relegated to the natural course of
things, this discovery can lack personal implication, can lack
potency even as a meandering stream lacks potency, while
the direct course of the torrent in a definitive channel can
generate vast force. Here Art Magick has its work to perform,
in shortening the way, in defining and deepening the channel
of purpose.

Robe and ring, the Chamber of Art and its equipment,
altar-cloths, lamps, incenses, the magical voice, the pattern of
the rite, music and battery and rhythm of movement, all
these things have their sense-impressions as well as their astral
effect, and can speak without words to nerve and brain. In
this, the mind of the Adept is the key, his body itself may be
considered as part of the lock: for by these indirect means he
must approach its autonomic system. From the most spiritual

to the most material levels of being, then, both the lock and the key extend: and the Adept has at every point the means of opening the lock if and when it be his True Will to do so.

His True Will is an essence which we might describe as having been distilled from all his components: and rather after the manner of a chemical compound, its "properties" (comparable to colour, form or odour) can come as a total surprise to the man which it represents. He may well find it distrubing, but he will accept it. It shall be the most potent of talismans, for in following it he follows his destiny.

Thus the Adept has found that which is his own, and knows his true path. Being and doing have converged, to a degree fairly close to that limit which is possible in incarnate life: for in terms of bodily fatigue and inertia they can never on earth converge completely. Nevertheless, he is as free as man on earth can be, inasmuch as he is conscious of doing that for which he was born. There remains no inner discord or tension, therefore, which could prevent him from looking directly into the centre of his own being. It is complete joy and peace: and to be able to realise this, is to know one's own divinity. FACITO VOLUNTATEM TUAM.

## POSTSCRIPT

Magick must answer to the spiritual needs of man's evolution. Historically, one can, broadly speaking, divide the development of religion into certain phases.* The spiritual evolution of mankind is a process of gradual self-discovery, while different times, circumstances and modes of life have necessarily changed the emphasis. All these factors are mutable, though the overall effect is of a cumulative exploration and maturing self-knowledge.

In the study of the psyche, on the other hand, we find that every development which is possible to the psyche is there in potential from the beginning. Psychosophy is concerned with the structures and phenomena of inner development, that is to say, it is concerned with the Way of Return which is inherent in the psyche, and which has been shadowed forth in various aspects of mythology from Sumeria to Cochise County. At the present stage of history, occultism has achieved a fairly comprehensive vision of this development.

High Magick, we say, is the sacrificial path of the Sacred King, the cult of individuality. In proclaiming this we do not lose sight of the cult of the Great Mother. From the beginnings of the known spiritual evolution of mankind, we find that the Great Mother was worshipped: alone in the earliest times, but also at a very early period, with her Son-Spouse. The sacrificial cults arose from the Mother-Son mythos, developing from the agricultural rites, when the Son was accorded increasing prominence, to the full concept of sacral kingship. The immense significance of the Mother-Son mythos in relation to the study of psychosophy will be obvious to all who have read the present book.

---

* *Myth and Ritual in the Ancient Near East* by E.O. James is a very fine introduction to this exceedingly complex subject.

Neither, for that matter, do we lose sight of the latest trend, the cult of the Child. He who comes forth from the tomb is the Child of Tiphareth: he comes beneath the law of the Mother, and he must grow to maturity: pre-Hellenic are the myths which surround him. This, the Hyperhelion of the Mysteries, we do not take as our ensign. We have written somewhat concerning this Child from the viewpoint of the twentieth century development of the Mysteries, others having considered this Child outside the traditional context.

Tiphareth is the heart of all Worlds: the manifest implications of the Solar Sphere are the fulcrum of the Western Mysteries and the ensign of our purpose. Rest where we may, sun after sun will set.

Concerning this viewpoint of the traditional Mysteries, which shows an eternal and ever-changing Now mediating between past and future, the great declaration of the West is inscribed as a palindrome in the floor of the octagonal XIII century Baptistery at Firenze for all who shall understand:—

*EN GIRO TORTE SOL CICLOS ET ROTOR IGNE*

# Appendices

## APPENDIX A
## THE LAMENT OF ATTIS

Sped over deeps of the sea in his boat's rapid gliding,
   Attis, his hurrying feet across Phrygia guiding,
   Entered the forested shades of the Goddess' abiding.
   There in such frenzy his spirit bewildered was driven,
   He from his members with flint-edge their burden has riven.

Afterwards, feeling that naught of his manhood remained,
   He, with whose bloodshed but lately the ground had been stained,
   She the light timbrel uplifted in fingers of snow—
   Timbrel and token, thy Mysteries, Mother, to show—
   Delicate fingers the echoing oxhide to shake:
   Tremulous voice, that a song for her fellows would make:
   "Seek we together, O Gallae, the woodland's deep hollow!
   Wandering kine of the Lady of Dindymus, follow!
   Come, ye self-exiled who sought for an alien home:
   Followers mine, will you follow me yet as I roam?
   Ocean's quick fury enduring with fortitude's merit,
   Daring your love-hating bodies from man to disherit—
   Forth let us speed for our Mistress, to gladden her spirit!
   Idleness leaving, at once and as one let us move
   Seeking the Phrygian shrine of the Goddess, the grove
   There, where the cymbals give voice and the timbrels reply,
   Where the curved flutes of the Phrygian sobbingly cry,
   Ivy-crowned Maenads their tresses tempestuous flinging,
   Shrilling their call as the sacred devices are swinging,
   Whither the vagabond cohorts of Cybele wander—
   Lead we the speed of our dancing, our offering yonder!"

Even as Attis, mock-woman, thus sang to the crowd,
  Sudden from quivering tongues rang the dance-cry aloud:
  Rang the light timbrel, and hollow the cymbals were clashed,
  Forth to green Ida the swift-footed company dashed.
  Attis, too wrought to the frenzy, all breathless was faring
  Through the dark forest the foremost, the timbrel yet bearing,
  Wild as a heifer unbroken the yoke to elude:
  Swiftly the haste of their leader the Gallae pursued.
  So it befell, at the house of the Goddess arriving,
  Foodless they sank to their slumber, all spent with their striving:
  Laden with weariness, sleep on their eyelids was pressed,
  Respite from raging releasing their spirits to rest.

Only when Sol with the gold of his countenance flaming
  Lit the pale heavens, the rockland, the seas beyond taming,
  Hunted the shadows with creatures of hoofbeat proclaiming,
  Sleep from awakening Attis was swiftly departed:
  Took him the Goddess Pasithea, tremulous-hearted!
  Now, by his slumber from flashing of fantasy freed,
  Attis himself in his heart could survey all his deed:
  Clearly his loss, and the place where he was, he could scan:
  Swift in the storm of his mind to the seashore he ran.
  Out on the waste of the waters her tearful eyes bent,
  Thus to her country she cried all her grievous lament:
  "O my dear country that bore me, that life to me gave!
  Fool that I am, I have fled like a runaway slave:
  Runaway, turning my foot towards Ida to hide,
  Here among snows, among frozen wild dens to abide,
  Dens where in frenzy I also my shelter may claim!
  Where, my dear country? — what region as thine shall I name?
  How do mine eyes of themselves seek in longing for thee
  While for a little my spirit from raging is free!
  Far from my home, in these forests my life shall I measure,
  Absent from friends and from parents, from birthplace and treasure?
  Absent from market and wrestling-ground, contest and pleasure?
  Sorrowful, sorrowful spirit, lament and lament!
  What is there human of form that my fate has not lent?
  I once a man, and a youth, and a lad, and a boy,
  I who was first in our games, and the wrestling-ground's joy:
  Crowded my gates, and to kindlier doors I was free:
  Mine were the blossoming garlands one morning to be

When I should rise with the sun, and my house all arrayed:
Ministress I of the Gods am, and Cybele's maid!
Maenad, and part of myself, shall my title be now,
Sterile, and dweller in snows of green Ida's cold brow.
Phrygia's summit: the rest of my life shall I view it,
Haunting the glade with the hind, with the boar ranging through it?
Now O my deed I repent, now O now would undo it!"

Thus from his lips as the hurrying syllables broke,
To the all-hearkening Gods a new cry to evoke—
Then of her lions great Cybele loosened the yoke:
Urging that terror to cattle, the left of the pair,
"Angrily harry him back to his place and his share!
Back to his frenzy impel him and back to the grove,
He who too freely away from my keeping would rove!
Smite yourself, spite yourself, flailing your flanks with your tail,
Bellow till Echo your fellow be, roar like the gale,
Flames of your mane by the strength of your shoulders be shaken!"
Thus the dire Goddess, and fastened the yoke half-forsaken.
Lashing and roaring, inflaming the rage of his heart,
Crashing through thickets the lion was swift to depart
Till in the plashing, the pallid domain of the tide,
There by the marble-cool waters poor Attis he spied.
Once leapt the lion, and Attis fled mad to the glade:
There for the rest of his life he was Cybele's maid.

Goddess, great Cybele, Dindymus' Lady, great Mother,
Far from this dwelling of mine be thy frenzy to gather!
Those whom thou drivest to rage, be they other, far other!

*Translated from the Latin of Catullus by M. D.*

## APPENDIX B
## HISTORIES
*An Experiment in Sorcery*


*In the present collection of histories, the experiences of untrained and for the most part involuntary participants in "occult" happenings have been selected, as giving the most informative view of the actions and interactions of the psyche in relation to such occurrences. The trained magician or occultist would have acted differently in many instances, would have averted disaster or would have rendered the consequences of an action less crudely obvious: the histories would then have been more complex and less suitable to our psychological study. This first history, "An Experiment in Sorcery," is probably the most stylised in the telling: it is however an authentic account of four schoolgirls and their encounter with the challenge of occult power, although it is told with more matured perception as a remembered episode. It is, in its simplest aspect, a serious warning to all dabblers: especially however it is a warning to the psychologically unready against placing themselves in the alchemical crucible. We see how each of the girls is at odds with, and yet a reflection of, the domestic, legalistic, economic or religious tensions of her home life. In their ordinary school friendship, the four girls balance and supplement one another: but as soon as the possibility of magical fulfilment touches each as*

457

*an individual, the parental problems come to the fore. That the principal victim of the experiment is not one of the participants, is a circumstance only too frequent when power is concentrated by those who are unable to control it.*

Imelda's dark pony-tail and Hilary's auburn plaits were tossed back as the two girls closed their books and sat up. Imelda pondered for a moment, "I like Satan," she said.

"He seems to have been Milton's favourite character too," replied her friend.

"Miss Atkins was talking to me after school the other day," Imelda went on, "and she said we don't have to agree with Milton about everything."

"We don't have to agree with anyone about anything, except for exams."

"No, of course not, but Miss Atkins told me that later in the poem, not in the piece we're doing, Milton says Adam prayed to God, and Eve prayed to God in Adam. She said that's out of date, and men and women should pray direct to God just the same as each other."

"Or to God through someone else just the same, I suppose, if they feel like it," said Hilary idly. She was an insatiable reader, and a line of Flecker that she had come across in the school's excellent library ran through her head: —

"And some to Meccah turn to pray, and I toward thy bed, Yasmin . . ." She slammed a mental door on it. "What went wrong in Latin this morning, Immi?"

"Oh yes, I wanted to tell you about that. You know that piece of translation about the entrance of Dido? — I wrote just what you told me, 'And now she comes among a large constipated crowd,' and the Hen crossed it out three times and nearly threw the book at me."

"Dear idiot, I did not tell you to put that. I said the word for 'densely packed' was related to the word—"

Outside in the corridor a hand-bell rang, and a moment later two other girls came quietly into the study. In the uniformity of white blouses and navy slips, hair became an outstanding individual characteristic, and plump Joan Winter's smooth primrose-blond bob was as conspicuous in its way as were Esther Marks' unruly red curls. They greeted Hilary and Imelda with friendly insults: the four were something of a sisterhood.

Esther pulled a crumpled paper from somewhere inside her slip and gave it to Hilary. "My uncle says the words don't mean anything, as far as he knows, but he's written down the way they would be pronounced. He asked where I got them from, and I told them they were in a book that one of my friends was studying at school. Next time I go to see him, he'll give me a little book for you, a children's book with the Hebrew letters, so that you can work them out for yourself."

Hilary gasped with real delight. It was not the fulfilment of a wish, for it had not occurred to her that an elementary knowledge of Hebrew could possibly come for the asking; but if she had thought of it, she would certainly have wished it. Already—but nobody else in the school knew this—she had coaxed Miss Henderson into teaching her the rudiments of Greek in Latin prep. time. Hilary's parents were against her going to a university: they said it was usually a waste of time for girls, who only married the first available man anyway—but however it might turn out, she was building up the essential tools for a lifetime's study.

"Please, Joan, get out the old book again, so that we can see how these words fit in," she asked. Joan went to her locker and brought back a square-shaped moderately-sized volume with all the signs of age about it. The leather binding was worn and flaked, and broken at the corners: the thick, unevenly-cut pages showed yellow wavy edges. She placed it carefully on the table in front of Hilary, and the other girls crowded round to look.

It was centuries old, with page after page of hand-set antique print interspersed with strange diagrams, circles and squares geometrically divided and inscribed with Greek and Hebrew letters: a sixteenth-century English edition of Cornelius Agrippa. "How did you ever come by that?" asked Imelda.

Joan blinked her sea-green eyes. "There was an old man in our parish, old Donald Black if you heard of him, and he had a wonderful library of old books. He bought them all his life, one at a time, and when he died he left them all to Daddy. Well, to the Church actually, but Daddy *is* the Church." She paused, and Hilary murmured "Lucrezia Borgia," but nobody took any notice.

"They were all stacked up in our parlour, and Daddy meant to look through them, but he had a sick-call the evening they arrived and so I got there first," said Joan simply. "I didn't have time to look at all of them, but this one seemed the most interesting, so I brought it away."

"Any chance of another look at them?"

"No, Daddy's sold them now. Towards the funds," the vicar's daughter added glumly.

Esther had picked up the book and was reverently turning the pages. "Oh, here's a ceremony with candles," she said. "They must have used a lot of candles. I love them. My uncle and auntie do something, lighting candles on Friday evenings: I don't know much about it, but I wish we did it in our house!"

"We have a lot of candles in church," put in Imelda.

"In church? Oh, you don't understand! None of you understand. Religion is for one's own home. Ours is the most beautiful religion in the world, and I've been robbed of it all, because my father and mother don't take it seriously!"

The quiet Jewish girl's outburst had shocked everyone, including herself. She flushed and fell silent. Imelda was not only shocked but also rather envious, and hastily gave voice to a paradox which had occurred to her some time previously: – "If I took my religion seriously as a Catholic, I should have to deny my own right to exist. I'm sure my mother wasn't married—my real mother, that is. They always tell me I was too young to remember her, but I do remember her, and I loved her."

Esther momentarily forgot her own troubles in this interesting mystery about Imelda. It might of course be fiction: one never caught Imelda out in a lie, but she had altogether too many strange stories, Esther thought. "You mean Dr. Ryan and Mrs. Ryan are not your real parents?" she asked cautiously.

"No. She's adopted," replied Hilary on her friend's behalf.

"Lucky thing to be adopted by Dr. Ryan!" exclaimed Joan. She had heard one or two regretful comments at home, because the prosperous physician-surgeon was not of her father's flock.

"Lucky?" Imelda cast around for some quick means of making her plight known. "Have any of you met Kathy? Hilary, you've met Kathy. Tell them."

"Won't you regret it?"

"No."

Hilary moved to face the whole group. "Kathy Ryan is Dr. Ryan's real daughter. They don't generally let people see her. She is—er—mentally defective." The tone in which Hilary spoke the last words was heavily loaded, and gave a gruesome impression of Imelda's home life. Imelda took up the tale:

"She's the one they really love, the one they really want. They only adopted me to be a companion for her. I have to play with her, read to her, try to explain things to her. I overheard them once saying what a success it was. They look after me well: that's my fee for being Kathy's companion: but if anything happened to her, I'm sure I could put on my coat and walk out, and nobody would trouble to ask where I was going or if I'd be back. I'm a bastard: I have no real place in the world"

"You're in it as solidly as the rest of us, so you may as well make up your mind to enjoy it," remarked Hilary. "I'm quite sure my wretched parents are legally married, everything they do is legal; I haven't a shred of pretext to get away from them for years, but I don't base my right to life on that. My right to life lis based on the fact that I have life and can use it. And so is yours. Now, who has the book?"

I have," said Joan. "I want to look for a page I found in it, that tells how you can know a good spirit from a bad one if it appears." She found the place and began reading, but quickly looked up with a puzzled frown. "It says an evil spirit can appear in the form of a goofie—!" She passed the book to Hilary, who looked at it and then laughed.

"In the form of a *goose*, you goose. It's you who are goofy. Haven't you noticed the long S's? These old books are all printed with them."

"Do spirits really appear, do you think?" asked Esther.

"The evidence seems to point that way," said Hilary.

"Of course they do, it's a known fact, but I'd be terrified if I saw one," said Imelda.

"Daddy told me of one that had to be exorcised out of a belfry, when he was a curate," said Joan. "It was quite real."

"But would a spirit appear, or anything else, according to the directions in this book?" Esther persisted.

"That," said Hilary, "we shall find out when we try."

"Then we are going to try?"

Hilary and Joan exchanged an almost inconspicuous glance, and nodded. "We are."

Three days later, they all met again in the Sixth Form study without any interlopers. They had chosen their ceremony from the varied assortment offered by Cornelius

Agrippa. "Some things we can't do, but most of them we can," said Hilary. "Most of the herbs we can buy at the herbalists."

"Blood of some sort we can get at the butcher's."

"Easier still, dried, at the gardening shop."

"We can't fast," said Joan, "it would attract far too much attention, here and at home. But we can wear white garments. I know of a whole cupboard full of them at home, that nobody ever looks at: about fifty years old, or more, solid white linen smocks. Mummy thinks they used to lend them out at one time, but nobody could possibly use them for anything now."

"You could bring some along and we could look at them," said Imelda.

"Now we come to the main points," Hilary went on, looking at the notes they had made. "The Magician has to proclaim the purpose of the ceremony. Who is to be the Magician and what is our purpose to be?"

For an instant Joan envisaged herself, a clergyman's daughter, as the Magician: then she decided she definitely did not want the role—the Magician would have to speak to anything that might appear—and she hastily replied "You, Hilary, or Esther."

"Hilary's doing Latin and I'm not," said Esther. "She'll pronounce all the names properly."

Hilary laughed involuntarily. An invisible cloak seemed to have descended upon her shoulders, and to fit there. Then she repeated her second question, "And our purpose?"

"First of all," Joan said, "who is taking part in the ceremony?"

"All four of us," replied Hilary. "You, Joan, you brought the book, besides being—er—born into the cloth. Esther is in because she likes ritual and understands it, and also because she is the one person I'm sure isn't goint to be scared by whatever may happen. It's true, Esther. I'm sure if anything unpleasant happened—though probably nothing will—you'd just hang right on to the God of Abraham, Isaac and your Uncle Benny. Somewhere in the book it mentions a consecrated sword. We are going to have a sword—I've seen an old brass-hilted affair that we can clean up beautifully—and you are going to carry it, Esther. I can just picture you."

"And Immi? She'll be frightened if—"

"She'll not be frightened if we are all there together," Hilary told them. Immi isn't going to be asked to do anything or say anything. I just want her to be there, and I'll tell you why. Do you remember last year when we were playing about with table-turning and so on? We had results all the time, certainly: but we only had messages that made sense and really worked, when Immi joined in. Immi couldn't have done it herself: she couldn't have predicted the tennis tournament results for instance, as we got them: but we got nothing like that whe she was away from the table."

"Why was it, do you think?" asked Esther.

"Haven't a clue," Hilary answered frankly. "But whatever it was, it was genuine. Immi, you'll be a great help. And now, this question of the purpose, please. Is there anything you'd like to ask for, Joan?"

"Only for Daddy to get the money he needs for repairing the old part of the Vicarage. He's really worried about
the roof: he says idt willl have to be done even if none of us go away for a holiday for years."

Fair enough. Esther?"

Esther shook her head. "No, thank you. Often I've lain awake, thinking and thinking. Everything will work out for me in time anyway; there simply isn't a nice way in which it could be hurried. I only need patience, and I think I have that. All I want just now, really, is to take part in this ceremony for its own sake, and to help you all. It doesn't seem evil, with all those prayers and things: it doesn't seem particularly Jewish or particularly Christian, but it should be interesting."

"Then thank you for helping us, Esther. Is there anything you'd like to ask for, Immi?"

"Yes." The dark grey eyes looked into the distance. "I want Alec Martin."

Her friends were stupefied. "Alec Martin? The boy who saw you home after the Christmas party? You never said you were keen on him. How often have you seen him since?"

"Once," said Imelda. "And I'm not exactly keen on him. I like him a lot. I want to make a wish, if that's possible, so as to marry him."

"But you hardly know him."

"That's true, but I have at least met him. I want to get married and to have my own home, as soon as possible. I want a husband and children, in-laws, a family of my own."

"Look, Immi, if that's what you want in life, why not go about, meet more boys—" Even as Joan spoke she knew it was hopeless.

"Go about? When? When I'm not keeping Kathy company I'm doing homework. I'm not like some of you, who can open a book and turn a page and know it well enough to answer a set of questions. I have to keep at it to learn anything, so as to be success enough for them to say 'Look what we've made of her, in return for helping our Kathy.' No. I just want to get off the merry-go-round."

Hilary sighed. "If that's how you feel, Immi, alas poor Alec. I think it's a waste, all ways round, but you're entitled to your chance."

"You haven't said what you want, Hilary," said Joan.

"I? I think I'm like Esther, I just want to do the thing for its own sake. No: not quite that. If I believed my whole life was handed to me like a blank paper, to make as I wanted with one wish, the world's so wonderful, what would I choose? To be a prima ballerina, to explore the Amazon, to play every musical instrument, to live for centuries? But I don't think it is quite like that, for me at any rate. What I want now is something else.

"I've been to Mass with Imelda, and in a way I like it. Don't worry, Joan, I don't want to discuss transubstantiation. My point is not whether or not it happens: my point is that the whole ceremony is geared for it to happen, and that makes it a better ceremony. But I'm not looking for some kind of Mass, because that is a ceremony to demonstrate the will of God, and I'm not all that keen on God. Look at an experiment in the chemi-lab. I suppose the main idea really is to give people practice in weighing and measuring, handling chemicals and fire, but it would be pretty dull without the experiments. A series of actions leads up to a bang or a stink, and everyone's happy. More than that, one of the laws of science has been demonstrated. It's the same with a trial at the magistrates' court. My father took me to see what went on, one day when he knew there'd be nothing but two or three motorists and a poacher. Every case went according to the book, right through to its conviction or acquittal—one man was actually acquitted—and as we came out, my father said 'There you are, Hilary. You've seen the laws of the land in action.' The laws of the land, the laws of science, the will of God, all with their ceremonies, all ending with a rap of the mallet, a conviction or an acquittal, a stink or a bang, Ite Missa Est, Q.E.D. But where do you find a ceremony to affirm the will of man?—of the individual person I mean?"

Joan thought hard for a moment. "The wedding service," she suggested, but Hilary ignored her.

"And yet all the rest depends on it, on the individual human will. You can't make a man a priest unless he's baptised, and you can't baptise him unless you suppose he has free will. You can't put a man on trial for a crime unless you suppose the same thing. A scientific experiment is only

valid if you suppose the scientist is free to choose at least
some of the conditions. Do you see what I'm driving at?—I've
got into a cloud myself now."

"Experiment to demonstrate the Will of Man," said
Imelda.

The cheerful villa which Chief Constable Armstrong
inhabited with his wife and their two children, Hilary and
young Michael, did not offer any hidden corners suitable to a
clandestine working in ritual magick. The manager's flat over
the bank, which was Esther's parental home, was even less
encouraging in that respect. For a brief while, preference
veered between a tool-shed screened by Dr. Ryan's
shrubbery, and a disused room in the oldest part of the
Vicarage; but soon it was decided that the most prudent
course would be to take advantage of a loose plank in the
school fence, and to conduct the ceremony in the summer-
house on a Sunday evening.

The ceremony itself was very much adapted, not only to
suit the resources of the girls but also to include attractive
passages from various parts of the book. Viewing the
completed preparations, Hilary felt exalted. A tremendous
line of Elizabethan drama came into her mind. "'Tis magic,
magic that has ravished me," she whispered to Imelda, who,
thinking it an original utterance, admired accordingly.

The summer-house was a square-based wooden structure
which was built true to the compass, and therefore almost
diagonally to the boundary fence which ran just behind it.
The two sides nearest to the fence were entirely walled in:
the other two, one of which contained the entrance, were
screened to a height of about four feet and completely open
in their upper part. A built-in bench-seat ran round three
sides of the interior: and the whole was covered by a
pyramid-shaped roof. In the centre of the floor, the girls had
placed for the occasion a small square card-table covered with

a large cloth to serve as an altar. In the centre of this, on a book-stand, rested the volume of Cornelius Agrippa: to one side stood a tumbler of holy water, provided by Imelda, with a sprig from the hedge to serve as a sprinkler: to the other side, on a small trivet, stood a bulb-bowl filled with sand, on top of which smouldered the charcoal and dried herbs on which the friends had decided. The project of white robes had been given up, as being too compromising in the event of discovery, so the participants were prosaically attired in their outdoor coats; but they filed into their places with dignity. Esther bore the brass-hilted sword, scoured and glittering, Imelda a goblet of the altar-wine which Joan had contributed: Joan followed with a silver salver on which was a quartered roll: and Hilary came last, with the wand which she had carefully fashioned for the occasion. The opening prayers and invocations were spoken, and unknown beings with curious resonant names were bound to the will of the Magician; then Esther put some more herbs on the brazier, and Hilary with upraised wand stated the purpose:

"That Imelda Ryan should—should win Alec Martin, and that Joan Winter's father should receive the money he needs."

Then they all tasted the bread and wine to seal their unity, and settled down to the repeated invocations, circling around the central altar. The smell of burning herbs hung in the damp air, strong as if in an enclosed room: Imelda developed an almost claustrophobic sense of being enveloped in it. Round and round they went, chanting and responding in hushed close-throated tones. To Joan, too, it seemed that the open spaces of the summer-house were being built-in around them. It reminded her of her sensations on the stage of the parish hall, during a dramatic performance, when the audience became a blur and then disappeared from her consciousness: only the immediate action was real. Round and round—round and round. Esther wished heartily that she had not come. According to the book, she knew, this part of the action should end in the operator receiving a vision concerning the purpose of the ceremony. She emphatically did not want this or anything like it to happen. With a detached fragment of her mind she could picture herself swinging out of the circle and crying aloud "Let this hideous nonsense stop!"—but the fragment was not operative, and she continued with the others.

Hilary felt strangely numb. She kept up the measured repetition of names and phrases, and she knew from the rhythm that the pace could not have changed very much since the beginning, but it was almost like walking on a moving escalator. The floor seemed to fly beneath their feet at a fantastic speed, and to be accelerating. An almost tangible vortex seemed to have built up around the central altar. Apart from this however, she had lost the very positive state of mind in which she had begun the action. Now she was passive, receptive, awaiting whatever would happen. Outwardly she would continue to direct the proceedings, but now she felt as if this was not so much her deed as an exterior fate laid upon her. She held her wand proudly and continued the circling. Suddenly Imelda stumbled and fell. "Well, really!" thought Hilary with involuntary distaste. Everyone halted in their tracks. The mysterious vortex shattered, and at once a tall flame leapt from the pile of burning herbs. A second time it leapt, though not so high: a third time, and then it vanished in smoking extinction.

Esther gave a cry. "Three days!" she exclaimed. "In three days you will hold him in your arms, and all will be settled!" She wondered at herself, ashamed of the strange dramatic words which she had spoken without forethought; but now she felt as if a giant hand held her jaws firmly together, and she could neither add to nor try to explain what she had said.

Imelda stood up, looking dazed and bewildered. Hilary

THE TRIUMPH OF LIGHT

went to the altar and brought the ceremony to its conclusion
as quickly as might decently be, dismissing the invisible
witnesses to their proper abodes, and giving thanks to the
Powers. Then all was dismantled and packed into satchels and
cases.

As they left, Hilary found herself overtaken by a mood
of complete scepticism. The whole affair had become empty
and absurd: she only hoped nobody would want to talk about
it now. A drop of rain fell across her cheek like a tear. "It's
going to rain," she announced thankfully. "We shouldn't
stand talking; we ought to hurry home at once."

The party broke up. She and Imelda went the same way.
They trudged along side by side, in a silence that tore at the
nerves.

Next day it became apparent that a wet week was
setting in. It rained intermittently by day and night. On
Wednesday, even the hockey teams abandoned the struggle in
their sea of mud. Usually on Wednesday evenings Hilary and
Imelda went for a fairly long walk together after school, but
now the rain set in too heavily for them to venture very far,
even in raincoats and boots, although Imelda was unwilling to
give up her free time.

"Let's call on Joan," she suggested, seeing they were
near the Vicarage; "she might have some interesting ideas."
As if by mutual consent, Sunday's experiment was not once
mentioned; it seemed to have been completely swallowed up
in the course of daily events.

The Vicarage was set some distance back from the road,
and a public footpath ran right across the glebe. The path
itself proved to be completely flooded by the heavy rain, and
the girls carefully made their way over the ground beside it.
As they approached the Vicarage, the cause of at least a part
of the trouble became apparent. From all parts of the wide,
many-gabled roof of the old house, gutter-pipes converged to

the near corner, where they discharged their rainwater into a huge urn-shaped receptacle of lead or iron which was fixed high up on the angle of the walls. Now, however, some obstruction—perhaps a bird's nest or a dislodged tile—had evidently blocked the pipe, so that the accumulated water was gushing in noisy cascades over the edge of the urn.

The girls were nearing the front-door, when a young man appeared, clad in oilskins and wheeling a bicycle. He was making a wide detour in following the flooded path. Suddenly Imelda recognised him.

"Alec Martin! Alec!" she called, her voice full of a curious assurance, subtly transformed by the prediction she had heard. Surprised and pleased, the young man turned and approached them. All at once there came a rending sound, and looking up they saw that the masonry holding the huge metal urn had given way under the strain, and the urn itself, gushing water, leaned out at a grotesque angle from the wall. For a moment it hung there, then fell, striking the paved ground with an explosive crash. A long fragment, whether of broken metal or stone, flew up from the wreckage and, striking Alec under the chin, continued its movement, taking his head back with it. It all took place so swiftly that the unnatural quality of the action could not at once be grasped. Then Imelda's lips parted in a long continuous shriek as she sprang forward, flung her arms round the young man's body and sank to the ground with it. Even in the pelting rain, she was covered with his blood.

When the Reverend John Winter, struggling with his umbrella, came out to see what had happened, the first firgure that he saw was Hilary, a very pale and shaken schoolgirl, kneeling down to vomit on the flowerbed.

## Crambo the Dwarf

*The following macabre history is included for the considerable psychological interest of some of the matters treated. The narrator is a student of psychic phenomena who kept a diary of all matters of occult interest which came her way: the occurrence here related has been only slightly rewritten to accord with our general principles of anonymity for the persons, and to limit its length by omitting some unnecessary details: much of it is therefore directly taken from the diary account, which was written as soon as possible after the events related. The methods employed differ from our methods: wine-glass divination and the like are not for the magician, though with regard to the automatic writing the narrator was admittedly confronted with the accomplished fact. We would further point out that never, in any circumstances, should alcohol be given to a person in a trance state: however, the people concerned in this case were completely unaware of the dangers to the recipient.*

*A point of especial interest lies in the symptoms of septicaemia which had been shown by Nada for a considerable time. The doctors at the prominent hospital at which she was examined and treated, could throw no light whatever upon either the cause or the disappearance of the malady. The present authors believe that they are contributing something to the study of such matters, by bringing to notice a curious parallel in a case encountered by Carl Jung:— to the paper on "The Psychological Foundations of Belief in Spirits" in his book "The Structure and Dynamics of the Psyche," he adds a footnote giving an account of a young East African woman who was suffering from what appeared to be a septic abortion, but whose malady completely disappeared after a local medicine-man*

*had carried out a procedure to free her from the ghostly
visitations of her deceased parents. Dr. Jung himself
witnessed both the symptoms and the recovery of the
patient. Needless to say, his works would not have been
known to any of the persons in the history given below: nor
could anyone have anticipated so strange a parallel between
the case of an African girl in the Twenties and an Irish girl in
London in the Sixties.*

At one time, Jim and Nada were the most attractive
couple that I knew. Jim was a young freelance engineer, with
a university degree to back him: his habitual air of somewhat
cynical elegance had rooted itself as aptly in the new
technocracy as it might have done in an older aristocracy.
Bernadette, or Nada as everyone called her, had no
background: she was entirely of the present. She was
beautiful in a strange moonlight way, with dark,
loosely-waving hair and a pallid skin. She dressed and spoke
excellently: her conversation ranged from brief comments on
current affairs to occasional cascades of repartee. Her
cooking was indifferently done, but served up to perfection.
Jim once told me that she had been a night-club hostess when
he first met her, and I could well imagine it. He had no close
relatives, and could marry to please himself. He had gathered
that Nada's earlier life had not been particularly happy, and
when he saw she was unwilling to speak of it he told her at
once that she need never do so: as far as he was concerned,
the past was dead. They seemed ideally matched in years,
looks and temperament.

With Jim I discussed science and philosophy, with Nada
men and cities. I was not especially either his friend or hers: I
was to some extent drawn to each of them, but chiefly to the
charming and vital interplay of personalities in their union.
For a few years, no social gathering was complete in my eyes
without them.

Then, imperceptibly at first, something went wrong. Nobody could put a finger on the beginning of it, but the unity between Jim and Nada was being destroyed, and it seemed as if they themselves were almost deliberately tearing it down. When at last they came to speak of it, their words were pitifully, exasperatingly banal: she said he was selfish and inconsiderate, he said she was sullen and lazy.

She would sit brooding, staring straight before her: if anyone tried to rouse her she would loosen the black curtain of her hair so that it fell completely over her face. It was a frightening and effective barrier, a veil that neither her husband nor I dared lift. It did nothing to diminish the mounting tension. At last we managed to coax her to see a doctor, but the doctor's findings at that time were altogether negative. Jim asked me once, in a confidential chat in the little restaurant to which he had retreated for a meal after coming home to an uncleared breakfast-table, if I thought Nada might be a solitary drinker. I told him honestly, no. Not only did she show no sign of it: I knew she had an acute aversion to alcohol, which she played down so as not to spoil other people's fun. Some other drug, I thought, might possibly have attracted her, but not that. She had lost some weight, and this suggested to me that she might be neurasthenic.

A specialist was consulted this time, but he again could find very little that was definite. He declared bluntly he thought it quite normal for a young married woman to feel frightened and resentful at being frequently left alone in a city flat till the small hours, as Nada had told him she was. Jim, who as an ambitious freelance seized upon work that more conventional companies hesitated to take, was at that time working under a contract which needed his presence fairly often during the hours when several large office-blocks were unoccupied. He had vaguely supposed Nada would amuse herself on such occasions by going to a show or visiting friends, and would whip up a supper for him on his return home. She had never before objected to late hours, and he thought she was being deliberately unreasonable about it now. Meanwhile, the specialist sent her back to her G.P., with a note suggesting slight anaemia. She was given some pills for this condition and took them without noticeable effect. She and Jim bickered incessantly.

If I had been altogether of his party, or of hers, I might have found the situation tolerable. As it was however, I did not. Happening at that time to move to another district, I decided that the activities of Jim and Nada were of no further interest to me: whilst, on the other hand, it seemed equally evident that I could be of no service to them. I omitted, therefore, to give them my new address: and on considering the matter further, I realised that there were no mutual acquaintainces to whom I need give it either. I could completely close that chapter of my life, and concentrate entirely upon other friends and deeper interests.

About eighteen months passed. February was approaching, and with it the ancient festival of Imbolc, the second of February, now known as the Purification of the Virgin, or Candlemas. With several of my new friends* I discussed how we should commemorate it. What we decided, we kept secret: and I need not disclose it here, only that I promised to contribute a quantity of snowdrops. So much must be told, to elucidate something which follows after.

On the night before the celebration, I went to bed early. This was fortunate, as I thus had about four hours' sleep. At about midnight I was awakened by a knocking on the outer door of my flat. Springing up, I slipped into a dressing-gown, and without switching on the light asked who was there. To my astonishment, Nada's voice answered, "Jim and I." Without more delay I put on the light and admitted them.

* The narrator had joined a small Celtic-style circle of psychics, to which reference is again made later in this history.

I put the kettle on, and Jim took the heavy fur coat from Nada's shoulders. In spite of her careful make-up and loosely-draped, expensive clothes, that first glance at her horrified me. She was thin, almost skeletal: I could only think of those photographs one used to see, of survivors from Belsen. In truth, I did not think her far from death. She looked round the room, and sighed, "Well, my dear, so we've found you! I'm sorry if we woke you up. Jim has some papers he wants you to see."

I asked about her health, and they told me while I set out the coffee and biscuits. A mysterious form of blood-poisoning, whose focal point nobody could discover, had set in, and was of necessity being combated with powerful antibiotics. The doctors had begun by suspecting a uterine infection, but had found absolutely no real evidence for this. Then they had tested her blood for every known disease, they had counted her red corpuscles and her white corpuscles, they had examined her glands, but to no avail: all their results pointed to the conclusion that her health should be better than average, but in fact they had to keep her alive with drugs in such massive doses as are usually only given for a short period. Every time the dosage had been stopped or diminished, the symptoms of septicaemia had flared up again. I could only express horror. Then she asked me, "Aren't you curious to know how we found your address?"

I admitted that I was. "Supposing I tell you," she went on, "that your address was given to us by automatic writing?"

Never in my life, until a few weeks before that date, had I seen an example of automatic writing although of course I had heard of it. Then one of my friends had made the acquaintance of a rather pathetic girl who had recently become—I might almost say—afflicted with automatic writing. She was very proud that the first scrawls had developed into words with some sort of legibility and sense, and had handed a sample to my friend, who had at once shown it to me. The incident had seemed pointless at the time, but now it looked almost as if I had had to be "primed" with a degree of knowledge as to the general appearance and quality of automatic script. "Can I see the writing?" I asked Jim. He showed it to me. It was a scrawl almost similar to that other which I had seen, but it continued for several pages. I asked how it had come about.

Nada began to explain. Jim had developed a small wart on his wrist, and she had offered to cure it by her grandmother's method. This was a charm requiring the use of a scrap of raw beef and a silver spoon. At that point in the story, Jim laughed and interposed: "I let Nada go through the whole potty performance to the very end, thinking, who knows, there may be some poor lost fragment of science or psychology buried in it, and at the finish she put the spoon under a running tap. A little later, I wanted the sink so that I could wash off some films I was developing, so I asked Nada how long the spoon had to stay there. She replied, 'My grandmother said the spoon must lie in running water for at least an hour, but I think that was just an old wives' tale!' "

"But after that," Nada went on, "I began telling him of some extraordinary things that my grandmother used to do, and that I used to do too when I was a little girl. Among the rest, I said that before I learned to write in the ordinary way, I used to do automatic writing. Then, to see if I could still do it, I took paper and pencil and sat quietly waiting. The writing soon began. Look at it: the first part is a cry for help, isn't it?"

Looking at the papers, in spite of the nearly illegible scrawl I saw that Nada spoke truly. I also saw a cryptic allusion to someone called Crambo the Dwarf, to someone named Helen, and, here and there, to a bag. "The bag was mine," was written clearly in one place: in several places also

was repeated the appeal for help, and "Bring her, bring her."
Then evidently Jim or Nada had asked whom they should
bring, because the next word was my surname. As a matter of
fact, neither of the questioners ever thought of me by my
surname, besides not having seen or heard of me for a year
and a half, so it was not strange if they followed this by
asking, "Who is that?" Then my address was given, exact and
entire, but since they did not know it they could not
recognise it. After that, there followed the words
"Snowdrops—circle—water" and finally my first name. This
at last they understood. With an extraordinary faith (when
one considers the nature of the document) they had found
the address upon a street-map, and had set out in their car to
seek me.

I pondered a little. However strongly I might again feel
drawn to these two most unfortunate people, I was not
inclined to accept their strange story instantly. Yet it seemed
that some unknown entity might possibly be offering a
means of saving Nada, and even if this entity were a fragment
of her own subconscious mind, it ought not on that account
to be disregarded. But what of my resolution not to be drawn
again into the affairs of these two?

One detail decided me. I looked again at the words,
"Snowdrops—circle—water." I went and dressed. I told them
I was convinced: those words referred to a matter which
neither of them could have known by ordinary means. If this
was an example of telepathy, it was telepathy with a guiding
purpose, since to me these words constituted an almost
obligatory appeal. I suggested that we should go to their flat,
where the writing had taken place, for the purpose of trying
to discover more.

When we had arrived there, I considered the best way to
make a beginning, and set myself to draw the letters of the
alphabet on a sheet of paper. When Jim saw what I was doing
however, he produced a set of stencils which he used for

labelling his professional work, and soon had a boldly legible
set of little alphabet-cards ready for me to arrange in a circle.
To these I added the words YES and NO. I was not anxious
for Nada to resume the automatic writing, and besides, in all
matters of paranormal communication I like to have
supplementary evidence obtained by a different method.

We all sat down round the small table on which the
cards were set out: Jim had brought writing materials to take
notes, and an inverted wine-glass in the centre of the table
completed our equipment. When we had each laid a finger on
the foot of the glass, I closed my eyes. I did not wish to
suspect myself of influencing whatever might come: while as
to other possibilities, the sense of touch is enough to let one
know if a glass in such a position is being deliberately
manipulated.

In the present case, the glass began its peculiar authentic
sliding almost at once. Soon I heard Jim ask, "Save whom?" I
opened my eyes to watch the glass, which moved swiftly to
the letters BERYN. Nada gasped: it was evident that she
recognised the name. "Save Beryn from what?" Jim
questioned. I closed my eyes again, and the glass moved a few
times. When I looked, Jim showed me the paper on which he
had written, CRAMBO. Then I asked, "Where is Crambo
now?" The response was given after some hesitation, THE
CLEARYS ARE THEM. This did not seem to answer my
question, so I repeated it. There followed a long series of
apparently meaningless syllables, ending with the words
GREEDY RASCAL. Suddenly I felt the glass gathering
power to itself as a horse does before bolting, and after
moving with swift energy through a number of letters, it
stopped dead. Jim showed me the paper. The words were
GIVE HIM BACK HIS MONEY FIVE TIMES OVER,
followed by some fragments which included references to
Helen and the bag. I heard the bell of some church or other
strike two o'clock. We re-settled our fingers on the glass, and

Jim asked, "What do you want now?" The reply came at once, the single word GIN.

"A libation!" he exclaimed. He took a bottle of gin from the sideboard and poured a tiny drop into the slightly concave base of the glass. The liquor evaporated almost immediately, but no further results followed. "That is certainly my grandmother communicating with us," Nada laughed, a little embarrassed:—"first the pet name of Beryn, which nobody else ever called me, and now this demand for gin!"

We sat waiting for some time, while I asked "How are we to give back the money?" but nothing happened. "This is too slow: I shall go and make some coffee!" cried Nada. While she was out in the kitchen, Jim said quietly to me, "Lately she has been behaving more strangely than ever, so much so in fact that the word Possessed has come into my mind, although, as you know, I should certainly never wish to define such a term."—"To my way of thinking," I murmured back to him, "that automatic script suggests a very ancient definition of the word." Nada returned now, so I said no more. We all drank our coffee and smoked our cigarettes: then Nada took the pencil and paper and, sitting silently, began to scrawl at random. From time to time we looked, but the words did not add much to our knowledge. At one point she wrote the name, Rosalisa. Soon afterwards, Jim said "Please write more plainly," which resulted in a name being written distinctly, Frederick Lambert. Then the scrawling began again. Presently Nada began drawing a map. I saw two streets shown, then a square, then, close to the square, a site marked X.

While she was drawing, her eyelids began to flutter. Beneath the long artificial lashes, I saw nothing but the whites of her eyes; then she went into a trance. Watching her carefully, Jim and I asked at once about the map, but the first replies were sullen and negative: "I don't know, I have never been there." But she, or the new personality, explained that the cross marked the position of a tavern. Our questions on the subject of Helen and the bag, however, produced better results, and the following story emerged. The narrator was evidently Rosalisa, Nada's grandmother; we already had some indication of her identity, and this was later to be supported in other ways.

It happened in Dublin, in the year 1908. Rosalisa, who gave us to understand that she had been the mother of twenty-one children all told, had at that time recently given birth to a girl, not her eldest, but distinguished by being born with a caul. She gave to this child her own names, Rose Isabel. She kept the caul in a bag, and boasted of it to her neighbours  because it was considered to be a precious talisman, especially among seafarers. A circus man, named Patrick but professionally known as Crambo the Dwarf, offered her five guineas for it. He said that if he sold the caul to a sailor, he could ask a better price for it than she could, because he had been born out of wedlock and a caul bought from such a one was considered doubly lucky. She promised to let him have it the next Sunday, and he gave her the money in advance, but in fact as the taverns were closed on Sundays she did not see him until the Friday following.

While telling her story, Rosalisa—for it was no longer Nada who sat at the table with us, but a cunning, uneducated old woman—had picked up the wine-glass and was playing with it as she talked. I stared at her, marvelling at the coarsening of her features: the slump of her shoulders, the puckering of her lips as they rounded to the peculiar sucking of her breath. Now suddenly, with obvious meaning, she looked into the glass and asked, "Is this empty?" When Jim asked what she would like to drink, she answered, "Gin."

"Gin and what?"

"And nothing, sir. Just plain gin."

"Plain gin?"

"Certainly sir, just plain gin if you please."

A number of times while she was recounting her history she made a similar appeal, sometimes saying that the glass was empty, sometimes that she was thirsty, sometimes that her chest was bad. Each time, Jim gave her a small quantity of gin, which she swallowed as if it were water. And yet Nada detested gin, and could not drink it even with orange or limejuice.

Rosalisa continued. She was keeping the caul for Crambo, but her chest was bad at the time, and money ran out quickly: and meanwhile she met a fisherman who offered her a pound for the caul, so she sold it again, and he took it away in the bag. On the Friday, she was in the tavern with her eldest girl, Helen, who was about thirteen years old, when Crambo came in and asked for the caul. Rosalisa told him what she had done, and that the money was all spent, and the caul gone with an unknown fisherman. Then the dwarf was seized with a terrible rage: he said that instead of the caul he would have the eldest daughter of her eldest daughter, that is, the first daughter Helen might have when she grew up.

Although she did not believe the dwarf had the power, Rosalisa did not wish to take any chances with the child in question. None of her own children took after her to any marked degree: she looked forward to a grandchild who might be more like herself, and according to old beliefs the eldest daughter of her eldest daughter should be the one. For this reason, on the spur of the moment she replied, "No, don't have the eldest daughter of this girl: it will suit you better to have the eldest daughter of Rose Isabel, of the one born with the caul." To which Crambo agreed, and went off.

This Rose Isabel, when she had grown up, "left the house to be married in shame." When her baby was a week old however, Rosalisa decided to go and see her. Then she saw that this baby, whom they named Bernadette, out of all her descendants was the only one to be her own absolute image. (This was the girl whom she called Beryn, and we called Nada.) As she put it, "All the others were either too fair or too feeble: they took after the other families." So the grandmother decided that she would have this baby girl for her own. She said to the mother, "Soon you'll want to go back to work: I'll take the baby." Seeing that Rose Isabel hesitated, she added "Money in your purse is always good: think it over." So for a short time she had her way. When Rose Isabel and her husband moved to England, they took her and the little Bernadette with them, although soon afterwards they placed the child with well-to-do foster-parents near London. Then Rosalisa received a postcard from Crambo: "He knew what was going on, oh yes: I don't know how he knew, but he knew!" So she got Rose Isabel's husband Fred Lambert to write a letter for her, saying she had made a mistake: the child Crambo should have was not Beryn, but was the one he had wanted at first, Helen's daughter. For Helen was by now married, and had a child: "I didn't care about that one," said the old woman: "she was a nice little girl, but she took after her father." Naturally Fred wanted to know what was afoot, but he was an ailing man, and shortly after writing the letter he died. Crambo's reply eventually came: Rosalisa's new offer was refused, the dwarf writing that he was very well pleased with things as they stood.

There followed the account of the old woman's desperate efforts, in the first place to regain Beryn for herself, and then to undo the damage done by the child's early unsettling and experience of high living with her foster-parents: then, again, to fight the slow and for years barely perceptible draining of Beryn's vitality. All these efforts, the grandmother lamented, had been too late, and the final breakdown of her own health had completed the disaster. We asked how the hold of Crambo upon his victim could be loosened. She told us there was only one way: we

must give him back five times his money, and must also
persuade Beryn to give up anything that she had come by in a
dubious manner. There were certain little pieces of jewellery,
she said, to the value of about another twenty-five pounds in
gold and silver, and these, with the money, ought either to be
given to Crambo himself or should be thrown into a river.
Best of all, they should be taken to Dublin, to the site of the
old tavern, which had been called the Bosun's Mate, on the
Waterloo Road. There were lodging-houses built on the site
now, said Rosalisa, but Crambo still stayed there whenever he
came to Dublin with Cleary's Circus. Mainly, although he was
now quite old, he was still up and down the country with the
circus: but if he were to be called nine times at the time of
the new moon, then he must come, either in body or in
spirit. If he came in flesh and blood, then we should throw
down the gold for him and run: but if he came in spirit, then
we should throw the gold into the Liffey and walk backwards
upstream for a mile and a half. At this point I asked, whether
we should call him nine times by his true name of Patrick, or
by his assumed name of Crambo. "Call him by his
chosen name, Crambo the Dwarf; then he must come,"
she said. "But you must make haste. He is old and sick:
and when he dies, if his hold on Beryn has not been
broken, he will take with him the best part of her and will
leave the worst to *you* and to *you*. She must be set free while
he lives."

In writing, I have considerably abridged the happenings
of that night. In fact, my watch now stood at 6.30 in the
morning. Jim asked Rosalisa why she had not told her story
sooner. She answered, that she had wished to bring Jim and
myself together, because to save Beryn we must act together.
We thanked her for her counsel, and promised to do all we
could. Then Jim said to her, "It is time for you to rest now."
She gazed imploringly at him. I added, "There's no need for
you to worry: you must be very tired, and besides I shall
have to leave soon. Also Nada will be exhausted. Go to
sleep now."

Rosalisa begged to stay with us. She tried to find excuses for delay, she went over the procedure for dealing with Crambo: "he is very greedy, he will accept the money." Then she besought us not to send her back to her own place, and I asked her what it was like there. "Sometimes I sleep," she said, "and I wish I could sleep all the time: but the awakening, ah, the awakening is frightful! Please don't send me back to those horrors!"

"Those horrors are only a kind of bad dreams," I assured her. "Have patience and they will wear themselves out." Then, seeing that we were resolved, she did not struggle as we led her to the bed: none the less, to secure her departure, we had to exercise both will and art. The recall of Nada, we found, was even more difficult. At last she opened her eyes, her appearance was normal, it was the real Nada: but when she sat up, suddenly with a groan she clutched her head:—"Oh, I'm drunk! Whatever have I had? There's a horrid taste in my mouth, and I feel so sick!"

"No wonder," said Jim, showing her the gin bottle. "You've swallowed a good half of this in the course of the night."

Nada could not credit this, since she had such a hatred of the stuff, and when we told her she had drunk it neat, she replied outright that this was impossible. "I've never seen anyone who could drink neat gin," she added, "except my grandmother." With that, she staggered off to the bathroom. I went to the kitchen to put the kettle on, and there she rejoined me presently. While we were making the coffee, she noticed my favourite ring on her own finger. Earlier, during a pause in her narration, Rosalisa, drinking her gin, had offered to bless the ring for me. I had hesitated: the old woman had been so individualised that for the moment I found myself thinking she might carry it off, but recalling the facts of the matter I let her have the ring, and was amused to see how instantly she slipped it on to her finger. There, naturally, Nada now found it, and was shocked at what seemed like her own unconscious appropriation of it. Her reaction showed me startlingly how her self-confidence must have been undermined by recent occurrences; however, I jokingly took back the ring, and transferred it, not to my finger but into a polythene wrapper and thus into my pocket. Then I helped Nada carry the coffee into the other room. Shortly afterwards she complained that something was hurting her, and pulled off the wellingtons that she had been wearing all night. Out fell several trinkets of her own, and Jim's lighter. "I didn't put them there!" cried Nada, appalled: and seeing how frightened she was I decided it would be better to tell her the truth. "Nada, don't worry. Of course you didn't do it. Think! You said a little while ago that nobody could drink neat gin, except your grandmother."

She understood at once. "Granny always put any valuables in her boots," she said. "Have I—has she been here?"

Then Jim made her lie down, and while he was telling her what had happened she fell asleep. Soon he took me home, and I had a short time to restore myself to rights before going on to the office, where I thought it advisable to explain that I had been up most of the night with a sick friend. By the evening, when I took my snowdrops and went to meet my other companions for the Imbolc celebration, I was practically back to normal. As soon as possible, I handed my ring to a sensitive who was there, and asked her opinion of the last wearer. She described a powerful force, essentially female, almost elemental, strongly associated with water, fluids, instincts and dreams, the domain of Neptune. I then told briefly the story of the previous night. Nada, my hearers agreed, must be helped.

A few nights later, as she consented to this, I took one of her photographs to another meeting, where the matter was looked into by the developed inner perception of those present. It was decided that Nada ought to be released, not only from Crambo but also from the well-intentioned but abnormal possessiveness of her grandmother: while Rosalisa herself apparently needed aid also, that she might be willing to forget the troubles of her past life and might go her appointed way in peace. Much work was undertaken to these ends. One man, however, especially wise in such matters, uttered a warning which I had to carry back to Nada: it was dangerous for her to brood in solitude, she must find activities on the material plane, and she ought never again to tamper with psychism in any form.

The results were slow in defining themselves, although about a week later the doctors decided to make another trial of taking Nada off her antibiotics. At this point however, it was Jim the sceptic, the man of science, who declared he could not be easy unless Granny Rosalisa's instructions were carried out to the letter. So twenty-five guineas in money, together with Nada's offerings of gold and silver, were made into a small packet wrapped in lead foil; and at the next new moon a swift week-end pilgrimage sped across England and across the Irish Sea to Dublin. We could not spare very much time, unfortunately, or I should have liked to seek out the truth as to whether there had really been a tavern called "The Bosun's Mate" in the year 1908; but we stood beside the Liffey when we felt reasonably sure of being unobserved at night, and we called on Crambo the Dwarf nine times over. After the ninth calling, a little cold breeze sprang up, and whirled in strange eddies, and fell again. So the lead-wrapped packet was consigned to the muddy waters of the river, and we stepped backwards, and so continued upstream for a considerable distance.

Nada stayed off her antibiotics. The infection in her blood had vanished as mysteriously as it had come, and her naturally strong constitution reasserted itself. In six months, although still painfully thin, she was quite evidently recovering completely. For about three years she carefully observed the advice which I had passed on to her, and had nothing to do with any form of psychism or divination. During that time all went well with her: she and Jim seemed as happy as when I had first known them.

After three years however, her curiosity led her into even stranger matters. She could still have been helped, but she was resolved to go her own way: and this time, it must be sadly recorded, she went altogether into the shadows where none of us could reach her.

### The Finnish Knife

*This history turns upon an aspect of prediction which might be interpreted as the laying of a curse, although the narrator does not emphasise this. The victim, indeed, does not make it clear whether he had known that a catastrophe awaited his hopes, or whether he had merely suspected this in consequence of his own sense of guilt. In either case, his sense of guilt seems to have been an operative factor in the matter.*

*Another operative factor is that the destiny set for him is not left to the mercy of his memory or of his changes of mood: he has a visible link with it, in the word engraved upon the blade of his knife. Why then does he keep the knife?—why does he not drop it overboard for instance on his way to England? The reason is surely that a great part of the prediction is desirable to him. He wants to cross the sea, he wants to become a violinist: like many another, he hopes to take the good and then by happy chance to avoid the bad. Some, it is true, in far more menacing circumstances have done this: but not sensitive souls burdened by an accusing conscience.*

Sometimes on first meeting with a stranger, a name leaps to one's mind and seems to attach to the newcomer so effectively, that no subsequent acquaintance with his real name will wipe it out. Thus it was on the evening in Oxford when I looked across the hotel lounge and set eyes for the first time upon Bruno. It is not merely a matter of suppressing his real name for the sake of prudence: to me, he was Bruno from that instant.

He was of medium height, aged anything between twenty-five and thirty-five, with rather small brown eyes set in a pale round face, and pale lips on which a nervous smile came and went, as if he were in the habit of commenting silently and quizzically to himself on all that occurred. He wore a dark brown suit of some cheap material which had creased badly despite evident care; a dark brown hat stood on the window-ledge beside him. At the moment when I noticed him, he was about to light a cigarette, but apparently the top of his lighter broke off as he flicked it.

He tried for a few moments to fit the pieces together again, his head slightly tilted as if he pleaded with them: then, as he saw it was hopeless, the two pieces of metal seemed to back away from one another in his hands, his face meanwhile taking on a playful snarl. With a shrug, he put the pieces away in opposite pockets.

This little act was not put on for my benefit, nor for the benefit of anyone else in the lounge. In fact, apart from myself, there was nobody else present except for a couple engrossed in flirtation on a settee, and three elderly men engrossed in discussion at one of the tables. Bruno was clearly only dramatising to himself the workings of his own mind about the lighter.

I gathered that he had a vivid imagination, that he was accustomed to solitude, and also, somehow, that he had an inward and almost unavowed preoccupation with some fear or other.

Perhaps he felt my eyes upon him, but in any case, if he

wished to light his cigarette, he had not much choice. As usual in such emergencies, no waiter was in sight. After a quick glance round the room, Bruno came to ask me for a light. He brought his hat with him.

I had been out of the country for a few years, and on returning a few days previously had made my way directly to Oxford, in the hope of clearing up a fragment of work at the Bodleian. So it came about that I was staying briefly at this small, comfortable hotel, and that I had with me a leather bag containing various of my possessions. It occurred to me that in the medley I had a lighter which I seldom used, and which I might be able to bestow without offence upon a fellow-guest whom I was unlikely in any event to meet again. With this in mind, I picked up the bag, opened it, and began laying its contents upon the little table before me. There was my passport-case, gloves, spare spectacles, the showy little sheath-knife which I had bought at a New Brunswick junkshop some years before, and which had accompanied me more as a mascot than—

A sudden gasp from Bruno made me look up. His face was almost blue-pale: he certainly was not acting now. He whispered something unintelligible, stood staring. I found the lighter, and he lit his cigarette but he was not really interested in it any longer. He sat down. "How did you come by that knife?" he asked.

I told him the history of the thing, as far as I knew it. For my part, I could not in the least understand his horror. Lying sheathed on the table, it looked more like a toy than a serious weapon. The handle was of polished horn, and was crowned with a little silver horse-head, stylised like a rough-cut chess-piece. The blade was hidden in a sheath of elaborately tooled buff leather, with broad silver mounts at the mouth and at the curved, oriental-looking tip. The silver, too, was heavily stamped with decorative patterns. The whole effect was barbaric but hardly sinister. If drawn from the sheath, the knife would reveal a slender, elegantly ground blade, single-edged but with a point which might be sharp enough for a stab. That was all. I had seen one or two knives of similar type. They were made in Finland, but in Canada they were usually called "miners' knives." When I had related the little that I could, I asked my listener why it troubled him.

He paused, trying to bring his thoughts into utterable form. Presently he said, "I was expecting to see this knife one day, but not now. You will have noticed that when you placed it on the table I said, 'The Finnish knife!'"

I had not noticed, because at that moment of shock he had spoken in a language which I did not understand: but this was not worth explaining. I let him continue.

"Many years ago, when I was a boy, I was travelling in my own country. A large number of people were meeting at a town in the mountains, to hold a fair. I was going there too." He paused again, and a sudden comprehension came to me. "Are you interested in puppets?" I asked.

"Puppets? You know, then? My father is a famous man with his puppets. I have worked with them too, when I was a boy, but I wanted to be a musician. I play the violin." An appreciative nod was called for, and I gave it. "So there I was," he continued. "It was evening when I arrived. I was driving a cart, with a pony, and I saw someone wearing a big coat, walking on the road in front of me. I thought it might be my cousin, because at that time he was wearing a coat that was too big for him. In any case, I said to myself 'I'll make that fellow jump,' and I shouted and made the pony gallop a little. Well, it was not my cousin, but an old woman wearing a man's coat, and as she tried to get off the road she fell down and was very frightened and angry. Of course I picked her up, and told her how sorry I was, and how it was all a mistake. Then suddenly she left off being angry, and told me to help her to her place. When we were there, she read the cards for me. She could read cards very well."

His lips twitched slightly, and he sighed. "She told me all that had happened to me, and all that would happen. They were wonderful cards that she had. She said my uncle would die soon, and he did. She said my aunt would marry again, a rich man, and it happened. She told me of an illness I would have, and of a girl I would love, and those things happened just as she said. Shè said I would be a musician."

Up to this point I had listened as one listens to any good yarn, not exactly disbelieving, but not exactly willing to stake anything on the truth of the story either. The next development, therefore, startled me.

"She asked me for my knife," said Bruno: and with these words he drew from inside his jacket a knife which, so far as I could see, was almost exactly similar to mine. Only the handle was of blue-painted wood, not of horn, and the sheath had perhaps a little less ornament: but the silver horse-head might have been cast from the same mould. In this quiet English hotel-lounge, the odds against such a coincidence seemed fantastic.

"Is there a word engraved on the blade of your knife?" Bruno asked me. I told him, no, and let him see for himself. He examined it carefully. "I was afraid to ask you at first," he said: then he resumed his story.

"There was a man at the fair, who engraved people's names on identity bracelets and such things. The old woman took my knife to him, and he engraved something on the blade. It is my destiny. Look: do you know what it means?" He unsheathed the knife and showed me. On the slender blade was engraved in cursive characters one word:—

*Zumarejit*

I shook my head in reply, and he answered "It means, To go across the sea." I nodded again: it looked as if it could mean that, although once again I could not identify the language. "Well, so I have crossed it, although I did not think it likely in those days," he added. "And the old woman also said that over the sea I should meet someone with a knife just like mine. It is an omen." He sat staring before him, and I was wondering what I could say, or how to end this strange conversation, when the clanging of a gong supplied the cue. Cheerfully referring to the imminent meal, I rose to my feet. Bruno stood likewise. "I shall have dinner in my room, but perhaps I shall see you tomorrow," he said sombrely.

Next day I concluded my work in Oxford, and removed to London. For some weeks I gave no further thought to the strange little incident at the hotel. Then one day as I chanced to be walking along a main thoroughfare in the West End, a sudden blackening of the sky and a deluge of icy rain sent me with hundreds of others dashing for shelter. Following in a stream of people who hurried through a glass swing-door, I found myself in a large self-service eating place. Good, I thought, a snack would certainly pass the time until the storm might be over. The tables were filling up rapidly, and I simply took my coffee and roll to the first vacant place that I saw. Not until I was safely established there, did I glance at my neighbours. The man opposite me, steadily eating a complete meal, was Bruno.

My astonishment at this second meeting was nothing compared to the complete dismay which he evidently felt, though with resolute urbanity he said only that it was a great surprise. We exchanged news like old friends. His dreams seemed on the point of being realised: he was to give "half a concert," as he called it, at Chandos Hall in a week's time. A lady pianist whom he hardly knew was giving the other half, but it was a beginning. I promised to be there. We seemed tacitly to have agreed that the omen of the knives signified a fortunate new epoch for him. I noticed, however, that he allowed his unfinished meal to be taken away without comment. Undeniably, he was badly shaken.

I went to the concert, although a late afternoon appointment in another part of London meant that I only arrived moments before the commencement. The lady pianist gave the first half, and it was not until after the interval that I found a change had been made. Bruno was not there. Not waiting for the rest of the programme, I went out into the foyer, where I found only a mask-faced commissionaire to give me any information. "The violinist? You didn't know? Well, then, I'm sorry to have to tell you, but he was run down by a lorry and killed almost a week ago." The commissionaire pulled a slip of paper from his vest pocket. "All enquiries to Sister Taylor, St. Elmo's Hospital," he read out.

Next day I visited the hospital. Sister Taylor came hurrying, but practically lost interest in me when her questions brought out the fact that I was not a relative of the dead man. The commissionaire at the hall had misunderstood her instructions, apparently. However, since I was here, what could she very quickly do for me?

Hardly knowing what to ask, I said "I only know that my friend was run down by a lorry. Did he recover consciousness at all?—did he say anything?"

Her head-shake was definite. "I can only repeat what was said at the inquest," she told me. "He was dead before the lorry reached him. He could easily have got out of the road when he saw it coming, but he fell, and seemed to think he could not regain his feet in time. His heart failed under the shock."

*(The narrator's Finnish knife was stolen a short time after the events here recorded: and this fact is perhaps also a significant part of the history.)*

*Fee Fi Fo Fum*

An unaccustomed sound awoke me one night. Something on the landing outside my room was snuffling at the crack under the door, as if trying to find a way in. This was not in itself alarming, for I immediately thought of the large black Labrador from the next house, and supposed that it must for some reason have decided to pay us a visit and had been accidentally shut in. Two subsequent ideas, however, were rather disturbing. One was the obvious thought, that I probably ought to leave my comfortable bed and go downstairs to let the dog out; the other idea, less distinct but far more disturbing, was that on some previous occasion, which might have been a few weeks before, I had heard that same snuffling but had not been sufficiently roused from sleep to consider it as more than an unpleasant fragment of dream.

Unpleasant the sound certainly was, with the rapid panting eagerness of the animal's breath. It had abandoned the crack under the door now, and was exploring the sides; now this side and now that it snuffled, then all the way up one side of the door *and along the top.*

This decided me. No dog, not even the big Labrador, could reach so high. I still thought however that it might be some other corporeal creature, such as a rat, capable of finding a foothold on the narrow projecting ledge of the lintel. Softly and rapidly I rose from my bed, and at once pulled the door open with one hand while I switched on the room-light with the other.

There was no sound, not a scurry, not a plop. The darkness seemed to whirl away into the other doorways, and into the well of the staircase. From my mother's room came the soft, scarcely-distinguishable sound of her undisturbed breathing: I asked myself whether this sound, magnified by my imagination, could be what I had heard, but I knew it was impossible. I switched on the staircase light and looked over the banisters. The house was silent, secure, empty. I put out the lights and went back to bed. About half an hour later, the snuffling began again.

This time I did not get up, but lay considering the situation. The intruder was not a dog, I now realised. Apart from the facts that no dog could have disappeared so quickly, and that no dog could have snuffled along the top of the door, there was the additional point that I would have heard the sound of its paws moving, the scrape of its claws on the floor outside. Likewise I had satisfied myself that it was not a rat. It was, then, a haunting.

Nevertheless, two details about it were apparent. Eager though it seemed to find an entry to my room, it apparently could not come in while the light was on, even if the door was open as it had been while I searched the landing; and it could not enter if the door was closed, or it thought it could not, which fortunately came to the same thing. To make sure however, I got up, switched on the light again, returned to bed, pulled the covers over my head and slept.

For the next few months there was no further sign from this particular annoyance; then, when I had mentally consigned it to the realms of nightmare, it returned for two nights in succession. A further silence of several weeks followed, after which the manifestations occurred more frequently, but always at apparently quite irregular intervals although now the longest gap between them was about six weeks. I installed a little table-lamp beside my bed, so that at the first sound from the landing I could switch it on. I did not again try to catch a glimpse of the cause of the trouble. I was convinced that on the first occasion I had done all that was necessary for success if the thing had been of the normal order; but besides this, the sounds outside the door had since that night become more unpleasantly suggestive of a material presence, and I did not particularly wish, now, to improve my acquaintance with it.

Of none of these happenings had I said a word to my mother, for fear of alarming her: her only comment on the reading-lamp had been to warn me against straining my eyes by reading for too long at night. One evening however, when she had been putting some linen in the bathroom airing-cupboard shortly after dusk, she came downstairs complaining of a peculiar smell upon the upstairs landing. When I asked her what kind of smell it was, she finally said that it could possibly have been caused by a dog of some kind. This gave me an opportunity to mention that I thought some dog or other was getting into the house from time to time, and, following from this, I asked whether she had ever heard the snuffling sound herself. She had not, and was plainly sceptical about it. Her suggestion was that I might have been snoring loudly, and might have partly awakened myself by the noise without recognising whence it came. This theory did not fit in with my experience, but all the same, it was such an intelligent idea that the next time I was awakened by the curious noise, I took care to listen to my own breathing so as to make sure I was not performing any unconscious act of ventriloquism. The results completely satisfied me that I was in no way consciously or unconsciously responsible for the noises.

It was on a night soon after my mother's remark about the smell, that a crisis occurred. The usual sound was accompanied by others, as of a large creature moving about; so I thought it best to get up and to sit, with a blanket over my knees, in a wicker chair facing the door. I was, therefore, already looking vaguely in that direction when, amidst a paroxysm of snuffling, the door-handle suddenly rattled and moved as if a heavy bulk had knocked against it. That was too much. I put on the main light so as to have a maximum of defence, and, not knowing what else to do, I also switched on a powerful little pencil-torch which I had, and aligned it with the keyhole. To any being that hated the day, the resulting beam of light out on the landing must have been rapier-keen, and searing as flame. There was a sudden harsh grunt, then silence. I spent the rest of that night in my armchair, with both lights on.

The next day, I gave a great deal of thought to the matter. I had resolved that something must be done without futher delay, but I had no real idea what measures to adopt. General reading had familiarised me with a certain amount of folk-lore to the effect that a few substances—garlic, angelica, salt, iron, silver—could be used effectively as defences against unpleasant visitants from other spheres of existence; but was my visitant of the right kind to be influenced by any of these things. If so, how should they be employed, bearing in mind that I did not desire mere passive defence from the creature, but to be rid of it? And what if it were in fact of some quite different kind?

The second question was beyond my competence so I concentrated on the first. I bought some oil of garlic and some dried angelica leaves. Various possible uses for the oil of garlic had suggested themselves to me, but on taking one sniff at it I changed my mind, corked it firmly again and placed the little bottle on my bedside table. Evening came before I had arrived at any decision regarding the other substances; I therefore merely placed the bag of angelica-leaves, an iron key, and a twist of paper containing salt, under my pillow. Probably what follows had nothing whatever to do with the presence of these things; but having little comprehension of the event, I can only record whatever may possibly have some bearing upon it. My action in placing these things under my pillow indicates, at any rate, that I had for the time stepped outside the realms of scientific method. It could also, on another level, be interpreted as a declaration of war. Both these considerations, I think, are relevant.

Having become accustomed to sleeping with the lamp alight, I found no difficulty about this. Presently, however, I dreamed that I awakened; or to put it in a different way, I did awaken, but on to the far side of consciousness instead of back to the waking state. In this condition, and as if obeying an instruction, my consciousness but not my body went out through the closed door and waited. I felt as it were protected, though I cannot say with what: and when something came rushing from afar and leapt upon me, aiming for my neck, the shock which I felt was the sheer horror of contact rather than fear of the event. Yet I felt I was battling for my life, albeit by choice.

It is difficult to describe this pseudo-physical grappling. The movements of it were instinctive, but not, I think, actually intended by either party for the infliction of bodily wounds had that been possible. The purpose was partly to instil fear, but chiefly, on either side, to make unceasingly felt the strength of one's own resolution and at the same time to test continually the resolution of the adversary. It was, in essence, a battle of wills.

Two other notions presented themselves to me as facts. One was, that as we struggled we were progressively rising into thinner, purer atmosphere; the other was, that we were not alone. Even apart from the darkness in which we still seemed to be enveloped, I could not have spared an instant's attention for anything but the contest: yet to some area of my mind which was free from it, it seemed that there were watchers, perhaps in the function of seconds in a duel. I do not know whether they would have intervened, nor upon what conditions; for all I know, they may indeed have intervened; but my one certainty is that there were a plurality of them, and they were present. As to my adversary, I can only state that it was all menace, with no possibility of compromise. I fought it in horror and loathing but I would not let it depart undefeated. And then suddenly, at what seemed my last resource of endurance, the thing fell away and was gone. I awoke trembling and gasping, but free.

*The above history describes the experience of a woman who was completely untrained in occult matters, but who showed a considerable degree of courage and resourcefulness which enabled her to fend off the manifestation for a time.*

*Subsequently she became intensely interested in the Western Tradition, and eventually joined the Aurum Solis, mentioning this experience as a contributory cause of her interest.*

*Several months after her entry into the Order the haunting began again, this time menacing her mother: and was then verified by the Order as being a Kappa-phenomenon,\* a type of visitation only to be brought to a conclusion by advanced magical means. In the event, this was successfully achieved.*

\*See Volume 3, *Mysteria Magica*

# ☾ LLEWELLYN ORDERING INFORMATION

## Order Online:
Visit our website at www.llewellyn.com, select your books, and order them on our secure server.

 ## Order by Phone:
- Call toll-free within the U.S. at 1-877-NEW-WRLD (1-877-639-9753). Call toll-free within Canada at 1-866-NEW-WRLD (1-866-639-9753)
- We accept VISA, MasterCard, and American Express

 ## Order by Mail:
Send the full price of your order (MN residents add 7% sales tax) in U.S. funds, plus postage & handling to:

**Llewellyn Worldwide
2143 Wooddale Drive, Dept. 0-7387-0810-0
Woodbury, Minnesota 55125-2989, U.S.A.**

## Postage & Handling:
**Standard** (U.S., Mexico, & Canada). If your order is:
$49.99 and under, add $3.00
$50.00 and over, FREE STANDARD SHIPPING

AK, HI, PR: $15.00 for one book plus $1.00 for each additional book.

**International Orders** (airmail only):
$16.00 for one book plus $3.00 for each additional book

*Orders are processed within 2 business days.
Please allow for normal shipping time. Postage and handling rates subject to change.*

## Mysteria Magica
*Fundamental Techniques of High Magick*

### DENNING & PHILLIPS

The magickal order of the Aurum Solis is best known to the world through the writings of Osborne Phillips and the late Melita Denning. Long out of print, *Mysteria Magica* was the third volume in The Magical Philosophy series, a complete curriculum of development within the Western Mystery Tradition. *Mysteria Magica* is the classic ritual text appearing on countless suggested reading lists.

   *Mysteria Magica* reveals essential and advanced teachings in terms that newcomers can follow, with a richness of inspiration embraced by experienced mages. It contains potent techniques and rituals for self-training, for constructing magickal defenses, and for consecrating your own magickal implements. The "Principles of Ceremonial" show how and why ritual acts can lead to their desired result.

0-7387-0169-6
448 pp., 6 x 9, illus. $24.95